Baseball For Dummies, 2nd Edition

Cheat Sheet

P9-CCR-307

Getting out

- A fielder catches your fair or foul ball before it touches the ground (unless it is a foul tip to the catcher with less than two strikes).
- You hit a foul tip (a ball caught by the catcher off your bat) for strike three.
- After hitting the ball, you or first base is tagged before you touch the base.
- The umpire calls three strikes during your at-bat (whether you swing or not).
- A ball that you hit fair hits your bat a second time while you are in fair territory.
- While running outside the foul lines, you obstruct a fielder's throw.
- You hit the ball with one or both feet outside the batter's box or step from one batter's box to another while the pitcher winds up.
- You obstruct the catcher from fielding or throwing.
- You run into your own fairly-batted ball while running from home to first base.

Getting on base

- You hit a fair ball that is not caught by a fielder before it touches the ground.
- You hit a fair ball that touches the ground and is caught by a fielder whose throw fails to beat you to a base.
- The umpire calls four pitches out of the strike zone during your at-bat.
- A pitch in the strike zone hits you without first touching your bat.
- The catcher obstructs your swing.
- You hit a fair ball beyond the playing field (for a home run).
- You hit a fair, catchable ball, but the fielder drops the ball, throws it away, and so on.
- A third strike skips past the catcher and you beat the throw to first.

The positions

Abbreviation	Player
P	Pitcher
C	Catcher
1B	First baseman
2B	Second baseman
3B	Third baseman
SS	Shortstop
LF	Left fielder
CF	Center fielder
RF	Right fielder

American League lineups include a designator hitter who bats for the pitcher without taking a defensive position in the field. DH is the abbreviation for that slot.

Baseball For Dummies, 2nd Edition

Cheat Sheet

Getting out on the base paths

- You are on the same base with a teammate when the ball is alive (the second runner is out).
- You pass a preceding runner on the base paths.
- You miss a base and the defense notices it.
- A fielder tags you with a ball that is alive while you are off the base. (However, no one can tag you out if you overrun first base provided you return immediately to that bag without making a turn toward second.)
- Your teammate hits a ball that touches you in fair territory without it first touching or passing any fielder except the pitcher.
- In the judgment of the umpire, you hinder a fielder from making a play.
- A batted ball forces you to advance to another base and the fielder possessing the ball tags that base before you reach it.

Major league baseball "mosts"

Most Games Played: 3,562, Pete Rose (1963–1986)

Most Career Home Runs: 755, Henry Aaron (1954–1976)

Most Home Runs in a Season: 70, Mark McGwire (1998)

Most Career Runs Batted In: 2,297, Henry Aaron (1954–1976)

Most Career Hits: 4,256, Pete Rose (1963–1986)

Most Consecutive Games Batting Safely: 56, Joe DiMaggio (1941)

Most Stolen Bases in a Season: 130, Rickey Henderson (1982)

Most Career Wins: 511, Cy Young (1890–1911)

Most Career Strikeouts: 5,714, Nolan Ryan (1966–1993)

Most Strikeouts in a Season: 383, Nolan Ryan (1973)

Most Strikeouts in a Game: 20, Roger Clemens (1986, 1996), Kerry Wood (1998)

Most No-Hitters Pitched: 7, Nolan Ryan (1966–1993)

Most Consecutive Games Played: 2,632, Cal Ripken (1982–1998)

Wiley, the Wiley Publishing logo, For Dummies, the Dummies Man logo, the For Dummies Bestselling Book Series logo and all related trade dress are trademarks or registered trademarks of Wiley Publishing, Inc. All other trademarks are property of their respective owners.

For Dummies: Bestselling Book Series for Beginners

Praise for Baseball For Dummies

"There may not be anyone alive who knows more about baseball than Joe Morgan."

— Bob Costas, NBC Sports Broadcaster

"Whether you are a first-day fan or a lifetime fan of baseball as I am, everyone can learn something from *Baseball For Dummies*. 'Little Joe' is truly Big Joe with this book."

— Chris Berman, ESPN Sports Broadcaster

"What Joe Morgan doesn't know about baseball is simply not worth knowing."

— Jon Miller, ESPN Baseball Commentator

"Joe Morgan knows baseball. In fact, he was one of the most intelligent players to ever play the game."

— Sparky Anderson, three-time World Series winning manager

"Joe Morgan could hit singles, doubles, triples and home runs. This book is a grand slam."

— Pete Rose, 1975 World Series Most Valuable Player, Cincinnati Reds

"*Baseball For Dummies* brings out the kid in every reader. A terrific book for people of all ages."

— Fred Opper, Coach of Fordham University

"NBC's Joe Morgan again showed himself a rare bird: an ex-jock with savvy and the ability to communicate it."

— *People Magazine*

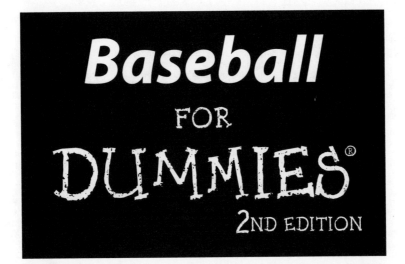

Baseball
FOR
DUMMIES®
2ND EDITION

by Joe Morgan with Richard Lally

Foreword by Sparky Anderson

Wiley Publishing, Inc.

Baseball For Dummies

Published by
Wiley Publishing, Inc.
909 Third Avenue
New York, NY 10022
www.wiley.com

Copyright © 2000 by Wiley Publishing, Inc., Indianapolis, Indiana

Published simultaneously in Canada

For general information on our other products and services or to obtain technical support, please contact our Customer Care Department within the U.S. at 800-762-2974, outside the U.S. at 317-572-3993, or fax 317-572-4002.

Wiley also publishes its books in a variety of electronic formats. Some content that appears in print may not be available in electronic books.

Library of Congress Cataloging-in-Publication Data:

Library of Congress Catalog Card No.: 99-68618

ISBN: 0-7645-5234-1

Manufactured in the United States of America

10 9 8 7 6 5 4

About the Authors

Joe Morgan, one of six children born to Mr. and Mrs. Leonard (Ollie) Morgan, moved from Bohnam, Texas to Oakland at the age of 10 in 1954. His principal residence has been in the East Bay Area since that time. Joe was an active participant in sports and social programs at the Brookfield Community Center. He continued his education in the Peralta College District, attending Merritt College from 1961 to 1963 and graduating with honors and an AA Degree. He also attended California State University at Hayward, earning a BS in Physical Education. Again, both scholastic and athletic honors were accorded him. Entering the ranks of professional baseball in 1963, Joe signed with the Houston Colt 45's. He participated with their farm club for approximately two seasons and became a regular player for the Astros in 1964. He was named National League Rookie of the Year in 1965, and his exceptional performance continued with the Astros until 1972 when he was traded to the Cincinnati Reds. He continued to be a dominant factor in the ranks of professional baseball throughout his career. Honors accorded him during this period are numerous. These honors include Most Valuable Player in the 1972 All-Star Game; Most Valuable Player in the National League in 1975 and 1976; the Commissioner's Award in 1976 for most votes by the fans for the All-Star Game; and the Comeback Player of the Year award in 1982. Before ending his career in 1984, Joe established a new career home-run record for a second baseman; played in a record 92 consecutive games without an error (by a second baseman); played in four World Series, winning two championships; played in seven League Championship Series; and established an All-Star record by playing in seven consecutive games with a hit. In addition, he won five Gold Glove Awards, played in ten All-Star Games, and recorded 692 stolen bases. These honors are indicative of his great abilities. He was elected to the National Baseball Hall of Fame in 1990 on the first ballot.

Richard Lally's articles and columns on baseball, politics, boxing, business, the arts, and general sports have appeared in prestigious publications throughout the world. He is the author or co-author of eighteen books, including the baseball autobiography *The Wrong Stuff* written with Boston Red Sox pitching ace Bill Lee. The book enjoyed a long run on best-seller lists in the U.S. and Canada and was selected as part of *Total Baseball's* Ultimate Baseball Library.

Dedication

Joe Morgan: To the Morgan family for their support and sacrifices when I was a player and their love that keeps me motivated today. Lisa, Angela, Ashley, Kelly — Dad loves you.

Richard Lally: To the SGI and the great desire for kosen-rufu.

Authors' Acknowledgments

Joe Morgan: I want to thank all of my former teammates who were part of my learning experience about the greatest game in the world. What are friends for? They are there when you need a favor. Thank you Johnny Bench, Ken Caminiti, Bob Gibson, Ken Griffey, Sr., Barry Larkin, Bill Lee, and Willie McCovey. A special thanks to the man who taught me the real philosophy of managing, the great Sparky Anderson. The Cincinnati Reds 1976 team was the greatest team ever. Richard, you are a great partner. The Wild Bunch would have cleaned up Dodge City easier than Doc and the Earp brothers. Thanks to IMG and IDG Books Worldwide, Inc.; your staffs do a great job. Your turn, Richard.

Richard Lally: I want to first thank my partner, Joe Morgan, for bringing the same dedication and intelligence to this project that he brought to the field in every game he played. Mr. Morgan is Hall of Fame in everything he does as well as being a grand fellow with great taste in westerns. (And remember, JM, if you ever want to take on Johnny Ringo and the Clantons, I'm your Huckleberry.) Joe's assistant, Lolita Aulston, kept us on track and on schedule. The staff at IDG could not have been more supportive: Stacy Collins, Kevin Thornton, Lisa Roule, and our meticulous editors Christine Beck and Joan Friedman made this project a pleasant task. Mark Reiter, our agent at IMG/Bach Literary, was a driving force behind the book. His encouragement and vision were constant sources of inspiration. Mark's former assistant, Sara Falkenberry, and her successor Michelle Yung, kept the lines of communication open and were extraordinarily patient (I tend to call a lot). I could never properly express my gratitude to Julian Bach. From the time I gave him my first manuscript, the skipper at IMG/Bach has been my most enthusiastic ally. And we all want to give special thanks to Ann Torrago, who kept the checks coming regularly.

We did not have a staff of researchers, but whenever data proved elusive, I was always able to turn to one of my gang of Usual Suspects: Billy Altman, Bill Shannon, Jordan Sprechman, Bill Daughtry, and John Collett (Our Man in the Ballparks). Mr. Shannon, a walking baseball database, also doubled-checked our work to cut out any glitches. Willie Mays, Bob Gibson, Rusty Staub, Bill Lee, Sparky Anderson, Johnny Bench, Willie McCovey, Barry Larkin, Ken Caminiti, Ken Griffey, Sr., and Harry Wendelstedt, Jr., our "all-star" team of advisors, could not have been more generous with their time and insights.

Every writer should be blessed with the friends and relatives who have encouraged me, many of them from the first time I picked up a pen. I thank and love them all: My brothers Joseph and Sean, my father Richard, and my late mother, Anne, who instilled in me my love for baseball; the late Brother Leo Richard who taught me to dream in wide-screen Technicolor; Aunt Kathy; Uncle Tommy (if for no other reason than that he was miffed over being left out of the first edition's acknowledgments); the ever alluring, violet-eyed Maria DiSimone ("Like *you* blend, pussycat?"); the estimable Natalie Ferrouw for her smoky voice and Barbara Stanwyck eyes; Barbara Bauer, who nurtured my love of the written word; the magical Eve Lederman, the best young writer in America and the second best second baseman I know; my pal for life Al Lombardo and his wife Cathy; Victor and Ellen Kiam; my buddy Charlie Ludlow ("Stay in the boat, young captain!"); Joyce Altman (who doesn't seem to mind when her husband Billy and I spend hours on the phone talking about this great game); Alan and Maralice Flusser; Richard and Jessie Erlanger, Karl and Margrid Durr, Alecks, Michaela and Rasmus Budny, Robert Moss, Florence Stone, W. Michael Gillespie and Vesna, Joey ("You are definetely insane . . . sir!") and the rest of my gang of renegades at Q Bistro in Forest Hills whose port and curried red snapper helped me keep body and soul intact throughout this project.

Publisher's Acknowledgments

We're proud of this book; please send us your comments through our online registration form located at www.dummies.com/register.

Some of the people who helped bring this book to market include the following:

Acquisitions and Editorial

Project Editors: Christine Meloy Beck, Joan Friedman

Acquisitions Editor: Stacy S. Collins

Copy Editor: Donna Frederick

Technical Editor: Bill Shannon

Acquisitions Coordinator: Lisa Roule

Editorial Manager: Jennifer Ehrlich

Editorial Assistant: Laura Jefferson

Special Help
Andrea Boucher, Corey Dalton, Amanda Foxworth

Cover Photo: FPG International LLC, © Jim Cummins

Production

Project Coordinator: E. Shawn Aylsworth

Layout and Graphics: Amy Adrian, Tracy K. Oliver, Brent Savage, Janet Seib, Brian Torwelle, Dan Whetstine, Erin Zeltner

Special Art: Precision Graphics

Proofreaders: Corey Bowen, Laura L. Bowman, John Greenough, Marianne Santy, Charles Spencer

Indexer: Steve Rath

Publishing and Editorial for Consumer Dummies
Diane Graves Steele, Vice President and Publisher, Consumer Dummies
Joyce Pepple, Acquisitions Director, Consumer Dummies
Kristin A. Cocks, Product Development Director, Consumer Dummies
Michael Spring, Vice President and Publisher, Travel
Brice Gosnell, Publishing Director, Travel
Suzanne Jannetta, Editorial Director, Travel

Publishing for Technology Dummies
Andy Cummings, Acquisitions Director

Composition Services
Gerry Fahey, Executive Director of Production Services
Debbie Stailey, Director of Composition Services

Contents at a Glance

Cartoons at a Glance

By Rich Tennant

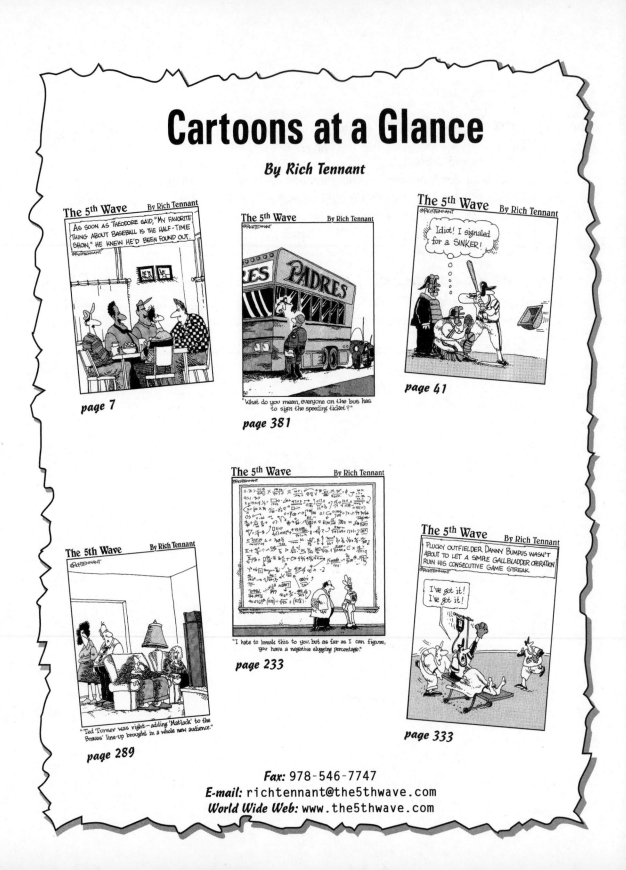

page 7

page 381

page 41

page 289

page 233

page 333

Fax: 978-546-7747
E-mail: richtennant@the5thwave.com
World Wide Web: www.the5thwave.com

Table of Contents

Chapter 23: Joe Morgan's Top Ten Fielders, All-Time and Current .357

Foreword

• •

*J*oe Morgan ("The Little Man," as I like to call him) knows baseball. In fact, he was one of the most intelligent players to ever play the game. And I should know, I had the distinct pleasure to know and work with Joe for more than two decades. During my years as the manager of the Cincinnati Reds, Joe was an incredible ball player — not just for his Hall of Fame abilities but for his genuine love of the game. Joe was an unselfish player with a healthy respect for the rich history and tradition of baseball. His first priority was always the team; he never tried to selfishly pad his individual statistics. I love and respect Joe for his giving attitude, and he is universally respected by both his peers and baseball fans worldwide.

Now Joe gives back to the game through this grand slam of a book, *Baseball For Dummies.* (I even helped out with a chapter or two.) Joe explains the game with insight and down-to-earth information so that anyone can understand and appreciate the game. I'm so glad Joe had the opportunity to share his vast baseball knowledge. His gift for understanding baseball and people sets him apart from the "average Joe."

Today, Joe continues to give back to the game through his expert analysis and commentary and, of course, through *Baseball For Dummies.*

Joe was a very special player who turned out to be a total person.

— Sparky Anderson

Major-league manager (two teams) for more than 26 years and three-time World Series winning manager

Introduction

● ●

Welcome to *Baseball For Dummies,* 2nd Edition, a book dedicated to the proposition that no one's education is complete unless it includes a thorough grounding in the principles of the greatest sport ever created. This book is much like a baseball game: orderly but spontaneous, filled with nuance and surprise, and packed to the brim with fun. We hope you enjoy reading it as much as we enjoyed writing it.

About This Book

We wrote this book to appeal to every level of fan, from the novice who just recently purchased his first pack of baseball cards to the loyalist who has been sitting in the same seat at the ballpark since the Coolidge administration. Whether you participate on the field or just watch, our mission is to increase your baseball pleasure by a factor of ten.

As a spectator, you'll have an easier time watching and appreciating baseball's finer points after you finish our book. You will not only know what the players on the field are doing, but you'll also know why they are doing it. If an extraterrestrial dropped out of the skies, we would hope it could read *Baseball For Dummies,* 2nd Edition, today and attend its first baseball game tomorrow without experiencing any confusion.

If you're a player, there isn't any component of your game that can't be elevated by studying this volume. Pitching, hitting, fielding, and baserunning — we cover it all with the aid of some of the game's legendary players. It doesn't matter if you're taking your first cuts in Little League or already sitting in a big league dugout; you can find something in this book to make you a better player.

Why You Need This Book

Novices need *Baseball For Dummies,* 2nd Edition, because no other book can offer you such a comprehensive introduction to the National Pastime. You're going to discover things about baseball that many die-hard fans still haven't learned. Do you know how the great outfielders are able to get a good jump on the ball? Where the first baseman should stand to receive a cut-off throw? How many stitches are in a baseball and who manufactures bats that meet major league standards? You can find the answers to these and many more questions within these pages. And if you already know a lot about the sport? You're about to learn a good deal more. This book is chock-full of inside tips and insights that you rarely encounter anywhere below the professional ranks.

To be honest, we believe that all human beings need this book because baseball is part of our genetic destiny. Archaeologists have unearthed evidence linking bat-and-ball games to our prehistoric ancestors. What compelled them to start smacking around a tiny sphere with a stick? No one knows for certain, but our guess is they did it because there was no television — no Oprah, no *Ally McBeal,* and no reruns of *Seinfeld.* What were the Cro-Magnons to do with all their leisure time? Cavemen would swing clubs to slay the odd raptor and throw stones to bring down an occasional pterodactyl. So it was a natural leap to utilize these talents for a less daunting sport.

Ever since the prehistoric days, the urge to strike round objects with a stick or club has been encrypted in our DNA. You can't escape it. Try suppressing this drive, and there's no telling how much damage you can do to yourself. (*Ripley's Believe It or Not* has reported cases of spontaneous combustion in which people burst into flames for no apparent reason. We think those people would still be alive today if they had only played a game of catch every few weeks.) So we offer this book to you as a kind of public service. Use it to find a safe release for your primordial urges.

How to Use This Book

You may use this book any way you like. Read it from cover to cover or just pick a section and dive in. If you're a novice, you may want to read the glossary first (or at least refer to it often) so you can understand the language we use. Then read Chapters 1 and 2 for an understanding of baseball's rules. If you're a more advanced player or coach, you may want to start with Part II to improve various aspects of your game. This book is designed so that you never have to read any chapter or part in its entirety; you can often find many short paragraphs that can stand alone as mini-chapters. And Joe's Part of Tens should appeal both to longtime fans and to those of you who are just learning the difference between a slider and a curve.

How This Book Is Organized

In each chapter, we start with the basics and build from there. For example, when Joe discusses hitting, we begin by advising you on what sort of bat you should use. Next, we focus on your grip, and then gradually we add all the other elements of a perfect swing until you're slashing line drives all over the field. Whenever we think a point needs further clarification, we cross-reference the appropriate chapter so you can immediately get any additional information you may need.

Part I: Getting Started (Before Your First At-Bat)

This is a baseball and this is a bat — yes, the book is that basic at the start. First, we give you a little history to tell you how baseball began. Then we review the rules, so you won't commit any *faux pas* on or off the field, such as running the bases in the wrong direction. Because you can't take the field without the proper equipment, we also identify the tools of the trade, tell you where to acquire them, and show you how to take care of your bats, balls, and gloves so they can take care of you.

Part II: Taking Your Swings — How to Play the Game

In this part, we help you shape up your game so you look like a pro no matter what your level of play. First, we get you into baseball shape. When you finish your workout, you'll be able to chew horsehide (it's terrific with a nice Bordeaux) and spit split-fingered fastballs. Next, a group of major leaguers joins us to improve every facet of your game. We smooth the kinks out of your swing so you can maximize your bat speed to hit for power and average. Would you rather take a turn on the mound? We can add some zip to your fastball and show you how to throw a major league curve. Fielding? You discover the proper way to turn a double play and catch a pop foul. And you'll never again get your feet tangled while chasing a fly ball hit over your head. (If you think a lot of major league outfielders won't be reading that section, you haven't seen a game lately.) For coaches and players, we include a playbook that reveals baseball's basic defensive alignments at a glance. No extra charge; we just threw it in as a bonus.

Part III: From Little League to the Major Leagues: Organized Baseball

In this part, we take you through every level of professional and amateur ball to impart some sense of where the game is played and how it is run. We also bring in future Hall of Fame skipper Sparky Anderson for some tips on managing. And we even show you some basic baseball math so that you won't be at a loss the next time your friends ask you to calculate their fielding percentages.

Part IV: We Don't Care If We Ever Get Back: A Spectator's Guide

If you'd rather watch than play, this is the part for you. In this part, you discover how to follow the game as a spectator, where to go for game coverage in various media, and — best of all — how to keep score. You also get an analysis of all the major league parks with an eye toward how they affect player and team performances. Want a little more involvement without going onto the field? We devote a whole chapter to Fantasy Baseball.

Part V: The Part of Tens

It wouldn't be a ...*For Dummies* book without this part. Our lists of all-time great players give you a taste of baseball history, and you can use our lists of current players as mini-scouting reports. The rest is just interesting stuff we thought you should know.

Part VI: Appendixes

You can't understand the game if you don't understand its language. Our glossary in Appendix A broadens your baseball vocabulary and gives you a timeline of famous baseball players. Appendix B is a contact list for the major baseball organizations around the world.

Icons Used in This Book

Baseball Speak: Talk like this and the folks in the bleachers will have no trouble understanding you.

Baseball Bookshelf: This icon cues you to some "must have" books to start or enhance your baseball library.

Joe Says: This icon signals tips from the Hall of Famer himself.

Heads Up: This icon gives you valuable information that can prevent you from making a bonehead play on or off the field.

Player Tip: This icon alerts you to sage advice from one of the greats of the game.

Viewer Tip: This icon signals an insight that can enhance your baseball viewing, whether you are in the stadium or in front of the TV.

Coach Tip: This icon alerts you to advice that comes from a coach and can be passed on by a coach.

Warning: Beware! This icon warns you that a situation can be dangerous.

Part I
Getting Started (Before Your First At-Bat)

The 5th Wave   By Rich Tennant

AS SOON AS THEODORE SAID, "MY FAVORITE THING ABOUT BASEBALL IS THE HALF-TIME SHOW," HE KNEW HE'D BEEN FOUND OUT.

In this part . . .

A father of one of the authors was a Marine drill instructor, who told him that the secret to succeeding in anything was to "have clear objectives." In this part, we start by describing baseball's objectives (to make sure you don't go wandering around the base paths during a game). We also tell you where to get the best ball, bats, and gloves — so you'll not only play like a pro, you'll also dress like one. We then share some of the rules that give baseball its structure.

Chapter 2

Suiting Up: Equipment

. . . .

In This Chapter

▶ Tossing a regulation baseball

▶ Finding the right bat

▶ Choosing a glove

▶ Dressing for safety and style

▶ Equipping your field

. . . .

When Pittsburgh Pirates shortstop Dick Groat was hitting his way to a batting title and MVP award in 1960, his manager Danny Murtaugh claimed, "Groat could hit .300 using a piece of barbed wire as a bat." Perhaps Groat could, but no one expects you to attempt that feat. When you take the field, you should take along the best equipment available. You don't need to spend vast sums to purchase top-quality accessories as long as you know what to look for and where to find it. Hence, as the late sportscaster Howard Cosell would say, this chapter tells it like it is.

Choosing Your Weapons: Balls, Bats, and Gloves

Unless you are under ten years old, buy equipment that meets all the major league specifications. Buying equipment that is licensed by a reputable body such as Major League Baseball, the NCAA, or the Little League offers you some quality assurances.

In this section, we show you how to shop for the basic tools you need in order to play the game effectively and keep yourself protected on the field and in the batter's box. With the right ball, bat, and glove, your chances of success on the playing field can increase dramatically.

Baseballs that last (and last and last . . .)

To be considered major league, a baseball must

- ✔ Have a circumference between 9 and 9¼ inches (22.9cm and 23.5cm). (Some youth league balls may have slightly smaller circumferences.)
- ✔ Weigh between 5 and 5¼ ounces (141.8g and 148.8g).
- ✔ Have an outer covering constructed from two pieces of white horsehide or cowhide stitched together with red thread.
- ✔ Have a cork core surrounded by two layers of rubber and wrapped in yarn.

Figure 2-1 shows a standard major league baseball.

Figure 2-1:
A standard
baseball.

You don't have to go to your local sporting goods store armed with a tape measure, scale, and scalpel (for filleting the ball to check its innards) to make sure you're buying a baseball that conforms to major league standards. Rawlings (800-729-5464, rawlings@accessus.net) is the only company licensed by both major leagues to manufacture their official baseballs. So if you buy one of their balls, you know you're getting the genuine article. Rawlings' major league baseballs carry the designation "Official Baseball of the American (or National) League" and are signed by a major league president. (In the near future, the baseball commissioner may sign official balls.) You can buy first-rate baseballs that other companies manufacture, but you have no way of knowing whether these products are of major league quality.

Rawlings tests its products by injecting them into an air gun and firing them against a wall nearly nine yards away. To pass muster with the company's ballologists (don't look up that word in your dictionary; we made it up), the hurtled sphere must rebound at 51.4 to 54.6 percent of its original velocity. Other machines roll each ball for 15 seconds to ensure roundness.

Reducing injuries with innovative baseballs

Many baseball-playing youngsters live in fear of being struck by a batted or thrown ball. Likewise, many parents fret while watching their children face live pitching for the first time. To ease such fears, Worth, Inc. (931-455-0691) manufactures Reduced Injury Factor (RIF) baseballs, softer balls that reduce the peak force of impact, lessening the chance of serious injury. Although slightly spongier, a RIF ball has the exact size and weight of a regulation baseball, giving children a safer yet realistic training tool.

Worth manufactures three types of RIF baseballs with varying injury protection:

✔ Level 1, the softest of the three, is recommended for players age 5–7 or as a training ball for all ages.

✔ Level 5 is a medium-firm ball recommended for players age 8–10.

✔ Level 10, the firmest RIF baseball, is recommended for players age 11 and up.

You can find RIF baseballs at many sporting goods stores; contact Worth, Inc., for the location nearest you.

A ball whose insides are poorly wrapped rapidly becomes misshapen with use. If your baseball is poorly stitched or constructed from inferior leather, it will fall apart. Avoid balls made with synthetic leather wrapped around a core of hard plastic. This kind of ball makes a good toy or first ball for a toddler, but if you're a young adult or older, you'll tear its cover off in one good afternoon of batting practice. The toy balls are also so light that you risk throwing out your arm if you use one for a serious game of catch.

Want to rip a few line drives inside a gymnasium during the dead of winter? Several companies manufacture balls with nylon covers and cloth centers so your best line drives won't shatter any windows. Honing your batting eye after dusk? Shop for orange-colored baseballs — a brainchild of Charlie Finley, the late, innovative owner of the Oakland A's — specifically designed for nighttime play.

Bats that really swing

Although pro players are required to use wooden bats, many people prefer the power that aluminum can offer. In this section, we cover how to buy a bat that will last, how to care for it once you've made your purchase, and what to expect if you choose the metal version rather than your standard lumber.

Professional wood

A major league bat must be a single, round piece of solid wood, no more than 2⅜ inches (7cm) in diameter at its thickest and no more than 42 inches (1.06m) long. Figure 2-2 shows what a standard bat looks like.

Choose a bat that you can swing comfortably with control and speed (see Chapter 5 for more details), but also look for one that will last. Bats made of white ash have greater durability than bats constructed from less dense woods. When you choose a bat, look for one with a wide grain, the mark of an aged wood. These bats are more resistant to breaking, denting, chipping, or flaking than bats made from less mature wood.

Hillerich & Bradsby (800-282-2287, lslugger@iglou.com), the official bat manufacturer for major league baseball, makes the Louisville Slugger, a bat that is very popular among major league hitters. Other makers of quality bats include Tri-Diamond Sports (509-891-6435, boatwa@aol.com), which produces a laminated ash bat with what the company has dubbed a boa constrictor handle. Laminating increases the wood's durability, and the boa handle decreases the likelihood that your bat will come flying out of your hands during a particularly strenuous plate appearance. For the color-coordinated among you, Glomar Enterprises (714-871-5956) sells a customized white ash bat that you can have stained in your favorite hue. Hoosier (219-531-1006, baseball@netnitco.net) manufactures an ultra-durable bat that is illegal for use in most professional leagues because it is made of three types of glued wood: maple for the barrel, ash for the handle, and hickory at the *sweet spot* (a spot, four to eight inches from the end of the barrel, where the ball can be hit most solidly). Former big-league pitcher Bill Lee will handcraft a bat for your on his lathe if you e-mail him for prices and specifications (spaceman@together.net).

Powerful aluminum

Aluminum bats are currently popular in many levels of nonprofessional baseball. The choice of aluminum over wood is largely an economic one. Most nonpro leagues find that the cost of regularly replacing broken wooden bats can bust their budgets.

Hitters love aluminum bats because they are hollow and light yet they have more hitting mass than heavier wooden bats. This quality enables the hitter to generate greater bat speed and power. Balls that are routine outs when struck by a wooden bat are out of the park when launched by aluminum.

Caring for your wood bat

Eddie Collins, a Hall of Fame second baseman with the Chicago White Sox and Oakland A's, reportedly kept his bats stored in a manure pile during the offseason to ensure their freshness. (When we told that to our resident left-handed sage Bill Lee, he quipped, "Well, at least Eddie knew no one would steal them.") We're not suggesting you do anything quite so exotic to keep your wooden bats in the swing of things (and won't your teammates be thankful). Instead, perform the following maintenance:

✔ Clean your bat with alcohol every day, especially if you cover its handle with pine tar. Alcohol cleansing prevents pine tar and dirt buildup.

✔ Keep the bat away from dampness. Absorbed moisture adds weight to your bat, which is why Ted Williams never, ever placed his bats on wet ground. If your bat gets wet, dry it off immediately and rub it with linseed oil.

✔ *Bone* your bat — rub it hard along the grain with a smooth piece of bone or another bat — to maintain its hard surface.

✔ Store your bats vertically, barrel down, in a dry place.

An aluminum bat's *sweet spot,* the launching point for so many base hits, is twice the size of that found on a wooden bat. Pitchers dislike these war clubs for obvious reasons.

Aluminum bats have a longer game-life than wooden models, but they aren't immortal. After 600 hits or so, metal fatigue becomes a factor.

Worth Sporting Company (800-423-3714) produces many of the aluminum bats used in the NCAA and Little League.

If your league insists that you use an aluminum bat, buy one that rings or lightly vibrates when you strike its barrel on something hard. Bats that don't ring have no hitting life left in them.

Other batting options

Ceramic and graphite bats are the new kids on the block. They have the durability of the aluminum bats but are closer in weight/mass ratio to wooden bats, so they don't give hitters an unfair advantage over pitchers. Their price, however, can be prohibitive: Top-of-the-line models can cost as much as $220.

Gloves that fit the job

Major league baseball rules regulate the size of gloves at each position. Most leagues for young adults and older players adhere to these directives.

(In Chapter 7 you can find out how to choose a glove for the position that you want to play.)

Catcher's mitts can be no more than 38 inches (96.52cm) in circumference nor more than 15½ inches (39.37cm) from bottom to top. The webbing should be no more than 7 inches across the top. It should also extend for no more than 6 inches to the base of the thumb.

The first baseman's mitt must be no longer than 12 inches (30.48cm) from top to bottom and no more than 8 inches (20.32cm) wide across the palm. The web of this mitt — which can be either a lacing, a lacing through leather tunnels, or an extension of the palm with lacing — cannot exceed 5 inches (12.7cm) from top to base or 4 inches in width.

Pitchers' and other fielders' gloves must not measure more than 12 inches (30.48cm) long from the tip to any one of the four fingers and no more than 7¾ inches (19.7cm) wide. If you work on the mound, your opportunity to make a fashion statement is limited: Pitchers' gloves must be a solid color other than white or gray (which could serve as camouflage for the ball).

All major league gloves and mitts are made of leather. Children can get by with using vinyl gloves and plastic balls, but once you're playing serious baseball, leather is the only way to go. Pick a glove that conforms to the major league standards and fits your hand comfortably. Gloves with open webbings allow you to watch the ball until you catch it, which is always a good policy. You don't have that advantage with closed-web gloves, which are also more difficult to break in (though if you're a pitcher, you need the closed webbing to better hide your pitches).

Major league baseball licenses Wilson Team Sports (800-272-4511) to manufacture fielding gloves (see Figure 2-3). Diamond King Sports (800-826-1464) produces the increasingly popular handcrafted Guerrero Gloves in 20 different models. The craftspeople at Barraza BBG, Inc. (714-252-5455) will customize a glove for you that fits like, well, a glove.

Caring for your leather glove

The best way to break in a leather glove is to play catch with it frequently. You can also make it more pliable by rubbing it with linseed oil, saddle soap, or — here's a Helpful Hint from Heloise — shaving cream (though you may want to avoid shaving gels, which tend to dry out quickly). If your glove gets wet, let it dry naturally. Placing it on a radiator or some other heat producer cracks the leather. When your glove is idle, place a ball in its pocket, and then tie the glove closed with a leather strap or wrap a rubber band around it to maintain its catching shape.

Figure 2-3:
A left-handed fielder's glove.

Ballplayers didn't always wear gloves to capture scorching line drives. During the sport's early days, athletes bravely fielded their positions barehanded. It wasn't until 1869 that Doug Allison, a catcher for the Cincinnati Red Stockings, set up behind the plate wearing a mitt (for which Joe's teammate, Hall of Fame backstop Johnny Bench, was eternally grateful). Allison's leather accessory, however, didn't become all the rage until the mid 1880s, when a livelier, faster moving baseball finally convinced players that they needed some padding to keep their digits intact.

Shodding Yourself Like a Pro

Most nonprofessional players give little thought to their shoes; they just put on whatever they can. In fact, standard baseball shoes are no longer obligatory for many pro players. I've seen Frank Thomas hit in tennis shoes. I'm a traditionalist in this area. I believe you should buy a light shoe with metal spikes so that you can get maximum traction in the batter's box and on the base paths. (Slipping in the batter's box, on the bases, or in the field could cost your team a ball game.) If you don't want to wear spikes, at least get shoes with rubber cleats so you can grip the playing surface as you run.

Your shoes should fit properly and offer your feet adequate support; otherwise you risk damaging your lower legs' connective tissue. Choose a sturdy shoe with support that runs its entire length. Because your shoes stretch with use, choose a pair that fits snugly when you first wear them.

Adidas (800-4AD-IDAS), Nike (503-671-6453), and Reebok (800-343-5658) — the Big Three in athletic footwear — all produce reliable spikes (the shodding of choice when you're playing on natural grass) and rubber cleats (preferably worn on artificial turf).

Equipping Yourself for Safety

Baseball is not as limb-threatening as football with its 300-pound human condominiums hurtling themselves into each other. However, there is some risk of injury whenever you take the field. You can minimize the chances of getting hurt by buying the proper protective equipment.

Catchers' gear

Besides their gloves, catchers have to wear the traditional tools of ignorance to survive behind the plate (as shown in Figure 2-4):

- Chest protector
- Mask
- Shin guards
- Protective helmet
- Throat guard
- Neck protector

Figure 2-4:
The catcher's equipment.

Protective helmet
Mask
Chest protector
Throat protector
Shin guards

If these items are of questionable quality, you are jeopardizing your health every time you drop into your crouch. All-Star Sporting Goods (615-526-2109) produces catcher's gear that meets major league standards, including the hockey mask headgear that is becoming de rigueur among professional catchers.

Batting helmets

Both major leagues require hitters to wear batting helmets with at least one earflap (protecting the side facing the pitcher). Anytime you go to bat against live pitching without wearing a batting helmet, you should have your head examined. And if you're unlucky, that is exactly what you will have to do. Even a low-grade fastball can permanently damage or even kill you if it collides with your unprotected cranium. A solid batting helmet with double earflaps is the best insurance policy a hitter can buy. American Baseball Caps, Inc. (800-345-8211) is the official manufacturer of batting helmets for major-league baseball.

Light plastic batting helmets, such as the freebies that major league teams give away on Helmet Day at the stadium, are too flimsy to protect your head from an errant fastball. Do not wear them to the plate. To offer effective protection, your helmet should

- ✔ Fit squarely on your head.
- ✔ Feature ear holes that center over each of your ears.
- ✔ Extend far enough to cover the delicate mastoid region.

Batting (and sliding) gloves

Batting gloves protect a hitter's most important tools — his hands — from painful blisters, cuts, and scrapes. Runners can wear them on the base paths to protect their hands while sliding; fielders can don them under their fielding gloves to reduce the sting of hard-hit balls. Franklin Sports, Inc. (800-225-8747) carries batting gloves designed to withstand the rigors of a major league season. For hitting, choose gloves that do not detract from your feel for the bat.

Pro-Hitter Corp. (914-634-1191) has created Direct Protect, a doughnut-shaped rubber accessory that fits over and protects your thumb, the digit most susceptible to injury when you're working in the batter's box. It can be worn over your batting glove.

The way you wear your hat

We're not sure who wrote the major league rule book, but it surely wasn't Ralph Lauren or Alan Flusser. The rule makers frown on any attempt at an on-field fashion statement that even hints at individuality. (As Jim Bouton, the irreverent pitcher for the New York Yankees and Seattle Pilots during the 1960s, once observed, "When baseball says it wants its players to show some flair, it means it wants us to wear our caps on a jaunty angle.") Baseball rules demand that teammates wear identical uniforms. Try to stand out by wearing different colored socks or donning a white fox cape, and the umpires won't permit you on the field (especially if they're part of the anti-fur movement). Home team uniforms must be white; visiting teams are required to wear a darker color. This requirement is meant to help fans, umpires, and especially players distinguish the teams from one another. If you have a base runner trapped in a run-down play and you slap the ball on a player whose uniform is the same hue as yours, you just tagged out your own third baseman.

Sweatbands

When the temperature is scorching and perspiration soaks your body, sweatbands help keep your hands dry at the plate. Two companies hold the major league licenses in this category: Wilson Team Sports (773-714-6800) and Easton Sports (800-632-7866). *Remember:* Make sure you clean those sweatbands regularly, or the aroma they exude will clear out entire stadiums.

Caps and Uniforms

Safety isn't the only consideration when dressing for the field; style and comfort matter, too. Want to dress your head like a major leaguer? New Era Cap Company (800-989-0445) is the official manufacturer of major league caps. Most major retail sporting goods chains, which include Foot Locker, Modells, Lids, Sports Authority, and Sears, carry baseball headwear. Your cap should fit snugly enough that the bill doesn't droop over your eyes to block your vision.

Russell Corporation (205-329-5089) holds the major league license to manufacture uniforms, batting practice jerseys, and baseball undershirts. However, Wilson and Rawlings also manufacture uniforms for several major league teams. Uniform fit is a matter of personal comfort; your pants and jersey should permit unrestricted movement at the plate and in the field.

Preparing the Field for Practice and Play

After you've equipped the players for some baseball action, your team may want to better equip its field and practice facilities for serious training and playing. In that case, consider contacting some of the companies listed in Table 2-1 that equip the professionals.

Table 2-1	Training and Field Equipment	
Equipment	*Manufacturer*	*Phone Number*
Bases	Beacon Ballfields	800-747-5985
Batting cages	National Batting Cages	800-547-8800
Field covers (tarpaulins)	Covermaster	800-387-5808
Foul lines (permanent)	Beam Clay	800-247-2326
Netting	Miller Net Company	800-423-6603
On-deck circles	AstroTurf Industries	800-233-5714
Pitching machines	ATEC	800-755-5100
Playing field sod	Beam Clay	800-247-2326
Radar guns	JUGS Company	800-547-6843
Scoreboards	Spectrum Scoreboards	713-944-6200
Turf mats	AstroTurf Industries	800-233-5714
Wall padding	American Athletic	800-247-3978
Wind screens	Promats Inc.	800-678-6287

And If You'll Permit Us an Indelicacy

Male ballplayers should never take the field without wearing jock straps (athletic supporters) and protective cups. You don't really need to ask why, do you?

A reminder on equipment

Be sure to play baseball with the best equipment that you can obtain. Remember, you don't always have to spend a lot of money to equip yourself well and to have fun. The great Willie Mays used to play stickball, and he seems to have done pretty well for himself. Who knows?

In an attic or a garage somewhere, your family may have some good equipment just waiting to see daylight again. (And if you run across the old baseball spikes shown here, you've just found some shoes worn by Hall of Famer Ted Williams.)

National Baseball Hall of Fame Library, Cooperstown, NY

Part II

Taking Your Swings — How to Play the Game

The 5th Wave   By Rich Tennant

In this part . . .

*B*aseball may not appear to be as physically demanding as basketball, hockey, football, or soccer, but don't kid yourself — you need to be in top condition to play a full season. In this part, we start our training camp by getting your muscles stretched and pumped (and stretched again). Then we've invited nine major league superstars to give you advice on your hitting, pitching, throwing, running, and fielding.

Our guest coaches have a combined 47 All-Star Game appearances, 30 Gold Gloves, 8 Most Valuable Player Awards, and 2 Cy Young Awards. In this part, they reveal some secrets of their success and help you strengthen any weaknesses in your own game. Read this part even if you intend only to be a spectator, because the information here gives you a deeper appreciation of what takes place on the field during a game. You'll quickly realize that something is always happening during a ball game, even when it looks like nothing is going on.

Chapter 4

Training: Getting into Baseball Shape

• •

In This Chapter

▶ Warming and stretching your muscles

▶ Jumping and bounding

▶ Using the medicine ball

▶ Sprinting

▶ Working with free weights

▶ Maintaining your rotator cuff

▶ Weighing in on the andro controversy

• •

*B*aseball players have to be in peak condition to survive the rigors of a long season. This game requires intense concentration and quick reactions; you can't allow yourself to be hindered by fatigue. A comprehensive training program can enhance your endurance, balance, coordination, speed and quickness (two different issues), flexibility, agility, and strength. The exercises described in this chapter are safe. However, you should have a complete physical before attempting any but the least stressful of them.

Trainers who transform 90-pound weaklings into Arnold Schwarzeneggers are of little value to you if they don't understand the demands of your sport. Ideally, you should work with people who possess a baseball background, either as trainers, coaches, or players. Stay away from drill sergeant types who demand one more rep even when the veins in your neck are flexed to bursting.

We've asked Gene Olivieri, who has trained pro athletes and helped get Richard Gere into buff shape for *An Officer and a Gentleman,* to oversee this chapter.

Warming Up

Your training program should start lightly and then gradually increase in intensity. Never start a workout cold. If you do, you risk an injury that could jeopardize your health and career. A good warm-up does exactly that: It raises your body temperature several degrees while rushing blood deep into the muscles and connective tissues you are about to challenge. A warm-up reduces the chance of ligament strains, muscle tears, and general soreness. You don't have to run a marathon to open up your capillaries; a continual 15-minute regimen should do the trick. Jumping jacks, bicycling, rowing on a machine, or bouncing on a trampoline can warm your muscle groups. Skipping rope is especially good because it also improves coordination.

A jogging circuit provides an ideal aerobic warm-up, and it requires no equipment except running shoes. Begin with a light 20-yard (18.3m) jog, going back and forth six times. Rest for a minute, and then repeat the exercise — only this time swing your arms in circles on both sides. Rest for a minute, and then repeat the exercise while raising your arms over your head. Now that your heart is pumping a tad faster, use the exercises in the following sections to further raise your muscles' temperature.

Jogging knee lifts

Start jogging again, but this time lift your knees toward your shoulders. Work your arms up and down in *opposite* step with your legs as you move. Repeat this three times over 20 yards (18.3m).

Skipping leg extensions

Extend both your arms in front of you to shoulder height. Skip forward slowly while extending your right leg toward your right hand, as shown in Figure 4-1. As you bring the right leg back down, extend the left leg in the same manner. Do this for 15 yards (13.7m). Do four repetitions.

Hamstring pulls are nagging injuries that too often sideline players whose legs are heavily muscled. Focus on your hamstrings during both of these exercises to ensure you are getting a full stretch.

Figure 4-1:
Skipping leg
extensions.

Stretching Out

Baseball is a game of sudden stops and starts, of instant acceleration. Tight muscles tear easily under such demands. Long, limber muscles increase your range of motion while decreasing the injury risks that accompany abrupt, jarring movements. Make sure to do the following stretches after your warm-up.

It is important to take long, slow breaths while you stretch. If you hold your breath or breathe too quickly during these exercises, you won't get the full benefits (and you may hyperventilate!). Breathe into the stretch and visualize exhaling any muscle tension. Hold each stretch for at least 10 seconds and as long as 30 seconds. Perform three sets per stretch, increasing your range of motion with each succeeding set. Do not bounce.

Torso twist

Stand with your feet shoulder-width apart, your knees slightly bent, and your head erect. Using only your waist and thighs to provide torque, slowly twist your trunk and torso to the left, and then to the right. Your head should follow the torso, as shown in Figure 4-2. Rotate until you can see directly behind you. Let your arms flail out so that they gently slap against your upper chest with each rotation. Keep your elbows, wrists, and shoulders loose, and your arm muscles relaxed. Do 30 repetitions. This exercise limbers the muscles supporting the spinal column.

Figure 4-2:
The torso
twist.

Forward bend

Stand with your feet shoulder-width apart, your knees straight and locked.
Loosely fold your arms across your chest. Bend forward gently. Slowly drop
as low as you can with your folded arms hanging down, as shown in Figure
4-3. Gradually lower your arms to a point a foot above your ankles. *Do not
force anything.*

Figure 4-3:
The forward
bend.

After you've reached your lowest point, take a deep breath and start rocking gently up and down. Your head and neck should be loose and dangling. Rock up and down 12 times, shift to the left for 12 more repetitions, and then do a final 12 on the right. This exercise stretches your vertebrae.

Forward leg bend

Stand in front of some form of waist-level support, such as a wall or a dance bar. Facing the support, raise up your right leg and place your heel on it. Starting at your thigh, slowly pull your hands up the upraised leg until you can wrap your fingers around your toes.

Place your forehead on your knee (or as close to it as you can get) while gently pulling the toes back toward your head (see Figure 4-4). Take ten deep breaths, and then switch legs. Do two repetitions. This exercise stretches the tendons in back of your legs.

Figure 4-4:
The forward
leg bend.

Shoulder roll

Stand with your feet shoulder-width apart and your knees slightly bent. Your arms should hang loosely at your sides. Roll your shoulders in a wide arc up toward your ears, circle toward the back, and then lower them (see Figure 4-5). Do 12 repetitions. Reverse the direction for a dozen more. Then simultaneously roll one shoulder forward and the other backward. Reverse those directions for the last 12 reps. This exercise stretches your shoulder muscles, tendons, and joints.

Figure 4-5:
The
shoulder
roll.

Triceps stretch

Stand with your feet shoulder-width apart and your knees slightly bent. Bending your elbow, bring your right hand behind your back and place the palm on the middle of your neck. Raise your left hand and place it on your right elbow. Gently pull the elbow to the left, as shown in Figure 4-6. Hold for 20 seconds, and then do the opposite side. Do two reps for each side. This exercise stretches your rear deltoids as well as your triceps. It limbers your throwing arm.

Figure 4-6:
The triceps
stretch.

Forearm and wrist stretch

Stand with your feet shoulder-width apart and your knees slightly bent. Extend your right arm in front of your torso with your palm parallel to the ground. Lift your right hand until its fingers point to the ceiling at a 90-degree angle.

Take the top of your right fingers in your left hand and gently pull the hand toward you, as shown in Figure 4-7. Hold the stretch for 15 seconds. Then point your right fingers to the ground and gently pull them toward you with your left. Hold for 15 seconds, and then repeat for the opposite side. Do one rep for each side. This exercise stretches the muscles of your lower arm.

Figure 4-7:
The forearm and wrist stretch.

V-stretch

Sit on a flat surface with your legs straight and, without straining, spread your legs as far as they can go in a V-shape. Place your left hand on your right knee to keep your leg straightened. Lowering your chest to your right thigh, slowly reach out with your left hand and grab the toes of your right foot, as shown in Figure 4-8. Hold the stretch, and then do the opposite side. Do two reps for each side. This exercise stretches the glutes, lower back, and hamstrings.

Figure 4-8:
The
V-stretch.

Seated groin stretch

Sit with your heels drawn together and as close to the groin as possible.
Gently push your knees to the floor with your elbows while keeping your
back straight. Then hold your ankles and pull your upper body forward while
maintaining your posture.

Knee pulls

Lie on your back with your knees up at a 90-degree angle. Place both hands
around your right knee and gently pull it toward your chest, as shown in
Figure 4-9. Hold for 15 seconds, and then do the left knee. Do four reps for
each side. This exercise stretches your lower back.

Figure 4-9:
Knee pulls.

Butterfly stretch

Sit on a flat surface with your legs in front of you in a V. Grab your ankles and pull them toward your groin. Let your knees raise off the ground. Then slowly lower your knees to their original position, as shown in Figure 4-10. Hold the stretch for 20 seconds. Do two reps. This exercise stretches the inner thigh and groin.

Dip splits

Stand upright with your feet together. Step forward with your left foot, as far as you can without straining. Balancing yourself on your left leg, slowly slide your right foot back while dipping your knee down. (You may want to brace yourself against a support the first few times you try this.)

Your left thigh should be parallel to the ground, and your right knee should be suspended just above the ground, as shown in Figure 4-11. If you don't use a support, extend your arms out to both sides for additional balance. While maintaining this position, gently rock up and down. Do six reps, and then repeat with the other leg. Do three sets for each side. This exercise stretches the hamstrings as well as the large muscles and tendons at the front of the thighs. It also strengthens your ankles.

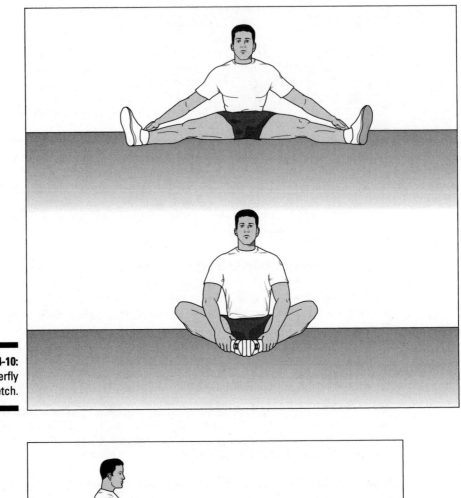

Figure 4-10:
The butterfly
stretch.

Figure 4-11:
Dip splits.

Jumping for Joy: Plyometrics

Plyometrics are a series of jumping and bounding drills to develop explosive leg muscles that react quickly and forcefully — exactly what you need to play a game filled with sudden, unexpected movements. To execute these drills, you need a padded, heavy-duty box with a solid base to support your weight. You can construct your own or, better still, buy one at an athletic equipment store.

Before taking to the air, warm up for ten minutes with a light jog. Jumping (or rather landing out of your jump) can jar your ankles, knees, and hips, so your shoes should be shock absorbent and provide your ankles with support. Gel-soled footwear is a good choice. If you have problems with your lower joints, don't attempt these drills without consulting your physician.

Good jumping form

Your upper torso should be relaxed but upright. As you prepare to leap, swing your arms up from your sides to create momentum. When you land, bend your knees to absorb shock. Start with a 12-inch-high plyometrics box and gradually progress to the 24-inch version. Position the box on a surface with give to it — grass is the best choice. Avoid doing plyometrics on a hard floor or concrete. Rest for several minutes between sets. Whenever possible, do these drills with an instructor or a partner who can monitor and correct your form.

The plyometric drills

The following sections describe the types of drills you can do for your plyometric workout.

The box jump

Stand approximately 12 inches (30.5cm) from the front of the box. (You can adjust the distance as you discover your jumping abilities.) Bend your knees and jump onto the box. (Don't forget to swing those arms up!) Jump backward immediately. As soon as your feet touch the ground, jump back on the box. Start with 5 reps and work up to 12. Start with one set and work up to three. This exercise works the calves and quadriceps.

The jump and run

Stand on the box. Jump forward to the ground, landing with your knees bent and feet shoulder-width apart. Immediately break into a 15-yard (13.7m) dash. Jog back and repeat. Start with four reps and work up to ten. This exercise improves your start-and-go reactions while working your glutes, quadriceps, hamstrings, and calves.

Box jumps at alternating heights

As you progress in strength and agility, you can use higher boxes. Attempt this exercise only after becoming comfortable with the 24-inch model. You need five plyometric boxes of varying heights for this drill. Their heights should increase from 12 to 24 inches (30.5 to 61cm).

Position each box (in ascending height order) 24 inches apart (61cm) from each other in a straight line. Take your usual stance in front of the smallest box. Jump onto it, jump immediately forward onto the ground, and then jump onto the next box. Complete the circuit without pausing. Rest for 30 seconds and begin again. Do four sets and work up to six. This exercise works a wide range of leg muscles while building endurance.

Side-to-side jumps

You don't need a box for this exercise. On grass, mark off two points 2½ feet (76.2cm) apart. Stand by one marker with your feet together and jump sideways to the other marker. Do 6 reps and then work up to 12. This exercise develops hip strength, which enhances your torque at the plate. (Read Chapter 5 to see how important torque is for hitting.)

Taking Your Medicine: Using the Medicine Ball

Medicine balls may seem like relics from the 1890s, but they are making a comeback with baseball's strength trainers. Used properly, the balls can work a wide range of muscles; they target your abdominals, glutes, hip muscles, upper leg muscles, and back muscles, while also working the upper torso. These muscles provide balance as well as explosive rotational power (just what you need whether you're pitching or hitting). Medicine balls come in a variety of weights — generally 2 to 16 pounds (7.3kg); if you've never used one before, start with nothing heavier than a 6-pound ball. Work slowly and concentrate on form. Rest one minute between sets. (You can slice that to 30 seconds as you build wind and endurance.) Do these exercises two or three times a week.

Basic rotation pass

Standing back-to-back with a partner, pass the ball back and forth in rapid rotation. You hand off the ball to your right and immediately accept the return on your left, as shown in Figure 4-12. Do this for 30 seconds for one set. Gradually work up to three sets and then start again with a heavier ball. This exercise builds your obliques and abdominals.

Figure 4-12:
The basic
rotation
pass.

Basic chest pass

You and your partner should stand approximately 10 feet (3.04m) apart. (If you don't have a partner, you can throw the ball against a wall.) Hold the ball at chest level. Using your wrists and fingertips, pass it to your partner as if your were passing a basketball. (See Figure 4-13.) Pass it rapidly back and forth for six repetitions. Work up to 12. Do two to three sets.

Basic toss

With your partner standing at your feet, lie on a comfortable, flat surface with your knees bent at a 90-degree angle. Raise your shoulders by slightly contracting your abdominals. From this position, toss the ball to your partner. Catch his or her immediate return, lie back, raise and contract again and repeat your toss. Start with 15 reps and work up to 25. Do one set. This exercise builds the chest, wrists, and fingers.

Figure 4-13:
The basic
chest pass.

Hip toss

Stand laterally 10 feet (3.04m) from your partner. (You can also use a wall for this exercise.) Hold the ball with both hands at your hip. While keeping your lower body stationary, twist your torso and arms toward your partner while firing the ball. Try to use the same motion you employ while swinging a bat.

Do a complete set, and then switch to work the opposite side. Start with 8 reps and work up to 12. Do two to three sets. This exercise works your obliques, hip, and lower back. It's another good drill for building torque.

Toe push

Lie on your back with the medicine ball on your chest. Bring your legs up to a 90-degree angle. Push the ball as close to the top of your toes as you can (as your shoulders lift from the ground). Hold this position for a moment, as shown in Figure 4-14, and then return to your starting position. Start with 15 reps and work up to 25. This exercise works the lower back, abdomen, chest, and shoulders.

Medicine ball jumps

Squat as close to the ground as your balance allows while holding the medicine ball in front of you at your knees. Jump up as high as you can while swinging the medicine ball upward. Land with your knees bent to absorb any shock.

Return to your squat and repeat the exercise. Start with 6 reps and work up to 12. Do one set and then work up to three. This exercise works your quadriceps, hip flexors, and hamstrings. It gives you explosive drive for leaping.

Figure 4-14:
The toe
push.

Lunges

Do this drill slowly. Hold the ball above your head while standing with your feet shoulder-width apart. Lunge forward with your right leg until your chest is behind your knee. As you lunge, bring the ball forward until it is just above or parallel to your right ankle. Return to standing and repeat the drill using your left leg. Start with 6 reps and work up to 12. Do two to three sets. This exercise works your leg's entire muscle group while limbering your hamstrings and lower back.

You can also build upper body strength by cradling the ball in your arms and jogging short distances. Start at a weight and distance that are comfortable and then gradually increase both.

High Intensity Leg Work: Sprinting

Jogging makes for a great warm-up and, when done over a long distance, builds wind and endurance. However, in baseball, running is done in short, sudden bursts, so sprints should be a regular part of your workout routine. The best place to sprint is a baseball field. When you lack access to one, go to any field and set up your own "diamond" with markers 90 feet (27.45m) apart.

Make sure you warm up with a light jog and stretch (especially those hamstrings!) before attempting any sprints.

Hurdling sprints

After warming up, do this drill prior to sprinting. It teaches you the arm swing, stride, and leg lift that compose proper sprinting mechanics. Place 12 1-foot-high (30.5cm) hurdles approximately 20 inches (50.8cm) apart in a straight line. (You should be able to take two sprinting strides between each hurdle.) Start by running the circuit slowly while pulling your legs up high (or you'll trip), and swing your arms up at your side with each stride. After you are comfortable, sprint back and forth across the hurdle line, as shown in Figure 4-15. Start with two complete circuits per set and work up to four circuits. Start with two sets and then work up to four.

Figure 4-15:
Hurdling
sprints.

Sprinting for home

When you are ready, stand at home plate as if you were at-bat. (You can use a real bat or an imaginary one.) Swing, and then sprint to first as if you were trying to beat out a close play. Jog back to home plate, swing again, but this time sprint to second. Retrace your steps with another jog, swing, and sprint at top speed to third. Catch your breath, and then sprint for home as if a teammate had just hit a sacrifice fly and you were challenging outfielder Raul Mondesi, one of baseball's deadliest arms. Finish the rotation by hitting an inside-the-park homer and circling all the bases. (If you want to fantasize that the pitch was delivered by Greg Maddux with the score tied in the bottom of the ninth of a World Series seventh game, it's all right with us.) Do one complete circuit and then work up to two.

You can add variations to your sprinting drill. Stand at first and pretend to be stealing second or sprint to third on a ball hit into the gap. Start at second and try to score on a single to left-center. By replicating these situations, you're gaining speed while practicing your game.

Playing Heavy Metal: Working with Free Weights

Baseball's approach to conditioning has changed radically over the last 20 years. Until the late 1970s, trainers frowned upon players lifting weights; they believed that weight training made you bulky and limited your range of motion. But in 1979, Brian Downing, a catcher with the California Angels, used a rigorous weightlifting regimen to transform himself into the Incredible Hulk. (Yes, that is what they called him.) In his new body, Brian added 70 points to his batting average and over 100 points to his slugging average. Those numbers caught everyone's attention. It wasn't long before clubs were opening weight training rooms and actively encouraging their players to press the metal. Today, most players train with weights. It's one of the reasons (genetics is the other) players are bigger and stronger than ever before.

However, before you even look at a dumbbell, a word or eight of caution. Start your weightlifting program with a certified trainer. A professional can teach proper form and devise a schedule that alternates body parts while allowing your muscles to heal. (Muscles do tear during lifting.) Proper form and a balanced schedule reduce injury risk and help you get better, faster results. Use a spotter — someone who assists you if you slip or need help completing a rep — whenever you lift a heavy weight (especially when you are benching). Generally speaking, you should be able lift a weight for at least eight reps. If you can't do eight, go lighter. After you can do 12 reps easily, go to the next higher weight and start at 8 reps again.

You are able to lift more if you work large muscles groups, such as the chest, before working smaller muscles like the biceps. To discover more about choosing trainers, proper form, weight-training equipment, vitamins, and nutrition, you may want to read *Fitness For Dummies,* 2nd Edition, and *Weight Training For Dummies* by Susan Schlosberg and Liz Neporent (from IDG Books Worldwide, Inc.).

Whatever weight-training program you follow, combine it with a regular stretching regimen. You don't want to sacrifice flexibility in pursuit of bulk. And remember, you don't have to pump iron to excel in baseball. Texas Rangers slugger Juan Gonzalez returned to the ranks of elite sluggers and won the 1996 MVP award after he *curtailed* his weight-training program. During the two prior seasons, his megamuscles had hampered his swing. Hall of Famers Mickey Mantle, Ralph Kiner, and Jimmy Foxx hit the ball as far as anyone playing today, and they didn't touch free weights. However, weightlifting drills can strengthen your baseball muscles, provided you know which exercises to use.

Performance specialist Jeff Sassone and the folks at the International Performance Institute (at the Bollettieri Sports Academy), a world-class sports facility devoted to improving all aspects of athletic performance (in Bradenton, Florida, 941-755-1000), have offered us some weight training exercises for any player who wants to pound some metal. Our experts are the same people who helped train 1997 Rookie of the Year Nomar Garciaparra, so listen closely to what they have to say.

Bench press

The bench press works your chest muscles. Lie with your back flat on a bench with your feet on the ground to either side. Grasp the barbell with an overhand grip at points that leave you a few inches wider than shoulder width. Tighten your abdominals and tuck your chin into your chest. The bar should be directly over your eyes. Lower the bar slowly to the middle of your chest, and then press it back up over your eyes.

Dumbbell bench press

This exercise also works the chest while emphasizing muscle balance. Lie flat on the bench with your feet on the floor. Grab the dumbbells in an overhand grip. Press them up directly over your shoulders with your palms facing forward. Lower them with control until your elbows are slightly below your shoulders. Push the weight back up while keeping your shoulder blades flat on the bench.

Close grip bench press

Lie flat on the bench with your feet on the floor. Grip the barbell with both hands, about 6 inches (15.24cm) apart. Lower the bar with control until it touches your chest. Then press back up to the starting position.

One arm dumbbell row

Grab a dumbbell with your palm facing in. Keep your abdominals tight. Bend at the hips until your upper torso is parallel or nearly parallel to the floor. Keep your back slightly arched, and your knees slightly bent. Place your free hand on the bench for support. Allow the arm with the dumbbell to hang straight down from your shoulder. Pull the dumbbell up to your waist. At the top of this motion, your elbow should be tight to your side (keep it tight throughout) and pointing straight in back of you.

Squats

Place the barbell across your shoulders so that the weight feels evenly distributed. Your feet should be parallel to one another and spread slightly wider than shoulder width. Place your hands shoulder-width apart on the bar. Keep your head up and your shoulders back. Maintain a straight back with a slight arch at its base. Slowly bend your knees until your thighs are parallel to the floor. Rise back up. Do three sets. This is a power-hitter's exercise; it works all the large muscles, including the hips and glutes, which help you to drive a ball for distance.

Lunges

Set up as you did for the squat. However, instead of bending with both knees, step forward with your right leg. Slowly bend your right knee and lower your body while bending your left leg behind you. Keep your chest behind your right knee. Push back to your starting position and work the other leg. As an alternative to using the bar, you can also do this while holding a dumbbell in each hand at your side.

You must use a spotter for this exercise and wear a weight belt to protect your back. You may also want to lightly wrap your knees for additional support. And don't let your front knee pass your foot.

Hammer curls

Grab a dumbbell in each hand. Hold them down at your sides with your palms facing each other. Raise the dumbbells simultaneously to the shoulders while keeping the palms facing each other and your thumbs up. Lower the weights with control and repeat.

Upright row

Grab a barbell with your hands about 6 inches (15.24cm) apart in an overhand grip. Start with the bar resting on your thighs. With your elbows to the outside, pull the bar up to your chin. Keep your elbows above your wrist and straight. Lower the bar to your starting point with control and repeat.

Curl to press

While standing, hold a dumbbell in each hand with your palms facing forward. Raise the dumbbells to your shoulders while keeping your elbows at your sides. With your palms facing forward, press the dumbbells overhead by extending your arms. Return the dumbbells to the starting position by lowering the weight with control.

Lying triceps extension

Lie on a bench while grasping your barbell in an overhand grip that is slightly less than shoulder-width apart. Without locking your elbows, straighten your arms until you raise the weight directly above midchest. Hold your elbows stationary as you bend your arms to *gently* lower the weight to your forehead. Raise the weight back above your chest and repeat. (See Figure 4-16.) Do three sets. This exercise builds up your triceps, the muscles that allow you to straighten your elbow. Strong triceps provide added insurance against elbow injuries and discomfort.

Figure 4-16:
Lying
triceps
extension.

When you are doing lying tricep extensions (a.k.a. brainbusters), one slip can cause serious injury. Start the exercise with a light weight; you may even use only the bar without any weights on it. And always use a spotter.

Keeping Your Rotator Well Oiled

Rotator cuff impingement has interrupted or terminated more pitching careers than any other baseball injury. It has also bedeviled position players. (All-Star shortstop Rick Burleson's career ended shortly after he blew out his cuff making rifle throws to first base.)

Simply put, the rotator cuff keeps your arm in its socket. Strengthening the muscles around the cuff helps to prevent a devastating injury. Julian Fantechi, a trainer certified by the American Council on Exercise, recommends the following exercises to keep your throwing arm from breaking down. You should gradually increase the amount of weight you use in each of these exercises as you grow stronger.

Circles

This exercise helps to strengthen the scapular muscles. Spread your feet shoulder-width apart, and bend your torso slightly forward. Let your right arm hang directly in front of you while holding a five-pound weight. Keep your left arm at your side or bend it behind you. Circle your right arm in a tight clockwise motion while keeping it straight at the elbow. Do two sets of 15 circles, and then repeat with your left arm.

External shoulder rotations

This exercise also strengthens the scapular muscles. While holding a five-pound weight, kneel down and rest your right arm across the top of a weight bench so that the arm is parallel to the ground. Without moving your upper arm, slowly raise the weight until your upper arm and forearm form a 90-degree angle. Lower the weight until you resume the starting position. Do two sets of 15 repetitions, and then repeat with your left arm.

Side lateral raises

This exercise strengthens the supraspinatus, a key rotator cuff muscle. While standing, hold five-pound dumbbells at your sides with an overhand grip. Laterally raise the weights to shoulder height with your palms facing down. Your arms should be parallel to the ground, and your elbows should be slightly bent at a 20-degree angle. Slowly return the weights to their original position and repeat. Maintain your elbow angle throughout. This exercise works the deltoids and strengthens the area around the rotator cuff. (You use the deltoids to swing your arms.) Do two sets of 12 reps.

Shoulder shrugs

This exercise strengthens the trapezius, rhomboids, and levator scapulae. Hold a pair of 10-pound dumbbells at your sides with your elbows locked. Slowly raise your shoulders up as if you were trying to touch your ears. Go as high as you can. Then slowly lower the weights back to the starting position. Don't roll your shoulders. (See Figure 4-17.) Do two sets of 12 reps.

Figure 4-17:
The shoulder shrug.

It Ain't Over 'til It's Over

Just as you had to warm up before working out, you have to cool down afterward. Do some light jogging or stretching. Then lie on the floor with your legs straight up and resting against a wall. Taking 10 or 15 minutes to gently come down from your workout limits your soreness while increasing your flexibility.

The andro controversy

Controversy broke out during the 1998 season when a reporter revealed that super slugger Mark McGwire was taking androstenedione. The nutritional supplement, which supposedly helps weightlifters build muscle mass, is sold over the counter throughout the United States. However, the International Olympic Committee considers andro a performance-enhancing drug; athletes who compete in Olympic trials and competitions are banned from using it. Major league baseball's executive council recently commissioned a Harvard University study to help it determine whether players should be barred from using andro. The study's initial findings were inconclusive. Any ban of the drug would have to be ratified by the baseball player's union.

If you're considering taking androstenedione (sales of the supplement skyrocketed when people found out that Big Mac used it), you should consider several issues. First, andro can't bulk you up on its own. It may help you do more reps using greater weight while speeding your recovery time. (Then again, it may not. Many physicians claim andro's effectiveness as a muscle builder has been exaggerated.) But you still have to put in long hours hitting the weight room if you want to build more mass. That means if you want McGwirean results, you have to demonstrate the same discipline as the ultra-dedicated first baseman.

Second, andro alone can't make you a better hitter. Bulging biceps do not a slugger make. Ken Griffey, Jr., for example, has never lifted weights, yet he has led the American League in

home runs four times. Ernie Banks, a member of baseball's 500 home run club, and Henry Aaron, the major league's career leader in four-baggers, were not especially large men. But they both had quick bats that enabled them to drive the ball great distances. When it comes to generating power, bat speed rather than size is what matters. (That's why the 5'7", 160-pound Joe Morgan was able to lead the National League in slugging in 1976.)

Finally, andro is relatively new. Because few human studies have been done involving this supplement, doctors can't predict its long-range health effects. We may discover 20 years from now that prolonged use of andro causes internal damage. Anyone interested in taking the supplement already has good reason to be wary. Manufacturers claim that andro works by triggering testosterone production. Many physicians believe excess testosterone may play a role in causing prostate cancer.

If you're looking for a muscle builder, you're probably better off taking something with a lengthier track record. And you shouldn't consume any bulk-enhancing supplements or hormones without first speaking to your doctor. (By the way, about a third of the way through the 1999 season, Big Mac announced he was no longer using andro. Forsaking the supplement didn't prevent him from hitting a major-league-high 65 home runs. Sammy Sosa had his second straight season of 60-plus home runs, and he has never taken andro. The muscular outfielder has, however, admitted a fondness for Flintstones vitamins; Dino is a particular favorite.)

Chapter 5

Swinging the Lumber: Hitting Like a Major Leaguer

· ·

In This Chapter

▶ Preparing to hit

▶ Taking your stance and stride

▶ Making contact with the ball

▶ Hitting the ball where you want

▶ Bunting and moving runners

▶ Practicing and troubleshooting your swing

▶ Taking some advice from Rusty Staub

· ·

I could talk about hitting for five minutes or five hours without repeating myself. Advice on the subject can be as complex as an in-depth explanation of hip rotation or as simple as saying, "See the ball, hit the ball." Ted Williams once said, "Hitting big-league pitching is the most difficult thing to do in sports." Coming from the greatest hitter of the past 50 years, that statement may seem like bragging. However, most athletes who have taken their cuts on a baseball diamond would agree with Williams. Just ask Michael Jordan how hard it is to get good wood on the ball. The greatest basketball player of our time — perhaps of all time — struggled to hit .220 during his season in the minor leagues. Bo Jackson was a football superstar, and as a major-league baseball player, he was a fine outfielder with great speed, a prodigious arm, and awe-inspiring power. But Jackson's lifetime batting average was a modest .250. Jim Thorpe, undoubtedly the finest athlete in Olympic history, also hit little more than .250 during his six-year stint in the major leagues.

What makes hitting so difficult? Geometry for one thing. As coaches have reminded hitters since baseball's earliest days, "The game is played with a round ball and a round bat, and you have to hit it square." Geography and physics complicate that challenge. Only 60 feet 6 inches (18.4m) separates the pitching mound from the batter's box. The average major-league pitcher throws his fastball 87 miles per hour, which means it takes the average fastball less than two-thirds of a second to travel from the pitcher's hand to your hitting zone. How quick is that? In the time it takes to think of the phrase "two-thirds of a second," strike one is already past you.

So unless the hurler is soft-tossing a *knuckleball,* a hitter has barely an instant to read the pitch. Is the pitcher throwing a *fastball,* a *slider,* a *change-up,* or a *curve?* If it's a fastball, is it a *four-seamer,* a *two-seamer,* or the dreaded split-fingered version? (Read all about these pitches in Chapter 6.) Where will it cross the plate — inside or out, up or down? Can you pull this pitch down the line or should you hit it to the opposite field? As you make these assessments, you must move your bat into the hitting zone. Of course, once you make contact, you have eight fielders in front of you (and one behind you) committed to transforming the ball you just hit into an out. No wonder the best hitters succeed only about three times out of ten.

A Hitter's Tools

If you're willing to put in the hours, you can overcome all these obstacles to make yourself a good hitter. How good depends on what you have to work with. To succeed, hitters need:

- **Excellent vision:** As the baseball adage declares, "You can't hit what you can't see." You need strong vision and depth perception to judge a ball's distance, speed, and spin. However, you don't have to have 20/20 vision in both eyes. Many major-league hitters have excelled while wearing corrective lenses. Michael Tucker, an outfielder for the 1997 Atlanta Braves, was not quite the nearsighted Mr. Magoo without his contacts, but he was close. Despite his poor uncorrected vision, Tucker hit .283 in 1997 while playing excellent defense. Frank Howard wore glasses as an outfielder/first baseman with the Washington Senators during the 1960s and '70s. He led the American League in home runs twice.

- **Quick reflexes:** After you recognize (or *read*) the pitch, your hand-eye coordination must be sharp enough to get your bat on the ball. The better your reflexes, the longer you can wait on a pitch.

- **Focus:** When you're up at the plate, fans, players, and coaches are yelling at you (and sometimes their words are not encouraging). Planes may be flying overhead, the wind may be swirling objects across your field of vision, the pitcher can have a funky motion, and you may be tempted to think about the error you made in the last inning. You must block out all of these distractions and concentrate on the task at hand.

- **Upper body strength:** To swing a wooden bat (which often weighs two pounds or more) with controlled velocity, you must build up your arms, shoulders, chest, and wrists. You also need strong hands. If you have a weak grip, a pitcher can knock the bat out of your hands.

- ✔ **Courage:** A fastball is a missile that can maim or even kill you. That is the hard reality that hitters bring to every at-bat, but you can't let it rattle you. If you're afraid of the ball, you're going to back off (or *bail out*) any time a pitch comes near you. You won't stay at the plate long enough to get a good look at the ball. You'll never be able to hit if you can't overcome your fear.

- ✔ **Sound strike zone judgment:** Hitters who come to the plate swinging at every pitch handicap themselves. You need to be able to recognize the strike zone while developing the patience not to swing at pitches outside it.

- ✔ **Adaptability:** You opened the season crushing inside fastballs. Now the pitchers around the league have gotten the message. (Trust me, they will. Federal Express doesn't operate as quickly as the pitchers' grapevine.) So you're suddenly seeing a steady diet of outside breaking stuff. Adjust to the change — or your batting average will plummet.

- ✔ **Hitting hunger:** Some batters get two hits in their first two at-bats and think, at least unconsciously, that they're done for the day. Great hitters are never content. As Stan Musial, the former St. Louis Cardinals out-fielder and batting champion, has repeatedly said, "When I got two hits in a game, I came up wanting a third. If I got a third, I had to get a fourth. I never knew when I might go 0 for 4, so I was always *hungry* for more base hits."

That last item is something you either have or you don't, but you can develop the other attributes. I help you work on most of them throughout this chapter.

Picking Your Lumber

Before we write another word explaining how to hit, take a look at what you hit with. The bat you choose should feel comfortable. Big-league bats gener-ally weigh between 32 and 36 ounces (907g to 1kg). If you can snap a 36- to 38-ounce bat through the strike zone with control and velocity, go for it. When a pitched ball collides with a heavyweight bat, it travels farther.

However, don't choose a large, heavy bat thinking it will magically transform you into a power hitter. Big bats don't necessarily produce big hits. If you can't control your bat, your swing becomes awkward and long. You may have to start it early in the pitcher's delivery — and once you get it going, it's hard to stop. Pitchers, taking advantage of that swing, can continually fool you with breaking stuff. Pretty soon, you won't be hitting for power, you won't be hitting for singles, you won't be hitting *period*. You may as well use that big bat for kindling.

Bats come in various shapes. Find one that suits you. For instance, a bat with a medium handle and large barrel offers you more hitting surface. However, you won't be able to snap it through the hitting zone as quickly as a bat with a very thin handle and a large barrel. Throughout most of my career, I swung an average-sized bat — it weighed 32 ounces and measured 34½ inches (87.6cm) long — yet I still managed to lead the National League in slugging in 1976. It had a thin handle and a large barrel. Bat speed was the key to my power. With my light bat, I could wait longer on the ball, which allowed me more time to recognize the pitch. I could whip through the strike zone with a quick, compact swing. The large barrel added momentum and gave me all the hitting surface I wanted.

Some big-league hitters change bats depending on the pitcher. I would occasionally go to a heavier bat against soft-throwing left-handers. I knew I didn't have to be quite as quick against them, and the bat's additional mass helped me drive the ball. Other than those instances, however, I stayed with my regular bat. It gave me the bat speed, control, and balance I needed to cope with most situations.

If you're a younger player, you may want to think "light." When you are unsure of the precise bat weight that is right for you, simply choose a bat that is comfortable.

Holding the Bat

The first thing you should consider when gripping a bat is *to glove or not to glove.* Almost all big-leaguers wear batting gloves — some because it gives them a better hold on the bat, others because they have large endorsement contracts with glove companies. I *didn't* wear a glove when I hit because I liked the feel of the wood against my fingers. (I did, however, wear a golf glove when I was on base to protect my hands while sliding.) Whether you wear batting gloves is a matter of personal preference. If gloves improve your grip, wear them. (Some players prefer substances such as resin or pine tar to improve their grip.)

Get a grip

When you hold your bat, your hands should touch so they can work as a unit. Begin by placing your bat handle at the base of the fingers of both hands. Grip the bat with your fingers rather than in your palm; holding it with your palm deprives you of wrist action, flexibility, and bat speed. Align the middle knuckles of your top hand between the middle and lower knuckles of your bottom hand.

Choking up on the bat gave me better control. I would slide my hands an inch or two above the knob of the bat. Many people believe that choke hitters can't generate power, but Ted Williams choked up, and he has over 500 career home runs on his résumé. You *do* sacrifice some power with an extreme choke (five or more inches above the knob). See Figure 5-1 for an illustration of both grips.

If you're strong enough, you can slide your hands down to the knob without surrendering any control; this grip gives you a tad more plate coverage. Some sluggers bury their little fingers beneath the bat knob; they believe doing so helps their wrists and hands to work in better sync. You have to be extremely powerful to do this, though. Most hitters should stick with one of the more conventional grips.

When you're at-bat, hold the bat firmly but don't squeeze it; tension slows down your wrists and hands. Your grip automatically tightens as you swing. Hold the bat more firmly with your bottom hand than with your top one. Your bottom hand pulls your bat through the hitting zone.

As kids, we were told that our bats would break if we hit a ball on the bat label. That's an old wives' tale, but you should keep the label turned away from the pitcher anyway. The grain side of the bat gives you a harder hitting surface.

Figure 5-1:
The basic bat grip and choking up.

Bat and body position

Now that you have your bat in your hands, how close should you hold it to your body? Again, let comfort dictate your choice, but it should be no less than 5 inches and no more than 7 inches from your torso (about 13 to 18cm). Holding your hands near your body keeps you on the inside of the ball. If you hold the bat out farther than that, your swing has too large an arc; you lose leverage and find it difficult to coordinate your hip and arm into your swing. If you bring the bat in too close, you restrict your movement and lose bat speed; your swing has a large loop, and it requires a long push to get your bat into the hitting zone. By the time you get the bat where you need it, that fast-ball is already past you (see Figure 5-2).

Hold your hands somewhere between the letters on your uniform front and your shoulders. Your elbows should be away from your body (as shown in Figure 5-3).

Figure 5-2: Holding your hands too near or too far from your body changes your swing.

Figure 5-3:
A proper
way to hold
your bat.

On chicken flaps and other eccentricities

Whenever I brought my arms too close to my body, I tended to upper-cut the ball. The result? Too many fly-ball outs. That habit was tough to break. The late Nellie Fox, a Hall of Fame second baseman and a player/coach when I played with the Houston Astros, suggested I flap my elbow whenever I was at the plate as a reminder to keep my arms away from my torso. I was only supposed to do this for a few days, but the "chicken flap" became part of my hitting routine. It kept my elbows out and also got me ready to hit.

Will flapping your elbows make you a better hitter? If you have the same problem I did, it may. However, rather than emulate my or some other player's quirk, you must develop your own method for getting comfortable at the plate. My Cincinnati Reds teammate Tony Perez — one of the best clutch hitters I ever saw — used to continually regrip his bat. First, the fingers of one hand would open and close on the handle, and then the fingers of the other would do the same. It was as if he were playing a flute as he waited for the pitch. This method was nothing more than a rhythmic device that relaxed Tony while preparing him to hit.

Some players step out of the box after every pitch to windmill their bats. Next time you watch a game, pay attention to the hitters as they enter the batter's box. You'll probably detect a different idiosyncrasy with each player.

The point of all this is you can do anything you want with the bat *before you start your swing*. However, as you attack the ball, your stride must carry you into your hitting zone. Stan Musial had a peek-a-boo crouch at the plate that made him look like a man peering around a corner (see Figure 5-4). Carl Yastrzemski, the great Boston Red Sox outfielder and batting champion, stood nearly upright at home — he only slightly flexed his knee and hip — while holding his bat high above his left ear. (Yaz was a left-handed hitter.) He looked as if he were ringing a church bell. Musial and Yastrzemski had dissimilar stances, but their strides and hip rotations left them in the same position as they made contact with the ball.

Figure 5-4: Musial demonstrates his unique hitting style.

National Baseball Hall of Fame Library, Cooperstown, NY

So however you choose to carry your bat to the plate — on your shoulders, close to your body, parallel to the ground — is fine, as long as it allows you to quickly reach your ideal hitting position. And you can't know what impact your quirk has on your swing until you get into the batter's box to practice.

Stepping Up to the Plate

When you come up to hit, the first thing you must decide is where to stand in the batter's box. This is a matter of personal preference. Edgar Martinez, an outstanding hitter for the Seattle Mariners throughout the 1990s, stands so far back in the box he's nearly out of it. This stance gives him more time to look over each pitch. Other batters stand in the rear of the box but far from the plate, up in the box and near the plate, or up in the box and far from the plate.

Any number of combinations is possible. I have short arms, so I stood close to the plate. This position gave me a better opportunity to reach strikes on the outside corner. (If your stance doesn't allow you access to those outside pitches, find another one.) Because I had a very quick bat, I felt comfortable standing far up in the batter's box. To discover what serves you best, hit from various positions in the box against live pitching.

The benefits of being up front

When you stand at the front of the box (see Figure 5-5), your stride brings you in front of home plate. Anything you hit in front of the plate has a better chance of staying fair. Standing in front also helps you against sinkerball and breaking ball pitchers; you are able to hit the ball before it drops below your swing. If you stand deep in the box against a good sinkerballer, you're giving him an advantage; his ball has more time to sink.

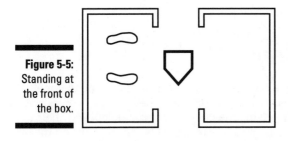

Figure 5-5:
Standing at
the front of
the box.

Standing at the front of the box also allows you to hit the curveball before it fully breaks. Even knuckleballs are easier to hit from this location; they have less time to dance. (I used to move as far up in the batter's box as I could against certain breaking ball pitchers; it took their best weapons away from them.)

Fastballs provide your up-front stance with its ultimate test. The closer you are to the pitching mound, the faster pitches reach you at the plate. If you can't handle fastballs from the front of the batter's box, you need to step back.

To develop bat speed and strength, I would swing a lead bat only with my front (right) arm. This exercise strengthens your front side, which pulls the bat through the hitting zone. I would do this 50 times a day during the off-season and 10 times before a game. Your daily regimen should also include 25 full swings with a bat that's heavier than the one you normally use in a game.

Stuck in the middle

Some batters take their swing from the middle of the box (see Figure 5-6). Hitting from the middle gives you a little more time to catch up with the fast-ball — but curveballs, sinkers, and knucklers also have more time to break. If you have only medium bat speed (something a coach can tell you), this is the place for you (at least until you develop a faster bat).

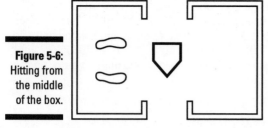

Figure 5-6:
Hitting from the middle of the box.

Tales from the deep

Obviously, standing deep in the box allows you the maximum time to cope with the fastball. But you have to be a great breaking ball hitter to consistently succeed in this location; you're giving the curve, sinker, and knuckler their best opportunity to work their magic. Because you'll be hitting balls on the plate and the angle of your bat is toward foul territory, their trajectory may carry more of them into foul territory. If you stand deep in the box and far from the plate, you may find it difficult to hit outside pitches (see Figure 5-7).

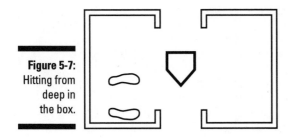

Figure 5-7:
Hitting from
deep in
the box.

Up close and personal

The toughest pitch to hit is the ball out and away from you. After getting in the batter's box, swing your bat to make sure you have full plate coverage. Stand close enough to home to reach pitches 4 inches (10cm) off the outside corner. When you're close to the plate, the outside part of it becomes your middle, and you take away a strength from the pitcher. Sure, the pitcher can throw even farther outside, but if you're a disciplined batter you can take those pitches for balls. In the ninth inning of the 1975 World Series final game, I drove in the winning run when Red Sox left-hander Jim Burton threw me a slider that broke down and away. It would have been a perfect pitch *if I had been standing farther off the plate.* Because I was close to the dish, I was able to reach over and hit it into left center field.

Tailoring Your Stance

Hitters can choose from three basic stances:

✓ **The open stance:** Your back foot is closer to the plate than your front foot.

✓ **The even** or **square stance:** Both feet are equidistant from the plate.

✓ **The closed stance:** Your front foot is closer to the plate than your back foot.

Figure 5-8 illustrates these stances for a right-handed hitter.

I always preferred the closed stance. Only hitters who can't rotate their hips out of the way properly need a somewhat open stance. (Your coach can tell you whether you have the right hip action.) The open stance frees your upper torso and automatically opens your hips, allowing you to drive your body and hands through the hitting zone while generating bat speed. The open stance also lets you turn your head so it faces the pitcher, which allows you to use both eyes simultaneously.

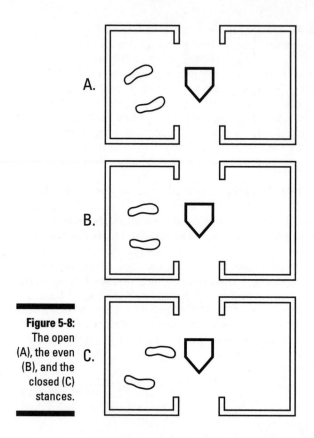

Figure 5-8:
The open
(A), the even
(B), and the
closed (C)
stances.

Everybody rotates away from the ball in order to hit. Open-stance hitters are already a half step away from the plate. They must, therefore, remind themselves not to *pull off* the pitch (move away from the plate a split second too soon) or they won't be able to hit the ball with any authority. For that reason, most major leaguers choose the closed stance or square stance.

Novice hitters should start with an even stance. It helps you keep your weight distributed evenly on the balls of both feet. (Now you know how the stance got its name.) As you gradually develop balance, reduce your stance an inch at a time until you find the closed stance that generates the most power.

Positioning Your Body

Your shoulders are slightly closed in a closed stance and more squared in the even or open versions. No matter which stance you choose, point your face toward the pitcher's mound so you can see the pitcher with both eyes.

Young hitters often make the mistake of looking out of only one eye. Sometimes they slightly cock their heads to the side so that one eye is closer to the pitcher than the other. This stance alters your depth perception. You need both eyes on a parallel plane if you are going to read the ball's spin and speed as quickly as possible. Tucking your chin behind your shoulder also limits your vision. Keep your head square and still throughout your stride and swing. You may hear broadcasters discuss how a hitter keeps his head down throughout his swing. That's always good policy. Keeping your head down keeps your eyes on the ball. Move your head, and your body follows — and your swing suffers.

When taking your stance, bend your knees slightly to allow greater freedom of movement. An erect stance restricts your lower body's maneuverability. How far you spread your legs apart is a matter of personal preference. I always felt more balanced with my feet spread slightly more than shoulder width (see Figure 5-9).

Figure 5-9:
A balanced
batting
stance.

Crouch for comfort

Some players, like the outfielder Rickey Henderson, go into an extremely wide crouch to shorten their strike zone. Rickey, the all-time stolen base king, will enter the Hall of Fame after he retires; he is proof that you can be productive hitting from a wide crouch. My former Cincinnati teammate Pete Rose hit out of a deep crouch with his bat on his shoulder. I don't think young players should copy that stance, but Pete used it to get more base hits than anyone in major league history. It all comes down to comfort. I recommend a slight crouch with some flex in the knee and your upper body only slightly tilted toward the plate.

Bending too much from the top hinders your swing; as you straighten up during your stride, you lose sight of the pitch. Stay in your crouch as you stride. If the pitcher takes a long time between pitches, step out of the batter's box to stretch so you don't become rigid.

Can you dig it?

You hear a lot about *digging in* at the plate. All that term means is that the hitter is planting both feet firmly in the batter's box. Digging in gives you more traction and prevents you from slipping. Power hitters do it all the time because they want to rotate off a firm back foot as their hips open. This position helps them to explode into the hitting zone.

Striding for Power

Try hitting without taking a stride. If you stand still and swing, you can't generate any power. Your stride releases your energy and takes you into the pitch. It helps you pivot while bringing your hips, arms, and shoulders into action. You must hit from a strong front side; your stride ensures that you are successful by allowing you to firmly plant your front foot.

Looking before you stride

When I was first learning how to hit, someone gave me a poem that taught me a valuable lesson about strides. It went

See the ball before your stride / Let it go if it's outside / If it's a curve and should break down / Jack up and hit it downtown.

This poem reminded me that I had to see the ball before starting my stride. If you move too soon, you're going to swing at the pitcher's arm motion instead of the ball. You won't get too many hits doing that. Always remember that you have more time to see and hit the ball than you think.

Some hitters watch the ball from the moment the pitcher puts it into his glove to start his wind-up. Don't bother with that because different motions may deceive you. Pitchers can rear back as if they are going to throw the ball through a wall, and then deliver a soft change-up. Or they can give you an easy, rocking-chair motion while throwing something hard and nasty.

Start looking for the ball when the pitcher drops his hand behind him to begin his throw to the plate. A pitcher's motion is like a batter's stance. A lot of idiosyncratic bells and whistles may be at the start of it, but eventually the pitcher has to come to a conventional release point. Concentrate on that point — say, the corner of a right-handed pitcher's right shoulder — because the ball comes out of that slot. As soon as you pick up the ball leaving his hand, react. Stride toward the pitch.

To make sure that you don't move too soon, try this exercise. Take batting practice and instruct the pitcher to occasionally complete his delivery *without throwing the ball*. If you find yourself moving into this phantom pitch, you need to discipline yourself at the plate.

Honing the length of your stride

Pitches lose speed from the moment they leave a pitcher's hand. When you stride toward the pitcher, you help the ball get to you quicker by shortening the distance it has to travel. So your stride should not be longer than your original batting stance. A long stride with a narrow stance also makes your head bob. The pitch seems as if it is jumping in and out of view. If your stance is 8 inches (20cm) wide, make sure your stride is no wider than that.

When you overstride, your upper body becomes unbalanced. Remember, the only purpose of a stride is to get your lower body into hitting position. Because your eyes are focused on the ball (at least they should be!), don't move your head or upper torso toward the pitch; you don't want to throw off your field of vision. Instead, stride into the ball with your lower body. After you stride, your head should still be in the middle of your body rather than leaning forward or backward. A hitter should glide and pop; don't leap and sweep.

As you move toward the pitch, step away from your hands, or push your hands back, to let your body move forward (see Figure 5-10). If you take your hands with you as you stride, you lose bat speed and power. Keep your hands and shoulders in the same position they held in your stance. I started my stance with my hands at the end of my left armpit, just off my shoulder. They would still be in the same position after I took my stride.

Figure 5-10:
Beginning
your stride.

Troubleshooting your stride

You know that your stride is too narrow and that you need to lengthen it when

- ✔ Your front side doesn't feel strong; or
- ✔ Your legs collapse in midstride.

You know your stride is too wide when

- ✔ You can't generate any hip action; or
- ✔ The ball seems as if it's jumping.

Players who overstride can draw a line or lay a bat across the batter's box during practice to remind themselves not to stride beyond it. I always thought the best remedy for overstriding was concentration. If you focus, you can eliminate most mistakes from your game.

Slapping Down or Cutting Up: Two Approaches to Hitting

Almost everyone agrees that the ideal swing starts about armpit high and levels out as your bat comes to the ball. How much it levels out is a point of divergence.

Some instructors tell you to hit slightly down or even chop at the ball. (Ted Williams has told me that hitters can't hit down on the ball; they can only hit the ball's top half.) When I was playing, Matty Alou, a center fielder with the Pittsburgh Pirates, won a batting title (.342 in 1966) and posted a .307 lifetime batting average by slapping the ball on the ground. He was obviously a gifted hitter. Matty scored 90 or more runs only twice, a low total for someone who usually batted at the top of a great hitting lineup. But to be fair, Matty had a slender, almost frail physique. Power was never going to be his game, so his hitting style was probably best for him.

The King of Swing, Ted Williams, took the opposite approach from Alou. Ted's swing ended with a slight, upward arc. His swing permitted him to hit for power without hurting his batting average (.344 lifetime). Ted still preaches the slight uppercut swing to every hitter he meets. He persuaded Tony Gwynn, the San Diego Padres outfielder and eight-time National League batting champion, to try it in 1997. Gwynn had his best all-around season at the age of 37; he won another batting title and drove in more than 100 runs for the first time in his career.

I'm in the Williams camp. Batters who hit the ball hard are going to put more runs on the board than those who can't. Runs, not hits or batting averages, win ball games. If you hit down on the ball, it is difficult for you to drive it for doubles or home runs. Keep your swing level; and if you stay behind the ball, your swing will have a slight upward arc as your body rotates into the pitch.

Making Contact

Don't swing as soon as the pitcher releases the ball; wait until you recognize the pitch (its spin and speed) before attacking it. You cocked your body with your stride, and you took that step away from your hands. As you go after the pitch, uncoil everything. Pivot forward, opening your hips as you transfer your weight from back foot to front. Brace your front leg. Bend your rear leg while pivoting your back foot. You know you have shifted your weight correctly if your rear toe ends up pointing directly downward (see Figure 5-11).

Figure 5-11:
The
anatomy of
making
contact.

During all this time, your hands and arms direct the bat's movement. Keep your elbows close to your body so that the bat travels in a tight circle. (Your hands and arms don't stay close to your body; good extension creates more bat speed.) Your bottom hand should pull the bat into the hitting zone while your top hand pushes and guides it (see Figure 5-12). The back surface of the bat should rest against your top hand's palm.

Figure 5-12:
Your hands
as you make
contact.

Your swing should bring your hands and arms in front of the plate with your bat trailing slightly behind for leverage — think of swinging an axe from the side. Make sure your wrists are firm as the bat moves into the hitting zone. Try to see the bat making contact with the ball. (You probably won't be able to, but just the attempt ensures that you are watching the ball throughout your swing.)

Remember that you want to hit the ball in front of the plate so it has a better chance of staying fair. As you finish your swing, the bat should make an almost complete circle around your upper body; most of your weight should be on your front foot.

Fine-Tuning Your Swing

Depending on a pitch's location, you can make small adjustments in your swing.

- ✔ **On pitches inside:** Rotate your hips out of the way quickly so that you can get the bat out in front faster. When you hit an inside pitch, the barrel of the bat should cover the inside of the plate.

- ✔ **On pitches outside:** Do the opposite of what you do with inside pitches. Keep your hips closed and go to the ball with your upper body. Try to drive the ball to the opposite field (to left field if you're left-handed, to right field if you're a righty).

- ✔ **On low pitches:** You shouldn't have to bend to hit a low strike. Give your swing slightly more arc as you go down to get the pitch.

- ✔ **On high pitches:** Many coaches tell you to get on top of the ball, but if you take that advice to an extreme you can develop bad habits. Because your hands should be at the top in your stride just before you start swinging, simply stay level (or high) a little longer and then hit through the ball.

- ✔ **When the pitcher has two strikes against you:** In this situation, you have to swing at anything near the plate. You can't count on the umpire calling a ball if the pitch is only an inch or so out of the strike zone. Shorten your stride and cut down on your swing by choking up another half-inch or so.

Following Through

Conventional baseball wisdom holds that the follow-through (shown in Figure 5-13), which occurs after the ball leaves your bat, is the last essential part of your swing. Some coaches tell you that if you don't have the proper follow-through, you can't hit the ball with power. It's true that concentrating on continuing your swing after the point of contact helps you to drive *through* the ball. But I think that people who emphasize the importance of follow-through have things backward. The reason you're not driving the ball with power is because you're not executing one or more of the other elements of your swing that produces a good follow-through. Following-through ensures that you hit *through* the ball, not *to* the ball.

By itself, a good follow-through doesn't help you hit. Why? Because the ball has left your bat! If you've done all the things we've talked about, your swing has already accomplished its purpose. A good follow-through results from properly executed mechanics; it is a finish, important only to the batter, not to the ball. A poorly balanced follow-through may tell you your swing is off, but the weak pop-up you just hit to the catcher already let you know that.

Figure 5-13:
The classic follow-through.

Dealing with the Strike Zone

The baseball rule book says the strike zone is a rectangle the width of home plate, extending from the top of the batter's knees to the letters across his uniform jersey. (See Chapter 1 for a diagram of the strike zone.) In practice, however, every player and umpire has his or her interpretation of the strike zone. Most umpires have a strike zone that starts at the bottom of the player's knee and finishes no higher than the top of his belt buckle. Rarely does an ump call a strike on a pitch at the letters.

Because the strike zone is supposed to have the same width as the plate, you wouldn't expect to see too much variance there. Yet some umpires call strikes on pitches 6 inches (15cm) off the plate (mostly pitches on the outer edge, rarely inside). And some umps never call a strike on any ball that just nicks the plate's corners.

When you take batting practice, swing at pitches in your legally defined strike zone; you can adjust to an individual umpire's zone after you determine what it is. The best hitters take most of their swings at pitches in the strike zone. Some players are so strong that they can hit a pitch that is 1 or 2 inches off the plate. However, these so-called "bad-ball" hitters are rare. Discipline yourself to swing only at strikes.

To get a sense of your strike zone without swinging a bat, play catch with someone. Stand 60 feet (18.3m) apart (nearly the distance between home plate and the pitcher's mound) and keep your throws between each other's chest and knees. Move your tosses up and down within this area. Because you are facing the thrower dead-on, you can immediately detect from the ball's trajectory whether it is a strike or a ball.

After you know your strike zone, find out where your hot hitting spots are within it. In his book *The Science of Hitting* (a must-read for every ballplayer), Ted Williams broke down his strike zone in a diagram, which demonstrated that he batted .400 when he hit pitches down the heart of the plate but only .220 when he hit pitches that were low and outside. This diagram reminded Ted that he shouldn't swing at those low, outside pitches unless he already had two strikes and the ball was over the plate. All athletes must develop that same kind of self-awareness. You can never be a good hitter or player unless you know your strengths and weaknesses. If you aren't a good low ball hitter, lay off that pitch unless you have two strikes.

Judging the First Pitch

Should you swing or take the first pitch you see in an at-bat? It depends on the situation. I remember a minor league game I played in Durham, North Carolina. My team was facing some rookie pitcher, and I opened the first inning by popping up on his first pitch. When I came back to the bench my manager, Billy Goodman, a former American League batting champion, asked me, "What does that pitcher have?" Well, I didn't know what the pitcher had other than a fastball, and I couldn't even tell you how hard he threw that. I hadn't seen enough of his pitches. And that was Billy's point: The first time you face a pitcher you don't know, *take* as many pitches as you can. Find out how his curve ball breaks, which way his slider moves. Does he have a change-up? Does he throw every pitch from the same angle?

When you face pitchers you *are* familiar with, however, there are no hard rules about swinging or not swinging at the first pitch. In that situation, I always went to the plate looking to hit the first good pitch I saw. If it came on the pitcher's first offering, I swung. However, I invariably *took* (didn't swing at) a lot of first pitches simply because so many of them were thrown out of the strike zone.

Going to All Fields

Novice hitters should learn how to hit the ball to all fields. If a pitch is thrown away from you, hit it to the opposite field (right field if you're right-handed, left field if you're a lefty). If a pitch travels down the heart of the plate, smack it up the middle of the diamond. If the ball is thrown inside, jerk (or *pull*) it into left field if you're a right-hander or into right field if you're a lefty. As you gain experience, you may discover whether you are predominantly a *spray hitter* (a player who hits to all fields, such as third baseman Wade Boggs, who picked up his 3,000th base hit during the 1999 season) or a *pull hitter* (a slugger like Mark McGwire). See Figure 5-14.

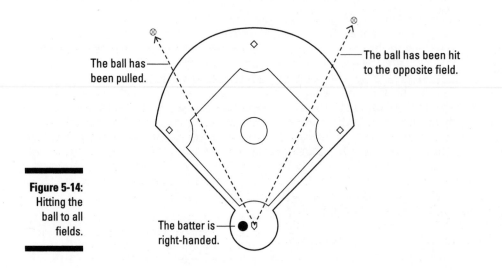

The ball has been pulled.

The ball has been hit to the opposite field.

Figure 5-14: Hitting the ball to all fields.

The batter is right-handed.

I started my big league career as a spray hitter but developed into a pull hitter as I got stronger. However, as a pull hitter, I could still slap a hit to the opposite field when the situation demanded it. A good spray hitter can pull the ball down the line when he needs an extra-base hit. The bottom line is you want to be as complete a hitter as possible.

Hitting up the center or to the opposite field

You have to hit the ball a little later in order to hit to center *(straight-away)* or to the opposite field. To do this, take an even stance at the plate. Aim everything through the middle. This strategy causes you to hit the ball later.

Pulling the ball

Hit the ball early enough so that the bat meets the ball in front of you. Right-handed hitters pull the ball to the left side; left-handers pull to the right. If you're using a closed stance, you're going to naturally pull a lot of balls. (See the section "Tailoring Your Stance" earlier in this chapter.) The more closed your stance, the more you pull the ball. Crowd the plate as much as possible. This position expands the area from which you can pull. Make sure to plant your back foot firmly because you want something stationary to drive from. Planting your back foot also gives your swing more arc. Don't uppercut the ball; let your body, stride, and swing give it power. As you start your swing, shift your weight to your front foot. This shifting keeps your bat level in the hitting zone for a longer period of time. Want to hit for more power? Keep your weight back a little longer.

PLAYER TIP

When the opposition gets shifty

Should you get a reputation as a pull hitter, opponents may try to stack their defenses against you. You could find yourself hitting against a *shift.* If you're a left-handed hitter, the shortstop moves toward the second base side of the infield (for the hitter, the portion of the infield to the right of second base), the second baseman shifts towards first, the center fielder leans toward right, and the left fielder comes closer to center. If you're right-handed, the fielders move the other

way. The most extreme shift in baseball history was the *Boudreau Shift,* which the Cleveland Indians employed against pull-hitter supreme Ted Williams. Whenever Williams came to bat, short-stop-manager Lou Boudreau would crowd the right side of the diamond with six fielders. (See the following figure.)

I hit against shifts during my career, though nothing as radical as the Boudreau version. The

(continued)

(continued)

best thing you can do when confronted by one is forget it's there. A shift's biggest impact is psychological. If you look at it and think, "I'll never get a base hit against this," you may as well drop your bat and return to the dugout. I always believed that if I hit a solid line drive, it wouldn't be caught no matter how many fielders they stacked against me. Attack this stratagem with that same confidence. Of course, you can always destroy a shift by *dinking* (softly hitting) a single to the opposite field or bunting, but that's what the opposition wants you to do. They are trying to make you move away from your strength. Don't fall for it. Take your normal cuts at the plate (unless a single can drive in a run).

Analyzing the Pitcher

Most hitters don't keep written notes on pitchers; they keep mental books documenting how pitchers have come at them in the past. If a pitcher has been unsuccessful trying to get you out with inside fastballs but has been burying you with outside breaking pitches, you can assume he's going to keep throwing those curves. However, you can't establish a pitching pattern off any one game. Maybe the pitcher's fastball was sluggish the night he never tried to bust it by you inside. He may have had an unusually wicked curve working that evening. The next time you face him, if his *heater* is hopping, he may get you out with fastballs inside all night. You may not even see his curveball. So you have to discover what a pitcher has working for him on game day.

I would watch the opposing pitcher warm up in the bullpen to see what pitches he was throwing for strikes. Generally, if a pitcher can't control his slider or curve in the bull pen, he won't be able to control them in the game for at least an inning or two. Take those pitches for balls until he proves he can get them over the plate.

The Dying Art of Bunting

When you *bunt,* hold your bat in the hitting zone and let the ball make contact with it. The idea is to deaden the ball so that the base runners can advance (or you can get to first) while the opposing fielders run in to make a play. There comes a time in every baseball season when anyone — even hulking sluggers like Sammy Sosa or Frank Thomas — should bunt. For example, say you're playing a game that decides whether you or your opponent clinches a championship. You come to bat with the winning run on first and nobody out in the bottom of the ninth inning. I don't care how many home runs you hit all season, your job is to bunt that runner to second base. Bunts can win ball games, so everyone who swings a bat should know how to lay them down.

It's especially important for pitchers to learn how to bunt, even if they play in a league that allows designated-hitters. Depending on how many substitutions are made during a game, pitchers can be called on to hit even in designated hitter leagues. (For more on this rule, refer to Chapter 3.) Or you may play an interleague game in the home park of a team whose rules don't provide for a designated hitter. In the fourth inning of the second game of the 1997 World Series between the Cleveland Indians and Florida Marlins, Cleveland pitcher Chad Ojea — who had never batted in the major leagues because of the designated hitter rule — bunted two teammates to second and third. It was a crucial play. A two-run single then broke open the game, which the Indians eventually won. Had Ojea failed to get the bunt down — or, worse, bunted into a double play — the outcome may have been different.

Choosing your bunting stance

The most commonly used bunting stance is the *pivot.* Take your normal stance at the plate while waiting for the pitch. As the ball comes to the plate, pivot your upper body toward the pitch while keeping your feet in their stance position (see Figure 5-15).

Figure 5-15:
An ideal
bunting
stance.

The pivot has several advantages:

- You can flow into a pivot quickly so you maintain an element of surprise.

- In the event of a fake bunt — where you "show" bunt to pull in the infielders and then swing away to drive the ball past them — the pivot allows you to easily resume a standard batting stance.

- With a pivot stance, getting out of the path of errant pitches is easier.

The *squared-stance* is your other bunting option — and perhaps the best option for players just starting out. Bring your feet parallel to home plate and each other while keeping them shoulder-width apart (see Figure 5-16). This stance gives you better plate coverage and a longer look at the ball than the pivot, but it also has its drawbacks. You become more vulnerable to being hit by a pitch, you risk stepping out of the batter's box (in which case the umpire may call you out), and, because you have to get set in this position early, you decrease your chances of surprising the opposition. I prefer the pivot, but you should adopt whichever position is most comfortable.

Whether you pivot or square around to bunt, make sure you drop into a slight crouch and square your shoulders toward the pitcher. Shift your weight forward as you stand on the balls of your feet. Hold the bat handle firmly with your bottom hand so you can control it, but don't squeeze the handle or you may hit the ball too hard. Slide your top hand up near the bat label. Pinch the barrel with your fingers and thumb, your thumb on top. This action shapes the hand into a U that absorbs any impact when the ball strikes your bat. It also protects your fingers (see Figure 5-17).

Figure 5-16:
The
squared-
stance bunt.

Figure 5-17:
Holding the
bat for the
bunt.

Many bunters hold their bats parallel to the ground while waiting for the pitch. I think it is better to hold the top of the bat barrel slightly higher than the handle. This strategy keeps you on top of the ball, which is where the bunter has to be. If you come up underneath the pitch, you pop it up. If you hit the ball dead center, you produce a soft line drive that can be converted into a double play.

Hold the bat near the top of your strike zone so you know that any pitch over your bat is a ball. This prevents you from offering at high pitches, which are the hardest to bunt. Try to bunt a low pitch. Watch the ball make contact with the bat in front of you and the plate. Give with the ball, don't push it. You should experience the sensation of "catching" the ball with your bat and guiding it to its destination. Let your bottom hand direct the bat's angle.

Bunting into a sacrifice

With the *sacrifice bunt,* the bunter advances the base runners while giving up a chance for a base hit. With a runner on first, bunt toward the area between the mound and the first baseman. With a runner on second or runners on first and second, bunt toward the third baseman to bring him off the bag (see Figure 5-18).

Figure 5-18:
Where to place the sacrifice bunt.

Bunt here with a runner on second base. — Bunt here with a runner on first base (and no one on second base).

Running the squeeze play

The *squeeze play* is a sacrifice bunt with a runner on third base. If a manager calls for a squeeze play, it's usually during the later innings of a close game with less than two outs. On a *safety squeeze,* the runner breaks for home only after you drop your bunt on the infield. If the bunt isn't good, the runner stays at third. As the bunter, your job is to push the ball away from the pitcher and towards first or third base.

The *suicide squeeze* is a riskier play. It requires the runner to dash toward home plate as the ball leaves the pitcher's hand. *He is coming home no matter what kind of bunt you drop.* So you can't take the pitch even if it is out of the strike zone. You must bunt the ball somewhere.

Don't be too finicky about placement. With the runner bearing down on home, just bunt the ball to the ground in fair territory, and you drive in a run. Even if you bunt it foul with less than two strikes on you, the worst that can happen is the runner gets sent back to third. If you don't make contact with the ball, the catcher has the runner dead at the plate (which is why it's called the *suicide* squeeze).

Bunting for hits

To successfully bunt for a hit, you must catch the opposition unaware. This is where the pivot gives you an advantage: It allows you to deceive the infielders longer than the squared-around stance. To bunt for a hit, you should be in motion as the bat makes contact with the ball. You should also grip the bat a little more firmly than you did for the sacrifice.

BASEBALL SPEAK

Left-handed hitters use *drag bunts,* so named because the bunter appears to drag the ball along the first baseline as he runs toward first (see Figure 5-19). I beat out a drag bunt to get a hit in the seventh game of the 1975 World Series.

Figure 5-19:
Brett Butler
executes
the drag
bunt.

National Baseball Hall of Fame Library, Cooperstown, NY

To execute the drag bunt, shift your weight onto your right foot as you pivot and step toward first base. Hold the bat solidly with its head pointed toward third. Don't pull back the bat or the ball will go foul. You should be moving into your second stride as you make contact with the ball. With your running start, you should beat out the bunt, if it stays fair (see Figure 5-20).

Right-handers and left-handers can execute *push* or *dump* bunts for base hits. If you bat right-handed, start with your weight on your right (the rear) foot. As you move to bunt the ball, quickly shift your weight forward into your left foot. Push the ball past the pitcher toward the hole between first and second. Run immediately after making contact. If you are a lefty hitter, reverse your weight shift and tap the ball down the third base line. Run immediately after making contact.

Faking the bunt

You can fake a bunt when a teammate is trying to steal a base. A successful decoy may get the infielders moving in the wrong direction. When you pull back the bat, you force the catcher to stay back so it takes him longer to get to the ball. You can also fake a bunt, pivot back to your hitting stance, and take a short, easy swing (a *swinging bunt*) to slash or chop the ball past the infielders as they mistakenly charge toward home. Square around when you're attempting to help the base stealer; use the pivot stance if you're using the ruse to get a base hit.

Figure 5-20:
The drag
bunt.

Executing the Hit-and-Run

As the batter on a hit-and-run play, your primary responsibilities are to protect the runner and to hit the ball on the ground. Swing and make contact with the pitch, no matter where it's thrown. If the pitch is out of the strike zone, lunge at it and try to get a piece of the ball. The runner takes off without a base-stealing lead, so if you miss that pitch, the catcher will have little difficulty throwing him out. If you hit a line drive at a fielder with the runner moving, it's virtually an automatic double play.

Take your usual swing, but hit slightly down on the ball. You may hit the ball through an area vacated by an infielder who moves to cover second base against the runner breaking from first. The manager usually initiates the play with one or no outs. However, a veteran hitter, suspecting the opposition is going to pitch him a certain way, can call the play with a sign to his base runner.

Turning the Run-and-Hit

The run-and-hit is generally called with a fast runner at first. The play is similar to the hit-and-run, but the hitter's task is less specific. The runner breaks for second after the pitcher commits to throwing the ball toward home. The runner should approach this like a straight steal. You are not obligated to swing at the pitch unless it's a strike (which is why the runner should be fast — if you take the pitch, he has to steal second). You can also put the ball in play anywhere rather than having to hit through the right side of the infield. With his running start, the base runner should be able to get to third on any ball hit out of the infield. An *extra-base hit* (anything more than a single) should score him from first.

Walking Aggressively

You can help your team by getting a base on balls, but you shouldn't go to the plate looking to draw a walk; you may lose your aggressiveness. Instead, work the count against the pitcher by expanding and contracting the strike zone according to the count.

 For example, I was a pull-hitter, so I preferred to hit the ball inside. If the first pitch to me was a ball, I shaved 2 inches (5cm) off the outside portion of my strike zone. The next pitch could be a strike, but I wouldn't swing at it if it was on the outer edge of the plate. If it *was* a strike, I'd expand my zone by 2 inches (but I'd never let it become larger than the umpire's strike zone). However, if the ump called it ball two, I'd cut another 2 inches from the outside of my strike zone. On a three-ball and one-strike count, my strike zone would be about half its normal width: from the middle of the plate in. To get me out, the pitcher now had to throw two straight strikes rather than one. That 3–1 pitch was exactly where I wanted it, or I wasn't swinging. If the pitcher came inside where I was looking, I could drive that ball a long way. If he threw a strike on the outside corner, I still had another crack at him. Ball four would put me on first base. All the percentages were working in my favor. On a 3–2 count, I'd expand the strike zone out again and protect more of the plate. By altering my strike zone on each pitch, I increased my chances of drawing walks while remaining aggressive at the same time.

Getting the Most Out of Batting Practice

Batting practice is usually divided into rounds. On most of the teams I played for, we would take ten swings in the first round, seven in the second, five in the third, four in the fourth, three in the fifth, and one in the last. Use your first round of batting practice to get loose. Start by laying down two bunts, one as a sacrifice, the other for a base hit. Then work on your swing.

This first round is essentially a warm-up. You are getting comfortable with your timing, stance, and stride while working on your batting eye. Don't try to kill the ball. A lot of hitters are playing *long ball* (trying to hit a home run) when they take batting practice. They're not working on anything in particular; they're just trying to see who can hit the ball farthest. That's a waste of time, especially if you aren't a home-run hitter. Just make contact and aim to hit the ball through the middle.

Starting with the second round, you should be simulating game conditions. Work on every aspect of your hitting. Try to pull the ball on one pitch and hit it up the middle on another. Poke one to the opposite field. Then let a swing rip without caring where the ball goes. Do this on every round.

If you want to play some long ball, do it on your last swing. After taking your last practice swing, trot around the bases to keep loose while practicing your left turns.

Working with Your Batting Practice Pitcher

During batting practice, have the pitcher throw you nothing but fastballs in the first round so that you can get your timing. Then have the pitcher work in some curves, sliders, and change-ups. If you take 30 swings, 8 of them should be against breaking balls. Facing a knuckleballer in tonight's game? If your pitcher can throw a knuckler, ask to see some of those, too.

You may discover that pitches in a certain location are giving you trouble. Ask the batting practice pitcher to throw to that spot so you can work on them. Usually you know what the pitcher is going to throw. However, every so often you should take a round in which the pitcher can throw any pitch to any spot at any time without telling you in advance. This element of surprise helps hone your concentration and prepares you for actual game conditions.

Other Practice Tips

Besides facing live pitching during batting practice, you can do a number of things away from the ballpark to improve your hitting. Here are some of my favorites.

Hit from a batting tee

I used one throughout my career. Adjust the tee's height (see Figure 5-21) and set its position so that you are hitting the ball inside, outside, or down the middle of your strike zone. No matter which side you choose, always set the tee up in front of the plate.

Figure 5-21: The batting tee is a great way to practice.

Hitting off the tee forces you to concentrate on hitting a particular spot on the ball. It helps to prevent you from *bailing out* (pulling away from the pitch) while quickening your bat.

Swing in front of a full-length mirror

I'm not advocating narcissism here. Swinging in front of a mirror lets you check your entire stance and stride.

Play pepper

In *pepper,* the batter stands no more than 10 feet (3m) opposite several fielders who are lined up side by side. One fielder throws the ball; the batter taps it back. (Don't take a full swing or you may decapitate someone.) The fielder who fields that ball quickly tosses it back toward the hitter, who taps it again. And so on. This game teaches you to keep your eye on the ball and make contact.

Work with grips and rollers

You need strong hands and wrists to hit. Use hand grips and wrist rolls to strengthen them. You can also squeeze a ball of putty to develop your grip.

Develop your hand-eye coordination

I used to punch a speed bag to develop my hand-eye coordination. Playing catch is also great practice. (Playing catch improves your fielding, but learning how to gauge the speed of the ball also helps you at the plate.) Play paddle ball, tennis, racquetball, or any sport that demands quick reactions and excellent hand-eye coordination. Table tennis is an excellent choice because the ball moves so quickly toward you and you have to hit it out front, which is precisely what you have to do with a baseball.

Troubleshooting Your Batting

You can work on specific problems during batting practice. Here are some common hitting flaws that often lead to slumps and some suggestions for correcting them.

Hitting off your heels

If you have your weight back on your heels, your body and bat move away from the plate as you swing. Outside pitches and off-speed stuff may give you trouble. You won't be able to hit with any power. **Remedy:** Concentrate on keeping your weight on the balls of your feet while you stride toward the pitcher.

Chopping

Slumping, novice hitters often chop down at the ball just to make contact. Swinging in this manner decreases your hitting area. Also, you can't drive the ball with this swing; you simply hit a lot of grounders (mostly for outs). **Remedy:** Make sure that you transfer your weight properly. When you transfer your weight to your front foot, your bat remains level. Keep your weight on your back foot, drop your rear shoulder (you can't chop with your shoulder down), and take your usual swing.

Uppercutting

When you *uppercut* the ball, you raise your front shoulder while dropping your rear shoulder and dipping your back knee. Batters who uppercut tend to strike out a lot. You can also forget about hitting high pitches with any authority. Raising your front shoulder moves your head out of its level plane, which prevents you from seeing the ball well. **Remedy:** Uppercutters keep their weight on their back foot too long; level your shoulder and make sure you transfer your weight from front to back. Finish your swing with a slightly upward arc, but avoid any exaggerated uppercutting.

Hitching

If you have a *hitch,* you are dropping your hands just before you swing. A hitch is okay, as long as you can get your hands in good hitting position before the ball arrives. Frank Robinson had a hitch; he dropped his hands below his belt, but he always got them back in time to hit. The last time I checked, his plaque was in the Hall of Fame. Unfortunately, too many hitters compensate for their hitches with rushed, upward swings. This hitch produces the same poor results as an extreme uppercut. **Remedy:** Keep your hands level and still.

Locking the front hip

Locking your front hip makes it impossible to transfer the weight from your rear foot to your front foot during your swing. You can't pivot properly. This fault significantly decreases your power. **Remedy:** Open your stance and concentrate on stepping toward the pitcher.

Lunging

Batters who *lunge* at the ball step into the pitch too early. This misstep throws off your timing, power, and bat control. Hank Aaron would occasionally lunge with his upper body, but he could drive the ball because he always kept his hands back. **Remedy:** Be patient. Wait until you read the pitch before you swing. Make sure your stride is no longer than your original stance. *Keep your hands back.*

Bobbing your head

If you bob or turn your head, you lose sight of the ball for a second. When you pick the ball up again (*if* you pick it up again), it is either almost past you or appears to be jumping at you. **Remedy:** Keep your head level and still throughout your stance, stride, and swing. If your stride is making your head bob, shorten it. Remember, your stride should be no longer than your stance.

Stepping in the bucket

Stepping in the bucket is another way of saying you are striding away from the pitch. The uneven weight distribution results in a loss of power. Because you're moving away from the plate, you can't hit the outside pitch. **Remedy:** Close your stance and concentrate on striding toward the pitcher.

Overcoming the Fear of Getting Hit

Some batters stride away from the pitch because they are afraid of being hit by the ball. To be successful, batters must be aggressive. If you can't overcome your fear, you won't be able to hit. I can't tell you how not to be afraid, but perhaps I can calm your concerns with a few facts:

✔ **It hurts only for a little while.** Many young players are afraid of getting hit by the ball because it has never happened to them before. They imagine the experience to be much more painful than it actually is. When batters do get hit, it's usually in a fleshy spot. Unless you've broken something (which rarely happens), the pain subsides quickly.

✔ **Pitchers don't often hit batters.** Rarely does a pitched ball seriously injure a hitter at any level — from Little League to the pros. I averaged around 600 plate appearances a season and stood way up front in the batter's box and close to the plate. Yet I rarely got hit by a pitch more than twice a year. Many of those pitches just grazed my uniform. I have been struck solidly by pitches, but I was never injured so badly that I had to leave a ball game or miss any playing time. Ground balls have hit me in the face during fielding practice (is that embarrassing!), but I've never been hit in the face by a pitch.

✔ **If your mechanics are sound, you can get out of the way.** Muhammad Ali, the great former heavyweight boxing champion, once said, "The punch that knocks you out is the one you don't see." Batters should remember that. If you keep your eyes (both of them!) on the ball, it's hard to get hit by a pitch, especially in the head. Your head is the easiest part of your body to move out of harm's way.

✔ **Batting helmets work.** Ron Cey, the former third baseman of the Los Angeles Dodgers, got hit in the head by a Goose Gossage fastball during the 1981 World Series. That's like taking a bazooka shell off the old noggin. However, Cey's batting helmet absorbed nearly the entire impact. He not only played the next game, he hit a home run. The moral: Never step up to the plate without wearing your helmet.

However, don't let the helmet give you a sense of false confidence. Getting hit in the head is dangerous and painful. It shouldn't happen to you, as long as you stay alert at the plate.

Post Script: Some Advice for Pinch Hitters from Rusty Staub

When your manager asks you to come off the bench cold and go to the plate in a critical situation, he is handing you one of the most difficult assignments in baseball. Pinch-hitting is a specialized skill. I rarely pinch-hit more than ten times in any one season, so I have enlisted an expert to give us some advice on the subject. My good friend and former Houston Astros teammate Rusty Staub wasn't just a great pinch hitter; he was a great hitter, period. He had a disciplined eye, superb bat speed, and excellent balance at the plate. During his career, Rusty amassed 2,716 base hits, 292 home runs, and 1,486 runs batted in while compiling a .279 lifetime batting average. He drove in 100 or more runs three times.

Some thoughts on slumps

If you go into a slump, take extra batting practice and focus on the hitting fundamentals that I describe in this chapter. Make sure your hands are properly positioned. Are they working together as a unit? Have a coach or teammate observe whether you're overstriding. Practice hitting the ball back through the middle of the diamond. Hitting the ball up the middle prevents you from uppercutting, pulling off the pitch, or hitting it too soon.

If practice doesn't seem to help, take a few days off. You may simply be fatigued. Remember that slumps are inevitable; there isn't a single Hall of Famer who didn't experience them. Babe Ruth was the greatest offensive force baseball has ever produced; he hit .118 in the 1922 World Series. Try to remain confident and optimistic. If you've hit before, you will hit again, so don't lose your aggressiveness. In 1976, I batted .000 in the National League Championship Series against the Philadelphia Phillies. I didn't get a hit or a run batted in (RBI). However, in the World Series that immediately followed, I hit .333 with one home run, three runs scored, and two RBIs in four games.

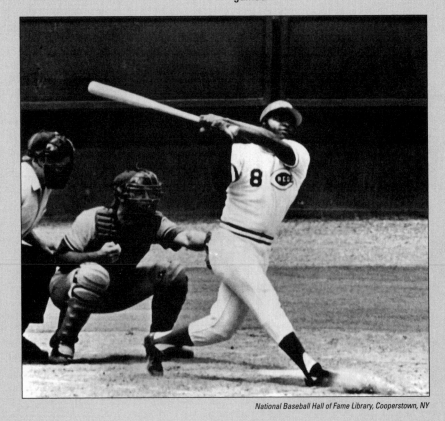

National Baseball Hall of Fame Library, Cooperstown, NY

As a pinch hitter for the New York Mets during his final three seasons, Rusty was the top of the line. He led the National League in pinch hits in 1983 and 1984. During the 1983 season, he tied a major league record with eight consecutive pinch hits; his 24 pinch hits that year also drove in 25 runs. That's delivering in the clutch. So when Staub talks about pinch hitting, he's like Smith-Barney on investing; we all have to listen.

"More than anything else, a pinch-hitter has to be emotionally strong. That season I tied the major league record for consecutive pinch hits, people forget that I was 0-for-April. I did walk a few times, but that didn't ease my frustration. It hurt because there were a couple of games we could have won if I had come through. And it's not as though you know you're coming back at the pitchers the following day like you do when you play regularly. A pinch hitter might go four or five games before he gets another at-bat. So you can't let your failures eat at you."

"When you are primarily a pinch hitter, you don't get to take as many batting practice swings as the regulars. Come to the park a little earlier and take extra b.p. (batting practice) as often as you can. Once the game starts, study that opposing starting pitcher intensely because you may be facing him in a later inning. What is working for him today? What is the catcher calling, and what does the pitcher seem to be shaking off? What sort of strike zone is the umpire giving him? If the umpire is giving him the outside of the plate, you have to adjust, not the ump. Just look at what happened during the (1997 National League) playoffs between Atlanta and Florida. You had that game where Eric Gregg was calling strikes on pitches way outside all day. What do you do as a hitter? Complain throughout the game while you go 0-for-4? If you're smart, you move up on the plate and make the pitcher try to get you out inside."

"You should also talk to your teammates after they take their swings against a pitcher. Find out what kind of stuff he has. Then see if you can pick up some nuance that tells you what the pitcher is throwing."

"I picked up enough pitches in my career to know what was coming about 40 percent of the time. It wasn't difficult if you observed closely. For example, Rick Wise (a pitcher with the Philadelphia Phillies and other teams) used to hold the ball with his hand in the glove. Then he put the glove right in front of his chest. If he dropped the glove all the way during the wind-up, almost to touch his body, he was throwing a fastball. But when he gripped the curve-ball or his change-up, he would drop the glove only 6 inches. That was blatant. When Tony Cloninger pitched for the Braves, he wore a long sweatshirt, even if it was 110 degrees. When he was at the top of his stretch, that sweatshirt would recede from his wrist. If you saw a lot of wrist, Tony was throwing a fastball. If you saw a little bit of wrist, it would be the curve or slider. No wrist? He was throwing the change. At one time, when Nolan Ryan had to pitch out of a wind-up, he would look down at the ground before delivering the fastball; if he looked at the catcher, he was bringing the curve. With the stuff he had, that didn't always help, but at least you got a little better shot at him."

"Besides studying the pitcher, you should also examine the park conditions. Is the wind blowing in or out? Is it blowing in different directions in different parts of the park? Is there a sun field (an outfield position that exposes a fielder's eyes to the glare of the sun)? If you hit the ball down the line, is it likely to stay fair or foul? Is the grass slowing down the ball? In Dodger Stadium, when I played, if you bunted the ball off the grass and it hit the mud, it stayed fair. In the old Astrodome, Joe and I knew that if you bunted the ball down the line, the turf moved the ball towards foul territory. Recognizing these idiosyncrasies helps you to bring as many plusses to the plate as you can. Every hitter should know these things, but it is especially important for pinch hitters. You only have that one chance per game; you have to make the most of it."

Chapter 6

Winning the Arms Race: Pitching Like a Major Leaguer

*P*itching is the most valuable commodity in baseball. Teams don't reach the postseason without possessing solid *starting rotations* (pitching lineups) backed by deep *bull pens* (relief pitchers). Any manager will tell you that strong pitching is the best insurance against long losing streaks. When your club surrenders only three or four runs every game, you can find a way to win even with the weakest offense. A gifted hitter can galvanize an entire lineup, but a dominant pitcher can do more to elevate a team than any position player can. Even a last-place club can compete like a world champion if it has a top gun on the mound.

Find that opinion hard to believe? Open up a baseball encyclopedia and look up the 1972 Philadelphia Phillies. You'll see a team whose .358 won-lost percentage was the worst in the National League that season. Yet when Steve Carlton pitched for the Phillies, they played .730 ball. No team came within 110 points of that mark. If Philadelphia could have cloned Carlton, the club would have won its division by 22 games.

And Carlton is only one of the many examples we could have presented. Tom Seaver, Walter Johnson, Bob Gibson, Ferguson Jenkins, Gaylord Perry, Grover Alexander — the record books are filled with the names of men who transformed their clubs from victims to predators every time they strode to the center of the diamond. Each of these pitchers had powerful arms, sound mechanics, a genius for pitch selection, and an unquenchable competitive spirit. Now we can't give you Randy Johnson's arm, Mike Mussina's drive, or

Greg Maddux's head. But in this chapter we show you the proper way to throw the various pitches you need to get hitters out. The rest you have to develop between the lines.

We've enlisted help from both sides of the mound for this section. Bob Gibson is our right-hander. During his 17-year career with the St. Louis Cardinals, Bob won 251 games, struck out 3,117 batters, posted five 20-win seasons, won two Cy Young Awards, and was named a National League Most Valuable Player — an award few pitchers have on their résumés. He is a Hall of Famer.

Bob was a power pitcher, so for help with *off-speed* (nonfastball) stuff, we have Bill Lee. As a member of the Boston Red Sox and Montreal Expos, Bill was one of the leading left-handers of the 1970s. He wasn't overpowering; Bill got hitters out with movement and great control.

Note: For information on special rules for pitchers, see Chapter 3. And be sure to check out the defensive strategies for pitchers in Chapter 7, which include the pick-off move.

It All Starts with Your Stance

Stances are as individual as the pitchers who assume them. Find a stance on the mound that leaves you balanced and comfortable. Your weight should be evenly distributed and your hands relaxed. Keep your glove hand and ball hand together so you don't let the hitter see your grip on the ball (it may tip him off to which pitch you intend to throw). As you take the sign from your catcher, your *pivot foot* (right foot for right-handers, left foot for left-handers) must touch the pitching rubber.

If you are left-handed, place your pivot foot on the left end of the rubber. If you are right-handed, do the reverse. Face the plate squarely.

Your Wind-up, Thrust, and Release

Your wind-up should get the full force of your body behind the pitch.

1. **Start releasing the momentum by taking a short step back behind the rubber with your striding foot (left foot for right-handers, right foot for lefties).**

   Avoid taking a large step or you will throw off your balance. You should be gripping the ball in the glove at some point between the top of your shoulder and high above your head. (See Figure 6-1.)

Figure 6-1:
Starting the
wind-up.

2. **Pivot as you lift your striding foot to bring it back over the rubber. Lift your striding knee to your chest.**

   This is your *leg kick,* but if you actually do kick out, you may disturb your balance. Keep your head steady and over your rear foot. (See Figure 6-2.)

3. **Bring your hands down (somewhere between your belt and chest) and separate them while shifting your weight to your pivot leg.**

   That leg should be slightly bent. As you pivot back, your foot turns until it is perpendicular to the rubber. Your hips and shoulders are closed to the batter.

"Don't try to copy your wind-up from some other pitcher. Find out what is comfortable for you. If someone were to give you a ball and tell you to go into your wind-up, 99 percent of the time that basic motion is what will serve you best because it's what's most natural for you. We may have to alter your mechanics — the positioning of your arm or something like that — but not your natural motion. If you are a coach and you have a youngster who isn't comfortable winding up, don't make him do it. Let him pitch without a wind-up." — Bob Gibson

Figure 6-2:
Beginning
your leg
kick.

4. **Maintain the weight on your back foot until your leg kick is at its highest point. Then start shifting your weight forward toward home plate. (See Figure 6-3.)**

Figure 6-3:
Starting to
come home.

5. **Bring your striding leg down and plant it with your foot pointed toward home.**

   As the striding foot hits the ground, your hips should open (but keep your front shoulder closed). Your throwing arm should be raised behind your head to its highest point with your wrist cocked back. Your striding leg should be slightly bent. Lower your body and thrust from the pitching rubber.

   "You have to get your hips into this. It's very much like playing golf or hitting. To play golf, you have to turn your hips away from the ball and then bring them back with your swing. To hit, you turn your hips away from the plate, and then come back. Same thing as a pitcher, you bring your hips to the side and then come back forward." — Bob Gibson

6. **As you bring your throwing arm around, bring your glove hand forward just above your elbow with the palm up.**

   Keep your elbow high so you can trace a wide arc with your throwing arm. Do not, however, trace so wide an arc that it throws off your balance. To get the most movement on the ball, deliver your pitch with a three-quarters motion.

   "If you were to stand erect while facing home plate and point your arm out straight from your shoulder and then put your elbow and hand up at a 90-degree angle, you'd see and feel the proper angle (for delivering a pitch). You'll see pitchers who go higher or lower, but the 90-degree angle is the easiest on your arm. Most pitchers — and a lot of them don't even know they're doing this — will have their arm in this spot just as they begin their thrust." — Bob Gibson

7. **Release the ball with your head over your striding leg and your arm fully extended.**

   Your elbow should be at or above shoulder level, your forearm parallel to the ground. Your pivot foot should come forward with its heel up as your hip (throwing-hand side) drives toward home plate. (See Figure 6-4.)

   "Don't try to muscle the pitch to get greater velocity. When you tighten the arm to throw, it's like a hitter trying to hit a home run and swinging too hard. His bat gets very slow. The same thing will happen with your arm. Keep your hand, wrist, and arm relaxed so you can pop the ball at the very last second. You get your velocity in front of the rubber, not behind the rubber. The ideal thing would be for you to use your arm like a whip, but not everyone is capable of doing that." — Bob Gibson

Figure 6-4:
Releasing
the ball.

The Follow-Through

"Follow-through is very important for a pitcher. If you cut off your follow-through, you won't be able to pop the ball for velocity." — Bob Gibson

After you release the pitch, your pivot foot should continue to move forward until it is parallel or slightly in front of your striding foot. Bring the elbow of your glove hand back toward your hip (as if you were elbowing someone behind you). Your throwing arm should sweep across your body on a diagonal and end on the first-base side (if you are right-handed) or third-base side (if you are left-handed) of your knee. (See Figure 6-5.) Ideally, this follow-through should leave you in perfect fielding position: weight balanced evenly on the balls of your feet, knees bent, and your glove ready to field anything hit your way.

"If your follow-through ends with you in perfect fielding position, fine. But don't let it get in the way of your main objective, getting the ball to the plate with location and something on it. If I had tried to come out in perfect fielding position all the time, I probably wouldn't have gotten anybody out because I would have had to cut my follow-through off. I wasn't willing to do that. So I just made sure I recovered quickly enough after my follow-through to field the ball." — Bob Gibson

Authors' note: Gibson's follow-through often ended with him facing first base, but he recovered quickly enough to earn nine consecutive Gold Glove awards.

Figure 6-5:
Following-
through with
the pitch.

Pitching from the Stretch

BASEBALL SPEAK

With runners on, you have to discard your full wind-up; it leaves your leg in the air so long that opponents are able to steal bases easily. Instead, pitch from the set or *stretch* position. Stand sideways with your rear foot against the front edge of the rubber and your front shoulder aligned with home. Your feet should be a little less than shoulder length apart with your front foot's heel even with the rear of your back foot's arch. (See Figure 6-6.)

Figure 6-6:
Getting into
the stretch
position.

Instead of winding up to deliver the ball, simply stretch your arms above your head and bring your ball and glove hands to a complete stop somewhere between your chest and belt. The rest of the delivery is similar to the one you use out of your wind-up except you need less kick and pivot and more push from the pitching rubber.

"Pitching from the stretch is no different from pitching with a wind-up. You're simply cutting off the wind-up, but at the point where you rotate your hips you should be in the same position as when you take your full wind-up."
— Bob Gibson

Heat and Other Weapons in Your Pitching Arsenal

Ninety-two mph, 94 mph, 100 mph — the numbers reported by the speed-obsessed media may lead you to believe that a fastball's velocity is its most important attribute. It isn't. More critical to a pitcher's success is the fastball's movement and location. Pitchers should also be able to change speeds to throw off the batter's timing. If a fastball doesn't move much, a competent major league hitter can time it after a few viewings no matter how many speed records it shatters. Case in point: When Hideki Irabu, the Japanese League pitching star, made his American major league debut with the New York Yankees, his best fastball clocked in at 98 mph. Few pitchers can match his speed. However, during his first season with New York, Irabu's pitches were straight as a string. After opponents got their swings grooved, they were hitting long shots off of him. After Yankee pitching coach Mel Stottlemyre taught Irabu how to make his ball move more (Stottlemyre altered Irabu's grip), the pitcher started winning more often than he lost.

"You can teach a pitcher to increase his movement on the ball. It's all a matter of how you hold and release the ball. If you release the ball with your fingers pointed straight up, there's a good chance the ball won't move. But if you just cock the ball to one side or the other, it will move if you work at it."
— Bob Gibson

Four time Cy Young Award winner Greg Maddux, on the other hand, rarely throws harder than 88 mph. That's only a little above average for a major leaguer. However, Maddux is nearly unhittable because he can put the ball wherever he wants it. His pitches not only move, they move late. A batter may think that he has honed in on a Maddux pitch, only to find that the ball has darted in on his hands at the very last second. The right-hander rarely throws two consecutive pitches at the same speed. Like most great pitchers, Maddux throws a variety of pitches, including a slider, curve, and change-up.

Every pitcher, no matter how hard he throws, should have at least three strong pitches — something hard, something that breaks (moves), and something off-speed — in his arsenal. With that in mind, take a look at your options in the following sections.

The four-seam fastball

The *four-seamer* is considered the basic fastball. Grip it with your top two fingers across the seams at their widest point. Nestle your thumb under the ball across the bottom seam. Curl your ring and little fingers along one side. Your middle and index fingers should be about a half inch apart. If they touch, the ball can slide, making it difficult to control. If you spread them too far, you can limit the wrist action you need to pitch. Hold the ball away from your palm with your fingertips. (See Figure 6-7.)

Figure 6-7:
The four-seam fastball.

Keeping your fingers in the center of the ball limits its movement. However, if you bring your digits a bit closer together and move them off-center to the left, the ball runs (moves to either side) or sinks. Placing your fingers off-center to the right causes the ball to break in on a left-handed batter and away from a righty.

The two-seam fastball

The *two-seam fastball* moves more than the four-seamer. To throw it, grip the ball along its two seams with your middle and index fingers. Position your thumb under the ball. Your ring and little fingers are off to the side of the ball, slightly behind your gripping fingers. Exert pressure with your middle finger and thumb. To throw a sinking fastball, move your top fingers so that they hook a seam. Throw the ball like a fastball and let your grip do the rest.

For a variation on this theme, you can grip the ball with your middle and index fingers across the two seams at their narrowest point (the portion of an official major league baseball that bears the league president's signature). Maintain pressure with your thumb and middle finger. With this two-seam grip, the ball should move more to the side.

Some pitchers turn their hands down and in when they release the two-seamer. This action slows the ball's break, which can throw off a hitter's timing; however, if it doesn't, that pitch is an excellent candidate for a home run.

"As a right-handed pitcher, if I threw the two-seamer to a right-handed hitter, the ball would usually sink or curve into him. If I threw that same pitch to the left-hander, it would sink and move away from him. Most left-handed hitters are low-ball hitters, which means that a two-seamer would be right in their wheelhouse. So I'm going to throw the four-seamer to him; that pitch will ride in on his hands." — *Bob Gibson*

The slider

A hybrid, the *slider* is part fastball, part breaking ball. It is listed with the other fastballs because it is more effective the harder it is thrown. The key to an effective slider is its late break. It should resemble a fastball until it approaches the hitter. Then it should veer sharply to the side.

Grip the slider with the index and middle fingers across the two widest seams. Keep your fingers slightly off-center, toward the outside of the ball. Your thumb is tucked under the ball, your ring and little fingers are off to its side. Exert pressure with your thumb and middle finger. (See Figure 6-8.)

Figure 6-8:
The slider.

When you throw the ball, *keep your wrist loose!* Throwing this pitch with a stiff wrist can strain and damage your elbow.

You also shouldn't twist your wrist as you release the slider (a mistake commonly made by pitchers who think twisting imparts greater spin on the pitch — it does, but it also increases the chances of injury). Instead, throw it like a fastball, but imagine cutting through the ball with your middle finger as you deliver the pitch. Keep your fingers on top of the ball until the moment of release.

"If you twist your wrist like you are throwing a curve, you won't get that extra bite on the pitch. That ball will have a big, slow break. Instead, turn the ball with your first two fingers and your thumb as if you were turning a doorknob." — Bob Gibson

The split-fingered fastball

The *split-fingered fastball* is the child of the *forkball,* a pitch that was thrown with great effectiveness by such relief-pitching stars as Elroy Face and Lindy McDaniel during the 1960s. Pitchers held the forkball between the first two joints of their middle and index fingers. When thrown by a good fastball pitcher, it was more like a good change-up than a power pitch. You don't hold today's split-finger (or *splitter*) as high between your fingers as the forkball, which means you can throw it with greater velocity. Split your middle and index fingers and grip the ball along its seams. Do not jam it past the midway point of your fingers. (See Figure 6-9.)

Figure 6-9:
The split-fingered fastball.

"Throw the pitch with a fastball motion and plenty of wrist. When properly delivered, the splitter should look like a fastball until it reaches the plate. Then the pitch should dive down as if the bottom had dropped out from under it."
— Bill Lee

The curveball

Good *curveballs* (also known as *deuces, hooks,* and *Uncle Charlies*) have put more hitters out of work than all the baseball strikes combined. If you have a hook that you can throw for strikes, batters can't *sit back on* (wait for) the fastball even when the count is in their favor. Hitters never look worse than when they swing at a curve after guessing a fastball.

To throw the curve, grip the ball with your middle and index fingers across the seams at their widest part. Hold it farther back in your hand than the fastball, but don't let it touch your palm or you won't get enough spin. Your object here is to get more of your finger surface in contact with the ball. Curl your ring and little fingers into your palm. Exert pressure with your middle finger and thumb; keep the index finger loose against the ball. (See Figure 6-10.)

Figure 6-10:
The
curveball.

"As you bring your arm forward in your motion, your wrist should be cocked and rotating inward. Your palm and ball should face you as your hand passes your head. While keeping your elbow high, turn your wrist and snap down as you release the ball over your index finger. The back of your hand should be facing the batter as the pitch leaves your fingers." — Bill Lee

Make sure you follow through with your motion, or your curve ball will *hang* (stay up in the strike zone where a hitter likes it). Pitchers who throw a lot of hanging curves often want to hang themselves because batters tend to smack those pitches a long, long way.

The three-fingered change-up

Change-ups make your fastballs more effective by making them seem faster by comparison. You can use a variety of change-up grips, but the *three-fingered change-up* is the easiest to master. Hold the ball back against your palm with your index finger, middle finger, and ring finger spread across the seams at their widest point. Nestle the thumb and pinky against each other under the ball. (See Figure 6-11.)

Figure 6-11:
The three-fingered change-up.

PLAYER TIP

"Exert equal pressure with all five fingers. Keep your wrist stiff. Bring it straight down as if you were lowering a window shade. Don't pick a corner with this pitch; throw it down the middle of the plate." — Bill Lee

The circle change-up

Hold the *circle change-up* like the three-finger change-up — only join the index finger and thumb in a circle on the side of the ball. (See Figure 6-12.)

Figure 6-12:
The circle change-up.

The palmball

The *palmball* is an off-speed pitch, a change of pace designed to mess with the hitter's rhythm. Unlike all other pitches, the ball is held tight against the palm. Your middle and index finger rest across the top of the two widest seams. Your ring and little finger rest against one side, your thumb is slightly raised along the other. Exert pressure on the ball with your ring finger and thumb. (See Figure 6-13.) Throw this pitch with your usual fastball motion. As you release the pitch, straighten out your fingers and make sure your hand is behind the ball rather than on top of it. You want the ball to slip from between your thumb and fingers.

Figure 6-13:
The palmball.

"Pitchers make the mistake of trying to underthrow their change-ups, reducing their arm's speed to slow the pitch. Throw the ball as if it were a fastball and let your grip and motion do the work." — Bill Lee

The screwball

Throw the *screwball* pitch only at your peril; it is murder on the arm. A reverse curveball, the *scroogie* is held like a four-seam fastball (see Figure 6-7). The index finger and thumb provide all the pressure, but you release the ball off your middle finger.

Come over the top with this pitch as if it were a fastball. However, just before you release the ball, turn your wrist, forearm, and elbow inward in a corkscrew motion. The rotation should be the opposite of your curveball. When thrown by a left-hander (which most screwballers are), the ball breaks down and away from right-handed hitters. However, it breaks down and in on left-handed hitters, which they like a lot; that's why left-handed hitters usually hit left-handed scroogie artists so well.

The knuckleball

The *knuckleball* is the one pitch that is more effective the slower you throw it. Knuckleballs are difficult to control because their movement is so erratic. Often, the pitcher who throws one has no idea how it will move or where. Knucklers dart, dance, jump, break, swerve, and rise. Sometimes these pitches perform two or three of these motions in the same flight. Most batters hate to hit against the knuckler; a good one can throw off their swings for weeks.

The trick to throwing the pitch is to eliminate as much of the ball rotation as you can. Despite its name, the ball is rarely thrown off the knuckles. Instead, dig the tips of your index, middle, and ring fingers (make sure your nails are always trimmed if you are going to throw this pitch) into just below the seams of the ball. Keep your thumb and little finger on the side. (See Figure 6-14.)

Figure 6-14:
The
knuckleball.

"Don't throw the knuckleball; push it towards home plate with a stiff wrist out of your usual motion. Imagine you are tossing a pair of socks into the hamper. As you release the ball, extend your fingers straight out towards home plate."
— *Bill Lee*

Before You Take the Mound

You can increase the effectiveness of all of your pitches if you throw them with the same motion. Have your coaches and teammates watch you on the mound to see if you are making any subtle gestures that may reveal which pitch you are about to deliver. Never throw a half-hearted pitch. If you don't agree with the sign from your catcher, shake him off (shake your head "no"). Wait until he calls for something that inspires more enthusiasm or comes out to the mound to discuss the options.

Don't let a hitter beat you on your second-best pitch. With the game on the line, go with your best stuff, even if it means matching your strength against the hitter's.

A word from Bob Gibson on throwing hard

"One of the lost arts in pitching is being able to throw the ball hard. Too many pitchers are throwing trick pitches at a very young age. Being able to throw the fastball with as much velocity as you can is more important. But the number one thing for any pitcher is control: being able to throw the ball where you want when you want to. Try using the same release point every time. If you don't know where your release point is, your ball is going to be everywhere. You also have to know yourself. For instance, if my ball was high, I knew there were two things I could be doing wrong. One was I had screwed up my release point, the other was I had taken too long a stride. When you understand that, you can make adjustments on the mound."

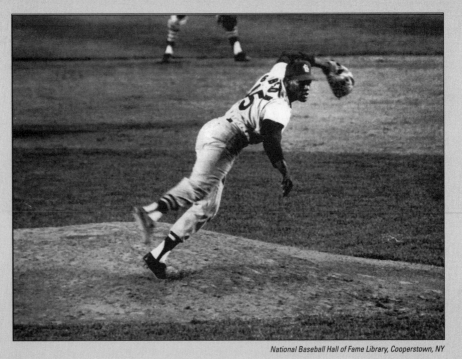

National Baseball Hall of Fame Library, Cooperstown, NY

Chapter 7

The Third Dimension: Defense

• •

In This Chapter

▶ Discovering the requirements for each position

▶ Getting your arm ready

▶ Fielding and positioning

▶ Playing catcher (Johnny Bench)

▶ Handling first base (Willie McCovey)

▶ Making it at second base (Joe Morgan)

▶ Taking your position at third base (Ken Caminiti)

▶ Trying your hand at shortstop (Barry Larkin)

▶ Being a defensive pitcher (Bill Lee)

▶ Roaming the outfield (Willie Mays, Ken Griffey, Sr., and Rusty Staub)

• •

*I*n 1997, each of the eight clubs in the major leagues that qualified for the playoffs had at least two Gold Glove recipients on its roster. (Gold Gloves are awarded yearly to the best defensive player at each position.) That shouldn't be surprising. Winning teams play good defense. We tend to think of power pitchers and sluggers as the dominant forces on a baseball diamond, but a great defensive player can be just as intimidating. When Seattle center fielder Ken Griffey, Jr. defies the earth's pull to make yet another leaping, rally-crippling snatch of what appears to be a sure double, watch how many shoulders sag in the opposing dugout. Plays like that can slaughter hope before it gains full maturity, deflating the victimized hitter and his club while elevating the team on the other side of the field.

Griffey, catcher Ivan Rodriguez, and shortstop Rey Ordonez are among the premier fielders playing today. These Gold Glovers have sure hands, fast reactions, and strong, accurate arms. They get to balls that other fielders merely wave at. However, you wouldn't call any one of them a "natural" fielder — someone who was born to steal base hits — because there is no such thing. The only way to become a great defender is to work at it.

This chapter begins with some general fielding tips. Then we turn the floor over to an All-Star team of consultants for advice on how to play each of the nine positions. (That's right, pitchers are part of the defensive mix, too.)

The Good Hands People

No matter which position you play, you need to have what ball players call *good hands*. However, *quick hands* and *soft hands* would be more accurate terms. If you have them, your hands adjust swiftly to bad hops, erratic bounces, or wild throws. Some people are born with quick hands, but most of us must develop them.

One way to develop quick hands is to play the game *short hop*. Stand 4 to 5 feet (1.2m to 1.5m) apart from a partner. Throw the ball to each other so that the ball bounces on a short hop, which forces the fielder receiving the throw to reach and adjust on every toss. Keep score to make the drill interesting. The first player to miss three short hops loses the round. Start again until you complete a five-round game. While practicing this drill, concentrate on using both hands for every catch. Training your hands to work in unison makes you a more coordinated fielder.

Picking a Position

Want to know which position is right for you? This section examines the particular qualities that each position requires so that you can see how you measure up.

Catcher

You must have a high threshold of pain to play catcher. Foul balls are going to ricochet off your fingers and feet, you may take an occasional fastball or bat on the mask, and you can count on at least one home plate collision every week. Catchers must have strong legs — you spend half the game squatting while wearing heavy equipment. If you are going to play the position properly, you must possess a powerful, accurate arm, although you can compensate for an average throwing arm with a quick release.

If you want an example of how a strong arm can completely neutralize base stealers, just watch Charles Johnson or Ivan Rodriguez intimidate a team from behind the plate. They both throw out a high percentage of potential base thieves, but what is more impressive is how few runners attempt to steal against them.

Besides having physical stamina, catchers must be mentally tough. Catching is draining work; you are in on every pitch of the game. If your pitcher takes the mound without his best stuff, you're the one who has to improvise a strategy to retire batters with his secondary pitches. With every hitter, that computer between your ears is working in overdrive, trying to recollect or decipher the hitter's weaknesses and strengths.

Are you immersed in a batting slump? No matter how many 0-fors you've taken, you need to put your hitting woes out of your mind the moment you squat behind home plate. You must place your entire focus on aiding your pitcher in the battle against the hitter.

Finally, you have to be a practical psychologist — if your pitcher is getting battered, you have to know whether he needs a pat on the back or a good swift kick in the rear.

What's glove got to do with it? (With apologies to Tina Turner)

Your glove (or mitt) is your most important fielding tool. It should fit snugly enough that it won't come off when you catch a ball in its tip. However, your glove should not be so tight that it restricts wrist flexibility or movement. How big should your glove be? That depends on what position you play.

- Catcher's mitts are always large, but yours shouldn't be so big that you cannot control it. Choose a mitt that you can open and close in a split second. (See Chapter 2 for some preliminary details on gloves and how to select them.)

- At first base, catching the ball is your primary concern. Digging the ball out of the mitt to get off your own throw is a secondary issue. Your first baseman's mitt should be as long as you can comfortably manage so that you can snag wide, errant tosses in the glove's webbing.

- Third basemen should also opt for large gloves. Balls are hit so quickly to third that you often only have time to block the ball or knock it down. You also have to field many balls hit wide to your left and right. A big glove helps you cover more territory.

- Second base is the position of quick throws; use the smallest glove possible here so that the ball won't stick deep in its pocket. Choosing a small glove to play second is also a matter of self-preservation — at times you may have 220 solid pounds of seething base runner bearing down on you to break up the double play (as well as any part of your anatomy he can reach). In these cases, you don't want to spend a split second more time than necessary searching for the ball before unleashing your throw.

- Shortstops must get the ball out of their gloves quickly, too. But they must also be able to catch grounders cleanly when they range wide in the hole. A medium-sized glove is in order for this position.

- Outfielders are primarily interested in catching the ball. They have little need for a quick release. If you are playing the outfield, use the longest glove that the rules permit. (See Chapter 2 for rules about gloves.)

Ideally, catchers should have a low center of gravity, like the 5-foot-8-inch Ivan Rodriguez. This body type gives the pitcher a better target and also offers the umpire a clearer perspective of each pitch. For example, seeing over a tall catcher like 6-foot-2-inch Charles Johnson can be difficult for an umpire; that size may occasionally cost his pitcher a low strike. (And that about sums up the only weakness — if you can call it that — in Charles's game. He is one of the best defensive catchers to ever pull on a pair of shin guards.)

First base

Left-handed throwers have an advantage playing first base. As a first baseman, all your throws to the infield go to your right; if you throw left-handed, the play is always in front of you. Right-handed throwers often have to whirl completely around before they can toss the ball to another base. First basemen don't need particularly strong arms; they rarely throw more than 60 feet. But your arm must be accurate, particularly on the 3-6-3 (first-to-short-to-first) double play when you are throwing into the runner.

First basemen should have enough range to cover their half of the hole between first and second. You need quick reactions and agility to cope with the opposition's bunting game. (Watch how San Francisco's J.T. Snow pounces on bunts with the nimbleness of a middle infielder.) First basemen catch more throws than any other fielders, with the exception of the catcher. Depending on how the thrower grips the ball prior to release, those throws can sink, rise, or dart to either side of you. You have to be prepared to gather in tosses from every angle. If catching the ball is a liability for you, move to another position.

Second base

Second base is a paradox. I've played enough of it to know that this can be the easiest infield position for catching the ball — you don't have to cleanly catch a ground ball to record an out. Your proximity to first base allows you plenty of time to simply knock the ball down and make the short toss to the bag.

However, second base is also the most difficult position because you are a sitting duck on the double play. You often wait for a throw with your back to some runner who is eager to tear you in half with his slide. (Think football and hockey players are the only athletes who relish a little hard contact? George "Boomer" Scott — a hulking bruiser of a base runner when he played with the Boston Red Sox and Milwaukee Brewers during the 1970s — often wore a necklace, which he gleefully claimed was constructed from retired second basemen's teeth. And George was one of the more genteel of baseball's crash artists.) Your attitude has to be, "The double play takes priority over my physical well-being. I'm going to turn the play first and *then* look for the runner."

Too many otherwise-skilled second basemen hurt their teams by letting their fear of injury prevent them from *turning two* (getting both outs on a double play). The key to not getting creamed is to catch your shortstop's ball cleanly so you have time to plant your left foot on the bag. When you throw toward first base, you gain the momentum to leap out of the way of the base runner. Second basemen who bobble that toss from the shortstop tend to freeze for a split second before they recover. This hesitation leaves them prone to collision.

In addition, a second baseman needs to be a take-charge type, an infield captain who can direct where a play should go. (Between pitches, the second baseman can indicate where the ball should be thrown if hit by the batter.) Because you move around so much — for example, when you have to cover first base on a bunt — you must concentrate on positioning a little more than the other infielders. Pokey Reese, a member of the 1999 National League Gold Glove team, is an excellent example of a second baseman who positions himself well on every hitter.

Because most of your throws are short, you don't need a powerful arm to play second base. However, your throws must be precise and quick (particularly when you are relaying an outfield throw to another base) and you must be able to throw under pressure (being exerted by that base runner bearing down on you).

Shortstop

Shortstop is the most difficult infield position to play. Shortstops must be able to field grounders cleanly because they rarely have time to knock a ball down and throw out the runner. Because you have more territory to cover than any other infielder, you have to be far-ranging.

Tall, lean players, like Derek Jeter (6 feet 3 inches) and Edgar Renteria (6 feet 1 inch), are built ideally to play shortstop; they can stretch out over more ground and reach out farther than smaller infielders. However, a relatively short player like 5-foot-9-inch Rey Ordonez can outplay almost anyone at this position because he is so quick. This position demands a powerful throwing arm to make the throw from the hole (near the third base side of the infield) or from deep behind second base.

Third base

Like the catcher, a third baseman must be willing to absorb a few body blows. You play close to home plate; if a right-handed hitter pulls the ball sharply, you often won't have time to get your glove into fielding position. That's when you have to throw your body in front of the ball, block it, get to your feet, and throw out the runner. That's why third basemen like Robin Ventura are studies in black and blue by midseason. You take a lot of punishment at third base.

Great third basemen usually have powerful arms; they need them to make long throws across the diamond. If you can throw with velocity, you can make up some of the time you lose blocking the ball and picking it up. However, Brooks Robinson, who is generally considered to be the best third baseman of all time, had an average arm at best. He compensated with a quick release and by positioning himself so that he seldom had to make the long throws required of most third basemen.

Third base is a reflex position; you must be able to react quickly to balls hit sharply to either side of you. Watch how third baseman Ken Caminiti can go to the line to his right as well as to the hole on his left. Ken's agility is one of the reasons he has several Gold Gloves sitting on his mantel. (A little later in this chapter, Ken tells you why he's so good at going to either side.)

Left field

Left field is the easiest position to play. Of the three outfielders, the left fielder makes the shortest throws, so he can get by with a below-average arm. Fly balls hit to left don't curve as much as fly balls hit to right. When batters hit the ball to the opposite field, it tends to *slice*. Because so many more hitters bat right-handed than left-handed, the left fielder doesn't have to handle many sliced balls (those fly balls that seem to keep moving farther away from the pursuing outfielder no matter how hard he runs).

Left fielders must be able to *charge the ball* (catch it while running toward it) properly; their close proximity and direct angle to home offer them numerous opportunities to throw out runners at the plate. Charging the ball gives them the momentum to unleash strong throws. Barry Bonds is the player who defines this position today. He's fast, goes back well on balls hit over his head, expertly plays balls hit down the line, and has an above-adequate arm that rarely misses its target. Watch how he lines up his entire body behind a throw. He's a walking clinic on left-field play.

Center field

Center fielders should have accurate, strong arms; they are going to run down more balls than the other two outfielders and consequently have to make more throws. (***Note:*** If you charge the ball quickly and have a quick release, you can get by without having a strong arm.)

Speed and quickness are two more requisites for center field. (A relatively slow player who positions himself well, on the other hand, can play either left or right field.) You cannot play center unless you can run; you have to cover too much territory. In addition to chasing after fly balls, you back up your fellow outfielders on any fly balls or grounders hit their way.

Center fielders must be able to get a good jump on the ball; they need to react and accelerate quickly. Players like Jim Edmonds and Andruw Jones move at the crack of the bat. Excellent lateral movement is another must. Edmonds and Ken Griffey, Jr. are among the best at going to either side to make a catch.

As a center fielder, you also have to understand your limitations. If you don't go back on the ball well, you cannot play too shallow. If you have trouble coming in, you cannot play too deep. A great center fielder like Griffey, Jr. has no difficulty coming in or going out, so he plays deep to steal extra base hits from the opposition.

Finally, the center fielder must be assertive — the entire outfield is your domain. If you call for a catch, the other outfielders must give way. On balls hit to the left or right fielders, you direct the play. (For more on where to go on a particular play, see Chapter 9.)

Right field

The first thing that managers look for in a right fielder is a strong arm. Right fielders have to make longer throws than anyone else on the diamond, sometimes throwing from deep in the right-field corner to third or home. (Larry Walker does that as well as anyone; he has a howitzer of an arm.) Because hits to right tend to curve or fade away from the fielder, you must be proficient at reading the ball's angle.

Pitcher

For this chapter, we are looking at the pitcher solely as a defensive player. You are 60 feet 6 inches (18.4m) away from the hitter, so you must have quicker reactions than anyone else in the infield. For your own safety, you should be able to catch the ball cleanly, but this skill is not a requirement. If you can simply knock the ball down in front of you, you usually have plenty of time to throw out even the fastest runners. Young pitchers often ignore fielding fundamentals; they seem to think all they need to win ball games is a lively arm. However, most of baseball's elite pitchers — players such as Gold Glovers Greg Maddux and Mike Mussina — are excellent fielders. They know how to execute, to do those little things that help them win close ball games. That's one of the reasons they are among their league's pitching leaders year after year.

Loading the Cannon: Getting Your Arm Ready for the Field

A poor throw can undermine the best glove work. Before exploring any other aspect of fielding, in this section we review the mechanics of throwing. To start, you need to warm up your arm. You and your throwing partner should stand 10 feet (3m) apart and gently lob the ball to each other. As your arm starts to feel loose and warm, gradually increase the velocity of your throws. If you are a young adult, toss the ball from four throwing angles:

- ✔ Over the top
- ✔ Three-quarters
- ✔ Sidearm
- ✔ Underhand

After you feel completely loose, stretch and strengthen your arm by gradually increasing the distance between you and your throwing partner.

Players under the age of 16 should throw only overhand or three-quarters; your arms aren't fully developed enough to withstand the strain of throwing sidearm or underhand.

Getting a grip

When you grip the ball, your middle and index fingers should be approximately 1 inch (2.54cm) apart, *across* the seams. Place your thumb on the ball's underside directly below your middle finger. Press the ball with your thumb and middle finger. Because you want your throws to travel straight and true, always throw with your fingers across the seams (see Figure 7-1). Placing your fingers *with* the seams causes the ball to sink or sail (a no-no unless you are a pitcher throwing to a hitter).

Make sure that you hold the ball out in your fingers, because if you hold the ball back in your palm as you throw, you won't generate enough velocity. Don't squeeze the ball; hold it just firmly enough to maintain control. Practice grabbing the ball and finding your across-the-seams grip without peeking.

Figure 7-1:
How to grip
the ball
before
throwing.

Delivering the throw

How you throw the ball depends on the position you play. Most outfielders throw the ball overhand for maximum power. The exception occurs on a *shoestring catch* (a ball caught, usually on the run, near your feet). If a runner is trying to advance on that play, the outfielder has to throw underhand or sidearm, or he won't get rid of the ball quickly enough.

Infielders rarely have time to straighten up and throw over the top; whenever you rear back to throw, you concede about 12 feet (3.6m) to the base runner. So you should throw three-quarters, sidearm, or underhand depending on the situation. On the double play, a second baseman or shortstop must throw from wherever he catches the ball. If you catch it high, throw overhand; if you catch it low, throw underhand.

To make an accurate, powerful overhand throw:

1. **Start the throw by squaring yourself toward your target and swinging your throwing arm back to your side in an arc.**

   Tilt your upper torso back on your throwing side, while keeping your other shoulder (and your eyes) pointed toward your target. Your wrist should be cocked and ready to throw.

2. **Step and thrust forward as you swing your arm directly over its shoulder and toward your target.**

   Make sure you extend your arm fully. Keep your elbow higher than your throwing shoulder (see Figure 7-2).

Figure 7-2:
Making the
overhand
throw.

3. **Plant your front (striding) foot while pushing off your rear (pivot) foot. To get maximum velocity on your throw, snap your wrist downward as you release the ball.**

   Your arm should continue to sweep in front of you and down to your side. As you follow through, your glove hand should come up behind you for balance. Allow your lower body to follow your upper body's momentum toward the target.

4. **Bring your pivot foot forward until it is parallel to your striding foot.**

   Use this same motion for the three-quarter throw from the outfield, but bring your elbow around on a 45-degree angle.

Infielders often throw sidearm and don't have time for a lot of motion when they throw. To throw sidearm, bring your throwing arm back in a short arc. Step toward your target and thrust forward as you swing your arm back in an arc that is parallel to the ground. You often cannot get your whole body behind this throw, so get as much shoulder and wrist into it as you can. Aim your throw for the middle of your target's torso.

You usually must throw underhand when you are close to your target or have to quickly toss a ball you have caught below your knees and to the side. Using a bowling motion, flip the ball toward your target's chest. Because you cannot get anything behind this throw, give it a good wrist snap as you release the ball.

Determining how hard is too hard

You don't have to air everything out on every throw you make. I don't believe throwing consistently hard is likely to hurt or tire your arm. However, if you are trying to throw the ball through a wall on every play, you can strain your muscles over the course of a season. Rick Burleson, a first-rate shortstop for the Red Sox and Angels from the mid-'70s to early-'80s, had a cannon arm whose power he demonstrated on nearly every throw. By age 30, a torn rotator cuff (an arm injury more common to pitchers than fielders) finished his career as a starting shortstop.

A Word about Errors

The first thing you have to remember is that every player makes errors. Don't let it get you down, though. In 1976, for example, I made 13 errors (nearly one every two weeks) while still winning a Gold Glove at second base. In 1980, when I was with Houston, our left fielder Jose Cruz led the National League with 11 errors, and he still managed to catch nearly 97 percent of the balls hit his way. (By the way, Jose was a fine outfielder; he just had one of those years.)

On the upside, if you have good range and play aggressively, you're going to commit fumbles on balls that other fielders don't even reach. Most errors come on grounders that are hit directly at you. (If you have any talent for catching a baseball, you rarely muff a fly ball.)

Fielders who fumble grounders tend to freeze for an instant instead of being aggressive. This lack of aggressiveness is what broadcasters mean when they say that the fielder *let the ball play him.* Whenever a ground ball is hit toward you, charge it immediately so you can gauge its hop; if you fail to charge right away, you can misperceive the ball's bounce.

When you do commit an error, don't let it discourage you. Dwell on it and you'll probably boot another ball because you're not concentrating on the play at hand. As National League Gold Glove third baseman Ken Caminiti says, "If you know in your heart that you gave a ball your best effort, you just shrug the error off as part of the game. Keep your focus on the game and get ready for the next play. Don't spend any time thinking negatively. Be aggressive. You should want that next ball hit to you because you *know* — not just *think* — you're going to make the play." That's the kind of confidence every fielder must have.

Don't short-leg

Fear of fumbles can sap you of aggressiveness. Some players, rather than charge a ball full-out, time their approaches so they and the ball arrive at a spot simultaneously. If they catch the ball, it looks like a dazzling play. If they miss it, the official scorer usually deems it a hit instead of an error. It's called *short-legging* the ball, and it is a capital crime. You aren't on the field to look pretty or compile a gaudy fielding percentage. You are there to help your team win. Short-leggers invariably cost their clubs victories. When you are on the diamond, give everything you have to every play.

Avoid those hidden errors

Mental errors don't appear in anyone's box score, but they are often more costly than physical mistakes. When you commit a *rock* (make a boneheaded play) like throwing to the wrong base, it's usually because you did not antici-pate the situation. As each hitter steps up to the plate, review all your options.

For example, you're the second baseman with a man on first and one out. Right away you should not only be thinking double play, but how to execute it. If the ball is hit to the shortstop or third baseman, you have to cover second. Hit to the pitcher? You are backing up the shortstop's play at second base. And so on. Cover all the possibilities so that when the ball hits the bat, you are ready to execute. You don't have to waste a second wondering what to do — you can simply react.

Six Tips for Fielding Grounders

Fielding a ground ball is easy if you have sound fundamentals. To put yourself in position to make a play, you should do the following:

- ✔ **Charge the ball whenever you can.** If you hang back, the ball has more time to take a bad hop. Maintain a short, quick stride rather than one that is long and uncontrollable. You should be able to stop abruptly.

- ✔ **Stay down on the ball.** Keep your body, including your buttocks, low to the ground. Standing straight up makes it difficult to gauge the ball's hop. You want your eyes down low for a good look at the ball. Keep your eyes on the ball; watch it go into your glove. After you catch it, look where you are going to throw it.

- ✔ **Keep your weight balanced evenly on the balls of both feet when you take your fielding stance (unless you are anticipating a specific play).** Having your knees flexed rather than bent allows you freedom of movement.

✔ **Use both hands to field whenever possible.** Catch the ball with your glove near the ground facing up and your bare palm above it facing down. If a ball takes a bad hop, using two hands gives you a better chance to corral it. The ball may drop into your glove after hitting the palm of your hand, or it may drop in front of you. Then you can pick it up in time to throw out the runner. If you use only one hand and the grounder takes a bad hop, the ball will get by you. Using both hands also allows you to get your throws off quickly.

✔ **Let your hands "give" a bit when the ball makes contact with your glove.** Cradle the ball in your glove as if you were catching a raw egg.

✔ **Keep your arms extended so that you catch the ball in front of you.** Try to field the ball in the middle of your body so that if the ball hits you on the bad hop, it drops in front of you. If it hits off to your side, the ball can bounce away from you.

Practice your throws so that you can take the ball out of your glove without looking at it. You should know whether you get more velocity on the ball by gripping it across or with the seams. You must be able to get your preferred grip on the ball while looking at your target, *not the ball.*

There will be times when you shouldn't even attempt a throw. For example, suppose that Kenny Lofton is speeding toward first on a slow hit grounder. If you realize that you have no chance to make an accurate throw, hold the ball. Yes, you just put a runner on first, but that decision is better than letting Lofton take second or third (and he will) if you throw the ball wildly.

Positioning Yourself for a Strong Defense

No matter where you play on the field, knowledge and anticipation are the keys to positioning. Prior to the game, your pitcher should have told you and your teammates how he plans to throw to the opposing batters. You need to combine that information with all the data you have on those hitters. For example, when I was with the Reds, Jack Billingham may have tried to catch Billy Williams (a terrifying left-handed hitter with the Chicago Cubs) off-balance with a slow curve. I knew Billy would probably pull that pitch toward right field. If Jack threw his fastball away, Billy would probably shoot it to the opposite field. However, if Reggie Jackson — a slugger who hit over 500 home runs in the American League — were the hitter, Jack may have thrown a fast-ball away. Most left-handed hitters would hit that pitch to the opposite field in left. But Reggie was strong enough to pull the fastball away into right field with authority. I had to know all these tendencies so I could position myself accordingly.

After your data file on the opposing players is complete, you can reposition yourself for each hitter that comes to the plate; you may even change your position from pitch to pitch. Say that your catcher calls for the fastball inside, you are going to lean to the left or right depending on the hitter's tendencies. Because smart hitters adapt to situations, you must do the same. For example, with the first baseman holding a runner on first, a left-handed hitting genius like Tony Gwynn can shoot balls through that big hole on the right side of the infield. If you were playing second in that circumstance, you would lean more toward first to get a better jump on balls hit toward the hole. If no one was on base, you would play closer to second. However, if the pitcher was going inside on Tony, you would cheat toward first.

Fielding Line Drives

Catching a line drive is a reaction play — you either catch it or you don't. However, if you can't catch a line drive cleanly, you must knock it down so you have some opportunity to pick it up and throw. Whenever you have to leap for a line drive, look the ball into your glove (watch the ball until it enters your glove).

Fielding Fly Balls

Later in this chapter, some fine major league outfielders give you tips on the proper way to catch a fly ball. For the moment, I want to talk about pop flies, those weakly hit fly balls that don't make it out of the infield. On pop flies, you should run to wherever you expect the ball to drop. Catch the ball in front of you on your forehand side. Don't play the ball so that you have to run to catch it at the last moment. If you have to go back on a pop fly, run sideways rather than backpedaling (though you can backpedal if it is only a few steps). You don't want to risk tangling your feet. Get stationary so the ball comes straight down into your glove. Position yourself so that if you fail to catch the ball, it hits you in the chest rather than the head or shoulders. Keep your arms extended but loose: That way, if you bobble the ball, you have a second chance to catch it before it hits the ground.

Whenever you see infielders or outfielders collide on a pop fly, you know that someone wasn't paying attention. I always told our outfielders to yell so I could get out of the way if they were going to catch a pop-up. If you both yell for the catch, you won't hear each other. When I was with the Astros, our left fielder, Jesus Alou, and our shortstop, Hector Torres, were both yelling as they went after a pop fly. They collided and Hector nearly choked to death on his tongue. Make sure that you have your signals straight before each game so you can avoid that kind of catastrophe.

The infield fly rule

Umpires may invoke the *infield fly rule* only when all three of the following conditions are met:

✔ There are less than two outs.

✔ Base runners must occupy first and second base; or first, second, and third.

✔ The batter hits a fair fly ball to the infield, which the umpire believes can be caught by an infielder making "an ordinary effort."

By yelling "infield fly!" (usually while waving his arms), the umpire automatically rules the hitter out, even if the ball is not caught. The runners may advance only at their peril.

Why have such a rule? When a pop fly is hit to the infield, the runners assume the ball will be caught, so they stay anchored at the bases. If there were no infield fly rule and the fielder deliberately dropped the ball, the runners would be forced to advance (to make room on the bases for the hitter). Because they could not begin running until the ball came down, the runners' late starts could make them easy victims of a double or even a triple play. Baseball's rule makers saw this as "stealing outs through deception," so they enacted the infield fly rule in 1895.

With a fast runner on first base, I've seen infielders deliberately drop pop flies so they could get the force-out at second. The idea is to erase a base-stealing threat or replace a speedy runner with a slower one. I don't believe that is ever good policy. Baseballs can take funny hops; if a pop fly hits the ground and bounces away from you, you may not get anybody out.

Playing the Field: Position by Position

I played second base my entire career. (Well, almost my entire career. I did play 16 games in left field while I was with the Astros and three games at third base for the San Francisco Giants.) So I've enlisted some of the best fielders of the last 30 years to help us grasp the nuances of the other positions. You can find examples of their expertise sprinkled throughout the rest of this chapter.

From behind the Plate: Catcher

Good catchers are field generals. Because they call the pitches from behind the plate, they dictate a team's defensive strategy. The better *receivers* (catchers) can also set a tone for an entire ball club. For example, when Johnny Bench joined the Reds, he brought an intimidating presence to the field that immediately transformed Cincinnati into a cockier, more aggressive team. Joe Girardi, a receiver on three New York Yankee world champion

A thought about mound conferences

Managers, coaches, catchers, or infielders sometimes initiate *mound conferences* when a pitcher is in a jam (the opposition is smacking his best stuff all over the lot). Mound conferences are sometimes used to stall for extra time while a reliever warms up (which usually means that the opposition is smacking the starter's best stuff all over the lot). The pitcher and his teammates discuss his mechanics (if anyone detects a flaw in his delivery), his emotional well-being (they want to calm and encourage him), the situation (as if he doesn't know that already), or even the weather (to take his mind off his troubles).

Participate in these meetings only when you have something specific to accomplish. I would go to the mound when I thought our pitcher was throwing a certain pitch too often or to give him a breather in a tight spot. If he had just thrown a long series of bad pitches, I may tell him to approach the next pitch as if it were the first one of the ball game, just to get him out of the rut. If you don't have anything constructive to add to these conferences, stay put — small talk slaughters genuine communication. The player who keeps running to the mound when he has nothing to say risks not being heard when he finally does have something to contribute.

teams, is an intense individual who raises his pitchers' concentration level the moment he squats behind the plate. Charles Johnson is the epitome of cool. When he caught for the Florida Marlins, he could even compose the emotive volcano that is Kevin Brown when that talented but temperamental right-hander got into one of his rare jams.

A catcher must be able to recognize the strengths and limitations of his pitchers and the opposing hitters. His arm must be powerful enough to provide base thieves with some incentive not to run. Receivers are often thought of as slow, blocky types. Most of them aren't speedy, but they need to be quick enough to scurry from behind the plate on bunts.

All of a game's action flows from the catcher's *signs*. (See the upcoming section "Flashing signs: The secret language of catchers.") Because everything starts with his position, this is an appropriate place to begin our defensive tour. Throughout this section, you get tips from the player who redefined the position — Johnny Bench. Johnny came to the major leagues with the Cincinnati Reds in 1968 and promptly won the first of his ten consecutive Gold Gloves — a record for major league catchers.

I could go on for pages about this Hall of Famer's accomplishments, among them two Most Valuable Player Awards and 12 All-Star Game starts. However, no roll of honors or litany of dry statistics could summarize the Bench career better than the words of his former Reds manager, Sparky Anderson, who stated, "Johnny Bench is the standard against which all other catchers must be compared. As the total package, no one who has ever played the position can touch him."

Setting up

Catchers are the only players in baseball who set up defensively in foul territory. How deeply you position yourself behind the plate depends on the hitter: You should get as close to home as you can without getting struck by the bat. Hitters who stand back deep in the box force you to stay back. If a hitter moves up in the box, you should also move forward. The closer you come to home plate, the better positioned you'll be to handle bunts, foul tips, wild pitches, and would-be base thieves.

Though each player brings a different wrinkle to his job, all catchers assume two basic stances behind home plate. The first is a set-up that puts you in position to deliver signs to your pitcher. Drop into a squat; keep your knees parallel with your weight evenly distributed on the balls of your feet. (See Figure 7-3.) To assume the second stance, put one foot slightly behind the other to help maintain balance. Spread your knees so that they provide a strong but comfortable base. Drop your rump until it is below your knees but slightly above your heels. Your upper body should be straight but never stiff.

Figure 7-3:
A basic catching stance.

"You don't have to follow any 'Spalding Guide' model when you get behind the plate. People have different physical makeups, so they are going to squat differently. If you try to assume a position that doesn't fit your body, it will not work. Do whatever feels comfortable and balanced so that you can move either way on a pitch or block a ball in the dirt. Don't restrict yourself by holding your elbows too far in so that you are blocked from reaching across." — Johnny Bench

Flashing signs: The secret language of catchers

To flash signs, extend your right hand between your thighs. Point your right knee at the pitcher; this position shields your signals from the opposition's first base coach. You can prevent the third base coach from stealing your signs by holding your glove in front of your left knee. Most catchers give signs by extending one or more fingers. To avoid confusion, keep your signals basic: one finger for the fastball, two for the curve, three for a change-up, four for any other pitch your pitcher throws, such as a slider or screwball. Spread your fingers as wide as you can when you give signs. You want to make sure your pitchers can see each digit clearly. (See Figure 7-4.)

Figure 7-4:
Giving signs.

"Depending on the shadows and your pitcher's vision, you might want to tape your fingers to give him a better look at what you're flashing. Sometimes you have to improvise. When I was with the Reds, one of our pitchers, Wayne Simpson, had a corneal abrasion on the day he was scheduled to pitch. He couldn't wear his contacts on the mound. I could have painted my fingers in neon and he wouldn't have seen them. So I set the glove on the side of my knee for a fastball, on top of my knee for a breaking ball. Wayne pitched a two-hit shutout." — Johnny Bench

You can also transmit signs through the *pump system*. Using this method, you indicate which pitch you want by the number of times you flash the sign. (Pump one fist for a fastball, two for a curve, and so on.) Call for pitch location by holding your palms up (for high pitches) or down (for low). Pointing away from or toward a batter tells your pitchers whether the next pitch should be inside or out.

"You might go to the pump if you have an indication that the other team has stolen your signs, or with a runner on second. Whatever method you use, always make sure you and your pitcher are on the same page. The worst nightmare is to be giving signs during a game and suddenly realize that you have no communication whatsoever with the pitcher." — Johnny Bench

After a runner gets to second, where he has almost as good a view of the catcher's signs as the pitcher, things get more complicated. You must alter your signs so the runner cannot decipher them. One way to confuse him is to give several different signs in sequence after first deciding with your pitcher which of these is the genuine article. Or you can prearrange with your pitcher to combine two signs to get the appropriate signal. For example, you can flash one finger (fastball) as your first sign, three fingers (change-up) as a second, and two fingers (curve) as a third. If you and your pitcher have agreed to combine sign one (one finger) and sign three (two fingers) when a runner is on second, the addition produces the three-fingered signal for the change-up. (It is important that your infielders are also privy to your signs in all their various guises so they can set up properly on each pitch.)

"You can use physical signs to indicate an addition. For example, I might go to my mask to add one, or touch my chest protector to add two. Hitters will try to peek at your signs to gain an edge. If you catch them doing it, you can set it up with your pitcher to throw an inside pitch after you call for something outside. And I mean way inside — like around the hitter's neck. That will give him some incentive to stop peeking. If you think he's checking out your location behind the plate, to see if you're setting up inside or out, set up inside — but call for something away. Or stay centered and don't move in or out until your pitcher starts to unwind with his pitch." — Johnny Bench

When you give signs, make sure that neither your fingers nor hands extend below your thighs (where an alert opponent can observe them). Keep your elbow as still as possible; if the opposition detects you wiggling your elbow when you call for a breaking pitch, they can feast on your pitcher's fastballs.

When you're ready to catch

After you've given your sign, you can hop from your set-up position into your receiving (or *ready*) stance. Bring your rump up to just below knee level while keeping your thighs parallel to the ground. Stay low to give your pitcher a good target. This alteration shouldn't raise you as much as it makes you more compact. Shift your weight forward onto the balls of your feet until your heels are lightly touching the ground. Your feet should be shoulder width, with your right foot a few inches in front of your left. Turn your knees and feet slightly out. (See Figure 7-5.)

Figure 7-5:
Getting
ready to
receive the
pitch.

In front of your knee, bend the forearm of your catching hand at a 45-degree angle from your body. Don't lock your elbows or place them inside your knees — if you do, catching pitches far out of the strike zone is nearly impossible. When nobody is on base, protect your bare hand by tucking it behind you. With runners on, keep your bare hand in a relaxed fist behind the webbing of your glove. Grab the pitch with your throwing hand as soon as it is delivered.

Your pitcher should be able to look directly into your mitt after you set up a target. Centering your glove to your body (while remembering to keep it outside your knees!) gives the pitcher a clearer view. If you call an inside pitch, you have to shift your target inside; do the reverse for outside pitches. Don't shift your body until the last possible moment or you'll tip off the opposition. Always keep your target within the strike zone. After you set up your target, maintain the target until the ball has left the pitcher's hand.

"You have to know what your pitcher wants to use as a target. For instance, Tom Seaver may have thrown to my shinguards — right shinguard, left shinguard — depending on which side the batter swung from and whether we wanted to go in or out. Or he would pitch to one of my shoulders. Other guys looked to my glove. When you set a target with your glove, do not hold it straight up so your wrist is cocked into a L-shape. Angle the glove so you can stay flexible enough to rotate to the left or right." — Johnny Bench

Receiving the pitch

Catch the ball in the strike zone. If you receive it on the edge of the zone, the pitch's force can move your glove enough to transform a strike into a ball.

Don't stab at the pitch; let it come to you. If you must, sway with the pitches on the borders of (or just outside) the strike zone. However, avoid any extreme movements: Any radical body shift may persuade the umpire that the pitch is a ball even if it is in the strike zone.

When a pitch is legitimately outside the strike zone, don't try to steal a call by pulling it back into the zone with your glove. Umpires resent this trick; they can punish you by refusing to call borderline pitches in your favor for the rest of the game. You can, however, *frame* a pitch by subtly rolling your wrists to rotate the glove up or down. To do this, keep your arm and torso stationary. Rotate the glove down on high pitches, up on low pitches.

"On an outside pitch to a right-handed hitter, keep the largest portion of your glove over the plate while catching the ball in your web. Do just the opposite against a left-hander. Always try to catch the ball in the web." — *Johnny Bench*

Tracking errant pitches

With runners on base, your pitcher must know he can throw a low pitch without having to worry that you'll let it skip by you. He'll have that confidence after you demonstrate your ability to dig those babies out of the dirt. To do that, you must forget about catching when runners are on base. Instead, concentrate on blocking the ball while anticipating that every pitch will be a bad one.

If the ball in the dirt comes directly to you, drop to your knees and face the ball squarely. Get your hands low and centered. Drop your chin onto your chest to protect your throat. With your shoulders hunched, push forward to smother the ball. Should the pitch look as if it will veer to your right, step toward the ball with your right foot while dropping to your knee with your other leg. Move your glove and bare hand to the space between your foot and knee. Keep both hands between your legs but close to your body. (See Figure 7-6.)

On high pitches, raise your glove slightly higher than the ball. Angle your glove downward so that if you miss the catch, the ball drops in front of you. If you keep your glove too low or angled upward, the ball can glance off it and skip in back of you. The runners will like that; it means extra bases for sure.

Figure 7-6:
Blocking
balls in
the dirt.

To catch a thief

Though it's not fair, catchers usually establish their defensive reputations with their throwing arms. (Though a receiver's game-calling ability provides a better measure of his value to a team.) Most teams prize those catchers who can curtail the opposition's running game. Like the other fielders, you must practice gripping the ball and removing it from the glove without looking. Your speed with this maneuver improves with repetition.

"You have to be quick. The good base stealers get down to second in about 3.1 seconds. It takes the average pitcher about 1.5 seconds to get the ball to home plate (from the start of his wind-up). That leaves you 1.5 seconds to throw the ball 127 feet, 3 inches to a target 6 inches above the bag on the first base side so the infielder has $\frac{1}{10}$ of a second to make the tag. And then you have to hope the umpire is in position to make the call." — Johnny Bench

As a catcher, your throws must be straight and true. A proper grip ensures that they are. Grab the ball across the seams where they are widest apart. If your grip is off on your first try, rotate the ball as you cock your arm to throw.

Your grip, cock, and release should constitute one continuous motion. As you grip the ball, bring your glove hand back to your right shoulder while closing your left one. With the ball in hand, bring your right arm slightly above and past your ear. As your right arm comes forward to throw, aim your left shoulder at the target. Keep your glove arm parallel to the ground. Throw overhand; side-arm deliveries tend to tail away from their targets. As you release the ball, snap your wrist downward.

"You can't practice enough the transfer of the ball from glove to hand. You have to keep doing it until reaching in and grabbing that ball across the seams becomes second nature. Practice this even when you are having a simple catch. When you're behind the plate and you make the transfer with your shoulder closed, step straight with your toes pointed towards your target so that your arm follows your body line." — Johnny Bench

To catch today's speediest runners, you have to get the ball off to your fielders quickly. Therefore, you must try to throw while still coming out of your crouch. Major league catchers generally choose from among three throwing styles.

- ✔ **The step and throw:** Recommended for catchers with average arms, it allows you to put more of your body behind each throw. Just before you catch the ball, step forward about 6 inches (15.2cm) with your right foot while pointing it toward second base. After you possess the ball, turn your hips as you draw back your arm, stride forward with your left foot, and throw.

- ✔ **The jump pivot:** The moment the ball hits your glove, jump to your feet and plant your left foot below the spot where you just gave your target while making a 90-degree turn to plant your right foot. Take a short stride toward second and throw.

- ✔ **The rock and throw:** This throw requires a powerful throwing arm because it entails little body movement. As you receive the ball, rock back on your right foot. Rise from your crouch with your arm cocked. Shift your weight forward to your left foot and throw.

"When people talk about throwing out baserunners, they are almost always thinking about arms, but they should be thinking about feet. A catcher has to have quick feet so he can 'get under himself' and move fluidly from a receiving position to a throwing position. Your feet will get your shoulders turned and in position to throw." — Johnny Bench

Derailing the double steal

With base runners on first and third, the catcher must be alert for the *double-steal*. On this play, the runner on first breaks for second hoping to draw a throw while the runner on third scores. Before stepping toward second to throw (if that is your choice), check the runner at third. If he has just broken for the plate, throw to third or hold the ball and get him in a rundown. You are virtually conceding second base to the runner on first, so failing to get the man at third leaves you with two runners in scoring position. If the runner on third breaks for home as your throw heads for second, be prepared for your second baseman or shortstop to cut off your throw and return the ball to you at the plate.

Blocking the plate

Throughout the season, the catcher is involved in numerous collisions at home. How well he blocks the plate determines if he gets the out while staying off the disabled list. As the runner steams toward home, spread your legs a little wider than shoulder width and anchor your left foot about 18 inches (45.7cm) in front of the plate. (See Figure 7-7.)

Figure 7-7:
Blocking the runner from scoring.

"When you block the plate, remember it is better to be a live coward than a dead hero. I always let the runner see at least half the plate, so he has the option of going around me. If he can't see the plate, he has no alternative but to try to go through you or over you. If you persuade him to slide, you have him on the ground, where you can control what he is trying to do. As you block the plate, keep your toes pointed up the third base line and aimed directly at the runner. Should you angle the leg, the impact of the collision could permanently damage your knee." — *Johnny Bench*

After you have the ball and the runner has committed to sliding away from you, move your left leg until you block the plate entirely. Grip the ball in your bare hand while turning the back of your glove toward the runner to protect your inner wrist. As the runner slides in, drive down on top of him with your shin guards to prevent him from reaching the plate. With the ball held firmly in the glove, you can tag him with the back of your mitt. If other runners are on base, see if any other plays are developing as soon as you make the tag at home.

These instructions assume that you are handling an accurate throw. If the throw is slightly off to either side, you can pull it in by shifting your right foot without leaving your position. However, if the throw is far off-line, abandon the tagging position and do what you must to get a glove on the ball. If the runner decides to come in standing up, roll away from him as you apply the tag. Avoid head-on collisions. *Note:* A catcher cannot block the plate unless he is receiving a throw or is already in possession of the ball — otherwise, it's obstruction.

Getting help

Catchers should have no difficulty seeing runners break from first when a right-handed hitter is at the plate. However, a left-handed hitter may block his view. Your first baseman has to let you know when the runner is taking off. (You should anticipate the steal on every pitch.)

Neither lefties nor righties can obstruct your view when a runner tries to heist third. However, with a righty at the plate, the angle of the pitch determines the launching point of your throw. On outside pitches, step forward with your right foot and then step toward third with your left so you can throw in front of the hitter. If the pitch arrives inside, throw from behind the hitter. Step to the side with your left foot, shift your weight to your right, step toward third with your left, and throw.

Pick-offs and pitchouts

Pitchers aren't the only players who can pick a runner off base. The catcher can also initiate a pick-off play whenever a runner strays too far from a bag. If the count is favorable (one ball or less), you can begin the pick-off play with a *pitchout.* After first signaling your pitcher, step into the opposite batter's box just as he starts to the plate; jump in earlier and you risk committing a balk. Ideally, the pitchout should come to you at your letters, but be prepared for a throw that is either too low or too high. As soon as you get the ball, throw to the fielder covering the targeted base.

When the count is not in your favor, call for a strike on the outside corner to set up the *pick-off.* As your pitcher delivers the ball, step back into throwing position with your right foot. Close your body by bringing both hands to the top of the letters. Pivot off your right foot, step in the direction of your target with your left foot, and throw. *Important:* You want the umpire to call a strike, so don't pop up too soon or you may obstruct his view of the pitch.

Fielding pop-ups

The best way to field pop-ups is to do it by the numbers:

1. **As the ball goes up, turn your back to the field and scan the sky for the ball.**

2. **Move toward the ball with your catcher's mask in your bare hand. (If you throw it too early, you risk tripping over it.)**

3. **After the ball reaches its apex and you sense where it will descend, toss your mask away and move in for the catch.**

4. **Catch the ball over your head with both hands.**

   The fingers of your glove should be slanted upward. Don't stab. Allow the ball to come to you.

After judging where a pop is going to come down, it's usually wise to back up one more step so that the ball doesn't wind up behind you — fouls usually drift back a little more than one expects.

Right-handed hitters usually pop up inside pitches to the right and outside pitches to the left. Left-handed batters do the reverse.

"The pop-up behind home plate reacts like a banana. The ball will drift towards the stands as it goes up and curve back towards the field when it descends. So when the ball is popped up in back of you, turn around quickly, stop, and slowly move towards the ball while remembering it will come back to you a few feet." — *Johnny Bench*

Thwarting the bunt

The catcher is in the best position to field and throw balls bunted directly in front of the plate. When the ball is bunted in your territory, stay low as you pounce in front of the plate, scoop the ball up with both hands, and then make your throw. (See Figure 7-8.) Your attention should be on the bunt, so call for the ball loudly to avoid a collision with any incoming fielders. When the bunt is beyond your reach, become a traffic cop. Call out which fielder should handle the ball and tell him where to throw it.

Figure 7-8:
Scooping up
a bunt.

Let the force be with you

When the bases are *loaded* (a runner on every base) and a ground ball is hit, anticipate that the infielder will throw home for the *force out*. You do not have to tag the runner to get the out. You simply must touch home plate while possessing the ball. When a force at home is in order, toss your mask away. Plant your right foot in the middle of home plate so you can move in either direction on a bad throw. Put your left foot in front of the plate. Be prepared to stretch like a first baseman to snare a short throw. With less than two outs, forget about the base runner as soon as you catch the ball. He's out! (Remember, your foot was on the plate.) Immediately pivot to your right, face first, and throw to complete the double play.

You Can't Hide at First Base

Willie McCovey is our guide at first base. This Hall of Famer played first base for 22 seasons, most of them with the San Francisco Giants and San Diego Padres. Willie won the Rookie of the Year Award in 1959 and was named MVP in 1969. His work at first base earned him the name "Stretch" — an homage to his ability to keep one foot on the bag while reaching wild throws.

"We have to dispel the myth that first base is an old man's position, and that you can put just anybody at the bag and expect them to play it well. The first baseman handles the ball more than anyone on the field except the pitcher or catcher. So you must have good hands. You have to have a little quarterback in you to lead the pitcher with your throws when he goes for the putout at first. A first baseman has to save wild throws from his infielders. Quick reactions are a must. If you charge in on a bunt, and the ball goes to the third base side, you must immediately retract to get back to cover first. First basemen have so many responsibilities. You cannot hide a player who is weak defensively at this position. One way to develop the quick reflexes and good hands you need to play the position is to stand about 20 feet from a wall, throw a rubber ball against it, and field the hot smash that ricochets back at you. Gradually come closer to the wall so you can practice fielding short hops." — Willie McCovey

Developing footwork and balance

"You have to be graceful; a first baseman should have loose muscles so he can move easily. Rudolf Nureyev, the ballet star, once came to me after a game and said I moved like a ballet dancer in the field. That was the greatest compliment I ever received for my fielding. If you are awkward, take a ballet class or study tai chi or some other discipline to improve your balance. If you weight train, make sure you stretch those muscles to stay loose." — Willie McCovey

Taking target practice

First basemen should generally play as deep as they can in the field. However, they must be able to get to the bag and set a target in time for the other fielders to make their throws. Taking those throws while putting your foot on first for the out has to become second nature. Your foot should hit the front inside corner of the bag. (See Figure 7-9.)

"If you're looking for the ball and the base simultaneously, or you have to spend time searching the bag with your foot, you'll miss making the out. Practice until your foot goes right to the bag without your looking. Avoid placing your foot on top of the bag where the runner can injure you by stepping on it." — Willie McCovey

You should have your target at first set when the infielder looks up to throw. Keep your weight evenly balanced on the balls of your feet so you can immediately shift to your left or right. Willie says, "A good first baseman will anticipate a bad throw on every play. That way he can easily adjust." Make sure your body is facing the fielder. Don't stretch for a ball until it is in the air and you are sure of its direction.

Figure 7-9:
Taking the
throw at
first.

Handling a bad throw

Low throws are usually the toughest to handle. Try to take the low throw
before it bounces. If you can't do that, get to it as soon as it hops so it won't
bounce away from you. On high throws, you can stay on the bag while
stretching for the ball, make a leaping grab off the bag, or move back into foul
territory.

*"Any time you get a bad throw, your first objective is to catch the ball. Don't
worry about keeping your feet on the bag or getting the baserunner out. If you
catch the ball but it's too late to get the runner, you have a man on first.
However, if the ball gets past you because you were stuck on the bag, the runners can advance an extra base."* — Willie McCovey

On plays where the pitcher or second baseman is too close to you to make a
hard overhand throw, he will probably try to feed you an underhanded toss.
Help him by setting a big target with your glove.

*"You would be surprised by the number of pitchers who cannot properly throw to
first base after making a play. On those soft toss plays, you have to anticipate
that the pitcher will throw it over your head."* — Willie McCovey

Holding on

When you *hold a runner on*, you shorten his lead off first to deny him a head
start to second. Place the back of your right foot against the front inside
corner of first while keeping your left foot along the base line. Your feet
should be no more than shoulder length apart. Give your pitcher a good
waist-high target with your glove.

As the ball is delivered to the plate, cross over with your left foot and bounce as quickly as you can toward second base. Get in a position to cover as much fair territory as possible. As the pitch approaches the plate, you should be in your crouch, facing the batter.

When runners are on first or second, or the man on first is slow, the first baseman can *play behind the runner* rather than hold him on. To play behind the runner, position yourself just inside the runner's left shoulder.

Make sure that the pitcher knows when you play behind a runner and second base is not occupied. Pitchers need to be reminded not to make a pick-off throw. Never assume that the pitcher knows instinctively that you've chosen to play behind a slow runner.

Covering bunts

Play bunts aggressively or you won't play them at all. Charge the plate as your pitcher delivers the ball home. Countless baseball instructional guides advise first basemen to listen for their catchers to tell them where their throws are going (first, second, or third). This advice is fine if you are not playing in a packed stadium where the roar of the crowd makes it impossible to hear yourself think. Under those conditions, you must be able to immediately recognize where the play is developing and throw accordingly.

*"Usually everyone in the stadium knows when a bunt is in order. However, there are some players and managers who will try to surprise you with a bunt. (**Note:** This usually occurs when the batter is trying to bunt for a base hit rather than a sacrifice.) If you study hitters closely, you can pick up some signs that telegraph a bunt is coming. For instance, some batters will look down towards you for an extra moment or two before bunting the ball your way. Other guys might choke up on the bat a little bit more. Watch what each hitter does when he bunts, and remember any quirks you can detect." — Willie McCovey*

Fielding cut-off throws

If runners are in scoring position, the first baseman is responsible for cutting off the throw on balls hit to right or center. The third baseman takes most cutoffs from left, but if he can't get into position, you have to cover for him. Give your outfielder a good target by holding your hand and glove chest high. (All infielders should do this.) Where should you stand to receive the cutoff? Some coaches advise that you take it at a midpoint between second base and the pitcher's mound. Others want you to cut the ball off from behind the mound.

"There is an advantage to cutting the ball off between second base and the pitcher's mound. If you are behind the mound, on the home plate side of the diamond, you risk having the ball hit the mound or pitching rubber and bouncing away from you." — Willie McCovey

As you accept the relay from the outfield, wave your arms so the outfielder doesn't waste time trying to find you. Listen for a teammate (usually your catcher) to tell you where your throw is going (or if you should let the ball go through). The instructions should be this simple:

- ✔ "Cut, Cut!" — Cut off the ball and hold it.
- ✔ "Cut and Relay!" — Cut off the ball and throw to a specific base.

If the fielder thinks you should let the ball go through, he shouldn't yell anything. When you are setting up for a relay, line up your body in the same direction as your target. For example, if you are throwing to third, your body should be facing left center.

"Catch the ball on your glove side so you don't have to turn all the way around to throw. Practice catching the ball, taking it out of your mitt, and delivering the throw all in one graceful motion. Too many first basemen break this down into two parts. That extra motion is often the difference between a runner being safe or out." — Willie McCovey

When the pitcher must cover first

If you play deep, the pitcher is going to cover many grounders hit to the right side. He heads to first base in case you can't get there in time to make the tag on your own. If you can get to the ball and field it near first base, make the tag yourself. Make sure you wave off the pitcher so he is out of harm's way.

When fielding the ball takes you too far from first to make an unassisted putout, you must get the ball to your pitcher. If the distance is short enough, lead the pitcher to first with a firm underhanded toss that hits him chest-high. Balls fielded on their way to the second base hole may require you to throw overhand. Again, you should lead the pitcher to the bag with a chest-high toss.

Doing the 3-6-3 (First-to-short-to-first double play)

Many first basemen will tell you this play is the most difficult play they make. To initiate this double play if you are left-handed (as most first basemen should be), pivot clockwise — to your glove-hand side — to unleash a throw.

If you are right-handed and the ball is hit directly at you, turn clockwise to throw. However, if the ball is hit to your left, you probably have to pivot counter-clockwise before throwing.

Your first throw is the key to making this double play. Nine out of ten times, you field the ball in the same line as the runner going to second. You must be able to throw the ball to your shortstop without hitting that runner. Then you have to get back to bag for the return throw. Because this play is always going to be close, you need to stretch before catching the ball on the return. (Sometimes this play goes 3-4-3, first-to-second-to-first. If he must throw to the second baseman, the first baseman's responsibilities remain the same.)

*"Make sure you get that lead runner. Too many first basemen are so concerned with getting back to the bag to get that second out, they end up throwing the ball away and fail to get anyone. If you don't have a clear shot, take an extra side-step to create a throwing lane to the shortstop. Try to get the throw to your short-stop in a spot to his liking. (**Note:** Many favor receiving the ball chest high.) But if you can't do that, make the best throw you can and depend on the shortstop's athleticism to complete the play."* — Willie McCovey

Second (Base) to None

Joe couldn't find a second baseman for this team, so he is doing the honors himself. His collaborator, editor, and publishers couldn't be more pleased. From 1973 to 1977, Joe's play at second won him five consecutive National League Gold Glove awards. He was tutored in the field by two of the greatest second basemen in baseball history — Nellie Fox and the Grand Master of the Keystone, Bill Mazeroski.

Setting up

A second baseman's stance in the field should distribute his weight evenly on the balls of both feet. This position allows you to move easily to one side or another. As the pitcher goes into his wind-up, look directly at the batter. But don't look at his body. Instead, imagine he is swinging through a rectangular box that is as wide as home plate and extends from his shoulders to the tops of his toes. Watch that box. The ball will come to you from some spot within it. Make sure you are on the balls of your feet and ready to move when you see bat and ball collide. (See Figure 7-10.)

Figure 7-10:
Getting
ready for
the play.

"Be relaxed but alert at all times in the field. If you stay in one position too long, your body will tense; this will slow your reactions when the ball is hit. To alleviate tension, move your hands while you are in your stance. I often rested my hands on my knees as the pitcher wound up. An infielder has to do that to ensure that he is bending forward far enough. But as soon as the pitcher released the ball, I would raise my hands about 5 inches to give myself greater freedom of movement." — Joe Morgan

Your skills and the situation determine how deeply you play your position. However, if you are fielding on artificial turf, the ball will shoot to you much quicker than it will on grass. Play two to five steps deeper. You should also remember that you cannot slide to a ball hit to either side of you on the turf. You have to field the ball and continue moving.

Whose ball is it, anyway?

On balls stroked up the middle of the diamond, who has first call, the short-stop or the second baseman? That's the shortstop's ball. Because he is moving toward first base on the play, he can make a stronger, more accurate throw than the second baseman (who is moving away from first).

"Just because it's the shortstop's play doesn't mean you don't have any responsibility. Get behind your shortstop and be ready to catch the ball in case it gets by him." — Joe Morgan

Blocking the ball

Nellie Fox was a three-time Gold Glove winner who led American League second basemen in putouts nine times. He taught me the best way to stop a ball you cannot catch cleanly from entering the outfield: Get down on one knee and block it with your body.

If this posture is not comfortable, find another way to get down on the ball. With a runner on second, do everything possible — dive in front of it if you have to — to prevent the ball from rolling into the outfield. Your methods can lack grace provided they get the job done.

"Because the second baseman rarely makes a long throw, he doesn't always have to catch a ball cleanly. Always remember that if you simply knock a ball down, you will usually have plenty of time to toss out the runner." — Joe Morgan

Getting the ball to first

When you have to throw the ball to someone like our friend Willie McCovey at first base, aim for an area between his belt buckle and his chest. This strategy allows you some margin of error if your throw is too high or low. Your throws should be on the money as often as possible. If you have to take a throw from a teammate, give him a chest-high target.

In most situations, you can wait until the first baseman reaches his bag before throwing to him. However, if the runner is some flash like a Lance Johnson or Eric Young, you may not have time to see if the first baseman is in place. Your job in that instance is to throw the ball across the bag; it's the first sacker's responsibility to somehow get to it.

"Make sure any player you are throwing to gets a good look at the ball. Take it out of your glove as quickly as possible so he can see it in your hand. This will help him to better gauge your throw's velocity and trajectory. When you bring back your arm to throw, make sure your glove doesn't block your target's view of the ball." — Joe Morgan

Preventing grand larceny: Defending against the steal

One of the oldest maxims in baseball dictates who covers second — the shortstop or second baseman — on an attempted steal. The shortstop covers if the batter is left-handed. When the batter is right-handed, the second baseman has to make the play. However, like all good rules, this one does have its exception. If the batter is a good hit-and-run man or opposite field hitter like Jay Bell, the second baseman and shortstop can switch assignments. Jay is a right-handed batter who excels at hitting behind the runner. Any second baseman who covers the bag on every steal attempt is inviting Jay to slap the ball through the vacated hole and into right field. So you have to play the major league version of cat-and-mouse with him. Your shortstop may cover for a pitch or even two. Then you may cover for the next couple of pitches. Keep switching so he doesn't know whether to pull the ball or go the other way.

"You and your shortstop must communicate to each other who will cover on the attempted steal. Before the game, decide between yourselves who will make the call. Keep the signals simple. Shield the front of your face with your glove. When you want your shortstop to cover second, open your mouth and purse your lips as if you were saying, 'You!' If you are going to take the catcher's throw, keep your mouth closed with your lips tightened to indicate, 'Me!'" — Joe Morgan

Picking runners off

On a *pick-off play,* the pitcher tries to catch a runner off base with an unexpected throw. You're not merely jockeying for an out with this play; you are also attempting to reduce the runner's lead. Just the threat of a pick-off can appreciably change the game. With the runner anchored at the base, your outfielders have a better opportunity to throw him out on a base hit; you have more time to execute plays in the infield.

"If the second baseman is covering the bag on the pick-off play, the shortstop must get behind him to back up any errant throws. If the shortstop is covering, the second baseman must reciprocate." — Joe Morgan

Pick-off plays come in two basic varieties:

- ✔ In the **time play,** the pitcher signals to the infielder covering second by glancing at him before looking toward the catcher. As the pitcher faces home, he and the infielder start counting, "One second, two seconds, three seconds." On three, the pitcher spins and throws; the infielder breaks for the bag. If everything is in sync, the infielder and the throw should arrive at second base simultaneously.

- ✔ **Daylight pick-off plays** don't require a count. The pitcher whirls and throws to second as soon as he sees a large enough space or "daylight" between the infielder and the runner.

"I dislike daylight plays because they can so easily backfire. Suppose you're trying to fake a runner back to the bag. The pitcher might mistakenly think you're breaking for second. If he attempts a pick-off, you have to scramble back to make the play. Often, you can't. The ball flies untouched into center field, the runner races to second or even home. Stick to the time play; there's less opportunity for error." — Joe Morgan

Executing the run-down

Run-downs occur (among other times) when a pick-off traps a runner between two bases. While tossing the ball to each other, you and your teammates chase the runner back and forth until he can be tagged. Making as few throws as possible is the key to an effective run-down. The more throws you make, the greater the chance one of you will toss the ball away.

After the run-down begins, you should try to force the runner back to the base he just left. The fielder with the ball should hold it high and away from his glove so the other fielders can see it. Whoever is waiting to receive the throw must give the player with the ball a target. For example, say a right-handed throwing teammate is chasing the runner back to you at second. You should stand to the left of the incoming runner. This position affords the thrower a clear view of your glove. If the thrower is left-handed, take a step to the other side. By using your glove as a target, your teammate is less likely to hit the runner with the throw.

During run-downs, fielders must stay out of the baseline while they await the ball. If you stand in line with the runner, his body may prevent you from seeing your teammate's throw. If the runner crashes into you on the base line when you don't have the ball, the umpire can award him the bag on fielders' interference, also called *obstruction*.

"Never fake a throw during a run-down; you might fake out your teammates as well as the runner. Always hold the ball high so your teammate can see it. Cock your arm back only when you intend to release the ball. When you're not involved in a run-down, choose an unoccupied base to back up. Stay out of the action unless the ball gets by someone and comes in your direction." — Joe Morgan

Tagging the big league way

When a runner slides into a base you're defending, tag him on his foot, toe, or whatever other part of his anatomy is closest to the bag. Try to tag his hand if he attempts a head-first slide. Tag a runner who arrives at the base standing up anywhere you can reach him.

Don't attempt a tag with the pocket of your glove facing the runner or he may kick the ball away from you. (And yes, that's a legal play. New York Giants second basemen Eddie Stanky pulled it on New York Yankees shortstop Phil Rizzuto during the 1951 World Series. The ball went trickling into center field. Instead of being called out, Stanky was safe. The Giants went on to score five runs that inning.) Instead, hold the ball firmly as you swipe the runner with the back of your glove.

Covering first

Both your pitcher and first baseman usually try to field any slow-hit balls between first and the pitcher's mound. With first base unattended, the second baseman must cover. You must become a first baseman. Go to the inside of the bag with your rear foot. Lean into the diamond to give the thrower a proper chest-high target with your glove. Maintain your balance so you can spring to either side on a bad throw.

Handling relays and cut-offs at second

You are playing second base. With a man on first, the batter smacks the ball down the right field line. Cinch double. What do you do? Don't stand at second waiting for a throw. Instead, turn to face the right fielder from a point midway between first and second base. If the runner on first tries to score, your job is to relay the right fielder's throw to the catcher at home plate. If the runner is heading toward third when you get the ball, try to nip him at that base. (Check out Joe's Baseball Playbook in Chapter 9 to study your assignments on all of baseball's basic plays.)

Any time the batter drives a ball into the gap (between the outfielders), there's going to be a relay. Make sure the outfielder makes the longest throw; between the two of you, he should have the stronger arm. Go out just far enough for the outfielder to reach you with a throw. After you get the ball, your job is to deliver a short, accurate throw to the appropriate base.

On balls hit to the left or left center field gaps, the shortstop accepts the relay. The second baseman must back up any balls that get by him. You must also let the shortstop know where to throw the ball. If he has to turn and look, he surrenders about 12 feet (3.6m) to the runner. While the outfielder's throw is in flight, observe the runners so you can tell the shortstop which base offers the best opportunity for a play. Identify the bag by yelling to the shortstop, "Home plate! Home plate!"

Turning two

Ask any infielder: The double play (DP) is the greatest play in baseball (other than the triple play, which is so rare you can't even think about it). When you turn a double play in a crucial situation, you immediately become the most popular guy on your club. Teammates shower you with high fives, pitchers want to buy you dinner, and managers name their firstborn after you. Nothing short of a win is more pleasing to a fielder than getting two outs with one ball.

Carly Simon knew the secret to executing the double play: Anticipation. (Great, now we're going to have *that* song humming in our heads for the rest of the month!) Whenever the opportunity for the double play presents itself — runners on first, first and second, or first, second, and third with less than two out — the second baseman must automatically think about turning two. Move a couple of steps closer to second and in toward the plate. You sacrifice a little range with this positioning, but it enables you to get to the bag quickly.

Charge for the base as soon as the ball is hit to the left side of the diamond. When you get within three steps of second base — and with practice, you instinctively know when you are — shorten your stride. Take choppier, quicker steps to ensure that you don't overrun the bag. You must maintain body control as you reach second, or you'll have trouble adjusting to a poor throw.

If you are a novice at second, look for the bag when you first run toward it. After you know where it is, put your focus on the fielder. Give him the best chest-high target you can. However, stay alert in case the ball veers off on an angle. As the fielder cocks to throw, your attention should go to the ball.

"The double play transpires so quickly, you must eventually learn to locate the bag without looking. When I first came up to the major leagues, I would work on starting the double play with our first baseman and shortstop for an hour and a half a day before practice. We did this until I was able to get to the bag without even glancing at it." — Joe Morgan

To complete the double play, you must catch the ball, force out the runner from first by tagging second base, pivot, and relay the ball to your first baseman. It sounds like several parts, but they are all parts of the same motion held together by your pivot. (See Figure 7-11.) You have different ways to pivot on the double play:

Figure 7-11:
The pivot
for the
double play.

✔ Many second basemen straddle the bag. As they catch the ball, second base is between their feet. They touch the bag with their left foot while throwing to first.

✔ Second basemen with unusually strong arms sometimes use the push-off method. They catch the ball behind the bag, tag the front of the base with their rear foot, and then push off it as if it were a pitching rubber for their throws to first.

"I learned the quickest and, in my opinion, best way to pivot by studying Bill Mazeroski. As a Gold Glove second baseman with the Pittsburgh Pirates, Maz led National League second basemen in double plays a record eight consecutive seasons (1960 to 1967). He was, and remains, the unchallenged king of the DP. Like Maz, I would catch my shortstop's throw out in front of my body. While crossing second, I would step on the center of the bag with my left foot. Then I would pivot and throw from wherever I caught the ball. If I gloved the ball high, my throw would be overhand or three-quarters. Feed the ball to me at my waist, and I relayed it sidearm. Any ball caught below my waist was delivered to first with an underhand toss. Your primary concern is to get rid of the ball as quickly and accurately as you can. Some players drag their foot across the bag when making the force-out at second. I think that practice upsets a fielder's rhythm on the double play. If you instead step on the center of the bag, your motion continues uninterrupted. This also helps build some momentum behind your throw to first." — *Joe Morgan*

The care and feeding of your shortstop

Some double plays require a role reversal: Your shortstop makes the pivot. You have to field the ball and then feed it to him for the relay to first. It is important to know where your double-play partner prefers to catch the ball.

Note: Many second basemen throw to the shortstop backhand in a double play — a backhand throw is less likely to sail high than an underhand toss. If you are close enough to the bag to do so, a backhand throw is preferred.

"For example, when I was with the Reds, our shortstop Davey Concepcion liked to take the throw on the outfield side of second. So I would give it to him chest-high (the easiest ball to handle and throw while on the move) on the bag's outside edge. I've also played with some shortstops who wanted my toss on the inside of the bag. However, no matter what your shortstop prefers, you shouldn't wait to make the ideal throw. If you're off balance, get the ball to your partner any way you can and let him make the adjustment. If your double-play partner hasn't reached the bag, feed the ball to him wherever he is. Never make him wait for the ball or you can disrupt his timing." — *Joe Morgan*

Dealing with the runner

As I have said, the second baseman's job is to make the double play before looking for the incoming runner. If you are continually concerned about getting hit at second, you can't play the position. One way to defend yourself against a collision is to get the ball to first as soon as you can. Don't worry about hitting the runner. Your quick throw will compel him to slide that much sooner. The sooner he slides, the longer it takes him to reach you at the base.

A last word on second

None of the suggestions I've just passed on to you are absolutes. Eighty percent of the time, you execute a play at second in the manner I've described in this chapter. However, some situations — such as when a throw is off line or the runner arrives at second faster than you anticipated — demand improvisation. When these situations occur, remember that your bottom line is to make the play any way you can. Get the out!

Cookin' at the Hot Corner

Third base is called the *hot corner* because the third baseman is so close to home plate he tends to field a lot of hot smashes. The position demands a strong arm, hair-trigger reflexes, and a ton of heart. All three attributes come to mind when we think about our third base "coach," the 1996 National League Most Valuable Player Ken Caminiti of the San Diego Padres.

The basic stance

Plays develop so quickly at the hot corner that third basemen must be able to shift out of position in an instant. Many third basemen set up in the lowest crouch on the field so they can spring up to their left or right. Ken has won three consecutive Gold Gloves without the benefit of an exaggerated crouch.

"For my basic stance — we're talking about when I don't smell bunt or some other play — I put my left foot slightly behind my right foot and bounce back on it. Now my focus is on the hitter, but I watch the pitcher with my peripheral vision. As he brings his leg down and arm through in his wind-up, I bring my left foot parallel with my right while transferring my weight evenly to the balls of both feet. As the ball crosses the plate, I bend forward a bit but not in a full squat. This leaves me balanced and open to move freely to either side." — Ken Caminiti

That word again: Anticipation

Ken doesn't rely solely on his reflexes and proper weight distribution to glove the bazooka shots aimed his way. Like all great third basemen, he combines a sixth sense with concrete data to anticipate where the batter is likely to hit the ball.

"Most of the time, I like to know what the pitcher is throwing to a batter, so I can prepare myself accordingly. So I will peek through the batter's legs to pick up a catcher's signs to the pitcher. Or I might have the shortstop relay the sign. I prefer to take them directly from the catcher, so there is no chance of miscommunication. Let's say the catcher calls for something offspeed. If the batter begins to swing before that pitch reaches the plate, you know he has to hit that ball down the line or into foul territory. You're going to lean towards the line. The trick is to focus not on contact but before the ball meets the bat." — Ken Caminiti

Checking the real estate

Before the first game of every away series, the third baseman (as well as the other fielders) should examine how a ballpark's topography may affect play. Never take anything for granted; groundskeepers or the elements may have altered a park since you last played there.

"I'll spend some time seeing just how far it is from my position to the stands; that tells me how far I can run without banging into a railing. I'm going to roll the ball down the line to see if it tends to stay fair or roll foul. That helps me decide if I'm going to pick up that bunt down the line or let it go." — Ken Caminiti

Fast hands for slow rollers

The grab and throw on bunts or slow rollers tapped to third is among the most difficult of all infield plays. Ken fields those balls as well as anyone who has ever played the position.

"To make those plays, you have to first get a good jump on the ball. On the bunt, try to key off the hitter to see if he gives it away (before trying to lay it down). His back foot can tell you a lot. For instance, a lot of right-handed hitters will drop that back foot before attempting a drag bunt. Left-handed hitters can be more difficult to spot. Kenny Lofton — who's probably the best I've seen at this — waits to the last moment and then just drops the bat on the ball. Brett Butler (one of the great bunters of the past 20 years) did the same thing. I try to take the bunt away from guys like him by playing all the way in and daring him to hit it by me. On those slow rollers, you have to bust it as hard as you can the moment you see the play. But you also have to maintain your timing. Get to the ball with stutter steps so that your left foot is even with the ball when you drop down to scoop it. Depending on how quickly you get there and the runner's speed, you glove the ball, take a step towards the base you're throwing to, and let it rip. On some plays, though, you just have to bare-hand the ball and throw in one continuous motion. That's a do-or-die play; you don't think, just react." — Ken Caminiti

Figure 7-12 shows how to bare-hand the slow roller.

Figure 7-12:
Fielding and
throwing
the slow
roller in
one motion.

Playing mind games

Persuade a runner to hang close to third base, and you decrease his chances of scoring on a short fly ball or hard hit grounder. How do you get a runner to anchor near third? Ken uses numerous fakes and moves to keep the runner honest.

"I'll make a move towards third or fake one to get the runner back, to keep him thinking. If you suspect a squeeze play is on (when the batter tries to bunt the runner on third base home), you can stand right next to the runner so he can't get too big a lead. When the pitcher starts up, I'll dart back to the bag just to cross the runner up." — Ken Caminiti

A basic rule to get two

Middle infielders usually attempt to get the ball to each other in a particular spot — at the letters, to the inside of the bag — on the double play. Their proximity to each other allows them this luxury. As Ken points out, third basemen don't need to be quite as specific.

"Things happen so quickly at third, many times the shortstop or second baseman hasn't reached the bag by the time you're ready to throw. So I just try to throw the ball directly over the base and let the fielders get to it. If a fielder is already at the base, I try to deliver it to his glove side." — Ken Caminiti

Some last words from third

PLAYER TIP

"You can't play this position scared. If you're just starting out, it may seem as if things happen too quickly at third, but your body will react in time if you let it. Take the field with the attitude you want every ball hit to you and that you are going to make the play. Third base calls for a lot of long throws, so you must be able to throw overhand. However, there will be some plays where you don't have time for anything but a sidearm throw; you've got to know how much time you have to make the play. Who the runner is, how the ball is hit, and the angle from which you are throwing all factor into that decision. You have to know all these things if you are going to do your job. The key to having good range and quick reactions at third is concentration. Lay back and you are going to miss some plays you could have made. You should be focused on every pitch of the game so that you can anticipate your next move. By the end of the game, the third baseman should feel drained." — Ken Caminiti

Ranging Wide: Playing Shortstop

All the infield fundamentals reviewed in this chapter — throwing, fielding grounders, positioning, and so on — can be applied to this position. Shortstops should also read our section on second base. The shortstop is nearly a mirror of the second baseman except he has more ground to cover and must make longer throws. A second baseman's longest throw to first is barely more than 90 feet. The average throw for a shortstop to the same base is 110 feet. Because of the greater distance, you must be able to catch grounders cleanly or you won't survive at this position. If you knock balls down as a second baseman sometimes does, you may not have time to throw out the runner. Because you are responsible for so much territory, you must study the hitters throughout your league so you can position yourself properly in every situation.

The shortstop on our All-Star team is Barry Larkin of the Cincinnati Reds. The National League's Most Valuable Player in 1995, Barry has won three Gold Gloves (1995–1997) at short. He is one of this era's great double play artists as well as being one of the best throwing shortstops ever.

Setting up

Because you must roam to either side at short, keep your weight balanced. Your feet should be a little more than shoulder width apart with your legs bent slightly in a semicrouch. You often have less time than any other infielder to make a play, so you must be continually thinking about how to react if the ball is hit a certain way. It is hard to turn on the jet packs from a stationary position, so put your body in motion by taking two steps forward as the pitch approaches the plate. You have a direct view to home plate.

Watching the catcher's signs lets you know what the pitcher is going to throw. If you feel the hitter is going to hit a certain pitch to your left or right, cheat a step in that direction.

"The most important thing is to field the ball cleanly, and — for the advanced player — catch it with your momentum carrying you towards wherever you are going to throw, second or first. You always hear that you should look at the ball into the glove, but you should also look at the ball as you remove it from the glove. A lot of times, guys catch the ball and immediately look for their target instead of at the ball — as if someone was going to move first base. Then they have to double-clutch or regrip the ball before throwing, and that can cost outs. When you throw, your weight should transfer to your planted rear foot as you cock to throw, then transfer back to your front foot as you release the ball."
— Barry Larkin

Getting the ball to first

Shortstops often run full-out, so you must avoid tangling your legs. When you dart to your right, pivot on your right leg and cross over with your left. On balls hit to your left, do the reverse.

"When you throw the ball to first, try to throw the ball through, not to, your first baseman's chest. If you just try to throw to him, and you're short, the ball will short-hop him. When you're in the hole and can't get on top of your throw, you might have to sidearm the ball to first base. You see a lot of inexperienced short-stops wasting a lot of motion trying to get something on that throw. If you are going toward first, get your wrist into the ball and snap off that throw. Your momentum will help put something on the ball. If I am moving toward third when I catch the ball, I contort my body to get off a throw. I try to keep my front (left) foot closed, so my toe is pointed toward the left field stands. Then I throw against my body and use torque to propel a snap throw. On a play like that, you don't have to throw the ball all the way to first. (Former Reds Gold Glove short-stop) Davey Concepcion taught me how to bounce the ball on one hop to the first baseman. Shortstops should work on that play in practice." — *Barry Larkin*

If you dive for a ball — something shortstops do frequently — you must get to your feet immediately. However, don't rush the play.

"Too often, young shortstops who dive start trying to throw the ball before they really catch it. Catch the ball, hit the ground, pop up, and make the throw. When a guy tries to throw the ball before he catches it, he stands a good chance of dropping it. With practice, you'll learn to pop up quickly after a dive with the ball securely in your possession. This should leave you plenty of time to get off a good throw. Studying martial arts helped me with this. One of the first things I learned was how to roll with a fall so I wouldn't be rigid when I hit the ground. If you can learn how to roll with your dive, your momentum will help get you to your feet." — *Barry Larkin*

Backhanded compliments

After ranging far to your right, you may still be unable to get in front of the ball. You have to make a *backhand play* in those situations.

"This should always be a play of last resort. You should be trying to increase your range daily so that you don't have to backhand too many plays. During practice, have your infield instructor hit balls to your left and right at ever-increasing distances away from you. Keep working your way around the ball. Your goal is not to let him get to your backhand. If you're not rangy, play a little deeper to compensate. When you do have to backhand the ball as you go towards the hole, try to catch it just beyond your left foot. Stop your momentum, plant on your right foot, step to your left and throw. Another way is to open up your right foot, catch your ball in front of it, bring your left foot through, plant on your right foot, and throw." — Barry Larkin

Figure 7-13 shows you the position for a backhand play.

Figure 7-13:
The back-
hand play.

The wisdom of an open-glove policy

This advice should be common sense: It is much easier to catch a ball with a glove that is fully open than with one that is half- or completely closed. All infielders should know this (although you would be surprised at how many major league infielders approach grounders with half-opened mitts), but it is especially important for the shortstop, who has little time to bobble the ball.

As you reach the ball, slow down and bend with your legs rather than your back. Lower your glove on an angle to the ground and open the glove wide.

The fingers should be touching the field and your palm should be lifted up slightly toward you. Keep the glove halfway open, or the ball can glance off its side. (See Figure 7-14.)

Figure 7-14: The short-stop's glove has to be ready.

Doubling up

Like the second baseman, the shortstop can start double plays (his usual function) or act as the pivot man. If the ball is hit within three or four steps of second base, you usually don't need to involve your second baseman. Simply step on the bag with your left foot, push off, and throw off your right foot. Do this in one fluid motion. In other double play situations, the shortstop's role changes:

✔ On balls hit near second, but not close enough to permit an unassisted play, give your second baseman a chest-high, underhanded toss. Throw sidearm to your second baseman on balls hit directly to you or just to your right.

✔ You must turn the pivot on the double play on balls hit to the right side of the infield. Get to the bag immediately.

✔ When the ball is hit so far to your right that you have to extend, take the time to plant your right foot and make a strong throw to second. You usually get only the lead runner on this play (which, by the way, should always be your priority), though the second baseman may be able to turn two if your throw is strong and accurate (and the runner heading toward first isn't very fast).

✔ On slowly hit grounders, forget about the double play. The shortstop must know the speed of each baserunner so he can decide whether to attempt the force at second or get the out at first.

"When I'm the pivot man on the double play, I prefer to receive the ball on the left field side of second. As I get to the bag, I slow my momentum so that I can adjust if the throw to me isn't where I expect it. On the pivot, if the ball is to my right, I step to it with my right foot and drag my left foot over the bag. If the throw is on my left, I step to it with my left foot and drag my right." — *Barry Larkin*

A last word on playing shortstop

"The great plays — the diving catches, the behind-the-back flips — are made because your fundamentals are sound. You've studied your positioning, you're aware of the situation and all the things that can happen. When you catch the ball, you look it into your glove and watch as you take it out. You do all the basics. Then when the ball is hit, your athletic ability and reactions take over. The great plays will come naturally because you will be in position to make them." — *Barry Larkin*

That Extra Infielder: The Pitcher

Retiring batters isn't the only responsibility pitchers have. When you are on the mound, you must cover a base or back up a fielder on nearly every play. (Refer to Chapter 9, the playbook, to learn your various assignments.) You have to be quick enough to flag down hot smashes up the middle (or at least get out of their way so one of your infielders can catch them) and pounce on bunts. When runners stray far from the bag, you have to drive them back with a look or a pick-off move. On many infield plays, you are the traffic cop directing your teammates, so you must stay cool and alert.

For advice on how pitchers can field their position properly, we turn to one of Joe's opponents from the 1975 World Series, Bill Lee. The Red Sox left-hander was one of the smoothest fielders in the game, quick on bunts, fundamentally sound on grounders, and capable of the amazing play. (The behind-the-back catch of line drives hit up the middle was a Lee specialty.)

Getting into fielding position: The follow-through

Pitching mechanics are covered in some depth in Chapter 6. Ideally, when you emerge from your follow-through, you should be in a position to field anything hit toward you. Your body should be squared toward home plate, your feet should be parallel and shoulder width apart, and your weight should be evenly distributed over the balls of your feet. Few pitchers on any level come out of their follow-through perfectly positioned to field. However, you should strive to come as close to the ideal we just described as you can.

"Never forget that your number one concern is getting the hitter out. If you can't come out of your follow-through in the ideal fielding position, you can compensate by keeping your eyes peeled on home plate and watching for the ball off the bat. Then let your reactions take over if the ball is hit towards you." — Bill Lee

Fielding aggressively

Try to field as many balls hit between you and first as you can. Anytime you can keep that first baseman near the bag, you are helping your team's defensive alignment.

- On bunt plays, charge balls that are hit directly toward you.
- On balls to the extreme side of you, field only those that look as if they will stop rolling before one of your infielders reaches it.

"As you go after the ball, don't focus on the runner. Instead, watch the ball into your glove. Don't rush your throw after fielding it. Get a good grip on the ball. Keep moving towards your target as you step and throw. If you have to spin and throw, keep a low center of gravity; it will make you quicker. If you are close to the base and the fielder isn't there, lead him to the bag with an underhand toss. However, if your fielder is on or near the bag and you aren't too close, hit the target he gives you with a strong overhand throw. Aim for his chest." — Bill Lee

On plays that require you to cover first base, go to a spot approximately 6 feet (1.8m) from first on the baseline. Run parallel to the base line as you cut toward first. As you reach the bag, shorten your strides so you can adjust to any bad throws.

"Touch the inside of the base on the home plate side with your right foot. This will prevent your momentum from carrying you into the runner (a must to avoid) or into foul territory." — Bill Lee

Keeping runners close

Anytime you keep a base runner anchored near a base, you not only reduce his chances to steal, you also make it more difficult to take an extra base or score on a long hit. Making numerous pick-off throws will chase a runner back to a base. Bill recommends three other things you can do to hold a runner on without making a throw:

✔ Use the same motion to first as you do to home. Don't give the runner any extra movement to key off of. Be especially careful that you don't reveal your intentions with slight head or eye movements. Good baserunners are studying you constantly and pick up on the tiniest quirks.

✔ Disrupt the runner's timing by altering your rhythm as you move into your set position and go into your wind-up. Remember you're not changing movement here, just the timing of your movement. Don't fall into any consistent rhythms. Hold the ball during your set position for varying time periods.

✔ If you are left-handed, just watch the runner. If you don't move to throw, he can't go anywhere. (Well, technically he can, but the odds are you are going to throw him out.)

"Always try to be quick to home plate. If the runner does take off, you will save your catcher a stride when he tries to throw the runner out. If you're slow to the plate, your catcher doesn't have a chance against the faster base stealers. He won't be able to get them unless he's Dirty Harry Callahan and he's toting his .44 Magnum." — Bill Lee

Catching the runner off base

You can attempt to pick off a runner anytime your foot is off the pitching rubber (that's to say when you are in the set position or going into your stretch). If you are a right-hander trying to pick off a runner at first, push off your right foot while pivoting toward the bag with your left foot. Keep your upper torso open so you throw overhand rather than across your body. (See Figure 7-15.)

If you are a left-hander, you don't need to pivot because you are already facing first. All you have to do is snap off a sidearm throw while stepping toward first. When you raise your striding leg out of the set position, there will be a moment when it is pointed toward first. Unlike the right-hander, you now have the option of throwing to the bag or continuing your motion toward home plate. (See Figure 7-16.)

Pick-offs at second are more complicated. As Joe points out earlier (see "Picking runners off"), you can employ a time play by signaling your second baseman or shortstop as you check the runner at second. On a 1-2-3 time play, the count begins when you turn back to face the hitter. On two, you should turn back toward second as the fielder breaks for the bag. On three, throw the ball at the fielder's knees and over the base. On the daylight play, the fielder sneaks up near the bag. You throw as soon as you see daylight between the fielder (usually the shortstop) and the runner.

Figure 7-15:
The right-
hander's
pick-off
move.

Figure 7-16:
The left-
hander's
pick-off
move.

"I know Joe prefers the time play, but, as a pitcher, I have to go the other way. I like the daylight play's spontaneity and the fact that you are reacting to your shortstop's movements. Time plays can go awry if you and your fielder aren't synchronized. That was always a problem for me. My middle infielders were usually on Greenwich time and I was on Somalian time." — Bill Lee

You shouldn't attempt many pick-offs at third because it's a bad percentage play. Few runners steal home, and if you throw the ball away, you've just given the opposition a run. To pick the runner off, the right-hander and left-hander reverse the mechanics they use when throwing to first.

"Don't even think about this play with two outs. The runner cannot score on an out and no one wants to face his manager after making the inning-ending out on an attempted steal of home. Concentrate on the hitter; he's the one who can hurt you." — Bill Lee

Avoiding balks

Deceptiveness is one of the keys to an effective pick-off throw. However, you can't be so deceptive that the umpire calls you for a *balk* (see Appendix A for a definition). You can avoid balking while attempting a pick-off at first by doing the following:

- When you are in the set position, take the sign from your catcher with your foot on the rubber and your hands visibly separated.

- After you have your sign, bring your hands together and pause one full second before going into your delivery.

- If you swing your striding foot past the rear portion of the pitching rubber, you must deliver a pitch.

- Move only your head while in the set position. If you shrug your shoulders or move your legs or hands, the umpire can nail you for a balk.

- If you make any motion toward a base, throw to it. You must complete any movement you

start without interruption until you are in the set position.

- Always step directly toward the bag you are throwing to. You may step and fake a throw to second or third, but you cannot fake a throw to first without first stepping off the rubber.

- If you want to move out of the set position without incurring a balk, step off the rubber.

- Never make a pitching motion unless you have the ball.

- Don't drop the ball during your delivery.

"It may sound funny, but don't even scratch your nose or wipe your mouth when you are on the rubber with a runner on first. I've seen guys called for balks for doing just those things. You're concentrating so hard on the hitter, something itches, and you just do the natural thing. Just make sure you step off the rubber first." — Bill Lee

Where Fly Balls Go to Die: Playing the Outfield

Oh boy, do outfielders have the life. They don't have to worry about kamikaze base runners bearing down on them during the double play, hot line drives sizzling towards their craniums, or which base to cover on any given play. All they have to do is saunter after the occasional fly ball, throw it back toward the infield, and work on their suntans.

Yeah, right.

Playing the outfield is like playing any other position. It demands discipline, hard work, and knowledge. You must be able to gauge fly balls that come at you from diverse angles, understand the mechanics behind a good throw, and know what to do with the ball after you catch it. On balls hit into the gap, you must sprint full out, time your extension and catch, and then throw to the right base in one fluid move.

Infielders can afford to take their time on many plays. Outfielders are so far from the action, they don't have a half-moment to spare on any ball that sets runners in motion. Infielders can bobble or even drop a ball and still record an out. If an outfielder drops a ball, the hitter is not only on first base, he probably takes an extra base. Outfielders don't collide with baserunners, but they can run into the occasional wall. (And unlike human beings, those structures have no "give" to them.) So you have to know what you are doing out there to avoid hurting yourself and your team.

Our chief outfield coach is Mr. Centerfield, the incomparable Willie Mays. We believe that Carly Simon, a die-hard baseball fan, was thinking of Mays corralling a flyball when she sang, "Nobody Does It Better." Willie holds the major league record with 12 consecutive Gold Gloves for outfield play. He is also the all-time major league leader in total outfield chances accepted. Runners rarely took liberties with May's powerful throwing arm. He once hit a long drive that fell just beyond the reach of a diving outfielder for extra bases. The broadcaster covering the game summed up Willie's fielding prowess by saying, "The only man who could have caught that ball, just hit it."

Ken Griffey, Sr., the 1980 All-Star Most Valuable Player, also shares his thoughts on outfield play in this section. Griffey patrolled all three outfield positions during a 19-year major league career spent largely with the Cincinnati Reds and New York Yankees. Sparky Anderson said, "Kenny is an example of how a person can make himself into an outstanding fielder through hard work. He was a defensive weapon wherever he played, and he charged the ball as well as any outfielder of his day." We're also going to bring in Rusty Staub, a smart outfielder whose powerful throwing arm was feared throughout baseball, for a word or two of expertise.

Setting up

Because they have more real estate to cover, outfielders have more positioning options than infielders. Where you play depends on the hitter, the pitcher, the situation, and the count. For example, Paul O'Neill is a left-handed hitter with good power to all fields. He can hit the ball with authority anywhere. However, against a hard-throwing right-hander like Pedro Martinez, Paul is more likely to pull the ball when the count is in his favor. Conversely, if a hitter is *behind in the count* (he has more strikes on him than balls), he tends to protect the plate and hit the ball to the opposite field. So if Martinez has a 3-ball 1-strike count on O'Neill, his outfielders should shade closer toward right field.

However, if you are playing the outfield behind lefthanded pitcher Randy Johnson, you may not move toward right if you don't believe O'Neill can pull Johnson's fastball. And even that is not an absolute. Suppose it's a close game in the late innings and Johnson has lost some of the hop from his fastball. You may think that O'Neill, who is looking to drive the ball for extra bases, may now indeed be able to pull on the tiring Johnson.

When setting up in the outfield, you must also consider your limitations and those of your teammates. Do you go back on balls well but have more difficulty on balls that pull you in? Play shallow. Do you move to your left better than your right? You have to compensate when a right-handed pull hitter is at the plate. Does your center fielder have a weak throwing arm? With the winning run on third and less than two out, you may have to take a ball that he would normally catch, so you can attempt the throw home. All of these factors — plus the field conditions for that day — determine where you play on each pitch.

Taking your basic stance

You should set up in the outfield with a square stance:

- ✔ Keep your feet parallel, shoulder-width apart, and pointed toward home plate.
- ✔ Get into a semicrouch with your weight evenly distributed over the balls of both feet.
- ✔ Rest your hands on your knees but drop them as the ball approaches the plate.

This stance gives you momentum to chase the ball if it is hit beyond the infield. (See Figure 7-17.) Because your weight is evenly balanced over both feet, you can move to either side quickly. If it looks as if the ball will be hit over your head, put the toes of whatever foot is on the ball side behind the heel of your other foot. (This is called a *drop step.*)

Figure 7-17:
The basic
outfield
stance.

"Get as loose as possible before the game starts. Give yourself 15 minutes to stretch, do calisthenics, and some light running. Don't bring any tension to the outfield; it will rob you of quickness." — Ken Griffey, Sr.

Taking off from jump street

What is the one thing you hear said about any great outfielder? He gets a good jump on the ball. Your eyes, ears, and head determine how quickly you break for a fly ball. If you've done your homework, you should already know where the batter most often hits the ball.

"Getting a good jump on the ball starts at home plate. You have to know who is hitting. If you don't know where the hitter tends to hit the ball, how can you get a good jump on it? If you start moving as you see the ball coming over the infield, you're too late. Study the hitters so you can anticipate what will happen before a certain pitch is thrown. For example, Billy Williams (a Hall of Fame outfielder with the Chicago Cubs) was a left-handed pull-hitter. But he would take the breaking ball to left-center (the opposite field). So I had to make sure our pitchers worked him inside, but way inside or he would hit the ball out of the park. I'd play him straightaway in that spot. If I knew we were going to throw him off-speed stuff away in San Francisco, I'd anticipate going towards left. Now, if you don't know the hitter, I would talk to the pitcher. Find out how he is going to work him. Tell him you're going to play straightaway until you see the batter over a few games." — Willie Mays

Concentrate on the pitcher-batter confrontation. You may not be able to tell what kind of pitch has been thrown, but you can at least observe its location. Notice if the batter is getting a late hack (swing) or is in front of the ball. Your knowledge of the hitter and pitcher should then give you some idea of where the ball is likely to land.

"Depending on who was on the mound, I would key off of the pitcher's fastball and how the hitter was reacting to it. That would tell me if the hitter could pull the ball, or, if he was a little late, hit it the other way. Or just hit it back up the middle." — Ken Griffey, Sr.

Another indicator of how far a ball will travel is the sound made when the bat hits the ball.

"Here's a little game my teammates and I used to play during batting practice to sharpen our ears. We would stand with our backs to home plate and try to identify where a ball would be hit without peeking. All we had to guide us was the sound of the ball against the wood. Practice that day after day and, after a while, you can take off at the crack of the bat. It becomes instinctive." — Rusty Staub

Outfielders usually move laterally on fly balls. To achieve maximum acceleration, pivot and push off the foot nearest the ball as you rise out of your semi-crouch. Cross over with your outside foot. If you must angle your run, stride first with the foot nearest the ball. Pivot on both feet whenever the batter hits the ball over your head.

"When you are going into the gap, don't keep your eyes on the ball. Train yourself to recognize where the ball will probably land and run to that area. After four or five steps, you can glance up to check the flight of the ball." — Ken Griffey, Sr.

You don't have to move much on balls hit right at you, but you do have to determine whether the ball will rise or sink. Don't take a step until you can read the ball's trajectory.

Making the catch

Pursue fly balls aggressively. If you drift over to time the catch of a ball, you aren't in position to throw. You may also be unable to adjust if you misjudge a ball's flight or a sudden gust carries it farther than you anticipated. Hustle on every play.

"The wind can be a factor when you go for a catch. You might run to the spot where you think the ball is coming down only to find out the wind has carried it another six feet or held it up so that it drops in front of you. Check which way the wind is blowing before the game starts. Then keep checking it every inning after that, because the direction can change. I always looked at the flags to see

where the wind was blowing. Some games would start with the wind blowing in, then it would start blowing out after only a few innings." — Willie Mays

Using both hands, catch the ball out in front of your body and over your throwing shoulder. (See Figure 7-18.) If you are left-handed, your right foot should be forward; if you throw from the right side, your left foot is out in front. This position leaves you in the correct position to get off a good throw. Take a crow hop to close the shoulders and hips on your glove side, and then move through the ball as you throw overhand with a cross-seam grip.

Figure 7-18:
Catching the
fly ball.

You will instill sound habits if you catch every ball as if you have to throw it to a base, even when there aren't any runners on the base paths. When you do have to unleash a throw, take a small hop to close the shoulders and hips on your glove side. Then move through the ball as you throw overhand with a cross-seam grip.

"Before a ball is hit, you have to be thinking baseball. What is the situation? How many are out? Are you behind or ahead and by how many runs? Who comes up next? When a ball gets by you in the gap with one out, you don't want that batter to get more than two bases. He can score from third without a base hit with less than two out. So your throw is going to third." — Willie Mays

"You should be practicing taking the ball out of your glove in a cross-seam grip until you can do it blindfolded. Do it every time you grab a baseball. For maximum power, throw the ball over the top whenever you can and have your momentum pointed towards your target. The best way to build your arm strength for these throws is to play catch as often as possible. And I don't mean just randomly tossing the ball back and forth. Play catch with a purpose. Make a game of hitting a target every time you throw. If you deliver the ball up near your catching partner's face you get two points, at his chest one. Low point man buys the soft drinks. Try to hit a specific target even when you're just loosening up."
— *Rusty Staub*

"I tried to make my throws so that my teammates didn't get hurt. What I mean is that I would give them a ball high that they could handle. I didn't want them to have to reach down as the runner was sliding in because that's where the fielder can get injured. But on a throw to the catcher, I would throw low, even bounce the throw, because he has all that protection and if he stays low he can block the plate better. Now when you make a throw, you're not always trying to get the base runner, you're trying to get the guy who hit the ball. If that hitter is slow, you might get him if he tries to take the extra base. So I would hit my cutoff man on purpose, try to catch that hitter running to second. I always tried to keep my throws to the cutoff man chest-high where he could handle them." — *Willie Mays*

Don't fall into the gap

Any time a ball is hit into the *gap* or power alley, one outfielder should try to cut off the ball, while another should run at a deeper angle to back up the play. Usually the fielder closest to the ball goes for it. On plays where the ball is equidistant from both fielders, the center fielder has priority. However, to avoid mix-ups, especially on balls hit between two players, you and your fellow outfielders should call loudly for any ball you pursue.

Coming in on a ball

During practice, learn how to read the trajectory of balls far in front of you so you can instantly decide if you should make the putout or catch it on a bounce. If you have to play the bounce, slow down while keeping your body and glove in front of the ball. That way, if you don't catch it cleanly, you can knock it down.

"Make sure you catch this ball belt-high or chest-high so that you keep your eyes on the ball. It will be easier to handle." — *Ken Griffey, Sr.*

"Again, you have to know your hitter. A strong hitter might hit a line drive that will hang up a little longer; someone not as strong, the ball might just die. And the wind might blow the ball up, down, or even to the side. Which is why you have to know what is happening in the ballpark at all times." — Willie Mays.

Going out on a ball

Most major leaguers will tell you the most difficult fly ball to catch is the one smacked over your head. Inexperienced outfielders often start back pedaling on that ball, which is the worst thing they can do. If you back pedal, you don't see the ball clearly because your head is bobbing up and down, you can't generate any speed (which is why marathoners do not run backward), and you can't jump if you need to.

"I would try to catch the ball like a wide receiver in football, over my left shoulder or right shoulder depending on where the ball is hit. And I'm getting in position to throw that ball while I'm making the catch. If you see a picture of my catch against Vic Wertz in the 1954 World Series, I caught the ball over my shoulder because I could see the ball better. I looked directly over my shoulder. And the left side of my body was ready to throw before I even caught the ball." (**Note:** *Mays is referring to perhaps the most famous catch ever made. With his back to the plate, Mays galloped full speed into deepest center to catch Wertz's booming line drive some 450 feet from home plate. He then uncorked a perfect throw.) — Willie Mays*

"Outfielders tangle themselves on that play when they start off on the wrong foot. If a ball is hit over your right shoulder, drop step back with your right foot. Cross over with your left foot and stay angled sideways as you go back. If it is hit over your left shoulder, do the reverse." (See Figure 7-19.) — Ken Griffey, Sr.

You have to catch grounders, too

With runners on, outfielders should charge ground balls as aggressively as infielders. They must catch the ball in a position that allows them to unleash a good throw. Field the ball on your glove side with your glove-side foot down. Close off your upper body with a crow hop, stride with your left foot, and throw over the top with a cross-seam grip.

"When there is no one on base, all you want to do is keep the ground ball in front of you. If it gets by, the runner is taking extra bases. Get in front of it, get down on one knee, and block the ball." (See Figure 7-20.) — Ken Griffey, Sr.

Figure 7-19:
Going back on the fly ball.

"You have to charge that ball and keep it in front of you like an infielder. I didn't practice doing that in the outfield. Instead, I took grounders at second or short-stop during practice. So when I went to the outfield, grounders were a piece of cake." — Willie Mays

Figure 7-20:
Keeping the ground ball in front of you.

Chapter 8

The Science of Baserunning

Baserunning has always been the most underrated aspect of baseball offense. Yet more games are won or lost on the base paths than most fans realize. The teams that consistently win close games are the ones whose players can go from first to third on singles, break up double plays, score on short fly balls or ground-ball outs, and take the extra base whenever it is offered.

Anyone can become a good base runner. You don't need speed; you simply need to be alert, aggressive, and smart. Pete Rose was one of the best base runners I ever played with or against. From the stands, Pete appeared to be fast because he hustled all the time, but he had only average speed. In a game I played against him in the Houston Astrodome, Pete went from first to third on a sharp single to right. You don't see that happen often on AstroTurf; singles bounce to the outfielders so quickly that base runners usually advance only one base. But Pete executed plays like that all the time because he was hustling from his very first step toward second. He also always knew where the ball was hit and the strength of the outfielder's arm.

Pete went from first to third as well as any player in the majors because of his head, not his legs. In this chapter, we show you how to take a page from his book by developing your baserunning savvy.

Accelerating Out of the Box

When you get a hit, you should be hustling toward first base the moment the ball leaves your bat. It doesn't matter which foot you lead with as long as you have good balance and your initial move propels you toward first. Always run in a straight line as close to the foul line as possible so that if a fielder's throw hits you, the umpire won't call you out for obstruction (see Figure 8-1). Don't overstride. Stay low for your first few steps to build acceleration and then explode into your normal running form.

Figure 8-1: The quickest way to first base is a straight line.

The foul line.

If a fielder is going to try to throw you out at first base, don't just run to first base, run *through* it. Always touch the front of the bag as you cross over it. Continue running several steps down the right field line before making your right turn into foul territory. If you do this after touching first, you can't be tagged out for leaving the bag. However, if you turn left toward second base, the fielder can tag you out before you get back to first. (See Figure 8-2.) As you run through first, glance over your right shoulder to see if you can advance to second on an error. (For instance, the fielder has thrown the ball past the first baseman and into the dugout, so you have time available to get to second base safely.)

Most of the time, you shouldn't bother to watch the ball as you dash toward first. Watching the ball slows you down. The only time you should watch the ball is if it is going toward one of the outfield gaps or over an outfielder's head. You can pick up most of those balls with a quick glance. If you can't, tilt your head slightly (and don't break stride) for a better view. Still can't pick it up? Then rely on your first base coach to tell you whether you should run through first or turn toward second.

Stay alert after singling to right field. If you make a wide turn at first, a charging right fielder may still get you out by throwing behind you to the first baseman.

If the play is at first base, run past the bag.

If you plan to head straight to second base, make a wide, smooth turn.

Figure 8-2: The proper way to run to first and beyond.

There may be times when you should slide into first base — for example, if a high throw draws the first baseman off the bag and he has to tag you for the out. If you slide while he's leaping for the ball, it is nearly impossible for him to get the ball down in time to nail you. Some players slide into first on force outs, but I think this is bad policy. Sliding or jumping into first on your final step doesn't get you to the bag more quickly; it slows you down.

Taking Your Lead

Baseball is, as they say, a game of inches; you are often safe or out by the barest of margins. Any time you can use your lead to shorten the distance from one base to another, you gain an advantage for your team — you are inching that much closer to your ultimate objective: home plate.

Leading off first

After you're on first, keep your left foot against the bag while you check the alignment of the fielders and pick up any signs from the third base coach. Remind yourself of the number of outs. Don't move off first until you know the pitcher has the ball. While closely watching the pitcher receive his signs, take several shuffle steps from the bag (do not cross your left foot over your right; you can get tangled if you have to dive back to first on a pick-off). This position is your *primary lead*. (See Figure 8-3.)

Your goal is to gradually get as far from first base as you can without getting *picked off* (thrown out). How far a lead you take depends on a number of factors: whether the pitcher is a righty or lefty, how good his move is, your size, and your reflexes. Tall players can take long leads — but so can short, quick players. Finding your ideal lead length is a matter of trial and error. However, most major league runners prefer to be a step or two and a dive away from first.

Figure 8-3:
Taking a primary lead.

When taking your lead, balance your weight evenly on the balls of both feet. Do not lean toward first or second. Drop into a slight crouch and flex your knees so that you can move quickly in either direction. This stance is known as a *two-way lead*. Your feet should be parallel to each other, shoulder width apart, and pointed toward the pitcher. (Maury Wills, who ran the bases well enough to steal 104 bases for the Dodgers in 1962, used to turn his right foot a little toward second base so he could pivot quicker.)

Let your arms hang loosely in front of you. Keep your eyes on the pitcher the moment you step from the bag. Watch for the pick-off play! Imagine a straight line leading from the outer edge of first base to the outer edge of second. Stand even with that line or a little bit in front of it. Leading off the bag from behind that line costs you extra steps. (See Figure 8-4.) It also makes it appear to the pitcher that there is a wider distance between you and first base than it actually is. You invite additional pick-off throws when you stand too far back.

As the pitcher throws toward home, you should assume your *secondary lead*. Take a crossover step and a hop toward second while watching the action at the plate. In a perfectly timed crossover, your right foot hits the ground a split second before the ball reaches home. When the ball passes the hitter or if the hitter hits the ball in the air directly at an infielder, stop on your right foot, turn, and get back to first. If the ball gets past the catcher or if the batter hits a grounder or a longer fly ball, push off your right foot and run toward second.

Remember: Don't leave the base until you know the location of the ball. Base runners must be constantly alert for pick-off plays and hidden ball tricks.

Line up your lead with second base.

Figure 8-4: Leading off first base.

Fly balls are tricky, because if a fielder catches one, you must get back to first before you get thrown out. If the batter hits a fly ball that looks catchable, you should move far enough off first base that you can make it safely to second (or beyond) if the ball is dropped, but not so far that you can't get back to first safely if it is caught. If the batter hits a medium fly ball, run no farther than halfway to second base until you see how the play evolves. You can run farther toward second on a deep fly.

Always remember that if the outfielder catches the ball before it touches the ground, you must get back to first. If the outfielder's throw reaches that bag before you do, you've just run into a double play. As you trot toward your dugout, you will notice a livid fellow with smoke coming out of his ears and the veins in his head threatening to explode. That is your manager. The dog-house you just slid into belongs to him.

Leading off second

You can take a longer lead off second than off first. Generally, no one holds you close to the bag because the pitcher can't look directly at you; he has to wheel and turn to pick you off.

If you are going to steal, set up in a straight line to third. Otherwise, stay a few feet behind the baseline. Take your primary lead. Advance as the pitcher delivers to the plate. You should be 15 to 18 feet (4.6 to 5.5m) from second as the ball crosses home plate.

If your team already has two outs, extend your primary lead off second to about 20 feet (6m) but set up about 3 to 5 feet (.9 to 1.5m) behind second base. This lead puts you in a better position to round third and head for home on a base hit. You don't have to worry about being part of a double play, so you can take off at the crack of the bat. (See Figure 8-5.)

Figure 8-5:
Two ways to
lead off
second.

Leading off third

Managers have exiled base runners to Devil's Island for getting picked off at third base. Therefore, your primary lead off third should put you no farther from the bag than the opposing third baseman. Take this lead in foul territory so you won't be called out if a batted ball hits you. (See Figure 8-6.)

Figure 8-6:
Taking your
lead off
third.

As the pitcher throws the ball home, take a two- or three-step walking lead toward home. You should land on your right foot, ready to break for home or return to third, just as the pitch approaches the plate. This movement leaves you in position to score easily on a wild pitch, passed ball, or ground out. It also allows you to pivot back toward third if the pitch is handled cleanly by the catcher.

Disguising the hit-and-run play

As the base runner on a hit-and-run play, don't depart from your normal lead or you may signal your intentions to the opposition. Timing is more important to the successful execution of this play than the size of your lead. You have to make sure the pitcher delivers the ball before you break from the base. (You can review how to execute the hit-and-run in Chapter 5.)

Reading Your Opposition

To be a great base runner, you must take the extra base *before* the ball is hit. Prior to your game, watch the opposing fielders during practice to see the strength and accuracy of their arms. When you reach first base during the game, observe how deeply the outfielders are playing the hitter. Are they leaning in any particular direction? If the left fielder is playing deep, and your teammate hits a shallow fly in his direction, you can take off without holding up to see if the ball is caught.

If the outfield is *shaded* (leaning) toward left, and the hitter smacks the ball down the right field line, you can go for at least two bases.

You should also observe if any of the outfielders are left-handed throwers. If a left-handed center fielder has to go to his right in pursuit of a hit, he has to turn and make an off-balance throw to get you out at third. On a single to right center field, a right-handed center fielder cannot throw to third until he turns completely around. That gives you an extra moment to slide in safely.

Rounding the Bag

All right, you've just pounded a ball into the outfield and you are thinking double all the way. You're not running through first and up the right-field foul line on this play. Instead, head straight for first as you normally would. When you are about 15 feet (4.6m) from the bag, veer slightly toward foul territory, and then cut in toward the infield. As you pass first base on a nearly straight line toward second, touch the bag with your foot. It doesn't matter which one you use. However, you have a shorter turn to make by touching the inside part of the bag with your left foot. (See Figure 8-7.) Make sure that you touch enough of first base for the umpire to witness the contact. Scamper to second base.

Figure 8-7:
How to
round first.

Tagging Up

After a fly ball is caught, base runners must touch the base they occupy before advancing to the next bag. This action is known as *tagging up*. If you are halfway between first and second when a deep fly is hit, you must return to first to touch the bag. Take off for second only *after* the ball and fielder make contact. You can advance in this manner from any base.

When you tag up from first, your right foot should be on the inside edge of the bag. This position leaves your right side open so you can follow the ball's flight more easily. If you are tagging up from third, your left foot should be on the bag. Tagging from second? The situation determines which foot you should place on the bag. On a ball hit to left or left center, it's your right foot. When the ball is hit to right field or right center, switch to your left foot.

As you tag up, drop into a crouch. Extend your front foot 18 to 24 inches (46 to 61cm), depending on your leg length, from the base. Shift your weight forward. Watch the ball! The moment it touches the outfielder's glove, push into your stride toward the next base. You don't have to wait for the outfielder to catch it cleanly.

BASEBALL SPEAK

The force out

Force out is a term that you need to be familiar with because it is a frequent occurrence in baseball — and often misunderstood by the novice player and viewer alike. (A trip to your local Little League game should convince you of that!) A force out (or *force play*) takes place when a batted ground ball forces a runner to advance to the next base, but that base is tagged with the ball before the runner reaches the base.

Under which circumstances does a batted ground ball force a base runner to advance?

✔ A runner on first must *always* try to advance to second base.

✔ A runner on second base must try to advance to third base if another runner is on first base.

✔ A runner on third base must try to advance home if runners are on first and second base (in this case, the bases are *loaded,* and a force out is possible at any base, including home).

Of course, if you are the defensive player, it is easier to tag the base in a force play situation (or throw to another fielder who may step on the base) rather than tag the runner — because tagging a runner may knock the ball out of your hand. You don't need to do both. And don't think that you must literally tag the base. Simply step on the base while holding the ball in either your bare or your gloved hand.

Under which circumstances does a base runner not need to advance when the batter hits a ground ball? (If this information seems like overkill, don't forget your visit to the Little League game.)

✔ A runner on second base need not run if no one is on first base.

✔ A runner on third base need not run if either first base or second base is empty.

✔ Runners on both third base and second base need not run if first base is empty.

In the preceding situations, go to the next base only if you can make it safely — and remember that the defensive player must tag you with the ball instead of simply touching the base that you are running to. If you don't think that you can make it to the next base safely, simply stay put!

HEADS UP

When two outs have already been recorded, don't wait for a fly ball to be touched before you run. If the ball is caught, the inning is over, anyway. So with two outs, be prepared to run on any fly ball — and hope that the fielder misses or drops it.

Using Your Coaches

PLAYER TIP

You may feel as if you are alone on those base paths; you're not. Think of the base coaches as part of your running team. Use them. When you get to first base, the coach there can be a fount of valuable knowledge. He can remind you how many outs have been recorded (if he doesn't and you're not sure, ask him), reveal a quirk he has detected in the pitcher's motion (so you can get a better lead or steal a base), or tell you something about the outfielders (such as which one seems hobbled or isn't throwing particularly well that day). This is just the kind of information you need to make appropriate decisions on the base paths.

The third base coach is your beacon. If you've lost sight of the ball or are unsure whether you should advance to the next base, watch his signs. No matter how much experience you have, heed the third base coach in most situations. He has a better view of the entire field than you do. You may think you are running faster than you are, or you may not realize how quickly an outfielder has gotten to the ball. A good third base coach can gauge all of that for you.

Sliding Safely

"Slide, Kelly, Slide" — the popular saloon song from the 1890s — was written in honor of Boston Red Stocking superstar Mike "King" Kelly. While the lone umpire was looking elsewhere, Kelly would often help his team to an extra base by cutting across the infield from first and sliding into third without touching second. (Kelly wasn't the only guy to try this stunt back then, by the way.) You can't pull that play today (too many umps and TV cameras to catch you), but you can grab runs and wins for your team if you know how to slide properly. Often, the only difference between the umpire calling you safe or out on the bases is the quality of your slide.

Practice sliding as diligently as you work on the other aspects of your game. You don't need to do this on a baseball diamond. My brothers and I used to practice in our backyard. Get into a pair of tennis shoes and sliding pads, wet some grass, put down a base, and practice all your slides. It's important to be able to slide on both sides. George Foster, one of my teammates on the Reds, could slide only on one side no matter how a play developed. Many times he could have been safe but was tagged out simply because he couldn't elude the tag. As you practice, you develop a feel for when you should start your slide.

The straight-leg slide

The *straight-leg slide* is my favorite. It gets you to the bag as quickly as possible while leaving you in position to bounce up and advance to another base if a misplay occurs. Because your top leg is straight and aimed at the bag, you have less chance of catching your spikes in the dirt (a leading cause of ankle injuries).

Start this slide about 10 feet (3m) from the bag. Push off your rear foot and lift both legs up. Your body should glide forward feet first. Slide straight in (you can do this on either side) with the toe and foot of your top leg pointed in a straight line toward the middle of the bag. Your bottom leg is bent under you. (See Figure 8-8.)

Figure 8-8:
The
straight-leg
slide.

The bent-leg slide

The *bent-leg slide* is a variation of the straight-leg slide. To launch the slide, push off your rear foot and lift up both legs. Then tuck your rear leg under your slightly flexed top leg at a 90-degree angle (this pairing should resemble a figure 4). Maintain a semisitting position with your torso arched back and hands held high as you slide. Hold your chin close to your chest so you can see the base and the ball. Aim for the middle of the bag with your top leg. Touch the base with your heel (which prevents your cleats from catching on the bag).

The *pop-up slide* is the bent-leg with a wrinkle. You start this slide about 8 feet (2.4m) from the bag. Don't lean back. As your top leg hits the base, push up with your bottom foot. The momentum brings you to your feet, ready to advance if a misplay occurs.

Lou Brock, the all-time National League leader in stolen bases, used the pop-up slide to great effect (see Figure 8-9). It left him in position to take an extra base on a misplay. However, I don't like to see it used unless someone has already overthrown the ball when you start your slide. Too many runners have been called out when they were safe simply because their pop-up slides didn't afford the umpires a long-enough look to make the correct calls.

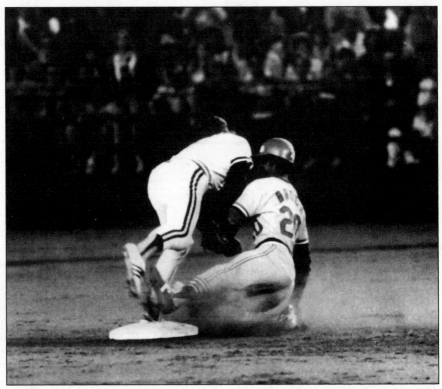

National Baseball Hall of Fame Library, Cooperstown, NY

Figure 8-9:
Lou Brock is
ready to pop
up and run
some more
in a misplay.

The headfirst slide

This slide is nothing more than a dive into a swimming pool — without any water. You are hurtling yourself at great speed onto a hard surface that has no give. Pete Rose slid headfirst for more than 20 years and never even cracked a fingernail (see Figure 8-10). Don't let that fool you. The headfirst slide can be dangerous. A descending fielder can spike your hands, the ball can hit you in the head, or you can jam your fingers and hands against the base if you hold them too low. In the 1997 National League Championship Series, Florida Marlin shortstop Edgar Renteria knee-blocked a headfirst sliding Kenny Lofton from reaching second base. If Kenny had slid straight in, Renteria couldn't have blocked him.

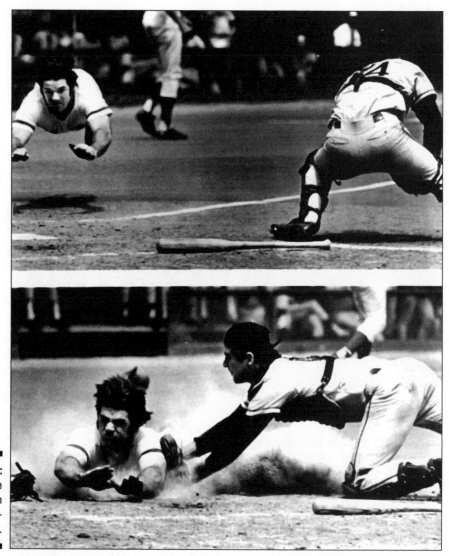

Figure 8-10:
Pete Rose
was known
for his head-
first slides.

National Baseball Hall of Fame Library, Cooperstown, NY

If you are still not dissuaded from going in head first, at least minimize your
risk by executing the slide properly. Start the headfirst slide by gradually lowering your body until you are about 8 feet (2.4m) from the bag. Extend your
arms while you launch yourself off your rear leg. Keep your body straight,

but relaxed, so that your forearms, chest, and thighs hit the ground simultaneously (this absorbs the shock). Stay alert and hold up your hands and head while sliding! (See Figure 8-11.) Should you attempt to execute a literal headfirst slide, you risk a sprained neck, concussion, or worse.

Figure 8-11:
The head-
first slide.

It's often hard to keep your hands up when attempting any type of slide. Wearing sliding gloves offers you some protection from injury.

The hook slide

The *hook slide* was supposedly the brainchild of Mike Kelly. It may have helped inspire that song they wrote about him, but it is basically a desperation play that you should use only when trying to evade a probable tag.

Let me set it up. You are on first. The batter hits the ball to right field. You cruise around second and burst toward third. The right fielder, however, has gotten a perfect bounce and has already fired the ball to the third baseman. As the ball beats you to the bag it pulls the third baseman toward his right. A hook slide to your right (the third baseman's left) is your only hope of avoiding an out.

Always execute the hook slide to the opposite side of wherever the tag will originate. If the throw comes in from the outfield side, slide to your left. Should it come from the infield side, slide to your right.

To hook slide to your left, push off on your right foot and drop to your left side. Your outer calf and thigh absorb the slide's impact. Keep your right leg relatively straight with a slight knee flex (your right leg slides to the right of the bag). Scissor your left leg out toward the base. While sliding past the base, reach out with the toes of your left foot or either hand. Touch the bag at its nearest corner. (See Figure 8-12.)

Figure 8-12:
The hook
slide.

If the fielder is about to tag your hand as you try to touch the base, you can pull your hand back. As the fielder's momentum carries him to one side, reach out to grab the bag with your other hand.

Remember to stay in contact with the bag until the fielder returns the ball to the pitcher or the umpire calls time.

To hook slide to your right (say, on a throw from the catcher), do everything I just described — only in reverse. Practice the hook slide from both sides. Don't use this slide on force plays; it slows you down when you need to get to the bag as quickly as possible.

Maury Wills was the greatest hook slider I ever saw. He could reach either corner of the base with the tip of his toe. This presented the fielder attempting a tag with the smallest target possible. With most runners, I only had to put the ball in the middle of the base to get them. They would slide right into it. I couldn't do that with Maury. You had to look for him, which is why he was so elusive.

You should also be aware of the risks involved with the hook. Your body's momentum can easily pull you too far past the base or make you miss it completely. Catching your spikes on the bag is another danger. Do this, and you can tear or break something. Keeping your knees slightly bent and both feet sideways offers you some protection. (See Figure 8-13.)

Figure 8-13:
Joe Morgan
himself
demonstrates
a hook
slide against
the master
hook slider
Maury Wills.

National Baseball Hall of Fame Library, Cooperstown, NY

Safety tips

To avoid injury while sliding, regardless of which type of slide you use, try to hold both hands in the air. Many major league ballplayers hold a clump of dirt in each hand to remind them to hold their hands high on the base paths. (Don't ask me how *that* custom started.) Wearing sliding gloves is a further precaution. And always remember the four cardinal rules of sliding:

- ✔ When in doubt, slide.
- ✔ Never be tentative (half-hearted slides are the most dangerous).
- ✔ It is always better to slide early rather than late.
- ✔ Never slide head first into home or when breaking up the double play (you don't want to expose your head and neck on contact plays).

Breaking Up Is Hard to Do: Preventing the Double Play

In the final game of the 1975 World Series, the Cincinnati Reds and I were losing 3–0 to the Boston Red Sox in the top of the sixth. Pete Rose led off that inning with a single against Red Sox left-hander Bill Lee. With one out, our catcher Johnny Bench hit a sure double play ball to Boston shortstop Rick Burleson. Burleson shoveled the ball to his second baseman Denny Doyle to start the double play. Doyle attempted to get a throw off to first, but Pete barreled into him just as the ball was leaving his hand. Though Pete was out, his hard (but perfectly legal) slide forced Doyle to throw wildly into the Boston dugout. Bench was safe; the inning, which should have been over, continued. The next batter, Tony Perez, hit a two-run homer that propelled us toward a 4–3 win and a world championship. Our comeback in that game started with Pete's slide.

Anytime you break up a double play, you snatch an out from the box score; you give your team an extra opportunity to score and win. To execute this maneuver, you must know how to slide properly. You should also know the rules governing the play:

- ✔ You must be on the ground when you make contact with the fielder.
- ✔ You must be able to reach the bag with some part of your body during your slide.

As the runner trying to break up the double play, your assignment is to get to second base as quickly as you can while making a good, hard slide. You're not looking to hurt anyone, so forget about any rolling blocks. (I had one thrown at me in 1968. It crumpled my knee and put me on the disabled list for the entire season. Inflicting that sort of injury is not your objective.) The idea is either to knock the pivot man (the second baseman or shortstop) off-balance or to disturb his timing by making him leap or hurry his throw.

You can start your takeout with your normal straight-leg slide. However, try to hook your top leg's foot under the pivotman's striding foot to knock it out from under him. Keep your weight on your bottom leg. When you take your usual slide, you aim for the base. Your objective here is to reach the fielder. Slide on whatever side of the bag he pivots from.

Though you don't have to hit the pivotman to break up the double play, you should try to do exactly that. This potential collision forces him to jump out of the way. Minimize the chance of injury by sliding with your spikes held below the pivotman's knee. Should you make contact, you will hit his shins or lower, where you won't break anything. Avoid hitting any fielder from the knee up.

Colliding with the Catcher at Home Plate

Catchers have this thing about base runners; they don't like to see their opponents sliding across home plate. So good catchers do everything they can to stop you. Catchers are usually built like small condominiums. They wear heavy protective gear, and many of them enjoy a good crunch at the plate. Getting through them can be a daunting task, but you have to do it whenever you have the potential to score a run home. Take the easy route whenever possible — if you can see the plate and know you can touch it, launch into your slide.

However, if the catcher has the plate completely blocked, you have to barrel through him. I know of no elegant way to do this. Just get low so you have your center of gravity working with you and keep your head away from the point of contact.

The catcher can block the plate only if he possesses the ball. If he blocks it without having the ball, he is guilty of obstruction, and the umpire will declare you safe at home after the collision.

Profile of a Base Thief

All great base stealers have a love of larceny. They derive joy from picking the opposing team's pockets, especially in pressure situations. To excel as a base thief, you have to be cocky. When you get to first base, your body language and demeanor should announce, "I am stealing and there is nothing anyone can do to stop me!" You have to embrace the role of intimidator.

Base stealers make things happen. During the 1975 World Series, Boston pitcher Reggie Cleveland walked me to open the sixth inning of the fifth game. He threw over to first base seven times before throwing a strike to the batter Johnny Bench. Then he made four more throws to first. When he delivered another pitch, I took off for second but Bench fouled off the ball. What did Cleveland do then? He made five more tosses to first. This didn't bother me a bit. Cleveland was concentrating more on me than the batter, which is precisely what I wanted. On Cleveland's next pitch, Bench singled, and then Tony Perez came up to hit a three-run homer. The lesson here is that you don't need to steal a base to help your team; just the threat of a theft can rattle a pitcher into making a critical mistake. If the pitcher is playing cat-and-mouse with you, he can't possibly focus fully on the hitter.

Stealing a lot of bases with your team far ahead or behind doesn't mark you as a great thief — many runners can steal in those situations because the opposing pitcher is paying little attention to them. He's either cruising to a win or concentrating solely on getting the batter out. Far more valuable are the runners like Tony Womack (see Figure 8-14), who ignite their offenses by stealing in the early innings or during the late portions of a close game.

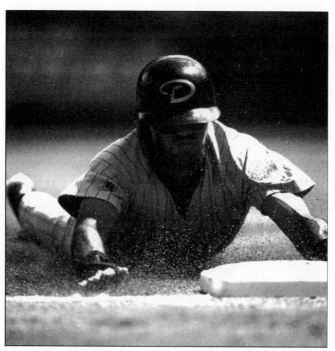

Figure 8-14:
Premiere
base stealer
Tony
Womack.

©1999 John Williamson / MLB Photos

A good base thief should be successful on at least 75 percent of his stolen base attempts. If your percentage is below that, your attempts are probably hurting your team.

What every base thief should know: Reading the pitcher

Ninety percent of all stolen bases come off the pitcher rather than the catcher. If you waited until the pitch reached home plate before you tried to steal, you would be thrown out 95 percent of the time. However, if you get a good jump as the pitcher delivers the ball, a catcher can do little to get you out, even if you aren't blessed with exceptional speed. In the fifth game of the 1997 World Series, Marlins first baseman Darren Daulton caught the Cleveland pitcher napping and stole second base. Darren has undergone nine knee operations, which have left him nearly immobile. Yet he got such a good lead that he was able to steal second against Sandy Alomar, one of the best throwing catchers in the business. Had the Indians' pitcher been paying more attention to first base, Darren never would have attempted a steal.

Base runners should study the opposing pitcher the moment he takes the mound. See if he has two distinct motions: one when he throws home and another when he tosses the ball to first to hold a runner on. Watch the pitcher throw to the plate from the stretch; note what body parts he moves first. Then see whether he does anything different when he throws to first base. See if he sets his feet differently on his pick-off move. Try to detect any quirk that can reveal the pitcher's intentions.

Ironically, good pitchers are often the easiest to steal on. Erratic pitchers typically use different release points from pitch to pitch (which is why they are erratic). You never know when they are going to let go of the ball. The better pitchers have purer mechanics. They establish a rhythm and stick to it. Pedro Martinez, the American League Cy Young Award winner in 1999, does the same thing to get to his release point on nearly every pitch. So a runner may be able to spot some clue in his motion when he plans to throw to first base.

After you have a pitcher's pattern down, take off for second the moment he moves toward his release point. He might indicate this with a hand gesture or some slight leg motion. Even a pitcher's eyes can fall into a pattern. Many pitchers take a quick glance toward first before throwing home; when they don't sneak a look toward you, they are throwing to your base.

You can also figure out pitchers by observing their body language. Watch the pitcher's rear leg. If it moves off the rubber, the throw is coming toward you. To throw to the plate, every pitcher must close either his hip or his front shoulder. He also must bend his rear knee while rocking onto his back foot. After the pitcher does any of these things, the rules state he can no longer throw to your base. You should immediately break for the next bag. If the pitcher breaks his motion to throw toward any base, the umpire should call a balk, which allows you and any other baserunners to advance.

If you are on first base, left-handed pitchers are traditionally harder to steal on than right-handers because the lefty looks directly at you when he assumes the set position. However, this also means *you* are looking directly at him so he is easier to read — if you know what to look for. Scrutinize his glove, the ball, and his motion. If a *southpaw* (a left-hander) tilts back his upper body, he is probably throwing to first; a turning of the shoulder to the right usually precedes a pitch to the plate. When he bends his rear leg, he is most likely preparing to push off toward home.

When a righty is on the mound, observe his right heel and shoulder. He cannot pitch unless his right foot touches the pitching rubber. Throwing to first requires him to pivot on that foot. If he lifts his right heel, get back to the bag. An open right shoulder also indicates a throw to first.

Lead — and runs will follow

Base thieves can choose between a *walking lead* and a *stationary lead*. Lou Brock, the former Cardinal outfielder, used a walking lead. Brock was faster than most players, but he wasn't especially quick out of his first few steps (most taller players find it difficult to accelerate from a dead stop). He would walk two or three small steps to gain momentum before taking off toward second base. If you require a few steps to accelerate, this is the lead for you. A walking lead does, however, have one disadvantage: A good pitcher can stop you from moving by simply holding the ball. If you continue to stroll, the pitcher can pick you off.

For that reason, I prefer the stationary lead, when a batter takes a few strides off first base then stands still while the pitcher prepares to throw. The pitcher can still hold the ball, but the batter is not budging until the pitcher makes his first move to the plate.

Remember: Whichever baserunning lead you choose, use the same one whether you are stealing a base or not. Set up the same way on every lead. You don't want to telegraph your intentions to the pitcher. He's watching you for clues as closely as you are watching him.

The key to stealing third

Stealing third is generally easier than stealing second. You can take a bigger lead at second than at first without drawing many throws. If your timing is good, you can also take off from second before the pitcher actually releases the ball.

Pitchers generally find it more difficult to pick runners off second than at first; the timing between the pitcher and his fielder must be precise. To catch you at second, either the second baseman or the shortstop has to cover or *cheat* (lean) toward the bag; this leaning opens up a hole for the batter. Alert coaches let you know when the fielders are sneaking in on you.

The potential to steal third depends on the batter at the plate. If a right-handed hitter is at-bat, you have an advantage because the catcher must throw over or around him to get the ball to third. But never try to steal third with a lefty at the plate, unless you get such a good jump that even a perfect throw cannot beat you.

Stealing third isn't a good gamble unless your success rate is 90 percent or better. Because you're already in scoring position at second, getting picked off can devastate your offense. Stealing third when your team is more than two runs behind is foolish. And making the first or last out of an inning at third, whether through an attempted steal or simply by running the bases, is considered a big mistake.

The only reason to steal third with fewer than two outs in a close ball game is so you can score on a fly ball or ground out. However, if you're a proficient base thief, it does makes sense to steal third with two outs; being on third rather than second in that situation offers you nine more opportunities to score. Memorize the following list and dazzle your friends with your baseball erudition.

If you are on third, you can score on

- A balk
- An infield hit
- A wild pitch
- A passed ball
- A one-base infield error
- A fielder's choice (where the hitter and any other baserunners are safe)
- Baserunning interference
- Catcher's interference
- A steal of home

Home, stolen home

Speaking of stealing home (how's that for a segue?), think long and hard about it — the odds are against you. If you must, only attempt a steal home during the late innings of a close, low-scoring ball game with two men out and a weak hitter at the plate. Obviously, home plate is the one base you steal entirely on the pitcher, because the catcher makes no throw on this play. Your best victims are pitchers with unusually slow deliveries or long wind-ups.

Having a right-handed batter at the plate when you attempt to steal home provides you with two advantages. First, the hitter obstructs the catcher's view of you at third. Second, if the batter remains in the box until just before you arrive at home, he can prevent the catcher from getting in position for the tag.

Delayed, double, and fake steals

With the delayed steal, slide-step into your regular lead when the pitcher releases the ball and then count 1-2-3. This should slow your takeoff just long enough to persuade the catcher and infielders that you aren't stealing. Race for second after you count. (You may also first break out of your lead and return to first to camouflage your intentions.) Catchers have no way of knowing who will cover second base on a delayed steal until either the second baseman or shortstop moves toward the bag. If you've caught those two infielders napping and no one covers second, the catcher has to hold onto the ball or risk throwing it into the outfield.

Double steals are possible whenever two bases are occupied. With runners on first and second, this play is nothing more than two straight steals occurring simultaneously. With only one out, the catcher will probably try to erase the lead runner heading to third. With two out, he may go after the slower of the two base stealers.

With runners on first and third, double steals become more complex. Imagine you are the runner on third. Your teammate on first should break full-out for second as the pitcher delivers the ball. You move down the line toward home. Halt as the catcher receives the pitch. Don't move until the catcher commits to throwing the runner out at second. Be alert in case he fakes a toss to the bag and instead throws to his pitcher, who fires back the ball for a play at the plate. The throw's *trajectory* should tell you if it is going to second base or to the pitcher — the throw will be higher if it is going all the way to second base, so hesitate long enough to see this. Dash home as soon as the second-base-bound throw leaves the catcher's hand.

Stealing: Know when to say no

The 1975 World Series serves as a great setting for a base-stealing lesson. In the bottom of the ninth inning of the fourth game, I was batting while our center fielder, Cesar Geronimo, was on second and Pete Rose was on first. We were trailing 5 – 4. Right-hander Luis Tiant was pitching for Boston. I was trying to concentrate on Tiant, always a difficult task because he had a thousand different herky-jerky moves and hesitations with which he distracted hitters.

Geronimo suddenly raced toward third just as Tiant went into his delivery. His unexpected movement pulled my attention away from the pitcher for a split second. By the time I looked back toward Tiant, the ball was nearly down the heart of the plate. A perfect pitch to drive for extra bases. However, that momentary lapse of concentration left me with little time to swing. My weak, late swing produced an inning-ending, rally-killing pop-up. That was the best pitch I had seen all night. I blew it.

Cesar should not have been running at that point. He was already in scoring position, we were trailing by a run, and Tiant was tiring (he threw an arm-wringing 163 pitches in that game). Given those circumstances, a base runner has to give his team's number three hitter — usually an RBI man — a chance to drive him in. To be a great base stealer, you must be aggressive, but you also have to know when to throw on the brakes for the good of the team.

If you are the runner on first for this play, helping your teammate at third to score is your primary goal. You may break for second while the pitcher is in his set position. Should your movement distract the pitcher, he may balk (see Chapter 3 for details on the balk). In that case, both runners advance one base. Attract a throw to first, and you can force a run-down. While you jockey to elude the tag, the runner on third can score.

Fake steals open the infield for the batter at the plate. You can bluff the opposition by taking two and a half quick strides out of your primary lead before coming to a halt. Your movement should draw the infielders out of position, because one of them must cover second base.

Chapter 9

Joe's Baseball Playbook

. . . .

In This Chapter

▶ Handling singles

▶ Fielding doubles or triples

▶ Covering bunts

▶ Setting up for pop flies

. . . .

*W*e could do an entire book devoted to defensive situations and strategies. These 24 plays are the ones you encounter in almost every game. It doesn't matter whether you coach or play in Little League, high school, college, a professional league, or for your company's softball team; make sure you have a handle on these plays.

If you want to know more about the defensive role of each player on the field as well as some of the vocabulary used to describe these plays, be sure to check out Chapter 7. To read the diagrams that follow, here is all that you need to know:

Symbol	Meaning
(P)	Pitcher
(C)	Catcher
(1B)	First baseman
(2B)	Second baseman
(SS)	Shortstop
(3B)	Third baseman
(RF)	Right fielder
(CF)	Center fielder
(LF)	Left fielder
⟶	Path of a player
------>	Path of the ball

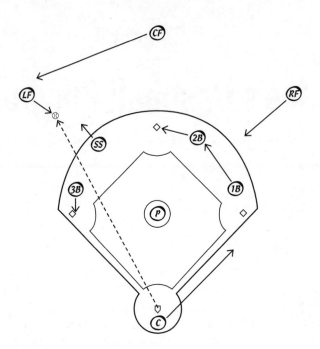

Single to left: Bases empty

Catcher: Cover first base in case the runner takes a too-wide turn.

Pitcher: Back up any throw to second base.

First baseman: Check that the batter touches first base and then back up the incoming throw to second base.

Second baseman: Cover second base.

Shortstop: Pursue the ball; then line up between the left fielder and second base to take the cut-off throw.

Third baseman: Cover third base.

Left fielder: Field the ball and throw it to the cut-off man (the shortstop). If the shortstop is out of position, throw to second base.

Center fielder: Run to back up the left fielder.

Right fielder: Move toward the infield to cover a poor throw from the left fielder to the second baseman.

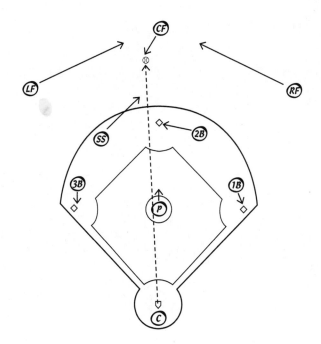

Single to center: Bases empty

Catcher: Cover home plate.

Pitcher: Stay near the mound and back up any throw to second base.

First baseman: Make sure the batter touches first base, and then cover the base inside.

Second baseman: Go to second base to take the throw.

Shortstop: Go out to be the cut-off man for second base.

Third baseman: Cover third base.

Left fielder: Back up the center fielder.

Center fielder: Field the ball and throw it to second base or the cut-off man (shortstop).

Right fielder: Back up the center fielder.

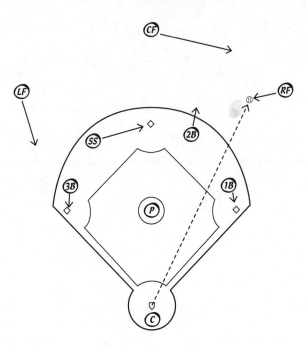

Single to right: Bases empty

Catcher: Cover home plate.

Pitcher: Follow the flight of the ball and then decide where to back up (usually second base).

First baseman: Check that the batter touches first base; then cover the base inside.

Second baseman: Pursue the ball; then take the cut-off position between the right fielder and second base.

Shortstop: Cover second base.

Third baseman: Cover third base.

Left fielder: Move toward the infield in case the right fielder makes a bad throw to second base.

Center fielder: Back up the right fielder.

Right fielder: Field the hit and make the cut-off throw to the second baseman. If the second baseman is out of position, throw it to second base.

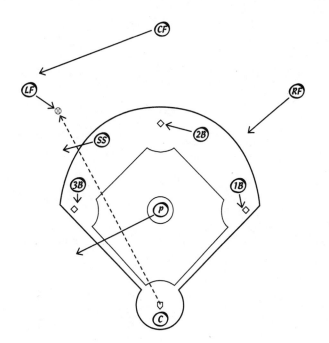

Single to left: Runner on first, or runners on first and third

Catcher: Cover home plate.

Pitcher: Follow the flight of the ball and then decide where to back up (usually third base).

First baseman: Make sure the batter touches first base, and then cover the base inside.

Second baseman: Cover second base.

Shortstop: Line up between the left fielder and third base for the cut-off throw.

Third baseman: Back up the shortstop (but also cover third).

Left fielder: Field the ball and throw it to the cut-off man (the shortstop). If the shortstop is out of position, throw it to third base.

Center fielder: Back up the left fielder.

Right fielder: Move toward the infield to field any bad throws.

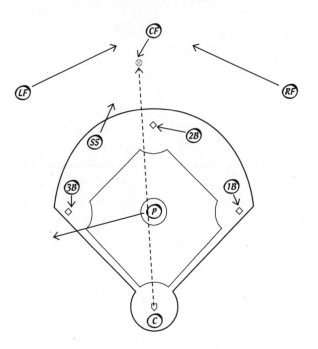

Single to center: Runner on first, or runners on first and third

Catcher: Cover home plate.

Pitcher: Back up the throw to third base.

First baseman: Check that the batter touches first base; then cover the bag inside.

Second baseman: Cover second.

Shortstop: Line up for the cut-off throw between the center fielder and third base.

Third baseman: Cover third base.

Left fielder: Back up the center fielder.

Center fielder: Field the hit and throw it to the cut-off man (the shortstop). If the shortstop is out of position, throw it to third base.

Right fielder: Back up the center fielder.

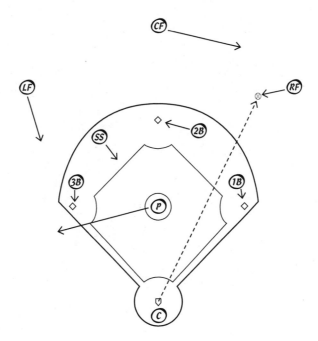

Single to right: Runner on first, or runners on first and third

Catcher: Cover home plate.

Pitcher: Back up third base.

First baseman: Make sure that the batter touches first base, and then cover the base inside.

Second baseman: Cover second base.

Shortstop: Line up for the cut-off throw between the right fielder and third base.

Third baseman: Cover third base.

Left fielder: Back up the throw to third base.

Center fielder: Back up the right fielder.

Right fielder: Field the hit and throw it to the cut-off man (the shortstop).

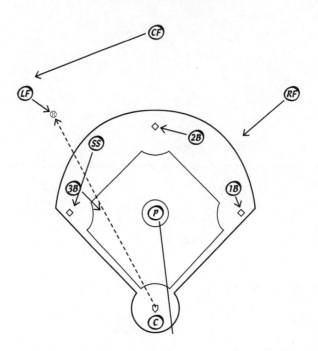

Single to left: Runner on second, runners on first and second, or bases loaded

Catcher: Cover home plate.

Pitcher: Back up the throw at home plate.

First baseman: Cover first base.

Second baseman: Cover second base.

Shortstop: Cover third base.

Third baseman: Take the cut-off position for a throw to home plate.

Left fielder: Field the hit and throw it to the cut-off man (the third baseman).

Center fielder: Back up the left fielder.

Right fielder: Back up any throw to second.

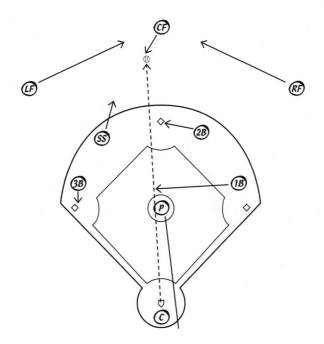

Single to center: Runner on second, runners on first and second, or bases loaded

Catcher: Cover home plate.

Pitcher: Back up the catcher at home plate.

First baseman: Take the cut-off position near the mound for a throw to home plate.

Second baseman: Cover second base.

Shortstop: Take the cut-off position for a throw to third base.

Third baseman: Cover third base.

Left fielder: Back up the center fielder and then become a quarterback. Tell the center fielder where the throw is going.

Center fielder: Field the hit, listen for the left or right fielder's instructions, throw to one of the two cut-off men: the shortstop (if the play is at third base) or the first baseman (if the play is at the plate).

Right fielder: Back up the center fielder and then become a quarterback. Tell the center fielder where the throw is going.

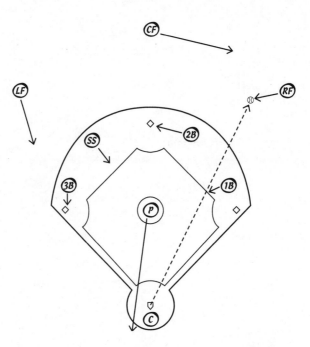

Single to right: Runner on second, runners on first and second, or bases loaded

Catcher: Cover home plate.

Pitcher: Stand outside the base paths between third base and home plate, watch the play evolve, and back up the throw (usually at home plate).

First baseman: Take the cut-off position for the throw to home plate.

Second baseman: Cover second base.

Shortstop: Take the cut-off position for the throw to third base.

Third baseman: Cover third base.

Left fielder: Come toward third base in order to be able to help out at third or second base.

Center fielder: Back up the right fielder and tell him where to throw.

Right fielder: Field the ball, listen for the center fielder's instructions, and throw to the appropriate cut-off man: the shortstop (on a play at third base) or the first baseman (on a play at home plate).

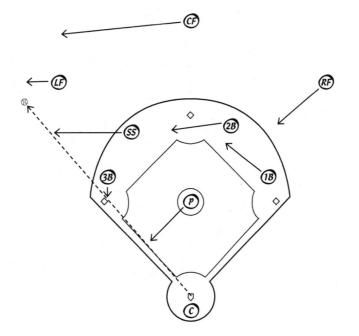

Double, possible triple down the left field line: Bases empty

Catcher: Cover home plate.

Pitcher: Back up third base.

First baseman: Make sure the batter touches first base; then trail the runner to second base.

Second baseman: Go to the trail position behind the shortstop. Stay near second base.

Shortstop: Take the cut-off position down the left field line.

Third baseman: Cover third base.

Left fielder: Field the hit and make the cut-off throw to the shortstop.

Center fielder: Back up the left fielder.

Right fielder: Back up any throw to second base.

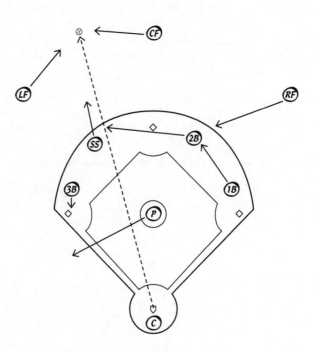

Double, possible triple to the left center field gap: Bases empty

Catcher: Cover home plate.

Pitcher: Back up third base.

First baseman: Make sure the batter touches first base and then trail him to second.

Second baseman: Go to the trail position behind the shortstop.

Third baseman: Cover third base.

Shortstop: Line up with third base and the fielder for the cut-off throw.

Left fielder: Back up the center fielder.

Center fielder: Field the hit and then make the cut-off throw to the shortstop.

Right fielder: Back up any throw to second base.

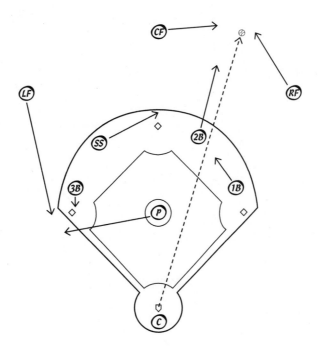

Double, possible triple to the right center field gap: Bases empty

Catcher: Cover home plate.

Pitcher: Back up third base.

First baseman: Check that the batter touches first base, and then trail him to second base.

Second baseman: Line up with third base and the center fielder for the cut-off throw.

Shortstop: Get to the trail position behind the second baseman.

Third baseman: Cover third base.

Left fielder: Back up any throw to third base.

Center fielder: Field the hit and make the cut-off throw to the second baseman.

Right fielder: Back up the center fielder.

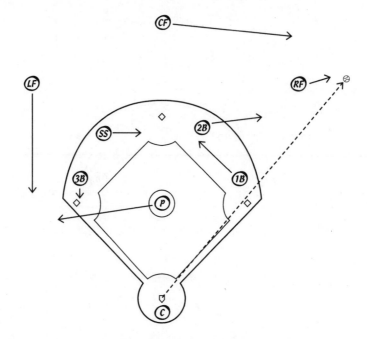

Double, possible triple down the right field line: Bases empty

Catcher: Cover home plate.

Pitcher: Back up third base.

First baseman: Check that the batter touches first base, and then trail him to second base.

Second baseman: Line up with third base and the fielder for the cut-off throw.

Shortstop: Get to the trail position behind the second baseman.

Third baseman: Cover third base.

Left fielder: Back up any throw to third base.

Center fielder: Back up the right fielder.

Right fielder: Field the hit and then make the cut-off throw to the second baseman.

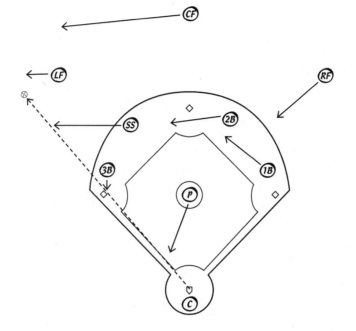

Double, possible triple down the left field line: Runners on base

Catcher: Cover home plate.

Pitcher: Stand between home plate and third base (closer to home), watch the play evolve, and back up the throw.

First baseman: Check that the batter touches first base, and then trail the runner to second base.

Second baseman: Get to the trail position behind the shortstop. Let the shortstop know where to throw.

Shortstop: Line up between home plate and the fielder for the cut-off throw.

Third baseman: Cover third base.

Left fielder: Field the hit and make the cut-off throw to the shortstop.

Center fielder: Back up the left fielder.

Right fielder: Back up any throw to second base.

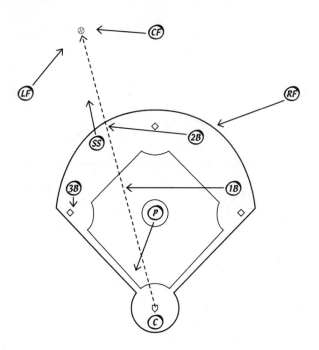

Double, possible triple to the left center field gap: Runners on base

Catcher: Cover home plate.

Pitcher: Stand between home plate and third base (closer to home), watch the play evolve, and back up the throw.

First baseman: Take the cut-off position for a throw to the plate.

Second baseman: Get to the trail position behind the shortstop. Let the shortstop know where to throw.

Shortstop: Line up with home plate and the fielder for the cut-off throw.

Third baseman: Cover third base.

Left fielder: Back up the center fielder.

Center fielder: Field the hit and make the cut-off throw to the shortstop.

Right fielder: Back up any throw to second base.

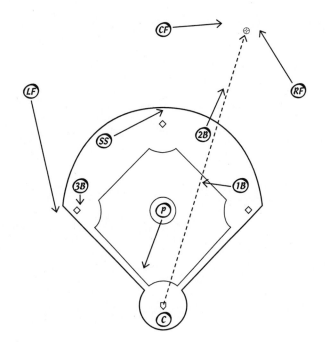

Double, possible triple to the right center field gap: Runners on base

Catcher: Cover home plate.

Pitcher: Stand between home plate and third base (closer to home), watch the play evolve, and back up the throw.

First baseman: Take the cut-off position for a throw to the plate.

Second baseman: Line up with home plate and the fielder for the cut-off throw.

Shortstop: Get to the trail position behind the second baseman. Tell the second baseman where to make the throw.

Third baseman: Cover third base.

Left fielder: Back up any throw to third base.

Center fielder: Field the hit and make the cut-off throw to the second baseman.

Right fielder: Back up the center fielder.

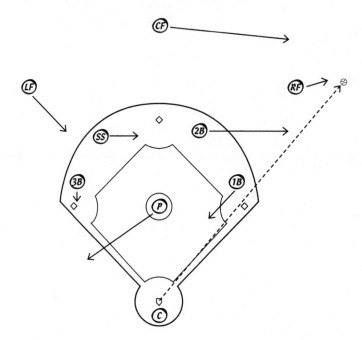

Double, possible triple down the right field line: Runners on base

Catcher: Cover home plate.

Pitcher: Stand outside the base paths halfway between home plate and third base, watch the play evolve, and back up the throw.

First baseman: Take the cut-off position for a throw to the plate.

Second baseman: Line up with home plate and the fielder for the cut-off throw.

Shortstop: Get behind the second baseman. Tell the second baseman where to make the throw. Be the cut-off man for a play at third base.

Left fielder: Back up any throw to second base or third base.

Center fielder: Back up the right fielder.

Right fielder: Field the hit and make the cut-off throw to the second baseman.

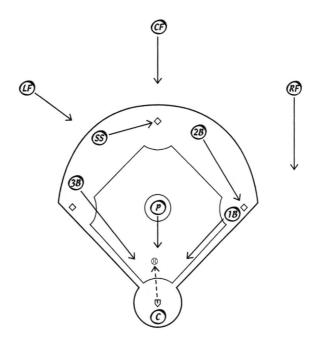

Sacrifice bunt: Runner on first

Catcher: Tell the infielders where to throw.

Pitcher: Cover the middle of the infield. If you field the ball, listen to the catcher's instructions, and then throw to the appropriate base.

First baseman: After holding the runner on first base, charge and cover the right side of the infield. If you field the ball, listen for the catcher's instructions, and then throw to the appropriate base.

Second baseman: Cover first base.

Shortstop: Cover second base.

Third baseman: Charge toward home plate and cover the left side of the infield. (Be prepared to retreat quickly to third base to prevent the runner from advancing there.) If you field the ball, listen to the catcher's instructions, and then throw to the appropriate base.

Left fielder: Come toward the infield in order to back up poor throws.

Center fielder: Back up any throw to second base.

Right fielder: Back up any throw to first base.

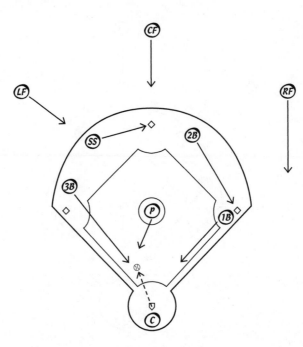

Sacrifice bunt: Runners on first and second, the infield goes for the out at first

Catcher: Tell the infielders where the throw is going.

Pitcher: Cover the third base line. If you field the ball, listen to the catcher's instructions and then throw to the appropriate base.

First baseman: Cover the right side of the infield. If you field the ball, listen for the catcher's instructions, and then throw to the appropriate base.

Second baseman: Cover first base.

Shortstop: Cover second base.

Third baseman: Charge and cover the left side of the infield. If you field the ball, listen to the catcher's instructions, and then throw to the appropriate base.

Left fielder: Back up any throw to second base or third base.

Center fielder: Back up any throw to second base.

Right fielder: Back up any throw to first base.

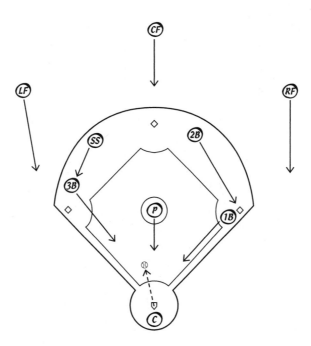

Wheel play: Batter puts down a sacrifice bunt with runners on first and second, the defense goes for the force out at third

Catcher: Tell the infielders where the throw is going. (Remember that the center fielder is covering second on this play.)

Pitcher: The shortstop should break for third base before you deliver the pitch. Cover the middle of the infield. If you field the ball, listen to the catcher's instructions, and then throw to the appropriate base.

First baseman: Cover the right side of the infield. If you field the ball, listen for the catcher's instructions, and then throw to the appropriate base.

Second baseman: Cover first base.

Shortstop: Get behind the lead runner's right shoulder and break for third base as the pitcher sets.

Third baseman: Charge and cover the left side of the infield. If you field the ball, listen to the catcher's instructions, and then throw to the appropriate base.

Left fielder: Back up any throw to third base.

Center fielder: Come toward the infield to cover second base.

Right fielder: Back up any throw to first base.

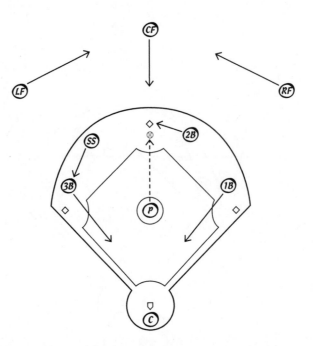

Wheel play fake: Runners on first and second with a pick-off play going to second

Catcher: Cover home plate.

Pitcher: As the shortstop breaks for third base, make your pick-off throw to second base.

First baseman: Cover the right side of the infield as if the wheel play were on.

Second baseman: Fake a step toward first base, and then break for second base for the pick-off throw.

Shortstop: Position yourself behind the runner's right shoulder. Break for third base as if the wheel play were on.

Third baseman: Charge and cover the left side of the infield.

Left fielder: Back up the center fielder.

Center fielder: Back up the throw to second base.

Right fielder: Back up the center fielder.

For the wheel play fake to work, everyone must go about his initial assignment as if the play is actually on.

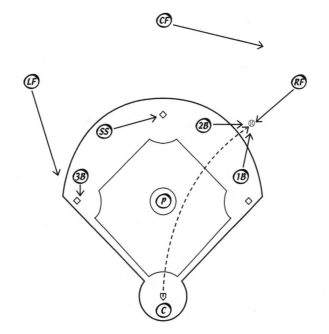

Pop fly to shallow right field

Catcher: If the bases are empty, back up a possible throw to first base; otherwise, cover home plate.

Pitcher: Call for a fielder if the ball is in the infield proper; if not, cover first.

First baseman: Call for a catch if you feel that you can make the play; however, you must back off if the right fielder or the second baseman calls for the ball.

Second baseman: Call for a catch, but back off if the right fielder calls you off.

Shortstop: Cover second base.

Third baseman: Cover third base.

Left fielder: Back up any throw to third base.

Center fielder: Back up the right fielder.

Right fielder: Call for the catch if you feel you can make the play. All other fielders must yield to you.

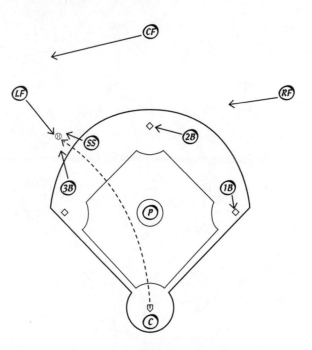

Pop fly to shallow left field

Catcher: If the bases are empty, back up a possible throw to third base; otherwise, cover home plate.

Pitcher: Call a fielder if the ball is close to the infield; if not, cover third base.

First baseman: Cover first base.

Second baseman: Cover second base.

Shortstop: Call for the ball if you think you can make the play. Give way if the left fielder calls for it.

Third baseman: Call for the catch if you think you can make the play. However, you must back off if the shortstop or left fielder calls you off.

Left fielder: Call for the ball if you think you can make the play. All other fielders must yield to you.

Center fielder: Back up the left fielder.

Right fielder: Back up any throw to second base.

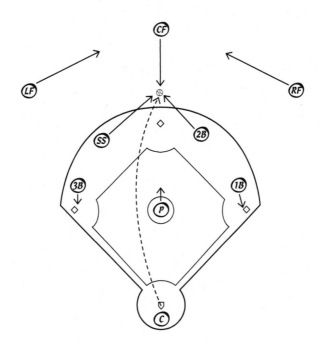

Pop fly to shallow center field

Catcher: Cover home plate.

Pitcher: Direct the infielders. If the shortstop and second baseman both go for the ball, cover second base if the first baseman is unable to do so.

First baseman: Cover first base unless the shortstop and second baseman both go for the ball. Then you must cover second.

Second baseman: Call for the ball if you think you can make the play. Back off if either the center fielder calls for it or if the shortstop calls for it before you do. Either you or the shortstop must retreat to cover second base.

Shortstop: Call for the ball if you think you can make the play. Give way if the center fielder calls for it or if the second baseman calls for it before you do. Either you or the second baseman must retreat to cover second base.

Third baseman: Cover third base.

Left fielder: Back up the center fielder.

Center fielder: Call for the ball if you think you can make the play. All other fielders must yield to you.

Right fielder: Back up the center fielder.

Part III

From Little League to the Major Leagues: Organized Baseball

The 5th Wave

By Rich Tennant

"I hate to break this to you, but as far as I can figure, you have a negative slugging percentage."

In this part . . .

Baseball is everywhere — you just have to know where to find it. In this part, we introduce you to the wide variety of organized baseball leagues. Weighing and comparing player performances is one of the great pleasures of baseball, so we also show you how to understand the measurements that do so — baseball statistics. Also in this part, Sparky Anderson joins us to show you how a major league manager's thought processes work. Veteran umpire Harry Wendelstedt, Jr. reveals how baseball's arbiters should conduct themselves on the field. You find out about baseball jobs that don't require you to swing a bat or throw a pitch. And finally, we explain major league baseball's playoff system and the World Series.

Chapter 10

T-Ball to College Baseball and Everything in Between

*W*hether you're 5 or 55, male or female, you don't have to regard baseball merely as a spectator sport. If you want to compete in an informal atmosphere, your local parks department can make a baseball diamond available for pick-up games. (You should always reserve field time in advance, especially if you have a number of leagues competing in your town.) Throughout the United States and Canada, thousands of baseball leagues and associations also offer nonprofessional players of all ages and genders an opportunity for organized competition.

The league you or your child joins does not have to be affiliated with **USA Baseball** (520-327-9700), but if it is, you are assured that the organization conforms to a rigorous standard. USA Baseball is the national governing body of amateur baseball. Its members include the Little League, the Amateur Athletic Union, the National High School Coaches Association, PONY Baseball, the Police Athletic League, the YMCA, and the NCAA. USA Baseball is also responsible for picking (with the help of a national network of college coaches) and training the U.S. Olympic baseball team. Team USA players who have gone on to star in the majors include Mark McGwire, Will Clark, Robin Ventura, Nomar Garciaparra, and Charles Johnson. In the land of Blue Jays and Expos, **Baseball Canada** (603-748-5606) is the prominent amateur organization.

T-Ball: A Good Place to Start

T-ball is baseball's version of miniature golf. The baseball is served on a batting tee, bases are never more than 60 feet apart, and everything else is scaled down so that children (usually eight years old and under) can experience the joys of the National Pastime without risking physical harm. The **T-Ball USA Association** (212-254-7911) in New York City does not run any leagues or teams of its own, but it does assist many leading amateur organizations with their T-ball programs.

This nonprofit association also runs clinics to teach coaches and parents the rudiments of baseball. For more information about the program, pick up a copy of *The Official T-Ball USA Family Guide to T-Ball Baseball* (Masters Press).

Amateur Leagues for All Ages

Little League Baseball (570-326-1921) is played in every state in the U.S. and in 87 countries. With three million participants (including over 400,000 female players), one million volunteers, and 22,000 leagues, Little League is the world's largest organized youth sports program. Leagues are required to play an annual schedule of at least 12 games. The organization maintains a museum and conducts instructional clinics for umpires and managers. It annually sponsors an international World Series in seven divisions.

Does Little League baseball provide a first step to the big leagues? An estimated 80 percent of all major league players participated in Little League baseball. Current major leaguers who played in the Little League World Series, held each year in Williamsport, Pennsylvania, include Gary Sheffield, Derek Bell, Dan Wilson, Charlie Hayes, and Wilson Alvarez.

You can keep up with the latest Little League news by ordering the organization's quarterly newsletter, *The Little Leaguer,* or its annual publication, *The Little League Magazine.* Little League Baseball also produces a number of excellent instructional handbooks and manuals. You can contact the Little League for a complete list of its publications.

The **Babe Ruth League** (609-695-1434) operates in 48 states in the U.S. (Hawaii and Alaska are the exceptions). Founded in 1951, the organization is currently composed of over 870,000 players on 43,800 teams in 6,200 leagues. Five- and 6-year-olds in this league play T-ball; 7- and 8-year-olds play with bases 60 feet (18.2m) apart and hit against a slow pitching machine or a coach. At ages 9 and 10, players face some live pitching. Babe Ruth League players do not, however, compete on fields with major-league dimensions until they are 13, when they enter a prep program. Age classifications top out at 18.

This league stresses player participation over winning and is famous for teaching the proper way to play the game. And Joe Morgan can tell you that reputation is well-deserved. He participated in the Oakland chapter of the Babe Ruth League as a member of the Qwik Way Drive-In team.

Over 400,000 players on 24,000 teams in 11 states participate in **Dixie Baseball** (334-242-8395), the leading youth baseball program in the southern U.S. Five divisions compose the association's baseball programs. The Youth T-Ball division caters to children ages 8 and under. The oldest division, Dixie Majors Baseball, is for players ages 15 to 18. Championship tournaments are held for the four oldest divisions during the first week of August. Dixie also sponsors softball leagues.

Competition is probably fiercest in leagues sponsored by the **Amateur Athletic Union** (407-934-7200), which boasts 50 associations in all 50 states in the U.S. Like professional clubs, many member teams travel out of their locales to play games. Players participate in 12 divisions with age limits ranging from 9 to 20. Amateur Athletic Union championships are decided in tournaments featuring double-pool play. Teams are seeded before the first round. Winners go on to play in the National Championship Tournament; losers participate in a consolation bracket.

Other youth baseball organizations include:

- ✔ **All American Amateur Baseball Association** in Zanesville, Ohio (614-453-8531)

- ✔ **American Legion Baseball** in Indianapolis, Indiana (317-630-1213)

- ✔ **Continental Amateur Baseball Association** in Westerville, Ohio (614-899-2103)

- ✔ **Dizzy Dean Baseball** in Eupora, Missouri (601-258-7626)

- ✔ **George Khoury Association of Baseball Leagues** in St. Louis, Missouri (314-849-8900)

- ✔ **Hap Dumont Baseball** in Wichita, Kansas (316-721-1779)

- ✔ **National Association of Police Athletic Leagues** in North Palm Beach, Florida (561-844-1823)

- ✔ **National Amateur Baseball Federation** in Bowie, Maryland (301-262-5005)

- ✔ **PONY Baseball** in Washington, Pennsylvania (412-225-1060)

- ✔ **U.S. Amateur Baseball Association** in Edmonds, Washington (425-776-7130))

Your child and the child within you can compete in the **National Amateur Baseball Federation,** which has 350,000 participants in 85 franchises across the U.S. Founded in 1914, this is the only all-volunteer amateur baseball organization in the country. For younger players, classifications advance from Rookie (ages 10 and under) to Senior level (ages 18 and under). Players between the ages of 19 and 22 compete in the college classification. If you are over 22, you can recapture your youth at the Majors level, an unlimited classification. Many former college players and professionals who have reacquired their amateur status compete in this division. Member teams play anywhere from 30 to 100 games per year in local competition. The best of these teams participate in round-robin championship tournaments scheduled between mid-July and late August.

Two other organizations have unlimited classifications. The **American Amateur Baseball Congress** (616-781-2002) holds its August tournaments in seven divisions named for Hall of Famers: Roberto Clemente (ages 8 and under), Willie Mays (10 and under), Pee Wee Reese (12 and under), Sandy Koufax (14 and under), Mickey Mantle (16 and under), Connie Mack (18 and under), and Stan Musial (unlimited). The **Continental Amateur Baseball Association** maintains competitive balance by spreading players out among 12 classifications (ages 9 and under to unlimited). You can find out everything you need to know about this organization from its Web site (www.cababaseball.com).

Founded by former Detroit Tiger minor leaguer John Young in 1988, **Restore Baseball in the Inner Cities (RBI)** annually brings the National Pastime to over 100,000 urban youths across the U.S. RBI teams compete to participate in an annual World Series, which is held in a major league park. Girls' softball has been part of the program since 1994. Major League Baseball contributes a portion of the RBI budget, and big league players such as pitching ace Kevin Brown have also pledged their financial support. To find out how you, your community, or your company can get behind this laudable organization, call 212-931-7897.

The Collegiate Talent Pool

The first baseball game played between two colleges took place on July 1, 1859, when Amherst beat Pittsfield 73-32. (Evidently they thought they were playing football.) Only 35 feet (10.6m) separated the pitcher from the batter, and the bases were a mere 60 feet (18.2m) apart. Few of the great college players of the late 1800s ever donned a major league uniform; most college men didn't consider baseball to be a respectable profession. However, the ascent of Christy Mathewson of Bucknell University, the elegant and erudite Hall of Fame pitcher for the New York Giants, considerably altered that attitude. Matty had been president of his class and a member of a literary society, and he could beat ten opponents at chess simultaneously. He demonstrated that one could play professional baseball without surrendering the title "gentleman." Largely due to his influence — as well as that of other turn-of-the-century college stars who turned pro (such as Hall of Famers Eddie Collins and Harry Hooper), American campuses became incubators for major league talent.

Today, over two-thirds of all major league players have a college education. Collegiate baseball — which is intensely scrutinized by major league scouts — provides the perfect stage for aspiring major leaguers to showcase their talents. The National Collegiate Athletic Association (NCAA) is, of course, the Big Kahuna of the college game. Over 250 colleges — among them Mathewson's beloved Bucknell — compete in its 29 Division I conferences. Other NCAA college baseball squads play in either Division II or III. The NCAA Division I College World Series takes place during the first week of June. Both championship series for the other two divisions take place during the final week of May.

Major-league baseball chooses its fledgling pros from among high school and college players in the annual Rule IV draft. Each team gets one pick per round until the talent pool is exhausted. Players picked in the first few rounds are considered the best prospects; however, getting picked in a high round is no guarantee of success. One-third of first-round picks never play a single inning of major-league baseball. And many late-round picks have gone on to All-Star careers. For example, Mike Piazza, perhaps the greatest hitting catcher of all time, was the Los Angeles Dodgers' 62nd-round pick in 1988. That means clubs preferred more than 1,600 players — enough bodies to stock the rosters for the entire major leagues and then some — to this almost certain future Hall of Famer.

Following are just some of the great players in the major leagues now who were passed over until the late rounds of the annual draft:

- ✔ Catcher: Mike Piazza (Dodgers, 1988, 62nd round)
- ✔ First Base: Mark Grace (Cubs, 1985, 24th round)
- ✔ Second Base: Jeff Kent (Blue Jays, 1989, 20th round)
- ✔ Shortstop: Mike Bordick (Athletics, 1986, signed as undrafted free agent)
- ✔ Third Base: Scott Brosius (Athletics, 1987, 20th round)
- ✔ Left Field: Richie Sexson (Indians, 1993, 24th round)
- ✔ Center Field: Marvin Bernard (Giants, 1992, 50th round)
- ✔ Right Field: Bernard Gilkey (Cardinals, 1984, undrafted free agent)
- ✔ Starting Pitcher (RH): John Smoltz (Tigers, 1985, 22nd round)
- ✔ Starting Pitcher (LH): Andy Pettite (Yankees, 1990, 22nd round)
- ✔ Closer: Robb Nen (Rangers, 1987, 32nd round)
- ✔ Long Reliever: Jeff Zimmerman (Rangers, 1998, unsigned free agent)

Chapter 11

The Minors and Other Leagues

In This Chapter

▶ American minor league action

▶ Japanese leagues and players

▶ Tropical teams and winter leagues

▶ Beisbol, Cuban style

▶ Good reads about the minor leagues

Major league baseball isn't the only game in town (especially if you live in Helena, Montana, or Brisbane, Australia). Thousands of amateur and professional baseball leagues offer games to fans all over the globe. Japan, Mexico, Australia, Cuba, Venezuela, Italy, Korea, and China are just some of the countries that have embraced our National Pastime. And who knows how many amateur leagues are flourishing throughout the world — the number must easily reach five figures. Baseball Fever . . . it's catching and spreading everywhere!

The American Minor Leagues

Major-league organizations often send their young players to the minor leagues to hone their talents before joining the big club. Veteran ballplayers sometimes visit the minors, too. A major-league player usually rehabs his injuries in the minors before returning to the big leagues, and if his performance has slipped and he is trying to recapture the magic, he may step down to the minors for a while. Most minor-league players have something to prove. And while the youngsters want to show their organizations that they are ready to step up to the big leagues, declining veteran players are eager to convince a team that they can still compete in the majors.

Because nearly everyone on the field is highly motivated, you often see a hustling, rollicking brand of baseball in the minors. The level of skills on display varies from league to league, team to team, and player to player, but the level of thrills is consistently high from Triple-A ball down to the Rookie Leagues. Most minor leaguers have large dreams but small salaries. They play a game they love not for dollars but for glory. Their innocent, fervid aspirations will fail to touch your heart only if you don't have one.

Minor league franchises — where are they?

Nineteen minor leagues were operating under one umbrella organization — the National Association — in 1999. For most of the 20th century, a second umbrella organization — the American Association — had also overseen minor league play. But at the end of the 1998 season, the American Association folded. Its member teams were dispersed among the remaining minor leagues.

The number of teams in each minor league may vary from year to year. Most minor league clubs are owned by major league organizations that absorb all of the operating costs. A few are independent entities, though even they have working agreements with clubs that underwrite much (if not all) of their overhead costs. Once the working agreement expires, a minor league club can switch its major league affiliation (which it might do if it has greater proximity to another big league team).

At the end of the 1999 season, the National Association leagues and franchises were competing under the following alignments. (1999 major league affiliations are listed in parentheses.)

Class AAA (Triple A)

- **The International League:** Charlotte (White Sox), Columbus (Yankees), Norfolk (Mets), Ottawa (Expos), Pawtucket (Red Sox), Richmond (Braves), Rochester (Orioles), Scranton/Wilkes-Barre (Phillies), Syracuse (Blue Jays), Toledo (Tigers), *Buffalo (Indians), *Indianapolis (Reds), Durham (Devil Rays), and *Louisville (Brewers).

- **Pacific Coast League:** Edmonton (Angels), Salt Lake (Twins), Las Vegas (Padres), Calgary (Marlins), Vancouver (Athletics), Tucson (Diamondbacks), Tacoma (Mariners), Fresno (Giants), Albuquerque (Dodgers), Colorado Springs (Rockies), *Oklahoma (Rangers), *Nashville (Pirates), Memphis (Cardinals), *New Orleans (Astros), *Iowa (Cubs), and *Omaha (Royals).

- **The Mexican League** is also a Triple A member of the National Association. All of its teams are independent entities with no major league affiliations. In 1999, the ML consisted of 16 franchises playing in three zones or divisions:

- **Central Zone:** Mexico City (Red Devils), Mexico City (Tigers), Cordoba, Aguascalientes, and Oaxaca.

- **North Zone:** Monterrey, Monclova, Union Laguna, Nuevo Laredo, Saltillo, and Reynosa.

- **South Zone:** Yucatan, Campeche, Chetumal, Tabasco, and Cancun.

Mexican League teams play a 122-game schedule that starts in March and ends in early August. The top two teams in each zone and the third-place clubs with the best records compete in a three-tiered playoff. The two finalists decide the Mexican League championship in a best-of-seven series.

*Indicates former American Association franchise.

The lower minors

We could present all the minor league teams and their affiliations, but then this would turn into a book of lists. Instead, in Table 11-1, we present one last list of the other National Association leagues.

Table 11-1	National Association Leagues	
Class AA (Double A)	*Class A (Advanced)*	*Class A*
Eastern League	California League	Midwest League
Southern League	Carolina League	South Atlantic League
Texas League	Florida State League	
Short-Season Class A	*Rookie (Advanced)*	*Rookie*
New York-Penn League	Appalachian League	Arizona League
Northwest League	Pioneer League	Dominican Summer League
		Gulf Coast League

Five independent minor leagues operated in 1999 (down from ten in 1997): the Atlantic League, the Frontier League, the Northern League (which recently absorbed the Northeast League), the Texas-Louisiana League, and the Western League. Most of these clubs operate without any major league affiliation. By the end of the 1999 season, major league teams had signed over 20 players from the Atlantic League alone, proof that the independent leagues have become a formidable incubator for professional talent.

Not just another minor league team

Bill Murray, actor-comedian-*Saturday Night Live* alumnus, is one of the principle owners of Minnesota's St. Paul Saints, a Northern League entry. Under club president Mike Veeck, the Saints have proven to be as entertaining as the brilliant Murray himself. Chia Pet Night, MASH Night (featuring a give-away of balls bearing camouflage patterns), Ron Popeil Vegamatic Day, Whoopee Cushion Night . . . no promotion pushes the envelope too far so long as it pulls fans into the Saints' home park. St. Paul has also become a proving ground for former major leaguers eager to return from injury, retirement, or some other career detour. Slugger Darryl Strawberry launched his successful major league comeback with the Saints. Veeck's commitment to fun (he once tried introducing Vasectomy Night — don't ask!) pays off at the box office. St. Paul is one of the few professional baseball franchises that sells out every game before opening day.

If you want to follow the progress of your favorite club's top farm team prospects, the bi-weekly publication *Baseball America* provides stats as well as reports on every player at every minor league level. If you want to know which teams are associated with any of the minor or independent leagues, refer to Appendix B for a league's address or phone number, or obtain the information from the most current copy of *Baseball America*'s directory. To order the directory, call *Baseball America* at 800-845-2726.

Experience not always necessary

Few players make it to the majors without first playing in the minor leagues. However, a fair number of those who made their professional debuts in the major leagues and were never sent down to the minors would eventually win baseball's highest honor — induction into the Baseball Hall of Fame in Cooperstown. Their ranks include

- Pitcher Walter Johnson (417 wins)
- Pitcher Catfish Hunter (224 wins)
- Pitcher Chief Bender (212 wins)
- Pitcher Ted Lyons (260 wins)
- Pitcher Sandy Koufax (165 wins, 3 Cy Young Awards)
- Pitcher Bob Feller (266 wins)
- Pitcher Eddie Plank (326 wins)
- Pitcher Eppa Rixey (266 wins)
- Shortstop Ernie Banks (512 home runs)

Banks, who played his entire career with the Chicago Cubs, spent half of it at first base. He won two consecutive MVP awards (1958–59) while playing shortstop.

✔ Shortstop Bobby Wallace (the greatest fielding shortstop of his era)

Wallace's glove work was so spectacular, he is one of the handful of men who played 25 years or more in the majors. In 1902, he was baseball's highest-paid player.

Minor league stars

Minor league audiences have witnessed some phenomenal performances over the years. In 1954, Joe Bauman, a first baseman with Roswell, hit 72 home runs to establish a minor league baseball record that still stands. Tony Lazzeri, who would eventually star at second base for the New York Yankees, drove in 222 runs for San Francisco of the Pacific Coast League in 1925 (his team played 197 games that year). In 1922, pitcher Joe Boehler won 38 games for Tulsa of the Western League. In 1951, Willie Mays compiled an astounding .477 batting average over 35 games for the Minneapolis Millers. Mays was promptly summoned by his parent club, The New York Giants, and never spent another day in the minors.

Some players' lifetime totals are equally staggering. Hector Espino, a slugging first baseman, hit a minor league career record 484 home runs, primarily for teams in the Mexican League. Bill Thomas won 383 games while pitching for various teams and leagues. Right-hander Frank Shellenback holds the Pacific Coast League career wins record with 295. Because he relied primarily on a spitball, Shellenback's major league prospects were shattered when the major league owners banned that slippery pitch. Ox Eckhardt spent parts of 13 seasons with various minor league clubs; he retired with the highest career batting average in minor league history — a dazzling .367.

Buzz Arlett won 108 games in his first six minor league seasons (1918–23). He won 29 games while pitching for Oakland in the Pacific Coast League in 1920. He also enjoyed two 25-win seasons. However, after hurting his arm, he switched to the outfield and hit 432 career homers. In 1931, the 32-year-old Arlett earned a spot on the Philadelphia Phillies of the National League. In his only major league season, he hit .313 with 18 home runs and 72 runs batted in. Despite this fine showing, the Phillies released him after the season and no other major league picked him up. (Apparently, Arlett was considered a dreadful fielder, though many minor league historians claim he was an adequate glove man.) And special note should be taken of lefthander George Brunet. Between the majors and minors, he pitched in professional ball for 33 years (1953–1985). In his final season, Brunet compiled a minuscule 1.94 earned run average in the heavy-hitting Mexican League; he was 48 years old.

The minors have also showcased their share of legendary teams. The best of these may be the 1937 Newark Bears, a New York Yankee affiliate that featured such future major league stars as second baseman Joe Gordon (an eventual American League MVP), outfielder Charlie "King

> ✓ Second baseman Frank Frisch (.316 lifetime batting average)
>
> ✓ First baseman George Sisler (.340 lifetime batting average)
>
> ✓ Outfielder Mel Ott (511 homers)
>
> ✓ Outfielder Al Kaline (3,007 career hits)

Though he wasn't eligible for induction until the year 2000, Dave Winfield (3,110 hits and 1,833 runs batted in) is a certain Hall of Famer who also bypassed the minor leagues.

Baseball in Japan

Historians credit Horace Wilson, an American professor based in Tokyo during the 1870s, with being the founder of Japanese baseball. Wilson's students called the game *yakyu* (field ball) or *beisu boru*. Amateur baseball flourished in Japan during the early part of the twentieth century. American teams regularly toured the country, and many top U.S. stars — including Frankie Frisch, Babe Ruth, and Casey Stengel — helped teach the nuances of the game to an enthusiastic Japanese audience. Ty Cobb, baseball's career hit king at the time, held baseball clinics in Japan in 1928.

Japan's major leagues

Japan's first professional team, Nihon Undo Kyokai, was formed in 1920. Two more professional teams appeared in 1921, but all three disbanded by 1923 due to a lack of competition. Matsutaro Shoriki, a newspaper magnate, reintroduced professional baseball to his country when he formed the all-pro team Dai Nippon (the forerunner of the current Tokyo Giants) in 1934. Two years later, Shoriki and a group of businesspeople formed Japan's first professional league. In 1950, that league split into the Central and Pacific Leagues. Today, six teams operate in each of the two leagues (see Table 11-2).

Table 11-2	Japanese Baseball
Central League	*Pacific League*
Chunichi Dragons	Chiba Lotte Marines
Hanshin Tigers	Fukuoka Daiei Hawks
Hiroshima Toyo Carp	Kintetsu Buffaloes
Yakult Swallows	Nippon Ham Fighters
Yokohama Bay Stars	Orix Blue Wave
Yomiuri Giants	Seibu Lions

Both leagues include tie games in their standings. Japanese teams carry 28 players on their major league rosters, though only 25 are eligible to play in any one game. Each organization has a 70-man roster, including minor lea- guers. Foreign (non-Japanese) players may hold four of these roster spots. Teams play a 135-game schedule (home and away game breakdowns vary each season) with no playoff format. Regular season games begin during the first week of April and end by the final week of September. The top teams in each league compete in the best-of-seven Japan Series — their version of our World Series — in mid-October.

The quality of Japanese baseball has improved dramatically during the last two decades, though it is not on par with the American game. Japanese out- fielders and catchers lack the throwing strength of American major leaguers. Power hitters are also scarce in Japan. However, Japanese pitching is impres- sive. Whereas the league used to be dominated by control artists, fireballers such as Hideo Nomo and Hideki Irabu have emerged over the past few years. American scouts also have enormous regard for Japanese infield play, which generally equals, if not surpasses, U.S. major league standards.

The stars

Like the United States, Japan has had its share of legendary baseball heroes, all of whom would have been stars no matter where they played. Their num- bers include:

- Sadaharu Oh, who won 15 home run titles, 9 MVP awards, 5 batting championships, and 13 runs-batted-in crowns while hitting — are you sitting? — 868 career home runs.

- Tetsuharu Kawakami, Japan's "God of Batting," who hit .377 in 1951 and managed the Tokyo Giants to 11 pennants in 14 years, including nine straight Japan Series.

- Katsuya Nomura, the "Johnny Bench of Japan," who hit 657 home runs from 1954 to 1980 while catching 2,918 games.

- Left-hander Masaichi Kaneda, who posted 400 career wins and 4,490 strikeouts from 1950 to 1964 while playing with a club that finished in the upper half of the standings only once.

- Yutaka Enatsu, who struck out 401 batters in 329 innings in 1968.

- Kazuhisa Inao, who won 42 games as the Nishitetsu Lions' ace in 1961.

Americans who have starred in Japan include:

- First baseman Randy Bass, a Central League Triple Crown winner (.350 batting average, 54 home runs, 134 runs batted in) in 1985.

- Outfielder Leron Lee, who holds the Japanese record for highest career batting average (.320).

> ✔ Pitcher Joe Stanka, who won the 1964 MVP award when he went 26–7 for the Nankai Hawks.

New Asian Frontiers

Over the past 15 years, professional baseball has become wildly popular in two of Japan's neighboring countries. Taiwan is home to the Chinese Professional Baseball League. Founded in 1990, the league's six teams play a 100-game schedule. Four teams compose the Taiwan Major League, which offers fans a 96-game schedule.

The Korean Baseball Organization has been operating since 1982. Its eight clubs compete in a 132-game season. Chan Ho Park, who made his major league debut with the L.A. Dodgers in 1994, is the first native-born Korean player to achieve stardom in the United States.

Tropical Leagues

In Mexico, Central America, and the Caribbean, baseball is nothing so sedate as a pastime; it's a passion. U.S. sailors and students introduced the game to Cuba around 1866. (See "The Cuban Juggernaut" later in this chapter.) The Cubans, in turn, brought baseball to Puerto Rico, the Dominican Republic, Panama, Mexico, Nicaragua, Venezuela, and Colombia.

The Caribbean Baseball Confederation

With the exception of the Mexican League, which is part of the American minor leagues, most other teams south of the equator play in one of the leagues that compose the Caribbean Baseball Confederation (CBC). These associations are referred to as *Winter Leagues* because their seasons begin in late October or November. There is no regular-season interleague play, but the league champions do compete against each other in the Caribbean World Series held each year in early February.

The following leagues compose the CBC:

> ✔ **The Dominican League:** Founded in 1951, its six teams play a 60-game schedule that begins in late October and usually ends just before the start of the new year. Each organization has a 30-man roster. At the end of the season, the four teams with the best winning percentages meet in a best-of-five semifinals. The two survivors play a best-of-nine series to

determine the league champion. Dominican League franchises include Aguilas, Azucareros, Escogido, Estrellas, Licey, and the Northern Giants (located in San Francisco de Macoris).

✔ **The Mexican-Pacific League:** Not to be confused with the Triple A Mexican League, the MPL was founded in 1958. Its eight teams play a 64-game schedule. The season opens around mid-October and ends in late December. Rosters are limited to 27 players. At the end of the season, the six clubs with the best winning percentages meet in a best-of-seven quarterfinals. The three winners of those series join the loser with the best regular season record in the best-of-seven semifinals. Two finalists emerge from those series to play a best-of-seven league championship. Mexican-Pacific League franchises include Culiacan, Guasave, Hermosillo, Los Mochis, Mazatlan, Mexicali, Navojoa, and Obregon.

✔ **The Puerto Rican League:** Founded in 1938, the oldest Caribbean league features six teams and a 50-game schedule. Clubs begin regular season play in early November and finish in early January. Twenty-six players compose each roster. At season's end, the league's top four teams meet in the best-of-seven semifinals. A best-of-nine final determines the league champion. Puerto Rican League teams include Arecibo, Caguas Criollos, Mayaguez, Ponce, San Juan, and Santurce.

✔ **The Venezuelan League:** Founded in 1946, the league has eight teams in two divisions. The teams play a 62-game schedule that starts in late October and usually ends by New Year's Eve. Rosters are limited to 27 players. Each division's top two teams join a wild-card entry (whichever third-place club has the better regular-season record) in a 16-game round-robin series. The two teams that win that series meet in a best-of-seven playoff for the league championship. Venezuelan League teams include Caracas, La Guaira, Magallanes, and Oriente in the East Division, and Aragua, Lara, Occidente, and Zulia in the West.

Other winter leagues

Four other leagues — three in the U.S. and one on the other side of the world — also provide fans with baseball during the fall and winter months. The Arizona Fall League, which begins its 50-game season in early October, is a terrific place to watch some of your favorite major league teams' top prospects improve their games. All of the league's six teams have multiple working agreements with various major league clubs. For more information, call the league office at 602-496-6700 or fax them at 602-496-6384.

Four teams play a 54-game schedule in the Hawaii Winter League. The season starts the first week of October and ends the first week of December. You can call the league office at 808-973-7247 or fax them at 808-973-7117.

The Maryland Fall League, a four-team confederation that features a 42-game schedule, debuted in 1998. Each club carries 28 players on its roster, many of them Class AA and A prospects putting in a little overtime to hone their skills. For more information, call 301-805-6012 or visit www.mdfallbaseball.com.

The Australian Baseball League (ABL) opens in mid-October and closes during the first week of February. Eight teams play a 60-game schedule. The top four teams meet in a best-of-three semifinal. The survivors of that series play a best-of-three final to determine a league champion. Dave Nilsson, a catcher-outfielder who joined the Milwaukee Brewers in 1992, and Graeme Lloyd, a left-handed relief specialist who helped the New York Yankees win the 1996 world championship, are two current major leaguers who have played in the ABL. You can call the league office at 011-61-2-9437-4622.

The Cuban Juggernaut

Emilio Sabourin founded *Liga de Beisbol Profesional,* Cuba's first organized league, in 1878. Cuba later had a minor league entry, the Havana Sugar Kings, in the International League (AAA). Players from the island who went on to star in the American major leagues included Tony Oliva, Minnie Minoso, Camilo Pascual, Dolf Lucque, Zoilo Versalles, Luis Tiant, Tony Perez, Rey Ordonez, and Orlando "El Duque" Hernandez.

However, shortly after Fidel Castro took power in 1959, the International League transferred the Havana franchise to Jersey City, New Jersey. Castro reacted by banning professional baseball throughout the country. He disbanded all pro teams and forbade Cuba's players from signing major league contracts. The flow of Cuban talent to the U.S. was stemmed at the source.

Castro, a rabid baseball fan who had once been a middling pitching prospect, sought to fill the void by establishing the amateurs-only Cuban League. Its 16 franchises (representing 14 cities) start by playing a 65-game schedule. Eight of these teams go on to participate in a 63-game second season called the Selected Series. Four clubs from that competition continue playing during a February postseason that culminates with the *Series Nacional,* Cuba's version of the World Series.

Most observers agree that Cuba is the world's epicenter for amateur baseball. From 1987 to 1996, the island's national team posted an 80–1 record in international competition. It has not lost a Pan American Games baseball tournament since 1963.

"I covered the historic game between the Baltimore Orioles and Cuban All-Stars in Havana on March 28, 1999. Five Cuban players made a lasting impression on me. Third baseman Omar Linares, long touted as the island's top baseball star, is an exceptional athlete with a good idea at the plate and obvious power. He's something on the order of the Phillies' Scott Rolen. Given some seasoning in the high minors, German Mesa and Marty Paret, both wide-ranging shortstops, could play in the big leagues. Pitcher Jose Ibar possesses pinpoint control although he's not overpowering. He'd probably make it as a long reliever in the majors. Another pitcher, Jose Contrares, is the real deal, gifted with a lively fastball, sharp control, and genuine mound smarts. He could come straight to the big leagues and win."

Required Reading for Minor League Fans

Your local library or bookstore is loaded with many fine books about minor league and international baseball. Here's a sampling:

✔ *Stolen Season* (Random House) by David Lamb. In this remarkable book, the author — a foreign correspondent — rediscovers America by traveling the minor league circuit.

✔ *The Society of American Baseball Research's Minor League Baseball Stars* and *Minor League Baseball Stars 2*. Both of these books offer complete surveys of minor league records. The two volumes include stats for 300 minor league stars as well as profiles of the most successful minor league managers. Both volumes are available through SABR, whose contact information is listed in Appendix B.

✔ *The Story of Minor League Baseball: A History of the Game of Professional Baseball in the United States with Particular Reference to Its Growth and Development in the Smaller Cities and Towns of the Nation* edited by Robert Finch, Ben Morgan, and Henry Addington. Its title is the length of some books, but this volume delivers what it promises. Packed with records and stats, it is the most comprehensive book ever written on minor league baseball as it was played during the first half of the twentieth century.

✔ *Sadaharu Oh and the Zen Way of Baseball* (New York Times Books) by Sadaharu Oh and David Falkner. No book offers more insight into the life of a Japanese baseball player.

Chapter 12

There Are Tricks to This Game: Coaching

*B*aseball managers are responsible for all on-field decisions affecting their teams. Professional baseball managers (usually with the help of an array of coaches) decide what to emphasize in training camp, which players make up the team's roster (though contract considerations determine much of that), who bats where in the starting lineup, and who sits on the bench.

Below the professional level, baseball managers — often called coaches — face even more responsibilities. In addition to making decisions about what happens on the field, managers must decide how to effectively encourage younger players while still offering them sound advice and constructive criticism. In this chapter, we explore how to do all these things and still find time to enjoy the game.

A Manager's Role

BASEBALL SPEAK

During games, managers decide which strategy to employ from inning to inning (though many professional managers trust their veteran players to make those decisions for themselves). Managers call for, among other things, sacrifice bunts, hit and run plays, and stolen base attempts. They occasionally flash the *take sign* when they don't want a hitter to swing at a particular pitch.

Managers impact a game most dramatically with their choices of substitutions. Picking the right pinch hitter or relief pitcher often spells the difference between victory and defeat. Some people say that a great major league manager can add six victories to a team's total during a 162-game season. That may not sound like much, but because every game you don't win is a loss, five additional wins translate into a ten-game spread in the standings. (For example, a team with a mediocre manager may go 81–81 during a 162-game season. If a great manager milks five more wins out of that team, it finishes 86–76). That spread can mean the difference between having a disastrous season or a respectable one, between being an also-ran or a pennant contender.

It is difficult to calculate how many games incompetent managers cost their teams. If a manager's strategy is unsound or the lineup selections fail to maximize a club's offensive potential, you may be looking at another 10-game spread in the other direction. However, much depends on the makeup of the club; a well-schooled, veteran team can band together to overcome a poor *skipper* (manager). But if the manager is also a divisive presence in the clubhouse, an entire season may be undermined.

Managerial responsibilities deepen and broaden below the pro and college levels. If you are coaching a high school or youth team, you must spend more time teaching fundamentals to your inexperienced charges. That task requires patience. Besides being a manager, you sometimes have to assume the role of psychologist and parent figure. This is particularly true if your players are preteens. Many of your young players may be going nose-to-nose with loss, failure, and rejection for the first time in their lives. If you guide them with compassion, each defeat becomes an opportunity for growth and insight. If you ignore their pain, or worse, exacerbate it with ridicule or cold silence, you may scar them for life. Your responsibility is nothing less than that.

Sparky Anderson's Winning Advice

If you're a coach or manager, you can find hitting, pitching, training, and defensive tips to pass along to your players throughout Part II of this book. You can also find 24 defensive strategies in Chapter 9. However, nothing written on any of those pages can illustrate how a manager thinks. To do that, we have brought in the most successful baseball manager of the last 30 years. In 26 seasons as manager of the Cincinnati Reds and Detroit Tigers, Sparky Anderson won 2,194 games (only two managers in baseball history have won more), three world championships, five league championships, and seven division titles. He is the only skipper to guide teams to World Series championships in both leagues. So sit back and discover how a master manager approaches the game.

Note: Although Sparky Anderson's advice stems from his experience as a manager in the major leagues, what he says can be applied to coaching baseball at almost any level.

Know your players

"You should develop enough of a feel for your players that you can sense if something is off just by walking through the clubhouse. This means you have to be able to read a player's face and body language, his whole demeanor so that you can head off a problem before it threatens the team. This also means you have to talk to your players constantly to get some insight into how they think. Knowing your players also means understanding their strengths and limitations. If there is a left-handed junkballer on the mound, and you send up a pinch hitter who has difficulty with slow stuff, whose fault is it when he makes an out? That's your out because you asked him to do something he couldn't do."

Avoid having a happy bench

"You hear about those utility players who play very little but are content with their role on the club. I love those guys — as long as they are on someone else's club. I never wanted anyone on my roster who was happy about not playing. You want guys who want to be out on the field, so that when you give them a chance, they're going to bring some fire to the lineup."

But don't let them get too unhappy

"Keep your bench and your regular starters fresh by weaving players in and out of the lineup all season. In 1976, the Reds had a tremendous starting lineup; we won the division by ten games and were 7–0 in the playoffs and World Series. Our eight regulars each had over 500 plate appearances, but we played them as a unit only 57 times during the season. We gave everyone a chance to contribute."

Know the elements of a winning team

"Pitching, defense, speed, and power, in that order. Power is marvelous, but when you put up eight runs and the other team puts up nine, it can be draining. When you have great pitching, you stop the other team from moving. You can create enough runs to win without using the long ball. On defense, if you give the other team only 27 outs, you have a chance. Give them 28 or 30 outs (by making errors or making mental mistakes), and you're handing their big sluggers extra at-bats to beat you."

"When you have speed, you can drive the other team crazy. I'm not just talking about stolen bases here. I mean going from first to third, pulling the hit and run, faking steals, doing anything that injects movement into the game. When you do that, it is hard for the opposition to get set defensively. I always liked playing against teams that could only slug; if you took away their long balls, you had them. But teams that are always on the go can beat you so many different ways."

The purpose of major league spring training

"Number one, your team should leave camp in top physical condition. If a player is not in condition when the season starts, you're dead with him because he'll be out of shape all season. Number two, drill those fundamentals constantly. For example, in spring training games, any time a runner was on first and a ground ball was hit through to center or right, I wanted him to go to third. I didn't care if we were down by ten runs. If they got thrown out, fine, it was part of the learning process. That's how they found out when they could take that extra base and when they couldn't. I never cared if we won a single game during spring training. My whole focus was on preparation for the regular season."

Use those first five innings

"Don't get the idea I don't like power. During innings one through five, I always wanted to destroy the other team, beat them up so badly that they went home crying to Mama that they didn't want anymore. So we'd play for the big inning and try to blow the opposition out of the park. One of the reasons you do that is that almost every club today has a big closer — a John Wetteland, a Jose Mesa, or a Mariano Rivera. You don't want to get into a war with those guys because nine times out of ten, you'll lose. If you bury the other team early, the closer never even gets up. However, come the sixth inning, if you don't have a lead, you have only 12 outs left to get something going. Now you have to grind it out, steal more, sacrifice runners, do all the little things to create some runs. If your team can't do that, you're stuck."

Criticize in private

"If you want players to be loyal, don't show them up. We had a game in Houston where a player on second was thrown out on an attempted steal of third for the final out of the inning. Now, you should never make the last out of an inning at third, and when a player does it, everyone knows he pulled a rock. When the reporters asked me about it after the game, I said, 'I had a hunch and I sent him.' Well, of course I hadn't, but I was deflecting the blame away from him. Why humiliate him when he already feels bad? You can bet he and I are going to have a long discussion about the mistake, but we'll do that in private. Once a player knows you're going to protect him that way, he'll be receptive to anything you tell him; he'll give you the best effort he's got."

"When some move you make doesn't pay off, never pass the buck. I was managing the Tigers in the ninth inning of a 2–2 tie. We put men on first and second with nobody out. Nine times out of ten, your next hitter is bunting, giving himself up to move those runners into scoring position. But if Cecil Fielder was coming up, there's no way I was asking him to bunt. Cecil was a slugger; bunting wasn't something he did well. So I would just let him do his thing, swing away, to drive in that winning run. If he hits into a double-play, I'm going to take the heat. After the game, I'm going to let everyone know it was my call."

Exercise tough love

"The hardest part of managing is letting a star player know he can't do it any-more. Stars don't want to believe that. Before breaking the news, you must evaluate if the player can still contribute in a different role. For instance, maybe this person can still be effective playing in fewer games against cer-tain types of pitchers. Perhaps he can contribute in a platoon role. Do what-ever you can to get the maximum out of whatever talent remains. Then you have to discover if the player will accept this limited role. If you decide he can't perform in any role on your club, give it to him straight. Some may want you to break the news gently, others may want it without any sugar coating. That's where your knowledge of the player comes into use. I would start by asking the player, 'Have I ever lied to you?' After he said no, I would continue, 'Then I'm not going to start now,' and I would give him my honest evaluation. Of course, this only works if you already built a foundation of trust with the player. That is one reason why you should never lie to your players."

Work with your coaches

"Grant them full authority in their area of expertise. Trust that they will get everything done exactly as you discussed it. Don't be checking up on them in the field. Never second-guess anyone. If your third base coach sends in a runner and the player is thrown out by 20 feet, don't say a word. In 26 years, I never questioned any of my third-base coaches' decisions. Once when a coach tried to apologize for sending a runner who was thrown out, I said, 'Hey, I'm glad you're out there and not me.' That should be your attitude. You also shouldn't think that just because you are the manager, you are superior to your coaches. Each of them will have an area of the game where they know much more than you ever will. Use that knowledge. Go to them for advice."

"You must also back up your coaches. My pitching coach with the Cincinnati Reds, Larry Shepard, used to lace into our pitchers so badly, you could hear him from down the hall. More than once I was tempted to go down to prevent what sounded like murder. I never left my chair. Larry knew his pitchers and understood what it took to motivate them. I had to put my faith in that. And it worked. Our pitchers respected him because he got the most out of their abilities."

Fear nothing

"You know what made Billy Martin (the late skipper of the New York Yankees and other clubs) one of the all-time great managers? Billy was absolutely fearless. He would make moves that he knew would bring him a lot of heat from the press and fans if they backfired, but he didn't care what they said. If he thought a play would win him a ball game, he put it on no matter how crazy it looked to everyone else. Managers can't be afraid of criticism. No one ever wins anything by playing it safe."

Keep it all in perspective

"I never knew any manager who put together a great record without great players. They are what it is all about. Once you think you're the most important part of the team, it's time to look for another line of work. If you're coaching Little League, baseball is supposed to be fun for these kids, so don't overemphasize winning or losing. The best part of your game should be the hot dogs and soft drinks afterwards. And parents shouldn't take things too seriously, either. How can any parent get upset when their child goes 0 for 4 when I can take them to Children's Hospital and introduce them to kids who have only six months to live? Wipe your little ones' tears, give them a big hug, and let them know you'll love them even if they never get another hit."

Choosing a pinch hitter

"I rarely picked pinch hitters on a strict *platoon* basis (lefty hitters versus right-handed pitchers, right-handed hitters versus lefties). Instead, I looked at how you matched up against the pitcher's stuff. If there was a hard-throwing right-hander on the mound, and I had a lefty whose bat wasn't that quick and a right-hander who loved to hit the fastball, the right-hander is going up to the plate. I was more interested in what kind of pitches you could handle than what side of the batter's box you stood in. When I brought in relievers, I applied the same thinking, only in reverse. If I knew a hitter hated the breaking ball, I was bringing in a curveballer even if it meant bringing in a left-hander to face a righty. Now this means you not only have to know what your team can do, you have to know the opposition's personnel as well. I also always tried to save my best pinch-hitter for the late innings when he could come up with the game on the line."

Chapter 13

Men in Blue: Umpiring Like a Professional

*U*mpiring is a demanding job. While a hitter must concentrate on maybe 15 or 20 pitches per game, a home plate umpire must maintain his focus for 260 to 300 pitches per game. On the bases, umpires must be as precise as microsurgeons. That's because baseball is not, as some claim, a game of inches; most of the time a tenth of an inch is the difference between a call of out or safe. So even though they never appear in a lineup, umpires make a critical difference in the outcome of a game.

If you choose to umpire, you assume a great responsibility. The job is demanding and difficult. For more than 33 years, one of the best in the business was National League umpire Harry Wendelstedt, Jr. A consummate professional respected for his fairness and integrity, Wendelstedt also served four terms as President of the Major League Umpires Association. The Harry Wendelstedt School for Umpires (see the end of the chapter for contact information) has sent more umpires to the major leagues than any other school.

In this chapter, we invited Wendelstedt to share his thoughts on umpiring. Listen closely to what he has to say; this is one umpire you don't want to argue with.

The Intangibles

"We can teach an umpire the rules and positions, but we can't teach judgment. You're born with that or develop it by the time you're ready to umpire. You have to be able to make the correct decision in stressful situations. You must be able to think on your feet. And you have to be physically fit so you can get into position in time to make the call."

"Good vision is another requirement. You can wear glasses or contacts to bring your vision up to speed, but you have to be able to see well enough to do your job. I was lucky. I had 20/10 vision for the first 25 years of my career, and then it went to 20/20. That's very helpful."

"You also have to possess the desire to do what is right. Sometimes it's easy to take the easy path. For example, if it's a tie score, two men out in the bottom of the ninth, bases loaded, the count is three balls, two strikes, and the pitcher throws a pitch that is just on the corner, you'd better be prepared to call that strike three and head into the tenth inning. If the pitch is just off the plate, again, you call it ball four, ball game over."

Going by the Book

"If you don't have a firm knowledge of the rule book and all its nuances, you will never be able to umpire on any level and do it well. I'm not just talking about memorization, either. I've had people come to my school who can quote you every rule in the book verbatim, tell you what page it's on and even the paragraph. But they wouldn't recognize that play if it happened right in front of them. You must be able to translate those words into practical application. The rule book must be firmly entrenched in your being as well as your mind."

Calling Balls and Strikes

"Behind the plate, you must assume a stance that allows you to watch the entire flight of the pitch without moving. A good plate umpire stays still throughout the pitch. If you have to move, it can distort your perception and cause you to miss some pitches. You sometimes hear umpires criticized for taking their time making a call. They are just doing their jobs. Good timing is a key element to good umpiring. By that I mean you have to let happen everything that can happen. When people talk about a delayed call, the umpire is just exercising good timing. There is nothing worse than a bang-bang play in which the umpire yells, 'He's out,' only to discover the ball has trickled from the fielder's glove before he made the tag."

On the Base Paths: Positioning Yourself to Make the Call

"Establish a 90-degree angle on each play on the bases as the ball is batted. If a play is going to be made at your bag, you watch the fielder make his throw to ensure it's true. Then your eyes go directly to the bag. You're looking for the runner's foot. You should be able to pick up the flight of the throw with your peripheral vision. Then you listen for the sound of the ball striking the glove and you make your call."

"You are using your ears as well as your eyes on that call, especially on a close play."

"An umpire in the field also has to be aware of where the ball is hit. You don't want to be in the path of a ball so that it strikes your body and interferes with a play. There is one secret for making sure this doesn't happen: Get out of the way! Ballplayers are taught to move instinctively towards the ball. As an umpire, you have to give up that instinct. Learn to pivot so you can get out of the ball's path."

Fair or Foul?

"On a fly ball hit down or near either of the foul lines (which, by the way are really fair lines since any ball that stays on the line is in fair territory), you must straddle the line. Follow the flight of the ball in conjunction with the foul pole. If you are off that line, it can change your perception and you could very well call a fair ball foul or vice versa."

"Any time you are not in the proper position to make a call, you are cheating yourself as an umpire. Below the major league level, there will be times when you are the only umpire or one of only two umpires on the field. If you are working behind the plate and another umpire is at first, it may be impossible for you to assume the correct position when a drive is smashed over third. The ball just moves too quickly. But you have to get as close to the right position as possible."

Umpiring Diplomacy

"When you find yourself in a heated dispute with a player, manager, or coach, you must try to defuse the situation. In order to control both sides, you must exert control over yourself. Don't allow yourself to be pulled into a screaming match. Keeping a level tone, calm the person down by saying something like,

'I want to hear what you have to say, but I can't do that if you're screaming. Just tell me what you have on your mind.' Get them talking in a conversational tone. Let them have their say, then move on. Don't tolerate any excessive abuse."

"With me, a person ran into trouble whenever they put the word 'you' in front of whatever they were yelling. There is profanity on the ball field; you have to tolerate some of that. But when they put a 'you' in front of an expletive, they're making things personal. That's when they're in trouble. You allow someone to heap personal abuse on you, and you will get buried, not just by other players and managers but by your own umpiring partners who won't take that abuse. It's important to maintain the dignity of the position."

"I've met a lot of people who think umpires enjoy throwing people out of games. We don't. The art of arguing in baseball, for an umpire, is to let someone say their peace, to let off some steam, but keep them in the game. I also found that if people know you are fair and reasonable, that you give 100 percent to your job, they give you a certain amount of respect on the field. So it doesn't become necessary to toss them."

Asking for Help

"There will be times when your vision is blocked on a play. For instance, a coach comes over and says, 'Harry, you blew that call — the ball popped out of his glove before he made the play.' If I suspect the fielder or runner's body blocked my view of the entire play, I have an obligation to talk to my partners, who saw the play from another angle, and ask if they saw anything happen. If my partner says, 'The ball popped out, Harry, the runner was safe,' I'm going to change the call."

Dispelling a Baseball Myth

"You often hear that established veterans like Tony Gwynn and Greg Maddux get more than their fair share of calls in their favor. Not true. Umpires don't favor anyone. The reason Greg Maddux has more strikes called for him by the umpire is because Greg Maddux throws more strikes than any pitcher in baseball. He can paint that corner all day long, which is why he is probably the best control pitcher of this decade. And you don't have to worry about the great hitters getting any calls, because if the pitch is close, they are swinging. You're not going to have to make too many calls on Tony Gwynn with a 3–2 count and a pitch on the corner because he's going to be hacking. You'll rarely see him take a good pitch in that situation."

Surviving the Pressure Cooker

"I have felt butterflies fluttering in my stomach before every game I ever umpired, particularly before a World Series or playoff game. That is part of the job. If you don't feel butterflies, then you don't care enough. I wanted to do my very best every time I walked on the field, and that creates pressure. But you learn to love the excitement. I worked five World Series, and, as with any game, you have to bear down on every pitch. That high level of concentration you take to the field will help you overcome any nervousness you might feel. After you call a pitch or two, the butterflies disappear and you settle into what you normally do. All distractions phase out. When I worked World Series games, there were as many as 50,000 or more screaming fans in the stadium. I wouldn't hear them. I was too focused on the pitch and the play. You go into a zone of total concentration, just like a player."

To contact Wendelstedt's umpiring school, write to 88 St. Andrews Drive, Ormond Beach, Florida 32174, phone 904-672-4879, or visit its Web site at www.umpireschool.com.

Chapter 14

Major League Baseball

*Y*ou can follow 30 teams — 16 in the National and 14 in the American League — under the current major league alignment. Spring training starts in late February (when pitchers and catchers report) and continues through March. Each team plays 162 regular season games (81 games at home, 81 in opponents' parks) that begin around April 1. Interleague play (which started in 1997) between National and American League clubs takes place during June, August, and September. The regular season ends during the final week of September, and postseason play starts in the first week of October with the two-round League Championship Series. These series produce a champion for each league (to find out how, see Chapter 17). The two league champions battle each other for the major league championship in the World Series in late October.

Major League Baseball Administration

The Office of Major League Baseball is in New York City (see Appendix B for full contact information). Allan "Bud" Selig, the former owner of the Milwaukee Brewers (his interest in the team is now in trust), was officially elected commissioner of baseball in 1999. His office enforces rules among the owners and proposes policy for both leagues. Paul Beeston, the former president of the Toronto Blue Jays, runs baseball's day-to-day business operations. James Martin is the executive director of Baseball Assistance Team (BAT), an organization that aids former players in times of need. Francis Coonelly of the Major League Baseball Player Relations Committee represents the owners' interests in labor negotiations. Rich Levin serves as major league baseball's executive director of public relations.

The American and National Leagues also maintain offices in New York City (and you can also find their addresses in Appendix B). As we went to press, Gene Budig was the AL president; Leonard Coleman was his outgoing NL counterpart. (Coleman tendered his resignation from the office during the 1999 season.) League presidents implement policy, issue directives, approve contracts, and have jurisdiction over all league matters — including player fines, protests, and other disputes. However, the roles of these positions are about to change radically as the commissioner's office assumes greater control over both leagues.

Donald Fehr doesn't own a club, swat home runs, or throw any high fastballs, yet he may very well be the most powerful man in baseball. Fehr is the executive director of the Major League Players Association, the baseball players' union. (The address for its offices is also in Appendix B.)

The Major League Franchises

In October 1997, Bud Selig announced that the Milwaukee Brewers of the American League Central Division would become the first major league baseball team in this century to switch leagues. The Brewers began play in the National League in 1998. Milwaukee's switch and the addition of the Arizona Diamondbacks expansion team currently give the National League 16 teams competing under the alignment shown in Table 14-1. (See Appendix B for contact information on all the major league clubs.)

Table 14-1	The National League	
NL East	*NL Central*	*NL West*
Atlanta Braves	Chicago Cubs	Arizona Diamondbacks
Florida Marlins	Cincinnati Reds	Colorado Rockies
New York Mets	Houston Astros	Los Angeles Dodgers
Philadelphia Phillies	Milwaukee Brewers	San Francisco Giants
Montreal Expos	Pittsburgh Pirates	San Diego Padres
	St. Louis Cardinals	

In the American League, the Detroit Tigers moved from the American League East to replace the Brewers in the Central division in 1998. The Tampa Bay Devil Rays, another expansion team, took Detroit's slot in the East (see Table 14-2).

Table 14-2	The American League	
AL East	*AL Central*	*AL West*
Baltimore Orioles	Chicago White Sox	Anaheim Angels
Boston Red Sox	Cleveland Indians	Oakland Athletics
New York Yankees	Detroit Tigers	Seattle Mariners
Tampa Bay Devil Rays	Kansas City Royals	Texas Rangers
Toronto Blue Jays	Minnesota Twins	

Each club carries 25 players on its regular-season roster (14 to 16 position players and 9 to 11 pitchers). Rosters expand from 25 up to 40 players on September 1. However, only those players who are on the roster before that time are eligible for postseason play.

A club captures first place in its division by compiling the best won-lost percentage. (You can discover how to calculate that percentage by consulting Chapter 16.)

Both leagues have a rich history that has been vividly captured in countless books. The best of these include:

✔ Harold Seymour's *Baseball — The Early Years* and *Baseball — The Golden Years* (Oxford University Press). Critics have hailed Seymour as baseball's greatest historian. His first volume covers the game from the pre-Civil War years to 1903. Book two continues to 1970. Seymour presents baseball against a historical backdrop that provides the reader with a sociological context for changes within the sport.

✔ Lee Lowenfish and Tony Lupien's *The Imperfect Diamond: A History of Baseball's Labor Wars* (Decapo Press). This book was first published in 1980 and has been recently updated to include events up to 1996. This is the one book you must own if you want to make any sense of the constant turmoil between baseball's labor and management.

✔ *Total Baseball* (Total Sports), currently in its sixth edition, is the game's ultimate reference work. It is chock-full of statistics on every major-league player who ever pulled on a pair of spikes. The 2,538-page volume also has league, team, and ballpark histories, all-time leader lists in every major category, and illuminating essays on such topics as Baseball's 400 Greatest Personalities (including players, managers, umpires, commissioners, and other executives), Caribbean baseball, Jewish ballplayers, Women in Baseball, and a new chapter (inspired by the Sosa-McGwire home run race of 1998) which traces the evolution of the long ball — "Going, Going, Gone." *Total Baseball* also comes in

CD-ROM, handheld, and Internet versions. Most major bookstores carry this 2,538-page masterwork. You can also order copies through the Total Sports Web site at www.totalsports.com.

Many of the best baseball books, such as Leonard Koppett's *Thinking Man's Guide To Baseball* and *Nice Guys Finish Last* by Leo Durocher (with Ed Linn), are currently out of print. You may be able to track them down at the Alibris Web site (www.alibris.com). Alibris couldn't be simpler to access. Key in the book title, press Go, and within seconds you have a list of copies of the book available at various prices based on condition. (For example, hardcover versions of Durocher's autobiography were available for prices ranging from $14–$62.) Alibris guarantees the condition of every purchase; if you're dissatisfied with a book, you may return it for a full refund. Transactions are by credit card only (Visa, MasterCard, American Express, Discover, and JCB).

Society for American Baseball Research

Is Mike Piazza the best hitting catcher of all time? Did Babe Ruth really call his home run against the Cubs in the 1932 World Series? What team originally drafted Tom Seaver out of college and how did they lose him?

You can find out the answers to these and many more questions by joining the Society for American Baseball Research (SABR). Founded in 1971, SABR is a nonprofit organization dedicated to the preservation of baseball history. Its two annual publications, *The National Pastime* and *The Research Journal,* are, by themselves, worth the $35 yearly membership dues ($20 for students or seniors; $45 for fans living in Canada or Mexico; $50 if you live overseas). However, members also have access to the SABR Lending Library, whose comprehensive inventory includes microfilm reproductions of *Sporting Life* (1883-1917) and *The Sporting News* (1886-1957). Besides the two annual publications, SABR annually sends its members nine newsletters and a special magazine dedicated to a specific topic, such as the Negro Leagues, Minor League baseball stars, or nineteenth-century baseball stars. You can also participate in various research committees with top baseball historians.

For membership information — and this is one organization every baseball fan should join — call SABR at 216-575-0500. (You can also find their address and fax information in Appendix B.)

Chapter 15

Off-the-Field Baseball Jobs and How to Snag Them

Alright, so you don't have Mark McGwire's awesome power, Greg Maddux's pinpoint control, or Rey Ordonez's astonishing reflexes. You can still get a position in baseball and even one day find yourself in the Hall of Fame. (Twenty former team executives are currently honored in that august shrine.) So don't abandon your Field of Dreams if you can't make the cut as a player. This chapter describes various positions you can pursue even if your batting average has never broken .100.

Bat and Ball Handlers

No, Bat Boys and Bat Girls are not denizens of Gotham City. They are the ballplayers' on-field valets, in charge of keeping their equipment — particularly their bludgeons of choice — ready at all times. Bat Boys and Bat Girls sit in the dugouts and clear the field of any bats that players toss aside. They then store the bats in their proper slots in the bat rack.

Ball Boys and Ball Girls usually sit on the field in foul territory. They are always gloved because their chief job is to retrieve foul grounders. They never retrieve fly balls because those remain in the province of the fielders. Ball Boys and Ball Girls must be able to defend themselves against the occasional searing line drive, which means good reflexes and manual dexterity are a must.

You can apply for bat and ball handling jobs by sending a letter to your local team's head of stadium operations. In filling these positions, clubs look for teenagers with solid academic records. High marks in deportment carry a lot of weight, so include some glowing letters of reference from your principal or teachers with your application.

Ticket Takers and Ushers

Ticket takers dispense tickets at the ballpark. Ushers must correctly read those ducats and then direct their holders to the appropriate seats. Ushers are also walking information centers. Throughout the game, patrons ask ushers a bevy of questions including where the restrooms are, how to get to the parking lot, and where to go for first aid.

A good usher is familiar with the entire workings of the ballpark and its surroundings. Ushers are also the first line of defense against rowdy customers. However, that doesn't make them members of ballpark security. If a fan gets out of line, an usher calls the head usher or security for assistance. Write your local team for an application for these positions.

Vendors

Vendors sell a variety of foods, beverages, and souvenirs throughout the ballpark. Most vendors work strictly on commission. Which products you sell on a particular night depends on seniority or a random number drawing. How much money you make is often simply a matter of what product you draw. If you're selling beer or hot dogs, you'll probably have a healthy bottom line for the evening. But if you're stuck hawking ice cream sundaes on a frigid night in September, the only compensation you're taking home is the memory of the game. Seniority also determines which part of the ballpark you work in, another important consideration.

Vendors should be physically fit. Those trays strapped around your neck can be heavy, and you are on your feet for most of the game. You can, of course, take the occasional rest, but when you're sitting, you aren't earning.

Teams or the companies that run their concessions advertise for vendors just before the start of the season. However, referrals are key to getting these jobs. If someone who is already vending in a ballpark recommends you for a position, you have a much better chance of getting it. If your application for a vending job is turned down, don't be discouraged. Keep checking back to see whether a position has opened up. Vendors have grueling jobs, and the attrition rate is high.

Groundskeepers

Groundskeepers maintain the diamond's sparkle. They keep the playing field smooth and dry and the grass trimmed (unless management wants it otherwise). Groundskeepers also smooth out the infield dirt in between innings. In more sophisticated parks, groundskeepers oversee a system of underground pumps and drainage devices.

Rain delays are the true test of a groundskeeping crew's mettle. They must cover the field with a tarpaulin quickly before that downpour renders the diamond unplayable.

Maintaining healthy sod is also one of the groundskeeper's primary responsibilities. For that reason, many groundskeepers study their craft in school. Many universities feature agriculture programs that offer majors in soil science with specialties in grounds management. If you want to be a groundskeeper for a team (or for your local golf course, park, or anywhere else the green stuff grows), earning a sheepskin from one of these institutions gives you a powerful advantage. Most groundskeepers start off as interns through their university programs and then go on to regular positions.

If you want to apply for a job with a club, call to find out the name of its grounds crew chief and then direct your resume to him or her.

Trainers

Trainers supervise a team's conditioning, strengthening, and injury rehabilitation programs. They also administer sophisticated first aid whenever someone is injured on the field. (And it isn't unusual for them to assist someone injured in the stands.) Teams look for trainers who are college-educated in sports medicine and board certified. You can send your resume to a team's head trainer for consideration, but many of these jobs come through referrals.

Public Address Announcers

"Now batting for the New York Yankees. . . ." If your baseball dream is to follow in the footsteps of the legendary, sonorous Yankee Stadium p.a. announcer Bob Sheppard, you have to have more than just a good set of pipes. Teams aren't necessarily looking for James Earl Jones to announce the lineups at their games (though they wouldn't turn down the voice of Darth Vader if he applied for the job). Teams do want announcers with clear enunciation. Anyone who sounds like Elmer Fudd with his voice box stuck in a blender probably shouldn't apply. You have to audition to win this spot, and some teams may want to first hear you on tape as part of a screening process.

Broadcasters

In the major leagues, at least two broadcasters work in both the TV and radio booths. One is a *play-by-play announcer* who describes the action of the game. His or her partner is the *analyst,* usually a former major league player or manager, who explains why something happened, speculates on what is about to happen, and shares some insights on a baseball nuance. Below the majors, most broadcasters work solo. If you haven't played or managed, a degree in broadcasting is almost a must here. Teams looking for broadcasters are going to require an audition tape, so it would be worthwhile for you to get a job calling games for your campus radio station.

Front Office Jobs

If you have ambitions of being a *general manager* — the executive honcho who wheels and deals while guiding a baseball franchise's fortunes — you must be willing to start at the bottom. Front office interns and administrative assistants often work long hours for little money. Each team offers a variety of entry-level executive positions. Clubs prefer to fill these slots with applicants who possess degrees in sports administration. If at all possible, choose a university whose sports administration program provides interns for local teams. Internships give you the hands-on experience that stands out on your resume. They also offer you an opportunity to network with the people who make the hiring decisions.

Note: Anyone seeking a front office or broadcast position should attend professional baseball's *Winter Meetings.* Usually held in December, this annual gathering is where you find everyone who is anyone from the executive ranks of the major and minor leagues. As soon as you discover where the meetings are being held (the office of Major League Baseball can give you that information), book your flight and hotel reservations. It's best to stay at the same hotel as the executives so you can do some schmoozing. Send your resume to the team you are targeting well in advance of the meetings. You should also enroll in the employment opportunities seminar annually conducted at this gathering by The National Association of Professional Baseball Leagues (P.O. Box A, St. Petersburg, Florida 33731). During the meetings, you will find any available front office or broadcasting jobs listed in the NAPBL office, usually located in the hotel where the executives stay.

Major League Team Owners

Playing hardball with the big boys doesn't require much. All you need to start is about half a billion dollars in discretionary income. . . .

Baseball job seekers should subscribe to *The Sports Market Place,* a directory published by Sports Careers, a division of Franklin Covey. *The Sports Market Place* carries a comprehensive listing of companies in the sports industry. Sports Careers also maintains a resume bank that is continually tapped by over 2,500 teams and organizations. If you want to contact a major or minor league team to inquire about a position or send off a resume, grab the latest copy of the *Baseball America Directory* (800-845-2726) which is published annually. This directory includes an Events Calendar that usually lists the dates and city for the upcoming Winter Meetings.

Chapter 16

Measuring Performance: Calculating Baseball's Statistics

In This Chapter

▶ Measuring offensive power

▶ Calculating pitching effectiveness

▶ Judging fielding ability

▶ Evaluating your team

*B*aseball fans are amazing. Math may have given them nightmares as students, but let their favorite player make a hit or an out, and they have his slugging average computed before he takes a step from the batter's box. Statistics provide the game's followers with a context that allows them to compare players and eras. To hold your own in any conversation about the sport, you have to know what the numbers mean. So here's an introduction to baseball's primary stats.

Calculating a Batter's Abilities

Mention the numbers 755, 4,256, and 70 to avid baseball fans, and they'll probably rattle off the famous baseball records that correspond to them. (Just for the record, Hank Aaron hit 755 homers in his career, Pete Rose had 4,256 hits in his career, and Mark Mc Gwire hit 70 home runs in 1998.) Even if you don't feel compelled to memorize baseball's legendary numerical feats, this section helps you make some sense out of the many ways that players and fans track and measure offensive ability.

Batting average

A batting average is the statistic used to measure what percentage of a player's at-bats results in a base hit. This statistic made its first appearance in 1864. To calculate it, divide the batter's total hits by his official times at bat:

Tony Gwynn, San Diego, 1997

$$\frac{220 \text{ hits}}{592 \text{ at-bats}} = .372 \text{ batting average}$$

(Yes, you might say Mr. Gwynn can hit a little.)

A hitter's at-bats do not include walks, sacrifice bunts, sacrifice flies, obstruction calls, catcher's interference, or being hit by a pitch. These events count as plate appearances but not as at-bats, so they aren't used to calculate batting average. When the hitter is safe on an error, you credit him with an at-bat, but not a hit.

To qualify for a major league batting championship (which means leading the league in batting average over the course of a season), a player must have 3.1 plate appearances (not at-bats) for every game his team plays. In a regulation 162-game season, a hitter needs at least 502 plate appearances to qualify for his league's batting title.

Today, the average major league hitter bats around .265. However, batting average alone doesn't tell you much about a hitter's ability. A player can have a high batting average, but if he doesn't draw walks or hit for power, he may not be as productive as a low-average hitter who does. For example, in 1969, catcher Manny Sanguillen of the Pirates batted .303 while Carl Yastrzemski, the Boston left fielder, hit only .254. Looking only at their batting averages, you might think Sanguillen out-produced Yaz. But consider these numbers:

Player	Homers	RBI	Runs	Walks	On-Base Pct.	Slugging Average
Sanguillen	5	57	62	12	.325	.407
Yastrzemski	40	111	96	101	.363	.507

When you consider these other numbers, Yaz was far more productive than Sanguillen. (Don't worry if you don't know what an on-base percentage or slugging average is — we address them both in just a moment.) Batting average alone couldn't adequately measure Yastrzemski's contribution to his team. To evaluate a hitter's full value, you must examine *every* aspect of his offense.

On-base percentage

Branch Rickey and Brooklyn Dodger statistician Allen Roth created this statistic during the 1950s. On-base percentage tells you what percentage of a hitter's at-bats results in his getting on base by any means other than an error, interference, or fielder's choice. To calculate this figure, add a batter's hits, walks, and hit-by-pitch (hbp) totals and divide by his at-bats plus walks plus hit-by-pitch plus sacrifice flies.

$$\frac{100 \text{ hits } + 100 \text{ walks } + 10 \text{ hbp} = 210}{530 \text{ at-bats } + 100 \text{ walks } + 10 \text{ hbp } + 10 \text{ sacrifice flies } = 620} = .3387 \text{ on-base average}$$

In this case, the on-base percentage rounds out to .339. The average major league hitter is right around that number. Ideally, the first two hitters in your lineup, the players who jump-start your offense by getting on base any way they can, should have an on-base percentage of .375 or better.

Slugging average

You can derive a player's slugging average by calculating how many bases he averages with each at-bat. To do so, divide the total bases he accumulated with hits by his at-bats. A single equals *one* base, a double *two* bases, a triple *three* bases, and a home run *four* bases. For example, in 1997, Frank Thomas of the White Sox had 114 singles (114 bases), 35 doubles (70 bases), 0 triples, and 35 home runs (140 bases) for a total of 324 bases in 530 at-bats:

$$\frac{324 \text{ total bases}}{530 \text{ at-bats}} = .661 \text{ slugging percentage}$$

The average major leaguer slugs around .420. A hitter with a .450 slugging average has good power; the elite sluggers are at .490 or better. Now you can see why pitchers refer to Thomas as "The Big Hurt."

Base-on-balls percentage

This statistic tells you what percentage of a batter's plate appearances results in a walk. Divide the hitter's total walks by his plate appearances.

Home run ratio

This statistic measures how often a batter homers. To calculate it, divide the hitter's at-bats by his home runs. An average major league hitter gets one home run for approximately every 35 at-bats. (In 1997, Ken Griffey, Jr. averaged one homer for every 10.9 at-bats!)

Stolen base percentage

You can judge a base stealer by the percentage of his stolen base attempts that are successful. Divide his stolen bases by his total attempts. In 1997, St. Louis Cardinals shortstop Royce Clayton stole 30 bases in 40 attempts for a .750 stolen base percentage. The average major league player is successful on 65 percent of his base-stealing attempts, but that is not a good rate. Expert base thieves succeed at least 75 percent of the time.

Strikeout ratio

The strikeout ratio discloses how often a hitter strikes out. Divide at-bats by strikeouts. An average major league hitter strikes out once every 5.5 at-bats or so. Some sluggers tend to chalk up a strikeout for every four at-bats. A great contact hitter like Tony Gwynn, however, may strike out only once every 14 at-bats or better.

Total Average

Washington Post baseball writer Thomas Boswell created Total Average to measure a hitter's complete offensive contribution. Simply put, Total Average is the ratio between the number of bases a player accumulates during a season and the number of outs he makes.

For example, in 1998, St. Louis Cardinal first baseman Mark McGwire hit 61 singles (good for 61 bases), 21 doubles (42 bases), 0 triples (0 bases), and — members of the pitching fraternity may want to avert their eyes now — 70 homeruns. He accumulated a staggering 280 bases with home runs alone, more than the average player totals with all his hits combined. McGwire walked 162 times, had one stolen base, and was hit by six pitches. Adding all these figures produces 551 total bases. Subtracting McGwire's hits (152) from his at-bats (509) leaves 357 outs. Boswell would add eight more outs for the eight double plays McGwire grounded into, bringing his final total to 365 outs. Dividing McGwire's total bases by his total outs gives you the first baseman's

Total Average: a mind-boggling 1.512. How good is that figure? Boswell considers any Total Average over .900 to be in All-Star territory. Anything over 1.000 is a season of Hall of Fame quality. Big Mac's 1.512 in 1998 was off the charts. Only four players in this century have topped it: Babe Ruth (six times), Ted Williams (twice), Roger Hornsby (once), and Mickey Mantle (once).

To learn more about Total Average, grab a copy of *How Life Imitates the World Series*, a collection of Thomas Boswell's finest baseball essays.

Measuring a Pitcher's Performance

Not to be outdone by the hitters, pitchers also have a whole slew of stats to measure pitching performance. The stats covered in this section help you determine how effectively pitchers get out opposing hitters. Although dozens of pitching statistics exist, the critical indicator for any pitcher is wins. Flashy statistics are nice, but the name of the game for any pitcher is winning.

Winning percentage

Simply put, this statistic tells you the percentage of games a pitcher wins in a season. Divide the pitcher's wins by his total decisions (wins plus losses):

Jeff Fassero, Seattle Mariners, 1997

$$\frac{16 \text{ wins}}{16 \text{ wins } + 9 \text{ losses} = 25 \text{ decisions}} = .640 \text{ winning percentage}$$

Generally, better pitchers post winning percentages of .540 or higher. However, if you pitch only .500 (which means you record as many wins as losses) for a club whose won-lost percentage is .400 or worse, your teammates probably call you *ace*. Pitchers who consistently post winning percentages of .600 or better are among baseball's elite performers.

Earned run average (ERA)

This statistic measures how many earned runs (runs that score without benefit of an error) a pitcher surrenders every nine innings. To calculate, multiply the number of earned runs on a pitcher's record by 9 and then divide the result by his innings pitched:

Roger Clemens, Toronto Blue Jays, 1997

$$\frac{60 \text{ earned runs allowed} \times 9 = 540}{264 \text{ innings pitched}} = 2.05 \text{ earned run average}$$

Clemens's 2.05 ERA led the American League in 1997 and helped him win his fourth Cy Young Award.

 Earned run averages have fluctuated widely over the years. When I played, an ERA under 3.50 was considered good. With all the offensive pyrotechnics in baseball today, a pitcher is doing well if he has an ERA of around 4.00. Because of the designated hitter rule, ERAs are usually .20 to .25 points higher in the American League than in the National League. (See Chapter 3 for information on the designated hitter rule.)

Opponents' batting average

This statistic reveals what percentage of batters faced by a pitcher hit safely. To calculate it, divide the number of hits a pitcher allows by the number of outs he records (innings pitched multiplied by 3) plus his hits allowed. As you can see in the following example, it's not as complicated as it sounds.

Getting a decision: The pitcher's dilemma

To earn a victory, a starting pitcher must pitch at least five innings (or four if the game goes less than six innings), and his team must have the lead at the time he leaves the game. If that lead is never relinquished, he gets the win. If the game is tied when a pitcher who has pitched at least five innings is removed for a pinch hitter, and his team goes ahead to stay during the inning in which he is pulled, he gets the win.

When the starter cannot get the win, the victory can go to any relief pitcher who is the pitcher of record at the time his team gains a lead it never loses. Credit a pitcher with a loss if he is charged with the run that beats his team.

If a reliever is the finishing pitcher for the winning team and does not qualify for the victory, credit the pitcher with a save in these situations:

✔ The pitcher gets the final three outs of a game that he entered with his team leading by three runs or less.

✔ The pitcher gets the final out (or more) when he inherits a situation in which the tying run is in the on-deck circle.

✔ The pitcher pitches the game's final three innings regardless of the score. (However, his pitching must be effective in the judgment of the official scorer.)

In 1997, Atlanta's Mark Wohlers recorded 208 outs in 69.1 innings pitched (69.1 × 3):

$$\frac{57 \text{ hits allowed}}{208 \text{ outs } + 57 \text{ hits allowed}} = .2237$$

This figure rounds out to an opponent's batting average of .224. The average pitcher has an opponent's batting average around .265. Outstanding pitchers, such as Randy Johnson and Pedro Martinez, consistently hold hitters below .220.

Determining a Fielder's Reliability

Fielding average reveals what percentage of attempted plays a fielder successfully completes. To calculate this percentage, add the fielder's putouts and assists, and then divide that number by his total chances for fielding a play (putouts, assists, and errors). Fielding average measures surehandedness, not range. Players who don't reach a lot of balls have fewer chances to make errors.

Crunching Your Team's Won-Lost Percentage

This statistic is something of a misnomer because the number only tells you what percentage of games a team has won. You determine it by dividing a team's wins by the number of games played. Want to see a mind-boggling won-lost percentage? Check out the 1906 Chicago Cubs:

$$\frac{116 \text{ wins}}{152 \text{ games played}} = .763 \text{ won-lost percentage}$$

Would you believe they lost the World Series that year? Every team wants to play at least .500 ball. Usually, a .550 winning percentage makes you a playoff contender. However, you can win a weak division with a relatively low won-lost percentage. In 1973, The New York Mets won the NL East with a .509 won-lost percentage and then went to the World Series by beating the — oh, must I relive this memory? — Cincinnati Reds in the league championship series.

The lowdown on statistics

Statistics are often misleading. Everyone believes that a .300 hitter is a good player and that a pitcher with a low ERA is a good pitcher. That belief is not necessarily the case. To be a good player, you have to either drive in runs or score runs (depending on where you hit in the batting order), and the great players do both. A .300 hitter makes seven outs for every 10 at-bats, and if his seven outs come with men on base and his three hits come with no one on base, these hits are not very productive. Run production is crucial. Likewise, many pitchers pitch just good enough to lose. Pitchers will tell you that it is just as tough to win a 5–4 game as it is a 1–0 game, because they have to pitch out of more jams.

Run production is how you measure hitters. Wins and losses are how you measure pitchers. Batting averages and ERAs are personal stats.

Chapter 17

Going All the Way: Postseason Play and the World Series

*G*etting to the World Series — that's the ultimate fantasy for every base-ball player, manager, owner, or fan. At least it ought to be.

I've participated in four World Series (including the Boston-Cincinnati classic in 1975, which many people have called the greatest World Series of all time) and seven National League Championship Series (NLCS). The moment I stepped on the field to play the Eastern Division champion Pittsburgh Pirates for the 1972 National League pennant in my first NLCS, I knew that the postseason is what baseball is all about. The stadiums are packed to bursting, and the spectators are continually on their feet or the edge of their seats. Adrenaline is running high in both dugouts, and the media are everywhere. It feels as if the whole world is watching. Every pitch, every at-bat, every play assumes ten times as much significance as it held during the regular season.

If you can't get excited about postseason baseball, you'd better check for a pulse. To understand what all the hoopla is about, we offer you a bit of the history of postseason play and examine the difficult path teams must tread to reach it.

The Humble Beginnings of the World Series

People who watch very little baseball during the regular season often find themselves riveted to the television when the World Series is broadcast in late October. At its finest, this best-of-seven confrontation between the champions of the American and National leagues has a gradual, dramatic build that makes the Series the most compelling event in sports.

The series was not always quite so compelling. Baseball's earliest "world series" took place in 1882 and consisted of two informal postseason games between Cincinnati of the American Association and Chicago of the National League. The teams split these contests, which received scant press coverage and were seen as little more than exhibitions. In fact, the National League chose not to see them at all. At that time, the National League refused to consider the American Association as a legitimate major league. A standing edict forbade National League clubs from participating in contests against American Association teams. To defy that order without risking expulsion from the league, Chicago had to release all of its players from their contracts before it could face Cincinnati. (The players re-signed with their club as soon as the games ended.)

The National Agreement of 1883 brought peace between the two leagues. One year after the pact was signed, the National League champion Providence Grays met the American Association champion New York Metropolitans for a three-game set. It was billed as a battle for the baseball championship of the United States. However, after the Grays won, the media hailed them as world champions. Subsequently, the phrase World Series began slipping into the baseball lexicon, though the major leagues would not officially embrace the name until the early 1900s.

Series setbacks

From 1885 to 1890, the American Association and National League pennant winners faced each other in series whose lengths varied from 6 games to 15. The National League won five of these six events. But friction between the two leagues forced the cancellation of the championship series in 1891, and shortly after that, the American Association folded.

In 1892, the National League expanded to 12 teams when it absorbed four A.A. franchises — Washington, Baltimore, St. Louis, and Louisville. The league then divided its season into two halves. Boston, the winner of the first half season, played Cleveland, owner of the second half's best record, for the league championship and "baseball's world title." The best-of-nine series was less than a sensation. Fans generally abhorred the split-season concept (it was abandoned after this one season), so they were unable to muster much enthusiasm for the confrontation it produced. A series packed with suspense may have won them over, but it was not to be. Boston shellacked Cleveland five games to none (there was one tie). Due to the disappointing response to the matchup, no championship series of any kind took place during the following season.

Postseason blues

William C. Temple, a noted Pittsburgh sportsman, tried to revive postseason play in 1894 by offering a prize cup to the winner of a best-of-seven series between the National League's top two finishers. For the next four years, baseball hailed the winners of the Temple Cup as world champions. Again, fans failed to embrace this concept and the trophy went back to its original donor.

In 1900, a Pittsburgh newspaper, the *Chronicle-Telegraph,* offered a silver loving cup to the winner of a best-of-five series between the National League's first-place finisher, the Brooklyn Superbas, and the second place Pittsburgh Pirates. Brooklyn won the set, three games to one, but the sparse attendance (the four games attracted fewer than 11,000 fans) convinced the National League owners to once again abandon postseason play.

Success at last

Fortunately, baseball owners gave postseason play one last chance in 1903 after a new National Agreement recognized the recently formed American League as a major league. Barney Dreyfuss, owner of the National League champion Pittsburgh Pirates, challenged the American League champion Boston Pilgrims to a best-of-nine confrontation. Boston established the American League's credibility by winning the series, five games to three. More important, the series generated enthusiastic fan interest.

When the National League champion New York Giants declined to meet the American League champion Boston Pilgrims in 1904, the public outcry persuaded baseball's ruling body, the National Commission, to officially establish the World Series for the following season. The 1905 series between the New York Giants and Philadelphia Phillies officially established the best-of-seven format, which is still followed today. (The leagues experimented with a best-of-nine format from 1919 to 1921, but deemed a nine-game series too long to hold the public's attention.)

The All-Star Game

Since 1933, the stars of the American and National Leagues have competed against each other in the All-Star Game, a midseason exhibition game (which means it is not counted as part of the regular season records) played in a different major league stadium each year. The managers of the previous season's pennant winners lead the AL and NL squads. Fans participate in a nationwide poll to choose the starting lineups (with the exception of the pitchers) for both clubs. The managers' own picks fill out the rest of their 28-player rosters. Each major league club must have at least one All-Star representative. The National League has a 40–27 lead in this "series," but much of that bulge was built from 1965 to 1985, when the NL teams — which were then much deeper in middle infield talent and power pitchers than their American League rivals — won 18 of 20 All-Star Games. Since then, however, the AL has won 9 games out of 12.

Except for 1994 when a players strike canceled the event, both leagues have participated in the World Series — or, to use its more elegant nomenclature, the *Fall Classic* — in every season since. The series has endured to become an American cultural icon.

To find out more about World Series records, history, and heroes, check out these titles:

- *The Complete Baseball Record Book,* published annually by *The Sporting News,* contains all the essential records from both the playoffs and World Series.

- Donald Honig's *October Heroes* is an oral history of the World Series as told by such players as Tom Seaver, Gene Tenace, Johnny Podres, and Lloyd Waner.

- *Eight Men Out* by Eliot Asinof is the best book ever written about the appalling scandal that occurred in 1919 when gamblers bribed members of the Chicago White Sox to lose that year's World Series against the Cincinnati Reds. The fallout nearly destroyed baseball's credibility. Director John Sayles later transformed Asinof's masterpiece into a compelling film starring John Cusack and David Strathairn. This movie is currently available on video.

The Ever-Changing Road to the Series

Before 1969, to qualify for the World Series, a team only had to be the last team standing when its league's schedule came to a close. If your team finished the season with the league's best won-lost record, you were on your way to the World Series. If you were tied with another team after playing all your regular season games, a playoff determined the league champion. (In the National League, a best two-out-of-three game series broke the tie; the American League used a one-game, winner-take-all playoff.)

Expansion and change

Major league baseball's 1969 expansion forever altered the postseason. Franchise owners voted to divide both the American League and National League — each of which had been a single league of ten franchises — into two six-team divisions. Intradivisional opponents played each other 18 times during the season and met teams from its league's other division 12 times per year.

Both leagues also introduced a playoff format (since named the *League Championship Series* or LCS) which required the teams that ended the season with the best records in their divisions to meet each other in a best three-out-of-five series. The winner of each playoff was declared league champion and went on to the World Series. If the season ended with two teams tied for a division lead, they met in a sudden-death, one-game playoff. Whichever club won that contest went on to the LCS. The survivors of those events represented their respective leagues in the World Series. Baseball tinkered with that format in 1985 when it expanded the playoffs to a best-of-seven game format.

Divisional Championships and Wild Card Teams

A more startling alteration to postseason play came in 1994 when the two leagues adopted their present alignment (see Chapter 14 for more details) of three divisions each. The addition of third divisions necessitated the creation of a second tier of playoffs — a three-out-of-five game series followed by a four-out-of-seven playoff to determine a league champion.

The division change also required the inclusion of a *wild card* (an additional playoff qualifier) team in the postseason mix. The rules governing the wild card team may seem a bit complex. To qualify for the wild card, a club must post the best record among its league's second-place finishers. If two teams tie for the division lead, but their records also qualify either for a wild-card berth, both teams make the playoffs. Whichever of the two teams holds the edge in its season series goes into the playoffs as the division champion. If the two are tied for the division lead, but neither team qualifies for the wild card (because a second-place team in another division has a better record than either of the two tied for the lead), the division championship is decided by a one-game playoff.

The club with the best overall record in its league retains the home field advantage throughout the playoffs. For example, after winning a record-setting 114 regular season games in 1998, the New York Yankees were scheduled to host three out of five games during the first round of playoffs (against Texas) and four out of seven games during the second round (against Cleveland).

Which teams oppose each other in the first round of playoffs varies from year to year depending on the identity of the wild card. Usually, the wild card team faces the club with the best regular season record in the first round of the playoffs. However, for whatever silly reason, the wild card team currently cannot play its division leader in round one. Boston was the wild card team in 1999, and it finished second in its division to New York, which again had the best winning percentage in the American League. Instead of playing the Yankees in the first tier of the playoffs, the Red Sox met (and defeated) Cleveland, the team with the league's second-best record.

In case of a tie, scream!

What happens if two teams end the season tied for both the division title and the wild card spot? Three formulas are used to determine which team enters the playoffs as a division leader:

1. The team with the better record of the two in head-to-head matchups is automatically declared the division champion; the other club enters the playoffs as the wild card.

2. If the two teams split their season series, the club with the better record within its division takes the title.

3. If both clubs have identical intradivisional records, the team with the better record over the season's final 81 games is declared the winner. If those records match, the criterion is extended to the final 82 games, then 83, and so on until it produces a clear-cut winner.

Part IV
We Don't Care if We Ever Get Back: A Spectator's Guide

The 5th Wave   By Rich Tennant

"Ted Turner was right—adding 'Matlock' to the Braves' line-up brought in a whole new audience."

In this part . . .

*I*t's time for our surgeon general's warning to baseball spectators: Once you're hooked on baseball, you won't be able to get enough of it.

In this part, we show you how to watch the game, where to sit, and how to keep score. As you become a diehard baseball fan, you'll undoubtedly want as much information as you can get on your favorite teams or players as soon as it's available. So this part covers where to get the most up-to-date baseball information. If you're on the Internet, we also tell you about a number of nifty Web sites to surf. Finally, we give you a brief introduction to the growing phenomenon known as "fantasy baseball."

Time to go to the park.

Chapter 18

Following the Bouncing Baseball

As a spectator, if you haven't experienced a baseball game live, well, you haven't experienced baseball. A ball field is more than mere backdrop; by juxtaposing speed against distance it provides a context for athletic miracles. Juan Gonzalez's latest 550-foot home run is merely a ball hit a long way when seen on television. But when viewed from a stadium seat, it becomes a majestic thing, almost unsettling in its celebration of raw, human power.

Baseball is a sport of nuance, and nowhere but the ballpark can these subtleties be explored and appreciated. Is the shortstop cheating toward second to gain a step on the double play? Is the hitter choking up with a two-strike count? How will the left fielder shade this right-handed pull hitter? Sitting in the stands, you can get an immediate answer to all these questions by simply looking out at the field.

A visit to your local ballpark is also a healthful experience. You get to bond with fellow humans, soak up the sun's vitamin D (if you go during the day), fill your lungs with air made fragrant by freshly trimmed grass, and escape from life's anxieties. It is sort of like going to an outdoor consciousness-raising group — only vastly more entertaining.

Picking the Best Seat (For What You Want to See)

Given the emphasis stadium architects put on unobstructed sight lines, nearly every seat in a modern baseball park (one built or refurbished in the last 30 years) is a good one. As you move around the stadium, you may find that each section offers a different, often contrasting perspective of the game on the field (see Figure 18-1).

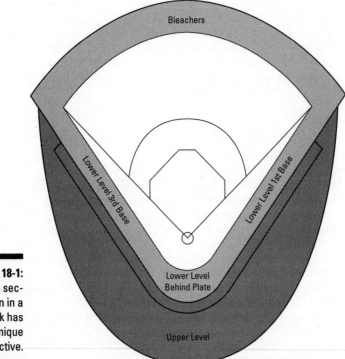

Figure 18-1:
Each sec-
tion in a
ballpark has
its unique
perspective.

Bleachers

Lower Level 3rd Base

Lower Level 1st Base

Lower Level
Behind Plate

Upper Level

Which perspective is best? It depends on what interests you.

- ✔ For the best view of the pitcher-hitter confrontation, camp out behind home plate.

- ✔ Want to watch the double play unfold and see the interaction between pitcher and runner? Head for the first-base side — a seat here also grants you a bird's-eye view of most of the game's putouts.

- ✔ From behind third, you can watch the relay and cut-off plays evolve as the runner races toward third or home against the right fielder's throw.

✔ Visit the upper deck and you can see the field as a giant chessboard with ever-changing defensive alignments.

✔ You get an appreciation of the various angles fly balls assume by sitting in the bleachers (if your park has them), which are located directly behind the outfield fence.

Looking for a Souvenir?

Almost everybody who goes to a ball game fantasizes about catching a foul ball or (even better) a home run. Foul-ball hunters have their best opportunities in the upper deck or lower boxes on the first or third base side of the park. If you want to add a home run ball to your trophy case, sit down near the end of the foul lines (just look for the foul poles to find out where those sections are) or in the bleachers (unless you are at Coors Field, where you can just wait out in the parking lot). Figure 18-2 shows you some of the best places to sit if you want to get your hands on a baseball.

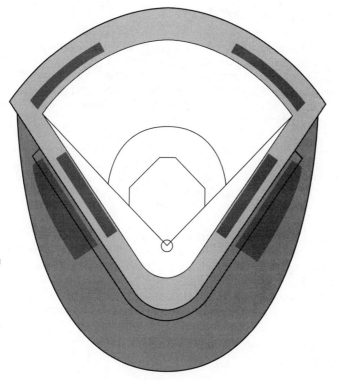

Figure 18-2:
Where to
await a
chance for a
free
souvenir.

Ballpark etiquette

When you visit a stadium, have fun and get loose — but not too loose.

- Refrain from using foul language (because children are usually nearby).

- Don't drink to excess. (In fact, why drink at all?)

- Never, ever throw an object onto the field, run onto the diamond, or do anything that interferes with play.

You are free to do whatever you want with any ball you catch, but you should know that in many ball parks, such as Chicago's Wrigley Field, hometown fans expect you to throw any home runs hit by the visiting team back onto the field.

Real Fans Keep Score

Nothing focuses your full concentration on a baseball game like keeping score. You can purchase *scorecards* from stadium vendors (who sell cards for each game) or at almost any sporting goods store (where they are sold by the book). Or you can make your own. For every game you score, you need two cards — one for the home team, another for its opponents. Figure 18-3 shows what a typical, blank scorecard looks like.

The first thing that you should do is write the date, the weather, and whether the game is a day or night game (or the first game of a doubleheader, and so on) on the top of your scorecard, along with the names of the teams competing. Lots of fans keep their scorecards (and ticket stubs) for a lifetime of memories.

The numbers running across the top of the grid represent innings. Spaces on the left-hand side of the grid are reserved for the players' names, positions, and uniform numbers. You summarize a team's output of hits and runs for each half-inning in the spaces provided at the bottom of the scoring columns. When the game is over, record the player and team totals (at-bats, runs, hits, runs batted in, and errors) in the grid's right-hand columns.

	P	1	2	3	4	5	6	7	8	9	10	11	AB	R	H	RBI	E
TOTALS	R H																

Figure 18-3: A blank baseball scorecard.

The scorekeeper's codes

The first time you encounter a completed scorecard, it may look as if some ancient sage has scribbled on it in hieroglyphics. Don't be intimidated. The scribbling becomes decipherable after you learn the basic symbols. Position players are represented by numbers (not to be confused with their uniform numbers), as shown in Table 18-1.

Table 18-1	The Numbers Assigned to Each Player
Player	*Number*
Pitcher	1
Catcher	2
First baseman	3
Second baseman	4

(continued)

Table 18-1 *(continued)*

Player	Number
Third baseman	5
Shortstop	6
Left fielder	7
Center fielder	8
Right fielder	9

All scoring systems adhere to this numerical code. The symbols and abbreviations used to record the outcome of each at-bat, however, can vary from scorer to scorer. Novice scorers should stick to the basic abbreviations shown in Table 18-2.

Table 18-2   Baseball Scoring Abbreviations

Event	Abbreviation
Single	1B
Double	2B
Triple	3B
Home run	HR
Base on balls	BB
Intentional base on balls	IBB
Balk	BLK
Caught stealing	CS
Double play	DP
Error	E
Fielder's choice	FC
Force out	FO
Fly out	F
Ground out	G
Hit by pitcher	HBP
Interference	I

Event	Abbreviation
Strikeout	K
Line drive	LD
Passed ball	PB
Stolen base	SB
Sacrifice hit	SH
Sacrifice fly	SF
Triple play	TP
Wild pitch	WP

Combine the position numbers and abbreviations to record the sequence of an out — which tells you who got the *assist* (a throw by a fielder that leads to an out), if anyone, and who made the putout. You can also pinpoint the location of a hit or assign blame for an error. For example, if a game's lead-off hitter is retired on a fly ball to left field, mark F-7 in the first inning grid alongside the batter's name. If that ball drops just in front of the left fielder for a single, the proper notation is 1B-7. However, if the official scorer thinks that ball was catchable, enter an E-7. A double-play ball that is fielded first by the second baseman who throws it to the shortstop for the relay throw to the first baseman is scored 4-6-3 DP (second-to-short-to-first double play).

Tracking the runner

Most scorecards have tiny diamonds within the scoring blocks. (If yours doesn't, you can draw them.) Use the diamonds to record the progress of the base runners. Treat the lower point of the diamond as home plate and work around the box counter-clockwise.

For example, if a batter singles to center field, darken the line of the diamond leading from home to first while recording the circumstances that put him on base in the lower right-hand corner.

1B 8

If the same player then advances one base on a wild pitch, darken the line from first to second and put the abbreviation WP in the upper right-hand corner.

When a short single to right moves this player up one more base, darken the line from second to third and note 1B-9 in the upper left-hand corner.

After a sacrifice fly to left field scores the runner, darken the line from third to home, fill in the diamond (to signify a run scored), and put a dot in the box of the batter who drove in the run. The result is a snapshot of a batter's entire one-inning history.

When the half-inning is over, draw a slash across the lower right-hand corner of the scoring block for any batter who makes the last out of a team's turn at-bat.

After you master the rudiments of scoring, you can adopt such advanced techniques as color coding — which requires you to record walks in green, strikeouts in red, and hits in blue. (You'd better own one of those multi-barreled pens, or you may need an extra seat at the ballpark just for your office supplies.)

Many books explain the various, complex scoring systems. But if you are looking for one that entertains as well as informs you, purchase Paul Dickson's gracefully written *The Joy of Keeping Score* (Harcourt Brace).

The Stadiums

We think of the player who hits 40 home runs while playing half his games in Coors Field as a fearsome slugger. But would we hold him in such high regard if his club's home address were the Houston Astrodome and he struggled to hit 15 home runs a season? Conversely, the Colorado Rockies pitcher whose earned run average (ERA) is over 5.00 appears to be one step away from his release. However, let him pitch half his games in Atlanta's Turner Field, and he may find himself among the league's pitching leaders. Ballparks matter. They not only provide a pleasant setting to watch a game, they also profoundly affect run scoring and our assessment of a player's ability. In this chapter, I examine the impact each major league stadium has on performance and perception.

You can find great details about each of these stadiums on the Web at www.ballparks.com/baseball/index.html.

The National League stadiums

William Hulbert founded the National League in 1876. Its original eight franchises were located in Chicago, New York, Philadelphia, Cincinnati, Louisville, Hartford, St. Louis, and Boston. National League stadiums tend to be a bit larger than their American League counterparts. With the notable exception of Coors Field, most of the stadiums seem to have been designed with pitching and defense in mind.

Turner Field: Atlanta Braves

Turner Field is a perfect example of how a stadium can affect our perception of a team. Through most of 1997, analysts struggled to explain Atlanta's loss of offensive vigor. Every Braves regular — with the exception of Jeff Blauser — was less productive than he had been in 1996. What was the cause of this hitting malaise? Age? Complacency? A shift in the setting of the Braves' sun sign? We'll answer the question by rephrasing a slogan from the 1992 presidential campaign: "It was the ballpark, stupid!"

Prior to 1997, the Braves played in Atlanta-Fulton County Stadium, also known as "The Launching Pad." If parents did not want their children to become pitchers, this was the place they took them for discouragement. Atlanta's former stadium was the best hitter's park in baseball.

However, their new field appears to have been custom-designed for the Braves' Cy Young Award-winning pitching staff. It has a huge foul territory; a lot of foul balls that would give hitters a second chance by dropping into the stands in other parks are dropping into fielders' gloves for outs at the Turner. The ball doesn't carry well, especially for the left-handed power hitters who flourished in Atlanta-Fulton County. For example, Atlanta first baseman Fred McGriff's home run production dropped dramatically in 1997. Ryan Klesko, another left-handed Brave, hit 34 homers in 1996; he hasn't hit more than 25 big flies in any season since then. One of the reasons for the decline in left-handed home runs is the huge right-center power alley where the fences are 390 feet from home plate. High fences along the outfield also contain a lot of hard-hit line drives that would be homers in other parks.

When it first opened, many players complained that the Turner had one of the worst infields in baseball. The grounds crew has made some dramatic improvements in recent seasons. The tightly-shorn grass and smooth infield produce few bad hops.

A final word here to prove the impact a ballpark can have: On the road, the Braves have been their usual, dangerous selves. The ballpark changed — not the team.

Wrigley Field: Chicago Cubs

Since its opening, Wrigley has been considered a hitter's paradise, but the park is deceptive. When the wind is blowing in, this stadium favors pitchers, particularly those who are adept at getting batters to hit ground balls. And during the late innings of day games, hitters can have a tough time picking up pitches coming out of the shadows. However, when the wind shifts outward, scoring goes up nearly 40 percent, and a batter's chances of hitting a home run double. I hit my first major league home run in this park. Right-handed sluggers tend to do well in Wrigley. The grass in this park is usually kept tall, so it can be difficult for hitters to drive the ball past the infield.

Cinergy Field: Cincinnati Reds

For me, this ballpark will always be Riverfront Stadium because that was its name when my teammates on the Big Red Machine and I called it home. This is not a park of extremes; it doesn't really favor hitters or pitchers. Home-run sluggers do get some help — though nothing like they receive in Camden Yards (Baltimore) or the Big A (Anaheim). It's difficult to hit a triple here. The turf is hard, but not to the point that it unduly hinders the infielders. Any fielder chasing a foul pop must keep in mind that the bull pens reside along each foul line.

When I was playing here, Cincinnati general manager Dick Wagner and I used to have a running debate about the hitting background. My teammates and I wanted something darker. However, some optometrist had told Dick that a gray background would make it easier for the hitters to pick up the ball. We couldn't convince him otherwise, but we still managed to score a few runs.

Coors Field: Colorado Rockies

Coors Field is baseball's black hole for hurlers. Pitchers who visit Coors are often never seen or heard from again. This is the greatest hitter's park of all time. Since the field opened in 1995, Colorado and its opponents have scored nearly twice as many runs at Coors as they do on the road. Because of this, the park's dimensions often surprise people. They expect Coors to be a bandbox. Its playing field is actually slightly larger than average. Home runs launch themselves into orbit because of the thin, mile-high atmosphere.

And this isn't just a home-run park. Because the visibility at Coors is excellent, you can get a good read on a pitcher's offerings. The spacious playing field inflates extra-base hit totals and batting averages. Teams whose outfielders possess below average speed are at a particular disadvantage here. Coors Field also features a defensive quirk: During the mid-summer months, the setting sun shines directly into the first baseman's eyes, at times making it difficult to pick up throws.

Complete games for a pitcher are a rarity at Coors. Few pitchers dare throw anything near the heart of the plate, so you see an unusually high number of walks and deep pitch counts. Any Rockies pitcher who maintains an earned run average (ERA) under 4.50 should be congratulated. In 1999, Colorado's Pedro Astacio was 17–11 with a club-leading 5.04 ERA. He did not get any Cy Young Award votes — one has to wonder if any Rockies pitcher ever will — but someone should have given him the Purple Heart.

County Stadium / Miller Park: Milwaukee Brewers

County Stadium won't be with us much longer; Miller Park is scheduled to be the Brewers' new home sometime during the 2000 season. County Stadium demonstrates a bias for pitchers: Run scoring here is annually below the league average. This is a daunting park for sluggers; if you don't pull the ball directly down the line, it's not easy to hit one out of the park. This makes it a good stadium for fly ball pitchers. However, County Stadium is a downright chamber of horrors for hurlers lacking pinpoint control. Apparently the mound is poorly maintained, so walk totals soar.

Miller Park was originally slated to open on April 1, 2000. However, a tragic construction mishap, in which three workers were killed, has delayed the stadium's debut until a date that remained undetermined as we went to press. The park's estimated dimensions indicate that, like County Stadium, Miller will be friendly to pitchers.

Pro Player Stadium: Florida Marlins

This stadium has two deep power alleys, so if you want to see baseball's most exciting hit — the triple — this is the park. Pitchers enjoy an advantage here because of the spacious outfield; the Marlins' ERA is nearly a full point lower at home than on the road. In 1997, Marlins ace Kevin Brown was an excellent pitcher no matter where he took the mound, but he was darn near unhittable on his home ground. Batters who spray hits to all fields also find success here, but hitters like that usually do well in any environment.

Pro Player is built for speed; a team needs an outfield composed of sprinters to track down those balls that shoot through the gaps.

The Astrodome / Enron Field: Houston Astros

The Astrodome's final season was 1999. The park had been where pitchers went to lick their wounds after a series at Coors. It was the best pitcher's park in the major leagues. The Astrodome was baseball's first fully enclosed stadium — the first to offer baseball played on a surface other than grass. Batted balls received no help from wind currents; your best shots often plummeted before they got anywhere near the fence.

After my days with Houston, the fences were moved in about 15 feet (4.6m). But it stayed a pitcher's park. To win in the Astrodome, your team had to be fundamentally sound. Playing tight defense was a must — runs were always at a premium so you couldn't give any away. And your team had to do all the little things on offense: steal bases, execute the hit-and-run, and bunt runners over. Of course, a club should be able to do those things in any park, but it was particularly important here.

Strikeout pitchers like J.R. Richard and Randy Johnson thrived in the Astrodome. It will be interesting to see how Houston's pitchers and hitters adjust to their new digs at Enron Field. This cutting-edge facility will feature a retractable roof and grass field (bye, bye AstroTurf!). After looking at its dimensions, Jimmy Wynn may want to come out of retirement. The new home of the Astros will probably be a hitter's haven. With the left field fence only 315 feet from home plate, the Toy Cannon would be on the heels of Sosa and McGwire in the home-run derby. However, pitchers will find some solace in the new stadium's deep center field. Enron Park is scheduled to open March 25, 2000.

Dodger Stadium: Los Angeles Dodgers

One of the reasons the Dodgers seem to have great pitching year-in, year-out is their ballpark. (Signing talented pitchers like Sandy Koufax, Orel Hersheiser, and Kevin Brown is another reason.) Hitters don't see the ball well here, and the ball doesn't carry. Maybe it's the smog's fault. There is also an unusually large foul area. Dodgers batters usually hit 10 to 30 points higher on the road with much better power numbers.

Olympic Stadium: Montreal Expos

This is another pitcher's park with a fast artificial surface. The fences were moved in a few seasons back to make life easier for pull hitters, but there is still plenty of outfield in which to lose hits. Olympic Stadium features a hard, marble-smooth turf; batters can get a lot of base hits driving ground balls through the infield. Former Montreal shortstop Mark Grudzielanek was a master at slashing the ball down either line for doubles when he played his home games here. Infield quirk: There is a metal door hidden beneath the portion of the infield located between first and second. It makes for some strange hops.

This is not a good park for ground-ball pitchers; the artificial turf infield is just too fast. Power pitchers who induce fly balls have an overwhelming advantage here.

Shea Stadium: New York Mets

It certainly isn't the Houston Astrodome, but Shea is a tough park for home-run hitters. In the park's first 36 seasons, only nine different Mets have slugged 30 or more home runs in a season. (In contrast, the Arizona Diamondbacks had three players with 30 or more dingers in 1999 — only their second year of existence.) As the ball leaves the pitcher's hand, it momentarily gets lost in the background and can be difficult to track. Pitchers are doubly tough at night. The field is relatively poorly lit and the air seems to thicken, making it hard to drive the ball. Strikeout pitchers — who don't give the hitter much time to see the ball anyway — can swagger as they take the mound at Shea. However, ground-ball pitchers who rely on brains rather than brawn don't usually fare as well, particularly during the day.

Hitters have an extra split second to recognize a soft-tosser's stuff, and the Shea infield isn't in great shape. Ground balls are an adventure on this surface.

Veterans Stadium: Philadelphia Phillies

They claim the field is composed of Astroturf, but put one cleat on it and you would swear that the Phillies are playing on cement. Managers can't regularly play a slow third baseman or first baseman in this park; the ball gets by them too quickly. Teams need rangy infielders with powerful throwing arms that allow them to play deep, particularly at third and short. Outfielders also have to be fast and strong-armed or the opposing team will bury them with extra base hits.

Veterans Stadium has always been a good park for left-handed line-drive hitters. When the Phillies won their last National League championship in 1993, their lineup often contained six left-handed hitters and two switch-hitters. Only one of that bunch (catcher Darren Daulton) hit more than 20 home runs that season, but Philadelphia still managed to lead the league in runs scored and doubles. The park was no small factor.

Three Rivers Stadium: Pittsburgh Pirates

This is a neutral park if there ever was one. Pirates hitters generally hit as well here as they do on the road. If the stadium offers a slight advantage to anyone, it is left-handed home-run hitters who hit towering fly balls. Three Rivers seems to work against batters with line-drive power.

This stadium — like Veterans Stadium, Busch Stadium, and Cinergy Field — is often cited as an example of the "cookie cutter" stadiums built in the late '60s and '70s. (See Figure 18-4.)

Busch Stadium: St. Louis Cardinals

This used to be an atrocious park for home-run hitters. The Cardinals won National League pennants in 1985 and 1987 with only one batter (outfielder/first baseman Jack Clark) hitting as many as 20 home runs. They also captured a world championship in 1982 without a single 20-home-run man. Busch Stadium was carpeted in Astroturf in those days, and the Cardinals game was built around speed.

Team management has moved in the fences a tad since then, so it's a bit easier to hit home runs. They've also torn up the turf and returned to natural grass. Despite these alterations, Busch is still a below-average power park; the ball gets no help in the still air. Of course, climate conditions don't matter when that Paul Bunyan among homer-run hitters, Cardinal first baseman Mark McGwire, strides to the plate. As they say around both leagues, Big Mac can hit the ball out of any park in America, including Yellowstone.

Figure 18-4:
Three Rivers
Stadium.

National Baseball Hall of Fame Library, Cooperstown, NY

Qualcomm Stadium: San Diego Padres

Here is all you need to know about Padres right fielder Tony Gwynn: He has won eight batting titles while playing in a park that decreases batting averages sometimes to an extreme. In 1997, Padres center fielder Steve Finley hit .216 at home while batting .303 on the road. It's as if he were two different players. Smog is a factor in the poor visibility, and the San Diego infield is slow. Would-be ground-ball base hits are gobbled up before they reach the lip of the outfield grass. Ground-ball pitchers are right at home here. Left-handed fly-ball/power pitchers, however, are at a disadvantage in San Diego. It is relatively easy to hit home runs in this park, particularly if you are right-handed. Qualcomm tends to suppress doubles and triples no matter which side of the plate you hit from.

3Com Park / Pacific Bell Park: San Francisco Giants

Whenever I think of San Francisco, I recall an image of Juan Marichal throwing that high curve against the wind so it would drop straight down as it got to the plate. Tough pitch.

Fielders always yearned to torch this place. When 3Com Park was called Candlestick Park, the gust could roll in off the bay to chill you even on a midsummer night. The wind was so powerful it blew 5-foot 11-inch, 185-pound reliever Stu Miller off the mound during the 1961 All-Star Game. Runners were on base so the umpires charged Miller with a balk.

After the park was somewhat enclosed, the wind no longer blew straight in anymore. Instead, it swirled around, like a giant whirlpool. Third basemen often danced fandangos under balls that were eventually caught by the shortstop. The minicyclone would even alter the path of softly hit ground balls. The left-field line at 3Com was only 7 feet closer than the right one, yet the park favored right-handed home-run hitters by a wide margin. Giants left fielder Barry Bonds would have posted better numbers in almost any park. Again, it was the wind. The currents pushing toward left field are usually stronger than those toward right field are.

A lot of Giant hitters won't be sorry to kiss 3Com/Candlestick goodbye as they move into their new Pacific Bell Park in April, 2000. The wind won't be as much of a factor, and left-handed pull hitters will salivate when they see that right field porch only 307 feet from home plate.

Bank One Park: Arizona Diamondbacks

When I first saw the model for this new park, its dimensions suggested a neutral field with perhaps a slight bias toward the pitcher. Forget it. This is another hitter's paradise. When Bank One's retractable roof is open — which is most of the time — long balls positively soar through Arizona's warm desert air. Bank One's deep outfield features a lot of quirky angles so triples come relatively easy here. The stadium is family friendly with a play area that features a swimming pool. By the way, the Diamondbacks' retractable dome is a state-of-the-art affair that supposedly opens and closes much faster than any dome in either league.

The American League stadiums

Ban Johnson founded the American League in 1900 and declared it a major league in 1901. It was not officially recognized as a major league until 1903. The original eight franchises were located in Chicago, Boston, Detroit, Philadelphia, Baltimore, Washington, Cleveland, and Milwaukee.

Edison International Field: The Anaheim Angels

For years this was a pitcher's park. Then in 1979, the Angels erected three-tier seating behind the outfield walls. That construction enclosed the stadium, cutting off the wind. As a result, the ball started flying out of there. From 1994–1997, the Angels played in the best home-run hitter's park in the American League. It was especially friendly to left-handed power hitters like Anaheim center fielder Jim Edmonds. However, in 1997, management started a second renovation that opened up the centerfield area. The wind once again became a factor as home run totals dropped, particularly for left-handed hitters. However, winds gusting about in right center still aided some right-handed sluggers. Edison International also depresses batting averages because visibility is poor.

For a long while, the infield of this stadium was notoriously rocky. You were more likely to see an infield error occur in this park than in any other American League stadium. Since the renovations, however, players say it is a much fairer infield.

Oriole Park at Camden Yards: The Baltimore Orioles

Visit Camden Yards and step into a time warp. This park is a throwback to the great bandbox stadiums of the 1930s, like Philadelphia's Bakers Bowl. Whoever the architect was, he had to be a hitter. The foul territory is tiny and the fences are cozy-close. You will see a lot of home runs and doubles in this park, but the small dimensions make triples a rarity.

Keep an eye on the right fielder. The ball can take any number of crazy hops off of that tall wall and scoreboard that stand behind him. Like Anaheim, this is a park where left-handed power hitters flourish.

Fenway Park: The Boston Red Sox

Think Fenway and you think of the Green Monster in left field, Ted Williams, Jim Rice, Carl Yastrzemski, and all those 10–9 slugfests. Great hitter's park, right? Not anymore. In 1989, Boston constructed 600 stadium club seats above the grandstand behind home plate. Broadcast booths and a press box were installed atop that. Fenway's home improvements altered the park's wind currents in favor of the pitcher. Scoring has decreased ever since. It's still a good place for enhancing your batting average (its small foul area contributes to that), but it actually suppresses home run totals. Outfielders have to be quick to cover the vast real estate in Fenway's right field. If you are playing shallow and a ball gets past you, it can roll into Triple City. Left fielders must contend with the crazy caroms balls take off of that Green Monster. (See Figure 18-5.)

Comiskey Park: Chicago White Sox

This stadium should warm the heart of any second baseman. Groundskeeper Roger Bossard and his crew maintain the infield so meticulously that the ball rarely takes a bad hop. This is a pitcher's park. Batting and slugging averages tumble when hitters spend any time here; nearly all the White Sox hitters fare much better on the road than at home. It makes you appreciate what an extraordinary hitter Frank Thomas has been throughout the '90s. Thomas once said that the park cost him more than 100 home runs over the course of the decade.

Figure 18-5:
The Green Monster looms at Fenway.

National Baseball Hall of Fame Library, Cooperstown, NY

Jacobs Field: Cleveland Indians

If it's late or early in the season, bring an overcoat. The wind off the nearby lake can be frigid. Jacobs Field has a well-deserved reputation as a hitter's park; visiting batters love to take their cuts here. However, The Jake can be hospitable to pitchers during those cold spring and fall evenings. Many make the mistake of calling Jacobs Field a home-run hitters park. It really isn't. Balls don't carry well to left field under any conditions and the 19-foot high left-field wall prevents many long drives from reaching the seats. A row of white buildings located beyond the centerfield fence makes it difficult for hitters to pick up certain pitches, another factor that diminishes offense. The reason people think of the Jake as a home-run haven is the Cleveland lineup, which is usually stacked with talented sluggers.

Tiger Stadium / Comamerica Park: Detroit Tigers

If you have a favorite left-handed slugger, Tiger Stadium was the place to watch him play. The short porch in right field was an inviting target for the likes of Ken Griffey, Jr. and Tino Martinez. Other hitters didn't fare as well. Many long fly balls — sure home runs or extra-base hits in other stadiums — were nothing but outs in this park's cavernous center field. The unusually high infield grass usually thwarted batters who hit the ball on the ground. Ground-ball pitchers, of course, flourished here.

Tiger Stadium closed its gates for good at the end of the 1999 season. In April 2000, the Tigers will take the field in Comamerica Park. Pitchers won't catch much of a break in their new surroundings. Comamerica features even dimensions similar to those found in Tiger Stadium, and its center field won't be nearly as large. However, plans call for a 398-foot left center field fence.

Kauffman Stadium: Kansas City Royals

Home-run hitters know that this is the toughest long-ball park in the American League. Its dimensions are actually smaller than Colorado's home-run paradise (Royals management recently brought in the fences), but the ball just doesn't carry well. Line-drive hitters who can drive the ball into the gap for doubles and triples fare best in this environment. George Brett, who hit nearly everything on the line, almost hit .400 while playing here. His teammate Hal McRae, a similar hitter, won the American League Runs Batted In (RBI) crown at the age of 37.

Kauffman Stadium's grounds crew is considered the crème de la crème of the American League. They keep the Royals infield in immaculate condition.

Hubert H. Humphrey Metrodome: Minnesota Twins

They called it the Homerdome when it first opened in 1982, but that was a misnomer. Only until very recently home runs were hit here at a rate below the league average. It is, however, a great park for doubles and triples. You won't see a lot of infield errors in the Metrodome; this is the fastest artificial turf in the game; the ball either scoots right to you for an out or zips past you for a hit. Visiting outfielders hate the place. If you aren't used to it, tracking a fly ball against the off-white backdrop of the Metrodome ceiling can be an imposing task. Balls seem to drop from out of nowhere and then they play hopscotch on the turf. This quirk contributes to Minnesota's enormous home field advantage. In 12 postseason games played in the Dome, the Twins are 11–1, including 8–0 in the World Series. The park has fond memories for me because I got my 2,500th major league hit here.

Yankee Stadium: New York Yankees

The myth is that Yankee Stadium favors left-handed power hitters. Actually it is a boon for left-handed pull hitters. If you can jack the ball down the line, you'll get some extra short porch home runs. Left-handed Yankees sluggers who often hit the ball to the opposite field — Babe Ruth, Lou Gehrig, and Reggie Jackson come to mind here — usually stroked more home runs on the road than at home. The park helps a hitter like first baseman Tino Martinez, though he is powerful enough to hit the ball out of any park. Right fielder Paul O'Neill, who is just as big, strong, and left-handed as Martinez, hits the ball to all fields, so the park deprives him of home runs. With its expansive center field and generous foul territory, Yankee Stadium, despite the long-ball heroics that helped make it famous, is a pitcher's park. After appearing on the mound here, Dodger pitching great Don Drysdale likened it to pitching in an airport.

Oakland Alameda County Coliseum: Oakland Athletics

This is the best pitcher's park in the American League. Visibility is poor at the Coliseum, so batters tend to strike out more often here than in other stadiums. Statistics demonstrate that the park gives a slight edge to right-handed power hitters, which makes the 30 plus home-run seasons by A's left-handed sluggers Matt Stairs and Jason Giambi in 1999 seem all the more impressive.

Safeco Field: Seattle Mariners

The Mariners moved from their former digs at the Kingdome to Safeco on July 15, 1999, so we still don't have enough data to know what sort of pitchers or hitters this park will favor. The Kingdome was a hitter's Field of Dreams. Management asserts that Safeco will be a neutral stadium with a slight bias toward pitchers. Early indicators support that assessment. In the 42 games played at Safeco in 1999, Seattle hitters hit 47 home runs, a healthy output, while the team's home ERA plummeted from 6.67 to 4.02. Long-ball lovers take note: A short right-field porch should prove friendly to left-handed pull-hitters.

Safeco features a three-paneled retractable roof; it doesn't seal the stadium, but it covers it like a gigantic umbrella so that an open-air environment is sustained even during inclement weather.

Opposing teams never relish visiting the Mariner's home field. Seattle's fans are the most raucous in baseball. They can electrify their team with their cheering while taking the opposition out of the game.

The Ballpark At Arlington: Texas Rangers

Strange park. Generally, hitter's stadiums promote power, but Arlington is brutal for home-run sluggers. Former Texas first baseman Will Clark, a 15-year major league veteran, once said it was the most difficult field he had ever seen for driving the long ball. And with its short right-field seats, the Ballpark was supposed to be tailor-made for left-handed hitters like Will the Thrill. Juan Gonzalez would probably hit 50 or more home runs if he played his home games in another park. Yet, the field is conducive to scoring a lot of runs because so many triples and doubles are hit here.

Players call the rock-hard infield the worst in baseball; grounders that would be outs in most stadiums rush past infielders for singles or down the line for doubles. When the sun resides in the gap between the Ballpark's upper and lower decks, outfielders can lose sight of the ball. Arlington's error rate is 25 percent above the league average, even though the Rangers have been a team of sure-handed fielders over recent seasons.

SkyDome: Toronto Blue Jays

Right-handed hitters who spray the ball around thrive here; left-handed sluggers don't. When the retractable dome is open, the wind tends to gust toward home plate making it difficult to hit the ball for distance. When the dome is closed, hitters gain a slight advantage. Otherwise, it's a fairly neutral park. SkyDome's artificial turf infield may be the truest in baseball. (Probably because it's held together by Velcro rather than the zippers used to bond other turfs.) You get the feeling that customs officials turn away bad bounce base hits at the border.

Tropicana Field: Tampa Bay Devil Rays

Tropicana Field features one of the smaller outfields in all of baseball. Pitchers who induce fly balls may have trouble here. Hitters who can drive the ball into the gap benefit. The park is asymmetrical so it doesn't favor righties or lefties. Tropicana's dome is nonretractable. Devil Rays play on artificial grass, though their turf infield does feature all-dirt paths. This means that groundballs shoot through the infield faster.

Stadium Statistics

Table 18-3 gives you the details on all the major league stadiums. (Because of space limitations, all these dimensions are in feet. If you want to talk meters, just divide the feet by 3.28.)

Table 18-3		Major League Stadium Statistics					
Park	**LF Line**	**Left CF**	**Center**	**Right CF**	**RF Line**	**Surface**	**Capacity**
Turner	335	380	401	390	330	Grass	50,528
Wrigley	355	368	400	368	353	Grass	38,884
Cinergy	330	375	404	375	330	Artificial	52,953
Coors	347	390	415	375	350	Grass	50,200
County	315	376	402	376	315	Grass	53,192
*Miller Park	342	374	400	378	356	Grass	43,000
Pro Player	330	385	404	385	345	Grass	40,585
Astrodome	325	375	400	375	325	Artificial	54,370
*Enron Field	315	n/a	433	n/a	325	Grass	42,000
Dodger	330	385	395	385	330	Grass	56,000
Olympic	325	375	404	375	325	Artificial	46,500
Shea	338	378	410	371	338	Grass	55,777
Veterans	330	371	408	371	330	Artificial	62,363
Three Rivers	335	375	400	375	335	Artificial	48,044
Busch	330	375	402	372	330	Grass	49,676
Qualcomm	327	370	405	370	330	Grass	46,510
3Com Park	335	365	400	365	328	Grass	58,000
*Pacific Bell	335	n/a	404	420	307	Grass	42,000
Bank One	330	374	407	374	334	Grass	48,500
Edison Field	333	376	408	365	330	Grass	45,050
Camden Yards	333	364	410	373	318	Grass	48,876
Fenway	310	379	420	380	302	Grass	33,871
Comiskey	347	375	400	375	347	Grass	44,321
Jacobs Field	325	370	405	375	325	Grass	42,865
Tiger Stadium	340	365	440	370	325	Grass	46,945
*Comamerica	345	n/a	420	n/a	335	Grass	42,000
Kauffman	330	375	400	375	330	Grass	40,625

(continued)

Table 18-3 *(continued)*

Park	LF Line	Left CF	Center	Right CF	RF Line	Surface	Capacity
Metrodome	343	385	408	367	327	Artificial	48,678
Yankee	318	399	408	385	314	Grass	57,545
Oakland	330	362	400	362	330	Grass	43,012
Safeco	331	390	405	387	327	Grass	47,000
Arlington	332	390	400	381	325	Grass	49,166
SkyDome	328	375	400	375	328	Artificial	50,516
Tropicana	315	370	407	370	322	Artificial	45,200

* Indicates new stadium; dimensions are estimated.

When You Can't Get to the Park

If you're like most fans, you see the majority of your baseball on television, which is a terrific way to learn about the sport. When you watch games on the tube, you don't have to do any work. The camera people direct your attention to all the important action. If you miss a critical event — a fielding gem, a clutch hit, or dramatic strikeout — replays give you multiple chances to view it. Stop-action and slow-motion shots help you to dissect a play from a variety of angles.

All the major networks are using computer graphics to analyze pitch locations, *hit spreads* (those places on the field where a batter's hits are most likely to fall), defensive alignments, and batter-pitcher matchups. You don't have to look at a single scouting report. The announcers always have a wealth of data at their disposal, so you're going to get information you can't find anywhere else. And, best of all, if there is a rainout, you're already home.

Be sure to check out Chapter 19 for information on where and when you can catch a game on TV (and on the radio, too).

Chapter 19

Keeping Up with the Show: Baseball Online, on the Air, and on the Newsstand

● ●

In This Chapter

▶ Surfing for baseball on the Web

▶ Finding baseball on TV

▶ Reading about baseball

● ●

*T*he enormous amount of media coverage devoted to baseball reflects the sport's enduring popularity. And the coverage doesn't end with the regular major league baseball season. You can lounge in front of the fire in the dead of winter and still enjoy plenty of baseball action — without leaving the comforts of your living room.

Baseball in Cyberspace

Back in the old days (last year, for some of us), you had to travel to your nearest newsstand to get the latest baseball scores and updates. Now you can get scores, news, and a wealth of other information at the click of a mouse. Thousands of baseball Web sites abound on the Internet. This section highlights some of the most popular ones.

Fastball

Baseball zealots should bookmark this Web site on their start page; you can access it at www.fastball.com. Want to know who won that late-night West Coast game that's so crucial to your favorite team's pennant hopes? This site gives you the answers you need. Fastball features all the latest scores (which are regularly updated), stats, and clubhouse gossip from both the major and minor leagues. Best of all, you can listen to live broadcasts of your favorite team's game by accessing Fastball's On the Dial feature. (You need to have Real Player in order for this to work correctly.)

MLB@Bat

In 1995, baseball became the first major league sport to go on the Internet (and the Seattle Mariners was the first team to have its own Web site). You can access the big league site, MLB@Bat, at www.majorleaguebaseball.com. Then get ready to dive into a treasure trove of baseball delights. You can find such goodies as the latest results from the Arizona Fall League, trivia contests, the complete records for last season, and a bevy of highlight films. During one online venture, we even stumbled onto a live conference call between all 30 major league managers. During the regular season, you can summon up the latest standings, league leaders, plays of the week, and live broadcasts of games you can't see anywhere else.

The Negro Baseball Leagues

James A. Riley, director of research for the Negro Leagues Baseball Museum, is the editor of this Web site at www.blackbaseball.com. The site is an archival resource that acquaints you with the rich history of the various Negro leagues, their players, managers, owners, and teams. This site also serves as a clearinghouse for Negro League books (sold through a discount bookstore) and memorabilia such as jackets, caps, and autographs.

The Baseball Server

Although it is chock full of major league information, the Baseball Server at www.nando.net/sportsserver/baseball/mlb.html is also the site to visit if you want find out what is happening in the minor leagues, from AAA ball to the independents. The Baseball Server features standings, stats, records, players of the week, and new highlights.

The National Baseball Hall of Fame and Museum

The National Baseball Hall of Fame on the Web at www.baseballhalloffame. org cannot give you the same thrills as an actual visit to Cooperstown, but it's the next best thing. This site offers users an online tour of the Hall of Fame, its museum, and its library. The Fall Classic page presents the history of the World Series as told through audio and video clips.

Total Baseball Online

Who holds the record for home runs by a National League switch-hitter? How many games did Babe Ruth win as a pitcher? The best place to find out is this Web site (www.totalbaseball.com), which is affiliated with *Total Baseball,* the official encyclopedia of the major leagues. You can download all the material found in that volume, including its illuminating articles on various aspects of baseball history. (By the way, the answers to our trivia questions are Howard Johnson, who hit most of those homers as a third baseman with the New York Mets, and 96 pitching wins for Babe Ruth.)

Ballparks by Munsey & Suppes

Are you a ballpark buff? Does just a glimpse of Wrigley Field's near-mythic ivy-covered walls set you to swooning? Have we got a Web site for you! Ballparks by Munsey & Suppes (www.ballparks.com/baseball/index.htm) has all the information you could ever want about major league ballparks present, past, and future — including seating plans, field dimensions, interior and exterior photos, turf type (for example, the Baltimore Orioles play on Maryland Bluegrass in Camden Yards), and historical summaries.

The Sports Network

This Canadian network's Web site at www.tsn.ca is one of the most creative in all sports. Besides the usual stats, standings, and records, it has featured interactive games such as Diamondball, which allows fans to perform as virtual managers. The Couch Master, fast becoming a Canadian Internet legend, runs a rollicking chat room. During the 1999 World Series, fans of this site had the opportunity to engage in lively chats with top baseball stars like pitching ace Roger Clemens and future Hall of Famer Dave Winfield.

Skilton's baseball links

This Web site, accessed by keying in www.baseball-links.com, links fans to nearly 5,000 baseball sites and updates. Talk about a baseball cornucopia.

Major league team sites

All 30 major league franchises now boast Web sites so you can keep up with your favorite team's latest doings with the click of a mouse (see Table 19-1).

Table 19-1	Major League Team Web Sites
Team/Site	*Neat Features*
Anaheim Angels www.angelbaseball.com	This site broadcasts quality video highlights of every game from the current schedule including clips from just completed games.
Arizona Diamondbacks www.azdiamondbacks.com	This site features a scoreboard you can store and refer to on your desktop while working on that great American novel or surfing other sites.
Atlanta Braves www.atlantabraves.com	This site gives the latest stats and scores, which are regularly updated by CNN/Sports Illustrated. It also has a virtual tour of Turner Field filmed from every perspective.
Baltimore Orioles www.theorioles.com	This site gives you immediate access through colorful icons to the Orioles minor league system. It's a terrific resource for Fantasy Leaguers scouting for the next Cal Ripken or Mike Mussina.
Boston Red Sox www.redsox.com	This site has a lively chat room that includes archival transcripts of past brouhahas between Red Sox fanatics.
Chicago Cubs www.cubs.com	This site has dazzling graphics featuring colorful video highlights of game actions and special events such as the introduction of the Cubs' All-Century Team.
Chicago White Sox www.chisox.com	This site has the most extensive archival section of all the team Web sites, featuring text by Richard Lindberg, author of *The White Sox Encyclopedia*.

Team/Site	Neat Features
Cincinnati Reds cincinnatireds.com	This site features Cyber Skipper, a game that offers fans www.the chance to win prizes for accurately predicting the game-by-game performances of their favorite players.
Cleveland Indians www.indians.com	Kids Stuff offers enough games, trivia quizzes, and playing tips to keep the younger Indians fans in your household glued to the keyboard for hours.
Colorado Rockies oradorockies.com	A handy Help page offers you www.col-all the plug-ins you need to access this site. Fastball Arcade lets kids take their cuts at Coors Field Stadium. A Blake Street Bash (a home run in the mile high city) turns on the water fountains.
Detroit Tigers www.detroittigers.com	This site has an all-time roster that includes everyone who ever wore a Tiger uniform. Want to know if shortstop Milt Bolling ever played alongside his second baseman brother Frank in Detroit? This site is the place to find out.
Florida Marlins www.flamarlins.com	Florida was redesigning this site as we went to press.
Houston Astros www.astros.com	This site offers a free e-mail account so Houston fans can give the front office an earful on how to run the team. And yes, the 'Stros do answer their mail.
Kansas City Royals www.kcroyals.com	This site has a sophisticated search engine that accesses information promptly.
Los Angeles Dodgers www.dodgers.com	This site has a broadcast clip of Brooklyn Dodger outfielder Al Gionfriddo robbing Joe Dimaggio of extra bases with a circus catch during the 1947 World Series.
Milwaukee Brewers www.milwaukeebrewers.com	Stadium buffs have heard all about the club's new home, Miller Park. This site offers those buffs the artists' renderings of the stadium, which are as beautiful as oil paintings.

(continued)

Table 19-1 *(continued)*

Team/Site	*Neat Features*
Minnesota Twins www.twinsbaseball.com	A daily poll invites fans to sound off on such burning Twins' issues as which player should be named the team's rookie of the year.
Montreal Expos www.montrealexpos.com	This site is available in both English and French.
New York Mets www.mets.com	This site features a wealth of video clips, including one of Mets great Tom Seaver pitching his fabled Imperfect Game against the Chicago Cubs on July 9, 1969. (Seaver didn't allow a single Cub to reach base until Chicago sub Jimmie Qualls ruined his perfect game bid with a two-out base hit in the ninth inning.)
New York Yankees www.yankees.com	Audio of legendary Yankee Stadium announcerBob Sheppard welcomes you to this Web site. A time machine icon links fans to this franchise's storied past.
Oakland Athletics www.oaklandathletics.com	This site has lively animated graphics and a speed link that helps you access information quickly.
Philadelphia Phillies www.phillies.com	This site offers Phanzone, an interactive section designed primarily for kids that includes mazes, coloring books, score keeping lessons, and screen saver downloads.
Pittsburgh Pirates www.piratesball.com	Construction images of the new PNC ballpark appear on this site. An icon provides fans with access to California Fall League information.
San Diego Padres www.padres.com	This is a bilingual (Spanish/English) Web site featuring chat rooms, a slew of video clips, and virtual Padre postcards.
San Francisco Giants www.sfgiants.com	This site features up-to-the-minute statistics from STATS Inc. and an interactive schedule that fans may download. Virtual Dugout gives fans a seat view generator, so you can check out the site lines from any section of Pacific Bell Park.

Team/Site	Neat Features
Seattle Mariners www.mariners.org	This site gives you your choice of 11 downloadable screen savers, live cam coverage of noteworthy events such as the construction of Safeco Field, and fun polls. (Fans were recently asked to watch and then vote for their favorite team commercials.)
St. Louis Cardinals www.stlcardinals.com	St. Louis's version of longball lover's heaven: a downloadable 20MB video of Mark McGwire's greatest hits (his record-smashing 70 home runs from the 1998 season).
Tampa Bay Devil Rays www.devilray.com	This Web site features a guide for those baseball warblers among you craving an audition to sing the National Anthem before a game at Tropicana Field.
Texas Rangers www.texasrangers.com	This site has perhaps the most comprehensive News and Notes section of any Web site.
Toronto Blue Jays www.bluejays.ca	For baseball history buffs, this site's unrivaled archival file offers thumbnail sketches of each Blue Jay season.

Baseball on the Tube

Who said that baseball on television was boring? This is your chance to prove that person wrong. Following is a guide to get you pointed in the right direction — toward your television screen.

ESPN

This cable network, based in Bristol, Connecticut, begins its regular-season baseball coverage on opening day. ESPN broadcasts Sunday night games as well as two games each Wednesday for a total of more than 75 regular-season exposures. It also carries divisional playoff games during the postseason. Fans can get the latest scores and game gossip on *Baseball Tonight,* which airs every evening throughout the baseball season.

ESPN also affords baseball wide coverage all year round on its flagship news program, *Sportscenter*. The show appears at regular intervals throughout each day. ESPN2, the little sibling of ESPN, does not offer live coverage of baseball. However, the ESPN2 sports ticker, which runs during its broadcasts of other sports, offers you up-to-the-minute game scores, transactions, and additional bits of news. ESPN2 also covers some off-field baseball events, such as the expansion draft and the Baseball Hall of Fame induction ceremonies. Both networks broadcast college baseball games. Consult your schedule to find out who plays and when.

Forgive us for mixing our media, but ESPN Sports Radio — a network with 375 affiliates around the country — broadcasts all postseason games (including the World Series), the All-Star Game, and a selection of regular season contests. Its All-Star coverage includes two events that take place the day before the game: the popular Home Run Derby and the All-Star Game Gala.

Fox Broadcasting

Ruppert Murdoch's Fox Network brings you 18 regular-season Saturday games starting in late May. Fox/Liberty, the network's cable arm, divides 52 national exposures between its Fox Sports Network and FX. As explained in the next section, Fox alternates its postseason coverage with NBC.

NBC

The network that made television history with *Baseball's Game of the Week* does not broadcast regular-season games under the current TV contract. However, it does alternate coverage with Fox Network for the All-Star Game, the League Championship Series, and the World Series. In 1998, NBC covered the All-Star Game and the American League Championship Series, while Fox covered the World Series and the National League Championship Series. The two networks switched assignments in 1999 and will trade back once more in 2000. (ESPN also covers some League Championship Series games as part of this postseason trio.)

The Sports Network

The Sports Network (TSN) is an independent cable network in Canada. In 1999, a typical broadcast year, TSN featured 80 Toronto Blue Jays games, 25 Montreal Expos games, assorted games from the Fox Network, and full coverage of the postseason.

The Classic Sports Network

Even when the snow is piled up to your rooftop, you can still watch baseball. Tuning in to the Classic Sports Network is like stepping into a time machine. The cable network doesn't carry any live baseball telecasts, but it does bring you some of the greatest games ever played in their entirety. You'll see the Brooklyn Dodgers win their first and only world championship, Nolan Ryan pitch a no-hitter, the storied sixth game of the 1975 World Series between the Red Sox and Reds, and much more. Check your cable listings to see if your carrier provides the network.

Caribbean League telecasts

Many Spanish-speaking networks carry baseball from the Caribbean leagues during the winter months. You can watch players like Juan Gonzalez, Bernie Williams, and Ivan Rodriguez strut their stuff while you wrap Christmas presents. Consult your local TV listings for times and schedules.

Baseball in Print

If you don't want to play or watch baseball (or look for it on the Web), perhaps you'd like to read about it. This section describes some great starting points for you.

- *USA Today* (703-276-3731) provides fans with excellent national baseball coverage daily. Unlike many local papers, it rarely brings a hometown slant to a game or story. *USA Today Baseball Weekly* (703-558-5630) is the best source of week-to-week coverage, particularly during the off-season. You can call its fine back-issues department to research any articles you may have missed on the stands.

- *The Sporting News* (314-997-7111) is an excellent weekly magazine/newspaper that covers all the major league teams throughout the year as well as other sports.

- For comprehensive coverage of a particular baseball news story or event, read *Sports Illustrated* (212-522-1212).

- *Baseball America* (800-845-2726) is published every two weeks; therefore, many of its major league stories are old news by the time a copy reaches your hands. However, no publication can surpass its coverage of minor league and college baseball. If you are in a fantasy league and want to chart the progress of an up-and-coming prospect, a subscription to this magazine is a shrewd investment. (See Chapter 20 for more information on fantasy leagues.)

Other publications for your baseball reading pleasure include:

- ✔ *Baseball Digest* (847-491-6440). A monthly compendium of baseball articles written by leading sportswriters from around the country.

- ✔ *ESPN, The Magazine* (212-515-1000). A sports fanzine published every two weeks whose mesmerizing graphics and illuminating sidebars pull the reader into the text.

- ✔ *Street & Smith's Baseball* (212-880-8698). The most respected of the preseason baseball annuals.

- ✔ *Street & Smith's Sports Business Journal* (704-973-1400). Gives you the story of the game off the field while offering a glimpse of the economic hardball played in front offices throughout both leagues.

- ✔ *Who's Who In Baseball* (212-807-7100). The complete minor and major league records of nearly every current major league player. It is updated annually.

- ✔ *Beckett's Baseball Card Monthly* (972-991-6657). A guide to the fluctuating baseball card market (the Dow Jones often exhibits less volatility) by the leaders in the industry.

Chapter 20

Fantasy Baseball

. . . .

In This Chapter

▶ Understanding the appeal of fantasy baseball

▶ Drafting, playing, and scoring

▶ Excelling as a fantasy team manager

▶ Playing computer ball

. . . .

Millions of people play fantasy baseball every year. "What's the big deal?" you ask. Fantasy leagues let you act as general manager for a team of major leaguers in a baseball universe of your own creation. You get to pit your executive skills against an entire league of virtual general managers who try to guide their teams to the pennant. After scouting and signing players, you spend the entire season modifying your club through trades, free agent drafts, and other transactions. If you win a championship, you get to take home a little prize money, bask in the applause of family and friends, and have a bottle of Yoo-Hoo poured over your head (one of Fantasy Baseball's more endearing rituals).

Daniel Okrent — whose contributions to baseball literature include the aptly named *Ultimate Baseball Book* (Houghton-Mifflin) — created the first fantasy league in 1980 while dining in the Manhattan bistro La Rotisserie Française with several other devotees of the National Pastime. The originators named the game Rotisserie Baseball after the restaurant. (Many players today often use the terms Rotisserie Baseball and Fantasy Baseball interchangeably.)

What the Heck Is Fantasy Baseball?

Fantasy baseball is a game you play with 10 to 12 people. Each team selects 23 major league players who compete against other teams of 23 players based on real-life players and their regular-season statistics. The week before the start of the major league season, you gather with the other "owners" in your league and hold an auction-style draft where each owner purchases players. After each of you fills his roster of players, the competition begins.

Your team battles against the other teams based on the real-life statistics of the players drafted. You don't play individual games in fantasy baseball; instead, you try to accumulate the best totals possible in each statistical category.

What baseball statistics do you use? Most fantasy leagues use the eight categories (four hitting, four pitching) shown in Table 20-1.

Table 20-1	Fantasy Baseball Scoring Categories
Offense	**Pitching**
Total runs batted in (RBI)	Team ERA (See Chapter 16 for information on calculating ERA)
Total home runs	Total wins
Team batting average	Total saves
Total stolen bases	Walks plus hits divided by innings pitched ratio (WHIP)

The goal is to select players who will amass the highest totals in the categories (except for ERA and WHIP, where the lowest total wins). Find out more about scoring in the section "Figuring your point total and winning" later in this chapter.

How Do I Play?

Covering all the nuances of fantasy baseball in a single chapter is impossible, so you get only the general stuff here. Check out Glenn Waggoner's *Rotisserie League Baseball* (Little, Brown) to find out more and help establish the official rules for your league. *Fantasy Sports Online For Dummies* by Jim Keogh and Gus Nunziata, published by IDG Books Worldwide, Inc., covers baseball in addition to many other fantasy sports.

Starting a league

Starting a league is easy. Here's what you do:

1. Recruit 11 friends.

Twelve is the usual number of teams for a fantasy league, but you can play with fewer.

2. **Select a date to hold your annual player draft.**

   Most leagues hold the draft the weekend before the major league season begins. If this date doesn't work for your busy schedule, try to hold the draft two weeks before the start of the season or the weekend after baseball's Opening Day.

3. **Choose to play with either National League or American League players. (See Chapter 14 for more information on the two leagues.)**

   Limit your fantasy league to selecting players from only National League teams or only American League teams. Nearly all fantasy leagues choose only one league.

4. **Agree on an entry fee.**

   This dollar amount can be as high or low as you like. Pool the entry fees together to form the *pot* — the cash paid out to the winners at the end of the season.

That's it. Start gathering information on your favorite players and get ready to draft!

Drafting a team

Fantasy leagues have a genuine salary cap; you can't spend more than $260 for your entire roster. You don't have to play with actual money, however; you may credit an imaginary $260 to each team. But you must keep the $260-to-23-players ratio. (See the next section, "Filling out your roster," for the position-by-position breakdown of the 23-player roster.)

Although no team must spend all $260, spending less isn't wise. Always try to spend all your money on draft day to maximize your chances of getting all the players you want.

Assign a drafting order for calling up players to the auction block. For example, Team A may start the draft by saying, "Ken Griffey, Jr. for $1." The other owners begin calling out bids, always upping the bid in increments of at least $1. When the bidding slows, the owner who started the bidding, in this case Team A, gives fair warning. ("Griffey going once, going twice. . . .") If no other owner ups the bid, the last bidder wins Griffey, Jr. Team B then calls up a player, and then Team C, and so on until all teams have drafted 23 players. Setting up a draft order ensures fairness because all owners get equal opportunity to call up players for auction.

Designate two people as official secretaries to record all the players, dollar amounts paid for each player, and remaining dollar amounts for each team. Accurate records help to resolve any potential conflicts.

Filling out your roster

Your roster must consist of the following:

- ✔ Two catchers
- ✔ One first baseman (first and third basemen are also known as *corners*)
- ✔ One second baseman
- ✔ One shortstop
- ✔ One third baseman
- ✔ A back-up second baseman or shortstop
- ✔ A back-up first or third baseman
- ✔ Five outfielders
- ✔ Nine pitchers

If you are playing with American League rules, you need to also draft a designated hitter. (See Chapter 3 if you don't know what a designated hitter is.) If you play by National League rules, draft a utility player (an extra outfielder, infielder, or catcher).

A player qualifies at a certain position by playing at least 20 games at that position during the previous year. For example, if a player appeared in at least 20 games each at second base and shortstop last year, you may play him at either position. If a player played 125 games at catcher and 15 at first base, you may only draft him as a catcher. The position qualifying rule varies widely from league to league; refer to Glenn Waggoner's *Rotisserie League Baseball* for more information.

Nearly all leagues also draft a group of *reserves*. Use these players to fill in for injured or traded players. Because so many leagues treat the reserve list differently, refer to the book *Rotisserie League Baseball* to help you formulate a reserve list policy for your league.

Managing your team after the draft

After the draft, you can kick back, relax, and watch your team in action. Or, to really have some fun, you can start calling fellow owners to make trades. Trading players with other owners adds spice to any league and can help you improve your team in the process. For every player you trade to a team, you must get a player in return. After completing a trade, all teams involved (yes, you can negotiate multiteam deals) must have 23 players on their rosters.

When a flesh-and-blood major league player is traded out of his league, released, put on the disabled list, or dispatched to the minors during the actual season, you can replace him in your lineup. For example, if Ken Griffey, Jr. breaks his leg in April and misses the entire season, you can replace him with a player from your reserves or acquire a new player.

Once again, thousands of rule variations exist for handling player movement during the season. Refer to the book *Rotisserie League Baseball* to help your league adopt a policy for picking up new players during the season.

Taking care of administrative tasks

As you may have guessed, running your own fantasy league involves some work. Here are some tips for minimizing the work and maximizing the fun:

- **Adopt a written set of rules.** Absolutely, positively do this or you'll face dozens of arguments throughout the season. Take an existing set of rules, such as the ones in *Rotisserie League Baseball,* and use them exactly the way they are or modify them to meet your league needs.

  Don't be afraid to tweak the so-called traditional rules of fantasy baseball. Create whatever rules you think will make the game as fun as possible.

- **Appoint a commissioner.** Choose someone, preferably the most ethical owner in your league, to wear the commissioner's hat to enforce rules and arbitrate all disputes.

- **Buy a good statistics software package or pay for a stats service.** A good software package allows you to download stats via computer and prepare detailed weekly reports and standings for each team. Appoint a statistician (preferably the computer guru in your league) to oversee the operation. If you don't have a computer or want to offload the work, subscribe to a statistics service which, for a fee, calculates all your statistics and standings and mails the weekly results to each owner.

  Check the classifieds in *Baseball Weekly* or search the Internet under "Fantasy Baseball" to see what's available in both stats software and services. Stats services usually charge a yearly fee per player; you can purchase the software for a one-time fee. A service definitely costs more but is convenient and involves almost no work on your part.

Figuring your point total and winning

Rank teams throughout the season from first to last in each of the scoring categories. In a typical 12-team league, you award 12 points for every first place finish, 11 for second, 10 for third, and so on down to 1 point for 12th place. For example, say your team has the rankings shown in Table 20-2 in a 12-team league.

Table 20-2	A Scoring Example	
Category	*Place*	*Points*
Total Home Runs	1st	12
Total RBI	3rd	10
Batting Average	6th	7
Stolen Bases	5th	8
Pitching Wins	2nd	11
Pitching Saves	10th	3
ERA	8th	5
WHIP ratio	12th	1
Total		57

You then compare your 57 total points to the other teams' total points. At season's end, the club with the most points finishes first. If you play for cash, award the prize money as follows (or create your own prize money distribution):

✔ 50 percent of the total prize money pool for the pennant winner

✔ 20 percent for second place

✔ 15 percent for third

✔ 10 percent for fourth

✔ 5 percent for fifth

Some Tips for Fantasy Baseball Success

Use the following information to keep your team near the top of the standings and your sanity on an even keel:

✔ **Gather info, more info, and even more info.** Gather as much information on players as you possibly can. Information gathering is the key to drafting success.

Check out as many preseason publications as you can. *USA Today*'s *Baseball Weekly* puts out an excellent preseason fantasy baseball issue in mid-March that contains loads of info, including projected draft dollar values for each player.

✔ **Carefully monitor your money during the draft.** Remember, you have only $260 to spend on 23 players. Plan wisely.

✔ **Choose players who stay healthy.** Injuries can destroy even the strongest team. Try to avoid the injury-prone players.

✔ **Beware of Spring Training phenoms.** Just because a rookie has a great Spring Training (baseball's preseason) doesn't necessarily mean his success will carry over into the regular season. Don't overbid for a player based solely on his success in the preseason.

✔ **Watch out for the World Series factor.** If a player had a great World Series the year before, chances are owners will overbid for him in the next year's draft. World Series heroes usually remain fresh in everyone's mind on draft day. Don't get suckered into overbidding for them.

✔ **Remember, there's always next year.** Is your team mired in last place? Don't worry, hope springs eternal; next year could be the year you win it all.

HEADS UP

Economics 101: Supply and demand in fantasy baseball

Here's where you finally find a practical use for that high school or college economics course you took years ago. Just as scarcity of oil in Saudi Arabia causes gasoline prices to rise in the U.S., supply and demand of players dictates the prices paid in fantasy baseball drafts. A short supply of certain types of players sends bids soaring through the roof. For example, each team in the majors typically includes a _closer_ (a relief pitcher who finishes off games). Because closers accumulate most of the saves (one of the scoring categories in fantasy baseball), most drafts place a premium on the short supply of each league's outstanding closers. (Count on paying $25–$35 for each closer.) Similarly, demand rages for _four category players_ — offensive players who excel in all four scoring

categories: batting average, home runs, RBIs, and stolen bases. For example, in 1999 Chipper Jones hit .319 with 45 homers, 110 RBIs, and 25 stolen bases — the type of season that fantasy owners drool over. Expect to pay around $35–$45 for scarce, four-category players like Jones.

Unique events during your draft may cause player values to fluctuate as well. For example, if three teams still need a first baseman and only one good first baseman remains available, you'll pay a pretty penny for him or else get stuck with a lousy first baseman. Also, watch out for the favorite team factor: If most of your league's owners follow the Cubs, for example, expect a high demand and overbidding for Cubs players.

Baseball on Your PC

Not content to draft a team of players and then follow their progress through the daily box scores? Want to know the thrill of managing your club to a World Series title? Computer baseball games put you right in the dugout, where you can watch the teams you draft and manage battle their way through a full season of competition. More than 100 such games are on the market today. The best of them include:

✔ **Strat-O-Matic Computer Baseball.** The undisputed king of tabletop sports games, designer Hal Richman's baseball simulation offers an extensive range of managerial and general managing options. Strat-O-Matic sells team discs from every year since 1901. You can replay entire seasons or recreate classic World Series, League Championship Series, and All-Star Games. You can even disperse the players within a league into a free agent pool and draft entirely new teams.

Strat-O-Matic allows you to trade and release players (you can match your swapping skills against your computer's) or augment your club with minor league call-ups. You can carry over your draft team's roster from one season to another.

Batters are rated for speed, performance against righties and lefties, base-stealing, bunting, clutch-hitting, and their ability to execute the hit-and-run play. Fielders are rated on range, fielding average, and throwing arm strength. Pitchers are rated for endurance (the latest version of the game allows for pitch counts), performance against righthanded and lefthanded batters, and their ability to close games.

Ballparks are also a factor in Strat-O-Matic (see Figure 20-1). That home run down the rightfield line in Yankee Stadium may be a harmless fly ball in Turner Field. Should your right fielder crash into the wall while pursuing that *can of corn* (easy pop fly), he might put in some time on the disabled list.

Playability is one of Strat-O-Matic's most attractive features. First-time users can have their leagues up and running in less than half an hour. In just minutes, you can play a nine-inning game against a friend, the computer, or solo. Clicking the Quick Play option lets you replay a full day's schedule of games in seconds or an entire major league season in under ten minutes (depending on the speed of your computer). Want to abandon the dugout for the field? With the Create A Fringe Player option, you can put yourself on a team's roster and lead it to the pennant.

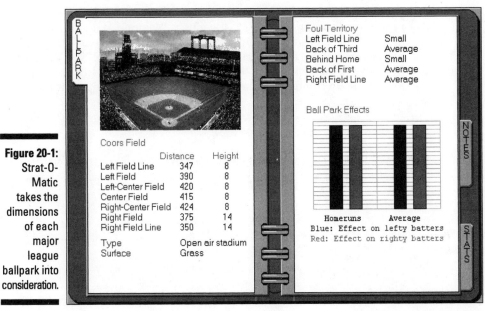

Bob Winberry, Strat-O-Matic Game Co.

Figure 20-1: Strat-O-Matic takes the dimensions of each major league ballpark into consideration.

✔ **Tony La Russa Baseball.** This game, from the Maxis company, allows you to replay recent seasons while receiving managerial tips from the esteemed La Russa himself. Outstanding features include rookie scouting reports, vivid player photos, stats on head-to-head matchups, and first-rate graphics. The General Manager Challenge is a fun addition that delivers trade proposals from the computer-run teams in your league throughout the season. Three play-by-play announcers give each game a realistic sound and feel.

✔ **Sports Illustrated presents MicroLeague Baseball.** Like Strat-O-Matic, MicroLeague offers you individual disks representing every major league team from the twentieth century. Its graphics contain more diverse camera angles than most of its competitors. MicroLeague also has a Rotisserie simulation feature for those fantasy gamers who want it all.

✔ **Hardball 5.** Not only can you replay recent and past seasons with this game, you can also run homerun derbies between baseball's legendary sluggers.

✔ **Baseball for Windows with Ernie Harwell (Miler Associates).** The legendary Detroit Tigers announcer provides the play-by-play for this realistic simulation. Baseball for Windows uses drag-and-drop technology so you can easily customize your league. The broadcast sound couldn't be more lifelike, and the latest edition features *Bill James's Baseball Encyclopedia,* a compendium of stats for every major leaguer who ever played.

✔ **Diamond Mind Baseball.** Another baseball simulation that includes nearly every season from the last century, Diamond Mind offers the most complex strategy options (even allowing for injuries during team brawls and umpire ejections) in easily accessible form. If you want your franchise to be backed by a deep minor league system, this is the game for you. Team owners can carry as many as 60 players on their rosters.

Part V
The Part of Tens

The 5th Wave   By Rich Tennant

PLUCKY OUTFIELDER DANNY BUMPUS WASN'T ABOUT TO LET A SIMPLE GALLBLADDER OPERATION RUIN HIS CONSECUTIVE GAME STREAK

©RICHTENNANT

I've got it!
I've got it!

In this part . . .

This part introduces you to Joe's picks of baseball's top players, pitchers, and fielders — past and present. One of our favorite chapters is our list of ten things Joe loves about the game. You can also read about ten legendary Negro League players who, though denied access to the major league stage by segregation, still managed to dazzle fans across the country during the first half of the 20th century. And we hope you get a hoot out of the list of player nicknames that have become a part of baseball lore.

Chapter 21

Joe Morgan's Top Ten Players, All-Time and Current

Some of these names are already household words — at least in a house inhabited by even the most rudimentary baseball fan. Other names may soon be household words. In any case, these players are the ones you'd want on your team.

The Ten Best Players of All Time

Just ask any group of baseball fans, "Who are the best players of all time," and then stand back and watch the fireworks. They'll debate for days. I should know — I argued with myself before finally whittling my list down to these ten megastars. To make my task easier, I restricted the list to players who are no longer active and whose performances I personally experienced as a spectator, teammate, or opponent. (That's why you don't find Babe Ruth and Ty Cobb on this particular list.)

Willie Mays

(New York-San Francisco Giants, New York Mets)

Willie could do anything on a baseball field, and he did it all with show-stopping flair. When I think of Mays, I think of him in a hurry: streaking around the bases or running out from under his hat to make another rally-breaking catch. He won as many stolen base titles as he did home run championships (four each). My favorite part of his game was his baserunning; I never saw anyone better at taking an extra base. Willie had an instinct for where the ball was hit, where he was on the base paths, and who was throwing from what angle. That's something you can't teach.

Hank Aaron

(Milwaukee-Atlanta Braves, Milwaukee Brewers)

Hank's 755 career home runs have overshadowed his other talents. (See Figure 21-1.) He was an underrated outfielder who rarely made a mental mistake, as well as an excellent base runner. Fans also tend to forget what an outstanding *base stealer* he was. A base stealer must be successful on 80 percent of his attempts to maximize his effectiveness. Aaron was right around that mark — and he usually stole his bags in crucial situations.

Figure 21-1:
Hank Aaron
was an out-
standing
base
stealer,
fielder, and
home run
hitter.

National Baseball Hall of Fame Library, Cooperstown, N.Y.

Mickey Mantle

(New York Yankees)

The best switch-hitter ever, Mantle was the fastest man in baseball during his prime, and he consistently hit the ball farther than anyone. (See Figure 21-2.) Mickey always regretted that his lifetime batting average dipped below .300. However, he finished up with an on-base average and slugging percentage higher than either Aaron or Mays. He didn't run as often as Mays; the stolen base was rarely a part of the Yankee attack. But when Mickey wanted to steal a base, few catchers could stop him. From 1955 to 1961, he stole 100 bases while getting caught only 13 times. He was a converted shortstop who turned himself into a Gold Glove outfielder.

National Baseball Hall of Fame Library, Cooperstown, NY

Figure 21-2: Mickey Mantle was the fastest man in baseball during his prime.

Frank Robinson

(Cincinnati Reds, Baltimore Orioles, California Angels, Los Angeles Dodgers, Cleveland Indians)

A great field leader, Robinson was one of the toughest competitors I ever saw. He is still the only player to win Most Valuable Player awards in both leagues. Frank hit for power and average. He was a punishing base runner who broke up the double play as well as anyone. In 1975, Frank became baseball's first black manager. He has always been a great leader. (See Figure 21-3.)

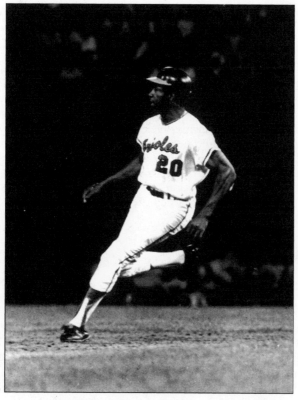

National Baseball Hall of Fame Library, Cooperstown, NY

Ernie Banks

(Chicago Cubs)

Banks is the godfather of today's power-hitting shortstops. As of the 1999 season, he still held the major league record for most home runs by a short-stop in a season. (The record is 47 home runs, set in 1958 — a season in which the average shortstop hit seven.) He had four straight 40 plus home-run seasons (1957–1960), another record for middle infielders, and he was the first National Leaguer to win two consecutive MVP Awards (1958–59). Ernie wasn't a one-dimensional player. He was an outstanding shortstop who, in 1958, set a record for highest fielding percentage at his position. In 1960, he was awarded a Gold Glove. When he lost some range, the Cubs moved him over to first base, where in 1969 he again led the league in fielding percent-age. Blessed with a lithe but powerful upper body, Banks could take a low outside pitch and pull it into left field. He hit 512 career home runs.

Johnny Bench

(Cincinnati Reds)

My teammate on the Big Red Machine of the 1970s is the greatest all-around catcher ever to don a face mask. We talk more extensively about Bench's defense in Chapter Seven. As a hitter, Johnny is the only catcher ever to lead a major league in home runs — something he did twice. He was that rare hitter who combined strength with quickness. Johnny was so talented at the plate, I always thought he could be a perennial .300 hitter if he chose to hit to the opposite field more often. But his role on our ball club was to drive in runs, so he sacrificed some average to hit with more power. You can't argue with the results. Bench led the league in runs batted in three times, had three other 100 plus RBI seasons, and earned two MVP Awards.

Willie McCovey

(San Francisco Giants, Oakland A's, San Diego Padres)

During the first ten years or so of my career (1965–1975), Willie was the most feared hitter in the National League. On any given pitch in any given situation, he could hit the ball 500 feet to win a ball game. Once he established himself as a full-time player, Willie displayed few weaknesses at the plate. He was especially dangerous with men on base: His 18 career grand slams represent the National League record. My former manager, Sparky Anderson, still admits to having nightmares featuring McCovey coming to the plate in some clutch situation. Most of the time, Anderson would order our pitchers to walk him if the game was on the line. And he wasn't the only manager to employ that strategy. In 1969, managers handed Willie 45 intentional walks, still the major league record. He has 521 career home runs to his credit.

Roberto Clemente

(Pittsburgh Pirates)

Willie Mays and Robin Roberts both told me that Clemente was the best player they ever saw. He won four batting titles, an MVP award, and a World Series MVP title. A right-handed batter, Roberto hit the ball to the opposite field harder than most left-handed pull-hitters could. He didn't achieve the home run totals of Mays or Aaron, but he played most of his career in Forbes Field, a terrible park for homers. I remember the center field at Forbes being so deep that the grounds crew would store the batting cage out in its farthest reaches during games! Roberto was a great right fielder with a legendary arm. After he threw out 27 base runners during the 1961 season, the league stopped running on him. His 13 consecutive Gold Gloves (1960–72) represent the record for outfielders.

Jackie Robinson
(Brooklyn Dodgers)

Jackie Robinson's career numbers aren't as lofty as the others on this list. Because of his color, the league didn't allow Robinson to play major league ball until he was 28 years old, so he missed some of his prime playing years. Despite the late start to his career, Jackie won the Rookie of the Year Award and National League MVP. He was the most intimidating base runner of his time, and he reintroduced the stolen base as an offensive weapon. As the man who broke baseball's color line, he played magnificently under more pressure than any player before or since. We'll never know just how great he was because of the stress he lived with every day. (See Figure 21-4.)

Figure 21-4:
Jackie Robinson broke baseball's long-standing color line in 1947.

National Baseball Hall of Fame Library, Cooperstown, NY

Ted Williams

(Boston Red Sox)

Williams was only an adequate fielder with a mediocre throwing arm. He was also an average runner. But once he got a bat in his hands, everyone forgot about his shortcomings. Known as the Splendid Splinter, Williams had the best combination of on-base percentage and slugging average of any hitter this side of Ruth. He won six American League batting championships and four home-run titles. Ted also led the league in runs batted in (4 times), runs scored (6 times), slugging average (9 times), on-base percentage (12 times), and walks (8 times). He is the last of the .400 hitters; his average hit .406 in 1941. Ted won his first batting crown when he was 23 and his last at the age of 40.

The Ten Best Current Players

Looking over this list, you immediately realize there is no talent drought in major league baseball. Most of these players are under 30 years old and possess multidimensional skills. I wouldn't be surprised if all of them reach the Hall of Fame.

Ken Griffey, Jr.

Ken Griffey, Jr. is like a young Willie Mays. He has the same tools, though he doesn't steal bases as often as Mays did. He also plays the game with Mays-like flair. When you watch Junior at the plate, notice the sound the ball makes when it jumps off his bat. He hits the ball hard almost every time, and his home runs are usually long line drives to straight-away right field rather than arching fly balls. Another sign of greatness: Though a left-handed hitter, Junior is deadly against left-handed pitchers. He hits them with even more power than he does right-handers.

Barry Bonds

In 1996, Barry Bonds became the first National Leaguer to hit 40 home runs and steal 40 bases in the same season. That record sums up Barry's game: an equal blend of flash and crash that no one else in the National League can equal. How much do major league dugouts fear him? During the 1996 season, Reds manager Ray Knight ordered his pitcher to intentionally walk Bonds even though Bonds was leading off the ninth inning and the Reds had only a one-run lead. Conventional baseball wisdom says never intentionally walk the potential tying run, especially with nobody out in the ninth. That's Barry; he forces managers to rewrite their strategy books. Barry won three National League MVP awards and easily could have won four or five. Though he's a 14-year veteran, he showed no signs of slowing down in 1999. He hit 34 home runs in only 355 at-bats and played solid defense in left field.

Jeff Bagwell

Another former Most Valuable Player, Bagwell is a great RBI man with power. He has deceptive speed and steals a base when his team needs one. Jeff is also aggressive on the base paths. If you're a second baseman, you don't relish hanging in on the double play when Bagwell is bearing down on you. He also plays Gold Glove defense at first base. He has the reactions of a third baseman — a position he played in the minor leagues — and is especially good at fielding bad throws.

Larry Walker

I rated Walker highly even before he hit .379 to win the National League batting title in 1999. Walker has one of the best arms of any right fielder in baseball. He can hit the ball to all fields with power, and he doesn't care which side of the mound a pitcher throws from. In 1999, Larry hit .395 against right-handers and .345 against southpaws. He also doesn't strike out much for a slugger. Walker's stolen base totals have dropped in recent seasons, but he's still one of the most intelligent base runners in the game. His hustling play and powerful arm in right field have earned him four Gold Gloves.

Mark McGwire

Here's how Larry Walker described a home run McGwire hit against the Rockies in 1997: "When the ball came down, it had moon dust all over it." Baseball has evolved into a home run hitting contest, and no one is better than McGwire at jacking the ball into the upper stratosphere. When he's on fire, no pitcher or ballpark can contain him. When McGwire set the all-time single-season homerun record with 70 in 1998, I thought it was a mind-boggling accomplishment. (See Figure 21-5.) But for him to follow that with a major-league leading of 65 homers in 1999 may be just as impressive, because maintaining such a high standard on the major league level is so difficult. Two years ago, I felt no one would ever approach Hank Aaron's career home run total of 755. Now I'm not so sure. Given McGwire's unprecedented production (he's hit 249 homeruns over the last four seasons) and Ken Griffey, Jr.'s youth and talent (he's just over 30 and already has 397 career homers), I think they both have a chance to break the record. By the way, Big Mac is more than just a hitter; McGwire is an excellent first baseman with surprising range, quick feet, and sure hands.

Figure 21-5:
Mark McGwire set the all-time single-season homerun record in 1998.

Brian Spurlock

Sammy Sosa

When he hit 66 homers in 1998, many people thought it was a fluke. Unlike Mark McGwire, Sosa had never hit more than 40 homers in a single season. Sammy's 63 homers in 1999, however, prove that he is here to stay. If he remains healthy, Sosa will be among his league's top sluggers for most of the next decade. When he first came to the majors, pitchers often got him out by muscling him inside. Cubs coach Billy Williams — himself a former batting champion and Hall of Famer — moved Sammy back and off the plate. This left him in a better position to handle anything thrown inside. Now Sammy deposits pitches that used to tie him up into the upper deck. What I like most about him is his ability to adapt to situations. He doesn't go up to the plate trying to pull everything. With a runner on second and his club short a run, Sammy smacks outside pitches to the opposite field for run-scoring singles.

Chapter 22

Joe Morgan's Top Ten Pitchers, All-Time and Current

From Sandy Koufax to Greg Maddux, these are the pitchers you'd want on the mound for any important game — well, for *any* game, to be honest. As I did in the previous chapter, I limited my all-time selections to retired pitchers whose performances I personally experienced as a spectator, team-mate, or opponent. Be sure to check out Chapter 6 for details on the pitching stuff that I mention here. Chapter 16 describes how you can figure out some of the statistics associated with pitching.

Joe's All-Time Top Ten Starting Pitchers

How good were these ten? Gaylord Perry won two Cy Young Awards while earning 314 career victories, and he didn't survive the cut.

Warren Spahn

(Boston-Milwaukee Braves, San Francisco Giants, New York Mets)

Spahn didn't record his first major league victory until he was 25 — a fairly late start — yet he won more games (363) than any other left-hander before or since. He was a crafty pitcher with power. Warren led the National League in strikeouts for five consecutive seasons. He lasted so long because he always made adjustments. When his fastball slipped, he added a screwball and change-up. When his curve flattened, he picked up a slider. Durability was his strength. At age 40, he led the league in wins (21) and earned run average (ERA) (3.02). Two years later, Warren won 23 games and had a 2.60 ERA. On July 2, 1963, he lost an epic 1–0, 16-inning duel to San Francisco's Juan Marichal. (He gave up a home run to Willie Mays.) Spahnie told me he mistreated his body in that game; he was never the same pitcher after that.

Steve Carlton

(St. Louis Cardinals, Philadelphia Phillies, San Francisco Giants, Chicago White Sox)

One way to judge a pitcher is to see how much better his record is than his team's. In 1972, Carlton pitched for a Phillies club that won only 59 games. Twenty-seven of those wins belonged to the man nicknamed Lefty. He had a great fastball, a good curve, and the best slider ever thrown on this planet. Nearly all pitchers throw sliders with a twist of the elbow. Carlton, however, pulled across the ball. But Steve's fingers were so strong that the result was a bat-breaking slider. Because the motion put no strain on his elbow, he maintained his power pitching into a relatively old age. (See Figure 22-1.)

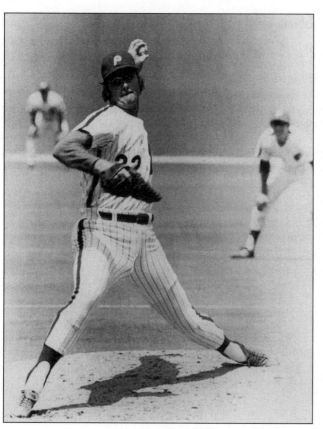

Figure 22-1:
Steve
Carlton
brings it
home.

National Baseball Hall of Fame Library, Cooperstown, NY

Tom Seaver

(New York Mets, Chicago White Sox, Boston Red Sox)

Seaver had a great moving fastball that overpowered most hitters. He also loved center stage in New York. When he pitched at Shea Stadium, it was as if he were appearing on Broadway. I had a few home runs against him and fought him off now and then, but I usually didn't hit him hard. Tom also had a good slider and, around the middle of his career, he'd surprise you with an occasional change. But mostly he attacked you with hard stuff. He really didn't have much of a curveball, but he really didn't need one.

Sandy Koufax

(Los Angeles Dodgers)

Sandy's fastball and curveball were the two best pitches I had ever seen. You couldn't pick up any spin on his curve. It was nearly as fast as his fastball, and it didn't just drop — it exploded out of the hitting zone. His riding fastball had everything on it. He threw as hard as Nolan Ryan did, but his control was better. I've faced a lot of great pitchers — Gibson, Seaver, and Carlton among them — on those rare days when they didn't have their best stuff. I never saw Sandy take the mound with anything less than his full arsenal.

Bob Gibson

(St. Louis Cardinals)

During a game against the Pirates in 1967, Roberto Clemente hit a line drive off Gibson's leg. Gibby pitched to another batter before he realized the leg was broken. He was the toughest competitor I ever faced. Great slider, great fastball, and a tremendous will to win. Gibson's expression always said, "You can't hit me." You had to admire that attitude if you were his teammate, but if you were hitting against him, it could get under your skin. Gibson was a gifted all-around athlete who won nine straight Gold Gloves and was a dangerous hitter with good power.

Juan Marichal

(San Francisco Giants, Boston Red Sox)

Marichal was a lot like Greg Maddux — only with better stuff. He was a magician on the mound. His bag of tricks included two different fastballs, a curve, a slider, a screwball, a palmball, a straight change, you name it. He threw them all for strikes from every conceivable angle. Juan pitched in and out, up and down within the strike zone, and he changed speeds. You could watch an entire game without seeing the same pitch twice. At Candlestick Park, where he usually threw against the wind, Marichal would take something off his curve so that it would break more. When he pitched at the Astrodome, where wind was never a factor, he threw a harder curve. That's pitching.

Ferguson Jenkins

(Chicago Cubs, Texas Rangers)

Jenkins had the best control of anyone on this list. He could nail the outside corner with his great slider, change-up, or curveball at any point in the count. That's why he was able to pitch successfully (Jenkins had six consecutive 20-win seasons as a Cub) in a slugger's park like Wrigley Field. Jenkins would surrender his share of homers; but because he rarely walked more than one batter per game, usually no one was on base when a hitter got a longball. It was especially difficult to get hits of any kind off of him in clutch situations. Jenkins had a potent fastball, yet he had such great control that you never knew what his best pitch would be in any particular game. He had 284 career wins.

Catfish Hunter

(Oakland A's, New York Yankees)

Another great control artist, Catfish could throw the fastball by you up in the strike zone, and then go down and get you chasing his bat-breaking slider. When he was behind in the count, he would use that slider to keep batters — who were often looking for his fastball — off-balance. Catfish was a master at changing speeds and hitting corners. As he got older, he developed a change-up that he could throw for strikes even when he was behind in the count. Cat won 20 games five times and led the American League in victories in 1974 and 1975. He also became baseball's first big free agent signing when he left Oakland for a five-year deal with the New York Yankees worth $3.75 million in December 1974.

Nolan Ryan

(New York Mets, California Angels, Houston Astros, Texas Rangers)

They called him the Ryan Express because his fastball never traveled on any local tracks. He and Koufax were the hardest throwers on this list, maybe the hardest throwers of all time. But their fastballs weren't quite the same. Koufax threw a fastball that seemed to ride up in the strike zone as it reached the plate. Most pitchers' heaters tend to drop a bit at that same point. Nolan's fastball didn't move quite as much, but it overpowered you with its sheer velocity. Three-quarters of the way to the plate, Nolan's fastball seemed to jump at you as if it were suddenly picking up speed. Ryan won 324 games, led his league in strikeouts 11 times, and threw a record-setting seven no-hitters. He will, however, always be remembered for all those Ks. Ryan struck out an all-time best 5,386 batters during his 27-year major league career. Is, that an unbreakable mark? All anyone has to do to top it is strike out 200 hitters a season for a little more than 28½ seasons. Good luck.

Jim Palmer

(Baltimore Orioles)

From 1970 to 1978, this three-time Cy Young Award recipient won 20 or more games eight times. Palmer had great control, especially high in the strike zone, and possessed a formidable overhand curve ball. Like Catfish Hunter, he mixed the two to devastating effect, except Palmer threw a little harder than Hunter did. Batters looking for Jim's high heater would often give up on his late-breaking curve. Jim was a workhorse. He pitched 270 or more innings in eight different seasons, led the American League in innings pitched on four occasions, and was usually among his league's leaders in complete games. He won 268 times while posting a 2.86 ERA, one of the lowest career marks of any hurler with 3,000 or more innings pitched.

The Ten Best Current Pitchers

Today's hitters are bigger and stronger than ever, and ballparks are becoming smaller. Fans expect every game to be a slugfest — except when these pitchers are on the mound. The following ten pitchers seemingly turn back the clock to the dead ball era of the 1900s, and teams become grateful for any runs that they score. (**Note:** David Cone and Tommy Glavine, two of the best pitchers of the 1990s, would have made the list except they both had a slightly off-year in 1999. Either or both could easily bounce back to resume positions among this group.)

Pedro Martinez

The most devastating pitcher in all of baseball, Martinez offsets an explosive fastball with a sinking, dead-fish change-up that destroys a hitter's timing. He also throws biting curveballs and cutters. Pedro doesn't allow many base runners. Mark McGwire says that Pedro — a Cy Young recipient in 1997 and 1999 — has the best stuff he has ever seen. In 1999, Martinez's major league best 2.07 ERA was 296 points below the American League average, one of the best differentials of this century.

Greg Maddux

Four Cy Young Awards make this an easy choice. If a strike is a pitcher's best friend, Maddux is never lonely. He throws more strikes than any other pitcher in baseball. Maddux gets 75 percent of his first pitches over the plate for strikes. When he's behind in the count, he displays a jewel cutter's precision; he rebounds with a strike in over 80 percent of those situations. Maddux features the standard assortment of pitches — fastball, slider, and curve. He doesn't throw especially hard, but his ball moves so much it doesn't matter. His biggest asset? A preternatural instinct for knowing what pitch the hitter *isn't* looking for; five-time batting champion Wade Boggs claims Maddux has a crystal ball in his glove. His best weapons? Control and changing speeds.

Roger Clemens

In 1997, Clemens tied his own major league single-game record by striking out 20 batters. Power pitchers tend to mix in a lot of fly-ball outs with their strike-outs. When you watch Clemens pitch, notice the high number of groundouts he records. His rising fastball accounts for most of his strikeouts, but his hard sinker and splitter induce batters to beat the ball into the ground when he needs a double play. Clemens was a little off his game in 1999 when he notched only 14 wins. But as he proved in the playoffs against Texas and the World Series against the Braves, the Rocket still knows how to finish games and finish off hitters. His fifth Cy Young Award in 1998 makes him a lock for the Hall of Fame. (See Figure 22-2.)

Figure 22-2:
Roger
Clemens
has racked
up five
Cy Young
Awards
so far.

©1999 Stephen Green / MLB Photos

Randy Johnson

How do you spell unfair? Johnson is 6 feet 10 inches, throws about 1,000 mph, has a wicked, slashing slider, and is just wild enough to make hitters call their insurance agents between innings. Everybody has a hard time hitting him, but this southpaw (left-hander) is particularly damaging to the fragile psyches of left-handed hitters. When the Colorado Rockies played Seattle in 1997, Larry Walker — who was only hitting .400 at the time — benched himself rather than face Johnson. The two did have a memorable confrontation in the All-Star Game later that year — the left-handed Walker came to the plate batting right-handed for the first time in his major league career (and even took one pitch). Like another legendary fireballer, Nolan Ryan, Randy may be getting better as he gets older. In 1999, at the age of 36, the lefthander won 17 games while leading the National League in ERA (2.48 despite playing in a hitter's park). His 364 strikeouts were the third-highest single-season total in baseball history.

John Smoltz

Pitch for pitch, Smoltz may have the best pure stuff in baseball this side of Pedro Martinez. His fastball hits the mid-90s, his *splitter* (split-fingered fastball) rates among the league's nastiest pitches, and his curveball is hard to pick up because it breaks late. However, his best weapon is a great slider. When John takes his full wind-up, he's virtually unhittable; he's more vulnerable pitching from the stretch. But to get him to pitch from the stretch, you have to get base runners on against him when he's pitching from that full wind-up. That's the kind of paradox that transforms a lot of batters into Amway salesmen.

Mike Mussina

Mussina complements his cutter, four-seam fastball, and knuckle-curve with the best change-up in the league. Mussina is always among the American League leaders in wins. He had some of his worst numbers in 1996, but in some ways it may have been his most impressive year. Mussina couldn't get the ball down that season; he surrendered 31 home runs and his earned run average soared to nearly 5.00. Yet he still scuffled to 19 wins. That's what you want to see from a starting pitcher. Forget about ERAs and those other stats; starters are paid to win. Mussina has proven he can do that even when he doesn't have his best stuff.

Chapter 23

Joe Morgan's Top Ten Fielders, All-Time and Current

You can't succeed in baseball without fielding. Getting leather on the ball (defense) is just as important as getting wood on it (offense). Be sure to check out Chapter 7 for details on how to play each position.

The Ten Best Fielders of All Time

Wide range, soft hands, and quick reflexes weren't enough to earn a player a spot on this list. All ten of these fielders made the grade because they also knew what to do with the ball *after* they caught it. Once again, we've restricted the All-Time list to fielders I watched perform as a fan, teammate, or opponent.

Willie Mays

(New York-San Francisco Giants, New York Mets)

You can't teach a person to play defense the way Willie Mays did — he got to balls faster than anyone. His quick release was a bonus because he possessed one of the best arms to ever disappoint a base runner. Willie was one of the few center fielders who came in on a ball as well as he went back on one. He could cut off a line drive over second before it had any chance to consider life as a single. Then, on the very next play, he would devour yards of real estate to yank yet another extra base hit out of the box score. Willie brought the same instincts to the field that he displayed on the bases. He always knew the pitcher, what he was throwing, who was hitting, how the ball left his bat, who was on base, what the score was, and the angles of the park. He won 12 Gold Gloves — more than any other center fielder in baseball history.

Ozzie Smith

(San Diego Padres, St. Louis Cardinals)

Gravity had no authority over Ozzie Smith. Ozzie brought an unprecedented array of acrobatic skills to his position. (He would do handsprings and backflips as he took the field.) The ultimate turf (artificial grass) shortstop, Ozzie was one of the few infielders nimble enough to change direction in midstep when a ball took a bad hop. His speed and agility enabled him to reach the deepest portions of his position in time to cut off grounders that slashed through the turf. A few years before he retired, Ozzie tore his rotator cuff — a devastating injury for infielders because it drains the strength from their throwing arms. He compensated by developing a hop and jump that put his entire body behind each toss. On balls hit into the hole, Smith's slide toward third base allowed him to firmly plant his foot to make a throw while he was catching the ball. I'd never seen anyone do that before him; he was the Rolls Royce of shortstops.

Curt Flood

(Cincinnati Reds, St. Louis Cardinals, Washington Senators)

Though he played a deep center field, Flood was nearly Mays's equal at catching line drives hit just over the infield. Curt had a strong throwing arm when he first came to the majors; after he broke it in midcareer, the arm never regained its former strength. Throwing would remain the one weakness in his defensive game from that point on. Nevertheless, he won seven consecutive Gold Gloves (1963–1969), led the league in total chances (a reliable indicator of an outfielder's range) three times, tied for the lead twice, and finished in the top two every season from 1962 to 1969. In 1966, Curt recorded 391 putouts without being charged with a single error.

Bill Mazeroski

(Pittsburgh Pirates)

Maz was Mr. Second Base. I modeled myself after him. In the field, Maz epitomized athletic economy. He rarely took an extra step to elude an incoming runner. Mazeroski was so quick on the double play that Pirates fans called him "No Touch." He seemed to relay the ball from the shortstop to first base without pausing to touch it. Maz had plenty of practice on that play; his 1,706 double plays represent the all-time record for second basemen. Perhaps the best part of his stellar game was his positioning; Bill knew where to play every hitter, even those he had never seen before. He had that sixth sense that is common to all great fielders. Maz led the National League in assists nine times, double plays eight times, putouts five times, and chances per game ten times. He holds the National League record for his position with eight Gold Gloves.

Johnny Bench

(Cincinnati Reds)

From the moment he came into the league, Bench was the best defensive catcher in the game. He had the quickest, strongest, and most accurate throwing arm of any catcher I have ever played with or against. Bench came straight over the top with his throws so they rarely sank or swerved. He was solid as a rock at home plate; enemy base runners had to find a way around rather than through him. He had huge, powerful but dexterous hands; he would take the padding out of his catcher's mitt so he could handle the ball with an infielder's flexibility. Bench was the first catcher to pick pitches out of the dirt backhanded with one hand — a signature maneuver that allowed him to capture balls that would have skipped past other catchers. From 1968 to 1977, he was the National League's Gold Glove catcher.

Roberto Clemente

(Pittsburgh Pirates)

In 1971, I played for the Houston Astros in a game against Clemente's Pirates. With two out in the eighth inning and Pittsburgh leading 1–0, I was on first with our left fielder Bob Watson at the plate. Clemente was playing medium deep in right center field when Watson hit a laser beam toward the right field corner. It looked as though the ball would strike just above the yellow home run line, which was 10 feet above the ground. Most right fielders would have positioned themselves to play *off* the wall a ball hit that high, that far, and that fast. Clemente, who was 36 at the time, wasn't having any of that. He galloped at full stride into the corner, leaped, and caught the drive while crashing into the fence. The inning was over, the Pittsburgh lead preserved. It was a memorable catch, the kind of brazen, heartbreaking play Clemente made repeatedly throughout his career. He won the Gold Glove every year from 1961 through 1972.

Brooks Robinson

(Baltimore Orioles)

No player at any position can match this third baseman's 16 consecutive Gold Gloves. Robinson introduced "The Dive" to hot corner play. (***Note:*** The *hot corner* is the third base area.) Before him, third basemen scurried or tumbled after balls hit far to either side of them. Robinson took to the air, and by diving, he got to balls no one else could reach. Brooks wasn't fast, but he was quick and heady. He positioned himself on every pitch. He would shift left or right on each batter depending on the pitcher, the hitter, and the situation. When he fielded a ground ball, his glove was always down (so the ball couldn't skip under it) and open to the hitter. Textbook stuff. Infielders with range like Robinson's often place among the league leaders in errors. However, Robby was so sure-handed that he led American League third basemen in fielding percentage a record ten times.

Keith Hernandez

(St. Louis Cardinals, New York Mets)

Hernandez was the most intimidating first baseman ever to play the position; no one could match him at covering the hole between first and second and charging bunts. He was also a master strategist. Keith would sometimes move up on the grass, obviously set for the bunt, and then back up several steps as the pitcher released the ball. He distracted so many hitters with this move, he practically eliminated the bunt as an option for many opposing teams. Most first basemen go directly to the bag to receive an infielder's throw. Keith would instead often loop back to the foul line, and then step toward first on a straight line. This maneuver kept the evolving play in front of him — always a good policy.

Mike Schmidt
(Philadelphia Phillies)

I played with Schmidt on the National League Champion Phillies in 1983. In terms of pure athleticism, he may have had more physical ability than any player I've ever shared a clubhouse with. He had tremendous range at third base, a strong, accurate throwing arm, tremendous hand-to-eye coordination, and the quick reactions you must possess to play baseball's hot corner. Mike could have played any position, including shortstop. In 1974, his first full season at third, Mike set a National League record with 404 assists. Three years later, he posted the second highest assist total in NL history with 396. Mike's eight consecutive Gold Gloves (he won a total of 10) are also a National League record.

Luis Aparicio
(Chicago White Sox, Baltimore Orioles, Boston Red Sox)

Aparicio was one of the few ballplayers who gained admittance to the Hall of Fame for his glove work. With his wall-to-wall range, Aparicio routinely made plays on the right-field side of second base. He would get in front of balls other shortstops backhanded; he backhanded balls other shortstops couldn't reach. Before Aparicio's major league arrival, shortstops, like other fielders, were taught to field the ball with both hands. Aparicio introduced a one-handed fielding style that left him in a better position to unleash a throw. He had an exceptionally strong throwing arm. Among shortstops, Aparicio holds the major league career records for games played, assists, and double plays. He led his league in fielding percentage eight times and earned nine Gold Glove Awards.

The Ten Best Current Fielders

Great fielders are exuberant; their pursuit of every batted ball is a dance of joy. When they take the field, these ten fielders aren't merely playing a position; they are playing out their passions.

Ken Griffey, Jr.

Ken Griffey, Jr., a Gold Glover from the moment he first stepped on a major league field, is the best of all young outfielders. Junior ranges far to his left and right. He plays so deep that he steals more extra-base hits from opposing hitters than any other center fielder. No one gets Junior's jump on the ball, and he is absolutely fearless. He crashes into walls, climbs fences, and makes body-jarring leaps to get to a ball. His arm is above average, and he rarely misses his target. Junior won his tenth consecutive Gold Glove in 1998 at the age of 30, putting him on pace to shatter Willie Mays's major league record of 12 Gold Gloves for center field play. (It should be noted, however, that during Mays's first five major league seasons, Gold Gloves did not exist.)

Barry Bonds

Bonds is my all-time left fielder. He studied for his doctorate in outfield play under the tutelage of his father, Bobby, a three-time Gold Glover in his own right, and Professor Willie Mays (who also happens to be Bonds's godfather). Even though he's left-handed, Barry is quick to the line; he has an accurate throwing arm, and he's the most fundamentally sound outfielder in the game. Barry consistently hits his cut-off man. He goes back on fly balls hit over his head as though he carries a built-in honing device; this talent allows him to play shallow enough to swipe enemy singles without leaving him vulnerable to the extra-base hit.

Ivan Rodriguez

Defensively, he's a Johnny Bench clone. Rodriguez has the best throwing arm of any catcher in the American League. He throws out better than 45 percent of would-be base stealers. (Thirty percent is about average.) Many clubs don't even bother to run against him. He also makes snap throws to first or second to pick off runners who stray too far from the bag. Every year, he enhances some aspect of his game: pitch calling, plate blocking, digging the ball out of the dirt. Only 28, Ivan has already won eight consecutive Gold Gloves. One more and he'll tie the major league record held by Mr. Bench.

Charles Johnson

In 1997, Johnson set a record among major league catchers for most games without an error. I don't know what kind of dishwashing detergent Charles uses, but he has *soft* hands; the ball nestles into his glove. His arm is even better than Ivan Rodriguez's — just as strong and a tad more accurate. He also has a quicker release. Though he's tall (6 feet 2 inches) for a catcher,

Chapter 24

Joe Morgan's Ten Negro League Legends

*B*aseball drew its color line during the mid-1880s when all-white professional teams, such as the powerful Chicago White Stockings, refused to take the field against integrated clubs. By 1899, baseball owners did not allow a single African-American to play in the major or minor leagues. But African-Americans continued to play on independent teams, and in 1920 Rube Foster created the Negro National League.

Major league baseball's unofficial policy of segregation (team owners never publicly acknowledged the color line's existence) remained in effect until Jackie Robinson joined the Brooklyn Dodgers in 1947. Up to that time, baseball's deplorable shortsightedness not only deprived African-Americans of the right to compete at baseball's highest level, it also robbed major league fans of the opportunity to see some of the game's most amazing talents. Many Negro League players would have been starters in the major leagues had they been given the chance. A number of them would have rewritten the game's record books. The ten men listed here — all Hall of Famers — would have been All-Stars in any league during any era.

Josh Gibson
(Homestead Grays, Pittsburgh Crawfords)

Many sportswriters and major leaguers who played against Gibson believe he was the greatest all-around catcher ever. Gibson was a superb defensive receiver. Hall of Fame pitcher Walter Johnson once said, "He catches so easily, he might as well be in a rocking chair and he throws like a bullet." Gibson was also a power hitter with few peers; Negro League and semi-pro box scores credit him with 75 home runs in 1931 and 69 in 1934. During a 17-season career, he batted .354 and topped .400 on two occasions. Gibson was also considered a leader, both on the field and off, of a powerful Homestead Grays team that won nine consecutive pennants from 1937 to 1945. Johnson said Gibson would have fetched $200,000 in an open major league market. Sadly, Gibson never found out what he would have earned in the white major leagues. The catcher died of a brain hemorrhage at the age of 33 in January 1947, only months before Jackie Robinson broke the color line.

Satchel Paige
(Chattanooga Black Lookouts, Birmingham Black Barons, Cleveland Cubs, Pittsburgh Crawfords, Kansas City Monarchs, New York Black Yankees, Satchel Paige's All-Stars, Philadelphia Stars, Cleveland Indians, St. Louis Browns, Kansas City A's)

The color line lifted just in time for this 42-year-old pitching legend — Paige was the Negro League's biggest drawing card — to join the Cleveland Indians in the midst of a grueling pennant race. All Paige did for the Indians was go 6–1 with a 2.47 ERA. He even pitched two shutouts. It has been estimated that the rubber-armed Paige won as many as 600 games during his 30-year Negro League and barnstorming career. A showman, Paige once reportedly made his entire outfield sit down while he pitched to Josh Gibson with the bases loaded. He struck Gibson out on four pitches. In 1952, 46-year old Paige pitched out of the bullpen for the St. Louis Browns; he won 12 games and saved 10 more. The following season, he was among the league leaders in saves with 11. Satchel made one last major league appearance when he pitched three innings for the Kansas City A's in 1965. He struck out one while allowing only one base runner and no runs. He was 59 years old. One can only imagine the big league records Satch would have set had only the owners let this baseball marvel play in his prime. Ted Williams and Robin Roberts, two Hall of Famers, told me that Gibson and Paige were as talented as any players they had ever seen. Both of them should have been on baseball's All-Century Team in 1999.

Oscar Charleston

(Indianapolis ABCs, Lincoln Stars, Chicago American Giants, St. Louis Giants, Homestead Grays, Philadelphia Stars, Brooklyn Brown Dodgers, and other teams)

Many of his contemporaries cite Charleston as the greatest player in Negro League history. At least one sportswriter, who saw both players in their prime, told me he would rate Charleston over Willie Mays! Blessed with great speed, Charleston played a shallow centerfield because he was confident in his ability to race back to catch anything hit over his head. He had so much lateral range that his other two outfield mates usually played right next to the foul lines. A powerful hitter, Oscar won at least four batting titles and several home run crowns. (Negro League records are sketchy and incomplete.) He is credited with a .353 lifetime batting average. Charleston, who also success-fully managed in the Negro Leagues, was known as an astute judge of talent. When Brooklyn Dodgers general manager Branch Rickey wanted to break major league baseball's color line, he hired Charleston as a scout. Charleston brought both Jackie Robinson and Roy Campanella to Rickey's attention.

John Henry Lloyd

(Macon Acmes, Cuban-X Giants, Philadelphia Giants, Columbus Buckeyes, New York Black Yankees, and other teams)

Many baseball historians cite Honus Wagner as the greatest shortstop — some even say the greatest player — of all time. Wagner considered Lloyd his equal. John Henry was in his early thirties when the Negro Leagues were founded; he spent his early career playing for independent black and Cuban teams. Yet he played in the Negro Leagues for a dozen years while compiling a career batting average of .344. In 1928, the 44-year old shortstop put together one of baseball's most remarkable seasons. He batted a league-leading .564 (no, that's not a typo) and led all comers in home runs.

Walter "Buck" Leonard

(Brooklyn Royal Giants, Homestead Grays)

This lefthanded, power-hitting first baseman combined with Josh Gibson to give the Homestead Grays one of baseball's great home run tandems. Leonard helped Gibson power the Grays to nine straight pennants. More than just a slugger, Buck won three batting titles. In 1939, he enjoyed his best season as he led the Negro Leagues in hitting with a .492 batting average. Leonard was also considered a Gold Glove quality first baseman, able to range far to his right to steal base hits headed for the hole.

Leon Day
(Bacharach Giants, Brooklyn Eagles, Newark Eagles, Baltimore Elite Giants)

As a second baseman and center fielder, the 5'9" Day played 16 seasons and hit over .300 in every one of them. Yet he is best known for his pitching prowess. Sporting a fastball (which some say was the equal of Satchel Paige's), a curveball, and a change-up, Day appeared in a record seven Negro League All-Star Games. In the 1942 contest, he faced seven of the league's top hitters and struck out five of them. Day holds the Negro League record for most strikeouts in a nine-inning game — 18. He was matched against the legendary Paige four times and won three of them. World War II carved nearly two seasons out of Day's career. In his first game back in the Negro Leagues, the fireballer picked up right where he left off with a 17-strikeout no-hitter.

Cool Papa Bell
(St. Louis Stars, Pittsburgh Crawfords, Detroit Wolves, Kansas City Monarchs, Chicago American Giants, Memphis Red Sox, Homestead Grays)

The story is as oft-told as it is apocryphal: Cool Papa Bell was so fast he could turn off a light switch and slip under the covers before the room got dark. That never happened, but there is no doubt that Bell was one of the fastest men ever to play baseball. He was once clocked circling all four bases in an astounding 12 seconds. Cool Papa often went from first to third on bunts and scored from second on sacrifice flies. On at least three occasions, he stole two bases on a single pitch. A line-hitter who was an inside-the-park home run threat any time the ball got past an outfielder, Bell hit .341 over a 25-season career.

Ray Dandridge
(Detroit Stars, Newark Dodgers, Newark Eagles, New York Cubans, Milwaukee Millers)

Willie Mays has said that Dandridge was the best fielding third baseman he ever saw. Panther-quick with a missile launcher for an arm, Dandridge could range to either side to subtract enemy base hits from the box score. A career .330 plus line-drive hitter (keep in mind that Negro League records are incomplete), Ray batted .370 in 1944 and led the Mexican League with a .368 average in 1948. That performance earned him a minor league contract with the Milwaukee Millers, a New York Giants American Association farm team. Though already 36 years old, Dandridge was the American Association Rookie of the Year in 1949 and its MVP in 1950. Despite these awards, he never got called to the big leagues.

Smokey Joe Williams
(San Antonio Bronchos, Leland Giants, Chicago Giants, Lincoln Giants, Chicago American Giants, Bacharach Giants, Brooklyn Royal Giants, Homestead Grays)

Ty Cobb, not the most generous of men, once said that Williams would have been a sure 30-game winner had he been allowed to pitch in the major leagues. Williams may have been the fastest pitcher of his time, regardless of league. Chicago Giants owner Frank Leland would boast, "If you've ever seen the speed of a pebble thrown in a storm, you have not yet seen speed the equal of this wonderful giant from Texas." In 1914, he went 41– 3. Sixteen years later, his fastball was still smoking as he struck out 27 Kansas City Monarchs in a 12-inning game.

Bullet Joe Rogan
(Los Angeles White Sox, Kansas City Monarchs)

Most contemporaries say that only Joe Williams's fastball was more torrid. In his prime, Joe *averaged* 30 wins per season over a 10-year span. Want to talk about a workhorse? During that span, which included over 450 starts, Joe didn't leave the mound for a reliever even once.

Chapter 25

Ten Things to Love about Baseball

*I*f we wanted to reveal all the reasons we love this great game, we could fill this entire book. But we wanted to cover a lot of other topics as well, so we had to keep this list manageable. Here are ten things about the National Pastime that keep us coming back to the ballpark game after game, season after season.

Those Magic 90 Feet

Daniel Adams must have been a genius. According to John Thorn, the estimable co-editor of *Total Baseball,* Dr. Adams is the man who fixed the bases at 90 feet. Just think what a difference 12 inches would have made either way. Had Adams set the bases 91 feet apart, pitchers would dominate low-scoring contests that would lull fans to sleep. At 89 feet, hitters would unleash a mind-numbing barrage of runs that fans would eventually find equally off-putting. Ninety feet is just right. This distance maintains the balance between offense and defense while giving baseball a sense of continuity. A runner out by a step 100 years ago would be out by that same step today.

The Perfect Diamond

Yankee Stadium's outfield configuration gives it a short right field for lefty sluggers to take aim at. In Fenway, hitters try to knock the ball over the Green Monster in left. Each stadium has a dimension that makes it unique. But the diamond, composed of four bases arranged around the pitcher's mound, remains the one constant in every park. Some infields may be harder or faster than others, but the layout of the game's core structure never favors one team over another.

National League Chess Matches

American League contests don't require as much strategy as those in the National League because the designated hitter rule removes many of a manager's late-inning decisions, such as choosing a pinch hitter for a pitcher late in a ball game. I like the way managers' wheels start spinning from the sixth inning on in a close National League contest. We saw a good example of that in the 1999 National League Championship Series between the Mets and the Braves. Every time Bobby Valentine made a move, Bobby Cox would counter it, and vice versa. They both showed the difference a manager can make in a tight ball game. American League managers can't make a similar impact because of the DH rule.

Showdown: The Pitcher-Hitter Confrontation

This is baseball's version of High Noon: Two gunslingers stare down each other's barrels, and only one can come away victorious. The pitcher controls the speed and location of the ball; the batter has only tenths of a second to adjust to whatever the hurler serves up. But the batter can set up a pitcher by working him into an advantageous count, such as two balls, no strikes or three balls, no strikes. This game within a game holds our fascination.

All in the Family

A ballpark is a great place for bonding. Parents and their children can go to a game and yell themselves hoarse together as they root for the home team. Then they talk for months about everything they saw that day. Every game is a shared gift that they store in the warmest folds of their memories. Baseball brings people together.

6-4-3

Maybe this is an infielder's bias, but I think few things are prettier than a perfectly turned 6-4-3 (short-to-second-to-first) double play. Twin killings require perfect synchronization between the shortstop and second baseman. The shortstop has to get the ball to his double-play partner so that he has enough time to step on second and nip the runner at first. And the second baseman often has to get the ball to first with 200 pounds or more of raging base runner bearing down on him. When you see two masters — like Roberto Alomar and Omar Vizquel — turn this trick, it's the closest thing baseball has to ballet.

Going for Three

The triple is the most exciting hit in baseball. When a hitter drives a ball into the gap in right or left center, we watch a mini-drama unfold: The runner revs into high gallop on the base paths, while the outfielder dashes to the ball as his teammates set up for what they hope will be a perfect relay to third. Ball and runner converge on third simultaneously, and only one can get there first. We hold our collective breath waiting for the umpire's call: safe or out!

Larceny on the Base Paths

When a great base stealer like Tony Womack or Rickey Henderson reaches first in the late innings of a close game, the entire park is electrified. We assume the runner is going to try to swipe second; the only question is when he will take off. Tension builds as the pitcher and runner engage in a game of cat-and-mouse, with the pitcher trying to hold his adversary close to the bag with side-steps and numerous throws. The top base thieves can take a pitcher out of his pattern by forcing him to abandon the change-up and slow curve. They change the entire pace and tone of a game.

Size Doesn't Matter

Baseball is a game that places emphasis on skill and hand-to-eye coordination rather than muscle. You can excel no matter how big or small you are. In the mid-1970s, a wire service photo showed Washington Senator first baseman Frank Howard towering over Kansas City Royals shortstop Freddie Patek as he held Patek close to the bag. Frank was 6'7", 255 pounds; Freddie was 5'4", 145 pounds. Yet they were both All-Stars. That's the beauty of the sport.

Going Deep for a Win

The *walk-off home run* — any homer that ends a ballgame — is baseball's exclamation point. The player who hits it — always a member of the home team — circles the bases while the visiting club walks off the field. We saw a perfect example of this dramatic blow in Game Three of the 1999 World Series when New York Yankee left fielder Chad Curtis's 10th inning blast crushed the Atlanta Braves. That night, Curtis was like a great matador who had just executed a swift kill. He brought the crowd to its feet before sending it to the exits.

Chapter 26

Ten Baseball Nicknames
That Hit the Mark

● ●

In This Chapter

▶ The Toy Cannon

▶ Cha Cha or The Baby Bull

▶ Doggie

▶ Charley Hustle

▶ Spaceman

▶ Le Grande Orange

▶ The Washington Monument

▶ Stretch

▶ The Bird

▶ The Monster

● ●

*E*ver since some sportswriter from the 1880s christened Chicago White
Stocking superstar Mike "King" Kelly with his royal moniker, nicknames
have been entrenched in the baseball lexicon. Following are ten of our
favorites.

Jim "The Toy Cannon" Wynn
(Houston Astros, Los Angeles Dodgers, Atlanta Braves, New York Yankees, Milwaukee Brewers)

Jim Wynn was tagged The Toy Cannon because he generated so much power
for his size (5'10", 160 pounds). Jim and I played together with the Astros
from 1963 to 1971. Pound-for-pound, he may have been the greatest slugger
ever. Jim had hands as strong as any blacksmith's. Though he swung a relatively heavy piece of lumber (36 ounces), he was able to snap it through the

strike zone rather than push it. The ball exploded off his bat. Jim played most of his career in the Astrodome when it was the worst home-run hitters park in the majors. Had he played on any other home field, he would have hit 40 or more homers every year. In 1967, Henry Aaron nipped Jimmie for the National League home-run title by only two dingers. Afterwards, the ever-gracious Aaron said, "As far as I'm concerned, Jim Wynn is the home-run champion this season because of the place he plays in."

Orlando "Cha Cha" Cepeda, a.k.a. The Baby Bull
(San Francisco Giants, St. Louis Cardinals, Atlanta Braves, Oakland A's, Boston Red Sox, Kansas City Royals)

Cha-Cha was the perfect nickname for Cepeda because he was so rhythmic in the batter's box. He was also an exuberant cheerleader in the clubhouse, one of the vocal leaders of the two championship St. Louis Cardinals teams. Fans and players also dubbed him The Baby Bull because his father Perucho, a shortstop whom many feel was the greatest player in Puerto Rican baseball history, was known as The Bull. That sobriquet also fit nicely, as Cepeda was one of the strongest right-handed hitters to play during the 1960s. Trivia fans take note: In 1958, as a rookie with the San Francisco Giants, Cepeda crashed the first major league homer ever hit on the West Coast. It came against the Giants's hated rivals, the Los Angeles Dodgers. Cepeda would go on to capture Rookie of the Year honors. In 1967, he became the first unanimous choice to win the National League's MVP Award.

Tony "Doggie" Perez
(Cincinnati Reds, Montreal Expos, Boston Red Sox)

Perez was one of the finest clutch hitters I've ever seen. On the Big Red Machine (Cincinnati Reds), we called him Doggie or Big Dog because any time he came to the plate with runners on base, you expected him to take a large bite out of the pitcher. He was able to do that because, unlike some sluggers, he understood what he faced in any given situation. With the bases loaded, if the pitcher gave him something to pull, Tony jacked it hard to the left, often for extra bases. But throw him a difficult outside pitch under the same circumstances, and Doggie would slash it to right field for a two-run base hit. He drove in 100 or more runs seven times and had five other seasons of 90 or more RBIs.

Pete "Charlie Hustle" Rose
(Cincinnati Reds, Philadelphia Phillies, Montreal Expos)

During a 1963 exhibition game against the New York Yankees, Reds second baseman Pete Rose ran top speed to first base. On a walk. Several Bronx Bombers, thinking the rookie was a *hot dog* (see Appendix A for an explanation of that term), derisively referred to Rose as "Charlie Hustle." Pete transformed the gibe into a compliment. Soon baseball fans were cheering his passionate, no-holds-barred style of play that helped him win three batting titles and made him a vital part of three world champion baseball teams.

Bill "Spaceman" Lee
(Boston Red Sox, Montreal Expos)

Before games, this wacky left-handed pitcher would hit *fungos* (see Appendix A for a definition) to himself in the outfield. Lee once publicly admitted to throwing two spitballs to Tony Taylor, one of which Taylor belted for a homer. When a reporter asked him how a singles hitter like Taylor could jerk out a spitter, Bill replied, "I guess he hit the dry side." If you asked him why he threw a certain pitch, Bill would do five minutes on Einstein's theory of curved space. Lee earned his nickname when a visitor to the Red Sox clubhouse asked his teammate, utility infielder John Kennedy, if he had seen a NASA launch that afternoon. Pointing to Bill's locker, Kennedy replied, "We don't need to look at anyone going up in rockets on TV; we have our own spaceman right here." Lee was a character, but he knew how to pitch. He had a funky moving sinker, a good slow curve, and pinpoint control.

Rusty "Le Grande Orange" Staub
(Houston Astros, Montreal Expos, New York Mets, Detroit Tigers)

Staub and I came up together with the Houston Astros. Rusty's dedication to hard work made him a star. He was not a good hitter when Houston first signed him; he was just a big guy who could handle only the high fastball. But he studied the pitchers and spent hundreds of hours in the batting cage honing his swing. Rusty became such a formidable player, he made the All-Star team six times. In 1967, his best season, he batted .333 to finish fifth in the NL batting race and had a league leading four doubles. I played with him that season, and almost every pitch he made contact with — including the outs — was hit hard. The 6'3", 210-pounder earned the nickname Le Grande Orange (meaning, of course, the big redhead) when the Astros traded him to the Montreal Expos in 1969. With his star presence and booming bat, Rusty became an instant fan favorite as he brought the expansion franchise some much needed on-field credibility.

Frank "The Washington Monument" Howard
(Los Angeles Dodgers, Washington Senators, Texas Rangers, Detroit Tigers)

When Howard was starring with the Washington Senators, the 6'7" 255-pound player was called The Washington Monument not only because he appeared to be as big as that landmark but because he looked as if he could hit a base-ball over it. Frank was one of the strongest men ever to play the game. When Ted Williams became manager for the Senators in 1969, he told Frank that he had seen only three men who could hit the ball harder than he could: Babe Ruth, Jimmy Foxx, and Mickey Mantle. Because Ruth once reportedly hit a ball 600 feet in an exhibition game and the Mick still holds the record for the longest regular season homerun (565 feet), that is mighty august company. Frank was the first player I ever saw who made the bat look like a toothpick in his hands. Nearly every pitcher who faced him was terrified that he might hit a line drive back through the box.

Willie "Stretch" McCovey
(San Francisco Giants, San Diego Padres, Oakland A's)

Another big man, McCovey was 6'5" and used every inch when he patrolled first base. Do you remember the comic book character Mr. Fantastic, the leader of the Fantastic Four? He could elongate his body for hundreds of yards to catch fleeing criminals. That's how Willie looked when he stretched out to take a throw from one of his infielders — as if his body shot out halfway across the diamond. He saved his teammates dozens of errors each season; it was nearly impossible to throw a ball by him. Gifted with soft hands, Willie caught anything he could reach, and he could reach just about any ball thrown in the same zip code as first base.

Mark "The Bird" Fidrych
(Detroit Tigers)

I felt so badly for Fidrych because a sore arm ended his career prematurely, and he would have been so good for the game. In 1976, Mark won the Rookie of the Year Award after winning 19 games for a Detroit Tigers team with a won-lost percentage below .500. Few players have ever been more entertain-ing on the field. Before throwing a pitch in a crucial spot, he would talk to the ball, imploring it to avoid the hitter's bat. If he thought a ball had a hit in it, he'd toss it out of the game and ask for a new one. ("I want that ball to go back in the bag with all the other balls so they can tell him to behave.") Mark would storm off the mound in mid-inning to throw his arms around an infielder after a good play. Fans called him The Bird — after the Sesame Street character Big Bird — because he would often flap his arms as if they were wings as he stood on the mound.

Dick "The Monster" Radatz
(Boston Red Sox, Cleveland Indians, Chicago Cubs, Detroit Tigers, Montreal Expos)

Facing Radatz was a real horror show for a lot of batters. This was the original Terminator. When this 6'5", 250-pound behemoth stomped in from the Red Sox bullpen, hitters started considering early retirement. He threw close to 100 mph, and whenever he took his warm-up tosses, he'd throw the first pitch all the way to the backstop. The idea that a guy who throws pitches you can barely see might be a little wild that day gets the hitter's attention in a hurry. When Radatz pitched in the early 1960s, most relievers alternated good and bad years. The Monster was a rarity because he strung together four seasons of All-Star quality (1962–1965). During that period, he registered 49 wins and 100 saves (when saves were much harder to come by than they are today) for Red Sox teams that never topped .500.

Part VI
Appendixes

The 5th Wave   By Rich Tennant

"What do you mean, everyone on the bus has to sign the speeding ticket?"

In this part . . .

*A*round the horn . . . bang-bang play . . . high heat. . . .
Baseball has a rich, colorful lexicon, and you must
understand it if you want to follow the action. We provide
a list of key phrases, slang words, and terms in Appendix
A. Appendix B provides you with contact information for
the world's major baseball organizations, from major
league franchises to youth and senior leagues.

Appendix A

Baseball Speak: A Glossary

• •

n this appendix, you discover the most common baseball terms (as well as a few uncommon terms here and there!) to help you in any baseball-lingo jam.

Ace: The top card in a deck, the top gun on a pitching staff. Strikeout kings and 20-game winners like Randy Johnson, Pedro Martinez, and Mike Hampton are all considered aces. Teams can have more than one. The 1997 Atlanta Braves staff featured a fistful of aces: Cy Young Award winners Greg Maddux, Tom Glavine, John Smoltz, and 20-game winner Danny Neagle.

Across the letters: Any pitch that passes the batter chest high.

Activate: To return an injured or suspended player to your team's active roster (in the majors, a 25-man squad).

Adjudged: Any judgment call made by the umpire, such as declaring a runner out at second base on a close play.

Advance: For a runner, to move along the base paths. ("Jeter advanced from first to third on O'Neill's single to right.") For a hitter, to move the runner at least one base. ("Griffey's groundout to Alomar advanced Rodriguez from second to third.")

Advance sale: The number of seats sold before game day.

Advance scout: A scout who follows opposing teams, trying to spot their strengths and, more importantly, their weaknesses.

Ahead in the count: If you're a pitcher, you have more strikes than balls on the hitter you're facing. If you're the hitter at the plate, the count contains more balls than strikes.

Alive: An inning that is extended by the offense after two outs. ("Base hits by Bagwell and Everett kept the inning alive.")

All-American out: A weak hitter. The phrase was supposedly originally coined by Babe Ruth to describe Leo Durocher.

Alley: The section of outfield real estate between the center fielder and the left or right fielders. It is also called the *power alley* (where hits go to become doubles or triples) or the *gap*.

Alley hitter: A batter who is an expert at driving the ball into the alleys for extra base hits. Edgar Martinez has been one of the better alley hitters of the 1990s.

Alligator mouth: A braggart. In his best-selling baseball diary *Ball Four,* Jim Bouton describes one player who couldn't back up his talk as having "an alligator mouth with a hummingbird behind." (Well, "behind" wasn't the word he used.)

Allow: To surrender hits or runs. ("Wright allowed three runs on five hits in the first.")

All-Star: Any player voted by the fans or chosen by the manager to appear in an All-Star Game.

All-Star break: A three-day hiatus in the major league schedule, which occurs in mid-July and coincides with the All-Star Game.

All-Star Game: The annual interleague contest between players representing the American League and National League. Fans choose the starting lineup for both teams in balloting currently conducted by *USA Today.*

Alphonse and Gaston Act: Two fielders charging after the same ball suddenly pull up short when they each think that the other is going to make the catch. The ball drops or goes through for a base hit. *They just pulled the old Alphonse and Gaston act.* The name comes from two turn-of-the-century cartoon characters, Alphonse and Gaston, whose deference to each other was so extreme, simple tasks like getting through a doorway took an eternity. ("After you, my dear Gaston." "No, after you my dear Alphonse." "No, I insist.")

Ancient mariner: A fielder who lacks wide range. The term comes from the poem *The Ancient Mariner* ("who stoppeth one in three") and was originally said of shortstop Joe Cronin during the twilight of his Hall of Fame career.

Appeal: When a player who has been fined or is subject to some other disciplinary action asks to plead his case to the league president or commissioner's office.

Appeal play: The defensive team's attempt to reverse a safe call by contending that a runner missed a base or left a base too early on a fly ball. An appeal must be called for immediately following a disputed play and before the pitcher throws another pitch toward home plate. Major league protocol requires the pitcher to step off the mound and throw to the base in question. The umpire at that base then rules if the runner was indeed safe or out.

Appearance: Taking part in a baseball game, either as a pitcher, fielder, or hitter.

Apple: A baseball. ("McGwire rocked that apple into the upper deck.")

Arbiter: Little-used term for an umpire, particularly the umpire working behind home plate.

Around the horn: A double play that goes from third base to second to first. The phrase comes from a time before the opening of the Panama Canal when ships had to sail around South America's Cape Horn to reach the Pacific from the Atlantic.

Arson squad: A bull pen that routinely allows the opposition to score. The relief pitchers are said to "throw gasoline on the fire."

Artificial turf: Any playing field surface that is not made of grass.

Ash: A baseball bat made from northern white ash.

Ash handle: The bottom portion of the bat.

Aspirin: A pitch thrown so fast that it appears to be smaller than it actually is. ("Millwood was bringing it so hard today, the baseball looked like an aspirin.")

Assist: A throw from one fielder to another that puts out the batter or a base runner.

At-bat: Any time the batter gets a hit, makes an out, or reaches base on an error or fielder's choice. If the batter draws a walk, is hit by a pitch, completes a sacrifice, or reaches base on catcher's interference, he is credited with a plate appearance but not an at-bat.

At 'em ball: A ball that is hit directly at a fielder.

Attempt: The act of trying to steal a base. ("Tony Womack has 55 steals in only 61 attempts.")

Automatic out: A weak batter who has such a poor sense of the strike zone that he rarely hits or walks. Most pitchers are automatic outs when they come to the plate.

Away game: When your team plays on your opponent's home field.

Babe Ruth's curse: The jinx that supposedly haunts the Boston Red Sox, who haven't won a world championship since the team sold Babe Ruth to the dreaded New York Yankees in 1920.

Backdoor slide: A difficult maneuver in which the runner reaches out to touch the base with his finger or hand as his body slides past the bag. Roberto Alomar is a master of the backdoor slide and used it to elude a home plate tag against the Boston Red Sox during a nationally televised game in 1999.

Backstop: The screen that sits behind and extends over the home plate area. It protects fans from foul balls. Major league backstops must stand at least 60 feet from home plate.

Back through the box: A ball hit sharply through the pitcher's mound.

Back yard: A team's home field.

Bad ball: A pitch thrown out of the strike zone, but just close enough to invite the batter to swing.

Bad-ball hitter: A batter who is adept at hitting pitches outside the strike zone. New York Yankee catcher Yogi Berra used to get base hits on balls thrown nearly over his head.

Bad bounce or bad hop: A batted ball that eludes the fielder when it takes an unexpected hop, usually because it has struck an object on the field such as a pebble.

Bad call: A call that the umpire misses.

Bad hands: An affliction attributed to poor fielders.

Bad hose: A sore throwing arm.

Bag: A term often used in place of *base.*

Bail out: What a hitter does when he falls away from a pitch that appears to be coming towards his body.

Balk: A pitcher's motion that is deemed deceptive by the umpire. Runners who are on base when a balk is called get to advance one base.

Ball: A pitch out of the strike zone that the batter doesn't swing at and the umpire does not call as a strike.

Ball boy or ball girl: The person who retrieves foul balls.

Ball club: A baseball team.

Baltimore chop: A batted ball that bounces so high it cannot be fielded before the hitter reaches first base. Wee Willie Keeler, John McGraw, and the cagey Baltimore Orioles popularized it during the 1890s.

Bandbox: A small ballpark, which favors hitters. The Baker Bowl, which was home to the Philadelphia Phillies until 1938, was a notorious bandbox. Only 280½ feet separated home plate from the right field wall.

Bang-bang play: The base runner and ball reach a base or home plate at nearly the same moment.

Banjo hitter: A batter who hits mostly singles.

Barber: A pitcher who throws close to the batter's chin. For example, "gives him a shave."

Barrel: The thickest part of a bat.

Base: The 15-inch (38cm) square white marker found at three of a baseball infield's four corners. (Home plate is five-sided.) Bases are placed 90 feet (27.45m) apart from each other.

Base on balls: What a pitcher surrenders whenever the umpire calls four of his pitches out of the strike zone (balls) during a hitter's time at bat. The batter takes first base, the errant hurler's manager takes a Maalox — and, if the pitcher allows very many of these, he takes a trip to the showers. Also known as a *walk.*

Baseball: The white, red-stitched sphere that pitchers throw, fielders catch, and hitters whack during a baseball game. It is composed of a cork core under layers of rubber, yarn, and cowhide.

Baseball mud: Umpires rub this auburn mud into new baseballs to remove the sheen from the leather. Why? So that pitchers can get a better grip on the ball. Also known as rubbing mud.

Base clogger: A slow base runner. When Casey Stengel's Yankees would play the Washington Senators during the late '50s, he would instruct his pitchers to walk such lumbering albeit dangerous sluggers as Roy Sievers and Harmon Killebrew so "we can clog the bases with those buffaloes."

Basket catch: A catch made with your glove at belt level. Coaches frown on the practice, but Willie Mays won 12 consecutive Gold Gloves with his signature catch.

Bat: The sculpted, wooden implement (usually fashioned from pine or ash) that hitters use to assault a baseball.

Bat around: What a team does when its entire lineup bats during an inning.

Bat boy or bat girl: The players' valet during the game. The bat boy or bat girl picks up the hitter's bat and helmet when the hitter's turn at bat ends. He or she also brings new balls to the umpires between innings.

Bat speed: The time it takes a hitter to get his bat through the hitting zone.

Batter: What a player becomes when he steps into the batter's box to take his swings.

Batter's box: The rectangle, marked by chalk, on both sides of home plate. The batter must stay within that box when hitting.

Battery: A team's pitcher-catcher combination for any given game.

Batting cage: A metal cage placed behind home plate during batting practice. It protects bystanders from being hit by foul balls.

Batting eye: A player's ability to judge the strike zone. Batters who average 100 or more walks per season (Frank Thomas, Barry Bonds, and Rickey Henderson) have excellent batting eyes.

Batting glove: Batters usually wear this soft leather glove on their bottom hand (right for left-handed hitters, left for righties), though some batters wear them on both hands. Batting gloves prevent blisters and give the hitter a better grip on the bat handle. Some fielders wear batting gloves underneath their fielding gloves to soften the impact of hard-hit balls.

Batting helmet: Hard plastic helmet that protects a hitter's cranium from errant pitches.

Batting order: The sequence in which a team's hitters appear at home plate during a game.

Beanball: A pitch that is deliberately thrown to hit the batter.

Beat out: When a runner reaches base just ahead of a throw, as in "Henderson beat out that grounder to short for a base hit."

Bees: The sting a batter feels when he hits a pitch off-center (usually felt in cold weather).

Bench: What players sit on while they are in the dugout. Players who are *benched,* are *grabbing some bench,* or have been forced to *ride the pines,* have been indefinitely removed from a team's starting lineup.

Bench jockey: A player, usually a sub who rarely appears in games, who hurls insults from the dugout at opposing players on the field to break their concentration.

Big bill: A ground ball's final hop. (It bounces as high as the bill on a crouched fielder's cap.)

Big leagues: The major leagues.

Bingle: A softly hit single.

Bird dog: A part-time baseball scout.

Black, The: The outer edges of home plate. Balls that are *on the black* are strikes and difficult to hit squarely. Control pitchers like Greg Maddux or Jimmy Key are often said to *paint the black* with their pitches.

Bleachers: The most inexpensive seats in the park. Located behind the outfields of most major league parks.

Bleeder: A base hit — usually one that barely makes it through the infield. It can also be a weak pop fly that falls in front of an outfielder.

Bloop: Or blooper. A weakly hit fly ball that just makes it over the infield. Also known as a *dying quail* or *Texas Leaguer.*

Blue darter: A hard hit, low line drive.

Bonehead play: A mental error. A typical boner by a player who rarely made one: Babe Ruth made the final out of the 1926 World Series when he was caught trying to steal second with the score 3–2.

Bonus baby: A young prospect, usually a college player, who signs for a large bonus before proving himself as a professional.

Book, The: A mythical compendium of traditional baseball strategies. Managers who *go by the book* play to tie in the ninth at home, bring in left-handed relievers to get out left-handed hitters, and have their pitchers bunt with none (and often one) out and runners on base. The best managers often go against The Book.

Boot: A fielding error. Also known as a *muff.*

Box score: The statistical record of a baseball game.

Breaking pitch: Any ball that curves.

Brushback: A pitch aimed at a batter, not to hit him (though they sometimes do, often to the pitcher's chagrin) but to move him off the plate. Also known as a *purpose pitch* or *chin music.*

Bug on the rug: A ball that eludes outfielders by bouncing about on the turf (artificial grass).

Bull pen: The area where pitchers warm up before entering a game. In most stadiums, it is located behind the outfield fence. In other parks, the bull pens can be found in foul territory along the left and right field lines. The term is also used to refer to the collection of relievers on a club. ("The New York Mets have a deep bull pen.")

Bunt: An offensive weapon in which the hitter holds his bat in the hitting zone and lets the ball make contact with it. If he is bunting for a hit, the batter tries to get to first before an infielder fields the softly hit ball and throws him out. If he is bunting to move a base runner up a base, the hitter only needs to push the ball to a spot where a play at first base is the infielder's sole option.

Bush: Any amateurish action or behavior. Publicly criticizing a teammate for a failed but honest effort is considered *bush*.

Butcher: A poor fielder.

Caddy: A substitute — generally an excellent fielder who takes the place of a mediocre fielder in the late innings of a ball game.

Cadillac trot (a.k.a. Cadillacing): A slugger's trot around the bases after hitting a home run. From a quote by Ralph Kiner, a homer king of the late 1940s and early '50s: "Singles hitters drive jalopies, homerun hitters drive Cadillacs."

Call: The umpire's declaration of safe or out, ball or strike, fair or foul. The term also refers to the official score's ruling on a play (hit or error, wild pitch or passed ball, and so on).

Called game: A game that has been terminated by the umpire-in-chief before its completion. Umpires usually call games due to inclement weather or curfews.

Called out looking: What is said to have happened to a batter when he takes strike three without offering at it.

Call up: Summoning a minor leaguer to the majors.

Camp under: What an outfielder does when he positions himself under a fly ball.

Can of corn: An easy fly-ball out.

Career year: The best season of a player's career.

Carry a club: Being the leading force behind your team's victories over an extended period. ("Bench's homerun splurge has carried the Reds for the last ten days.")

Castoff: A player cut from a team.

Catch: The act of a fielder getting secure possession of the ball in his glove or hand. Whether you have secure possession is sometimes obvious, but it is often a subjective call by an umpire.

Cellar: Last place in your division or league.

Cellar dweller: The team in last place in the league.

Challenge the hitter: To throw your best pitch, usually a fastball, to the hitter, daring him to make contact.

Chance: Any opportunity for a fielder to catch a ball.

Checked swing: A swing that is terminated before a batter *breaks his wrists* (brings his top hand over the bottom hand while taking his swing). Whether the hitter went around too far is the umpire's subjective call.

Choke hitter: A hitter who grips the bat at least an inch or two from the bottom of its handle. Using an extreme version of this grip (four inches or more) sacrifices power for contact.

Circus catch: A spectacular, unusually acrobatic fielding play.

Cleanup: The number four hitter in a lineup. He is expected to *clean* the bases by driving in runs.

Closed stance: A hitting stance in which the batter's front foot is nearer to the plate than the back one.

Closer: The relief pitcher who finishes games, usually in *save* situations. Mariano Rivera, Trevor Hofman, Armando Benitez, and Robb Nen are all considered premier closers.

Clubhouse lawyer: A player who is outspoken and critical about club, league, or union policy.

Clutch: A situation when the outcome of a game or series is on the line. It often occurs in the late innings of an important ball game.

Collar: From *horse collar* (which resembles a large 0). A batter who doesn't get a hit in a game is *wearing the collar.* Collars come in all sizes — size three when the batter is hitless in three at-bats, size four when he suffers a quartet of failures, and so on.

Come-backer: A ball hit back to the pitcher.

Corked bat: A bat with a deep hole drilled into the center of its barrel. The perpetrator (corked bats are illegal) fills the hole with cork, shredded rubber, or mercury, and then plugs it with glue and sawdust to make the bat appear normal. Bats filled with these substances propel the ball faster and farther than those made strictly from wood.

Count: The numbers of balls and strikes called on a hitter during a time at bat. The balls are always listed first. A 2–1 count means the batter has two balls and one strike.

Cousin: A pitcher who can't get a particular hitter out with any regularity, as in "Edgar Martinez hits (fill in the name of any New York Yankee pitcher) as if he were his cousin."

Cup of coffee: A brief stay in the major league. A minor league player who fills in for an injured major leaguer for a few weeks and is then sent back down has been up for *a cup of coffee.*

Cycle: When a hitter hits a single, double, triple, and home run in the same game. Of these four, the triple is hardest to collect (unless you are a hitter like Chicago Cubs outfielder Lance Johnson, who rarely homers but annually leads his league in triples).

Dead ball: A ball that the umpire has ruled is no longer in play because play has been suspended. (A base runner is *dead* when a fielder throws him out.)

Dead from the neck up: A phrase used to describe a player who is gifted physically but is intellectually challenged.

Deep in the count: Two balls and two strikes or three balls and two strikes against a batter.

Defensive indifference: An undefended stolen base. The defensive team makes no attempt to throw out the base stealer.

Defensive interference: Any act by a fielder that interferes with a batter's swinging at a pitch.

Designated hitter (DH): The hitter in the American League lineup who bats without having to take the field. He always bats in place of the pitcher, though the rules state he may bat in any position in the batting order.

Diamond: A baseball field (more correctly, the *infield*).

Dig out: To successfully field an inaccurate throw.

Dish: Home plate.

Domeball: Baseball games played in enclosed stadiums.

Double: A two-base hit.

Double play: A single defensive play that produces two outs; it usually occurs in the infield. In an *unassisted* double play, one fielder records both outs.

Double steal: Two base runners attempting to steal on the same pitch.

Doubleheader: Two consecutive games played between the same teams on the same day.

Down the line: A hit that closely follows the foul line.

Downtown: The place where Petula Clark hangs out and where deeply hit home runs are said to land. During the late 1960s, a San Diego Padres outfielder was known as "Downtown" Ollie Brown.

Ducks on the pond: Base runners.

Earned run: Any run charged to the record of the pitcher. These runs can develop as the result of a hit, a sacrifice fly, a fielder's choice, a walk, a hit batsman, a wild pitch, or a balk. Runs that develop as the result of an error, passed ball, or catcher's interference are *unearned.* (See Chapter 16 for how to figure a pitcher's earned run average, or ERA.)

Ejection: Banishment from the field of a player, manager, or coach by an umpire.

Error: A defensive misplay.

Even count: One ball and one strike or two balls and two strikes against a batter.

Even stance: A hitting stance in which both of the batter's feet are equidistant from the plate.

Everyday player: A player who appears in his team's starting lineup for most of its games.

Exhibition games: Any game that does not count in the season's standings. All spring training games are exhibition games.

Expansion: Adding new franchises to a league. The first major league expansion in the 20th century occurred in 1961, when the Los Angeles Angels and new Washington Senators (the old Senators had moved to Minnesota) joined the American League.

Extra-base hit: Any base hit other than a single.

Fadeaway: The original term used for what we now call a screwball. Hall of Famer Christy Mathewson reportedly created the appellation.

Fair ball: A batted ball that: 1) Settles in fair territory between the foul lines; 2) Remains in fair territory until it passes first or third base; or 3) Stays within the foul lines while it passes over the outfield fence for a home run.

Fair territory: The part of the playing field between and including the first and third base lines, from home base to the outfield fences.

Farm system: A major league team's system of minor league clubs.

Fielder's choice: When a fielder handles a ground ball and attempts to throw out a base runner other than the hitter.

Finding the handle: Getting a firm grip on the ball before throwing it.

Finesse pitcher: A hurler who gets hitters out more with guile and control than speed. Greg Maddux is probably the greatest finesse pitcher of the last twenty years.

Fireballer: The opposite of a finesse pitcher, this stud overpowers hitters with a blazing fastball. Randy Johnson has been the king fireballer of the 1990s.

Fireman: A relief pitcher, usually one who is brought into a precarious situation. He is there to put out the fire.

First ball hitter: A batter who usually swings at the first pitch. Such hitters rarely walk and usually have low on-base percentages.

Five o'clock hitter: A low-average hitter who hits his best shots during batting practice.

Five-tool player: A player who runs the bases quickly, fields his position expertly, demonstrates a strong, accurate throwing arm, and hits for both power and average. Ken Griffey, Jr., Vladimir Guerrero, and Larry Walker are five-tool players.

Flake: Any player who behaves eccentrically. Reliever Turk Wendell, who brushes his teeth between every inning, is said to be a flake.

Flare: A looping fly ball hit to the opposite field, just beyond the infield. It usually plunks in for a base hit.

Fly ball: A ball hit into the air on an arc.

Force out: When a batted ball forces a runner to advance to another base and the fielder possessing the ball tags that base before the runner reaches it.

40-40 Club: That group of rare players who have hit forty homeruns while stealing forty bases in the same season. Oakland's Jose Canseco became the first 40-40 man in 1988. As of 1999, Barry Bonds and Alex Rodriguez were the only other two members of this select group.

Foul pole: The yellow poles along the outfield walls that mark the end of the foul lines. They indicate whether a ball hit into the seats is foul or a home run. Balls hit to the left of the left field foul pole are foul, as are balls hit to the right of the right field pole. A ball that hits either pole is, for reasons no one understands, called fair. (That being the case, why don't they call it the fair pole?)

Foul territory: The section of the playing field outside the first and third base lines.

Foul tip: A batted ball that careens sharply toward the catcher's mitt and is caught. It is a foul tip *only* if it is caught. Any foul tip is also a strike. The ball is in play. If the catcher catches a foul tip with two strikes on the batter, the batter has struck out. If a foul tip is not caught (in which case it remains a foul ball), the pitch is called a strike if the batter has less than two strikes. With two strikes on the batter, the count holds and the at-bat continues.

Franchise player: A star player, usually young, around whom management can build a team. Boston's Nomar Garciaparra and Montreal's Vladmir Guererro are both franchise players. When the young Tom Seaver was leading the New York Mets out of oblivion in the '60s, he was nicknamed "The Franchise."

Free agent: A player who is not contracted to play for any team. He is free to negotiate with any club interested in his services.

Full count: When the pitcher has three balls and two strikes on the batter.

Fungo: A long, thin bat used by a coach or player to hit grounders or flies during fielding practice. The hitter tosses the ball into the air before striking it.

Game face: A look that tells you a player is all business. ("When Dave Stewart wears his game face, his glare penetrates the hitter like a laser.")

Gamer: A player who thrives in pressure situations, handles adversity well, or has a high threshold of pain. Also, the bat a hitter uses during a game. Out of every dozen bats he orders, the average major leaguer usually finds three or four gamers. He uses the other bats during batting practice or gives them away as souvenirs.

Games back: The number of games your team is out of first place.

Gap: The area between the left fielder and center fielder or the right fielder and center fielder. See *alley.*

Gap shot: An extra-base hit that lands in the gap and usually rolls or bounces to the wall. Also called a *tweener or gapper.*

Get a piece of the ball: When a hitter is just trying to make contact with a pitch, usually with two strikes on him.

Getaway game: The final game in a series for the visiting team.

Glove: The padded leather covering that protects a fielder's hand and makes it easier for him to catch a baseball. All fielders use gloves except the catcher and first baseman, who wear *mitts.* (The difference between a mitt and a glove? Mitts have more padding.)

Glove man: An expert fielder. Often used to describe a weak hitter whose fielding prowess keeps him in the lineup.

Goat: A player who makes a glaring mistake that contributes to a defeat. It's a term used almost exclusively by reporters and fans. Most professional players will tell you that no one play ever costs a team a game.

Go deep: To hit a home run.

Go nine: To pitch a complete game (something that is becoming increasingly rare in modern baseball).

Gold Glove: The annual award given in the major leagues (AL and NL) to the best fielding player at each position.

Goose egg: A scoreless inning. ("Jose Lima has put up nothing but goose eggs through nine.")

Gopher ball: A pitch that is hit for a home run.

Grand slam: A home run with the bases loaded. (*Note:* The popular phrase "grand slam home run" is a redundancy.) Also known as a *grand salami* (a term popularized by broadcaster Tim McCarver).

Green light: Not an actual sign. When a player has the green light, his manager has told him he can steal a base whenever he chooses, or he can swing away on 3–0 and 3–1 counts.

Ground ball: A batted ball that rolls or bounces on the ground. Also known as a *grounder.*

Grounds-rule double: A fair ball that goes over the outfield fence on a bounce. The runners take two bases.

Gun: A fielder's strong throwing arm. The term is usually applied to an outfielder or catcher. ("Texas catcher Ivan Rodriguez has a gun behind home plate.")

Gun shy: Being fearful of getting hit by a pitch.

Hack: To swing at a pitch ("take a hack").

Handcuffed: What an infielder becomes when a ball is hit so hard that he can't handle it, even though it was hit right at him.

Handle: The end of the bat gripped by the hitter. It is the thinnest part of the bat.

Hanging curve: A curveball that breaks little except a pitcher's heart. Hanging curves don't hang for very long; hitters usually quickly deposit them into the upper decks for home runs.

Headhunter: A pitcher who throws at hitter's heads.

Heads-up play: A smart maneuver on the base paths or in the field.

Heat: An above-average fastball. Also known as *cheese, high cheese, smoke, gas, high heat,* and *hummer.* Dennis Eckersley used to call his fastball a *yakker.* Want to flash some retro-cool? Try on a term popularized by the Cincinnati Reds pitchers during the mid-1960s. That hard-throwing lot — they led the National League in strikeouts four times in five years — measured their fastballs by how much *hair* they had. The faster the pitcher, the more hair he had on the ball. ("Did I have much hair out there today?" "You were positively shaggy, son.")

Hill: The pitcher's mound.

Hit: A ball batted into fair territory, which allows the hitter to reach base safely without benefit of a fielding error or a fielder's choice.

Hit by pitch: A plate appearance that results in the batter being hit by a pitch. The batter is awarded first base. It's also known as *taking one for the team.*

Hit-and-run: An offensive strategy called by a manager with a runner on first. As the pitcher winds up, the runner takes off for second base. The batter must make contact so that the runner can safely take second on an out or go for extra bases on a hit.

Hitch: The term used to describe a hitter's habit of dropping his hands just prior to swinging his bat. It disrupts the timing of most batters, though for some players (like former slugger Cecil Fielder) a hitch is part of their timing mechanism.

Hole: In fielding, the term refers to an area deep and to the far right of the shortstop or deep and to the far left of the second baseman. In hitting, when a pitcher has a ball-strike advantage over a hitter, the batter is said to be *in a hole.* ("Clemens has Buhner in an 0–2 hole.") Also, a batter who doesn't make contact often is said to have a lot of *holes in his swing.*

Home plate: Home plate is a 17-inch (43cm) square with two of its corners removed to leave a 17-inch long edge, two 8½-inch (21.5cm) adjacent sides, and two 12-inch (30.5cm) long sides angled to a point. The result is a five-sided slab of white rubber with black borders. A runner scores by safely rounding all bases and touching home plate.

Home run: A fair fly ball that travels over the out-field fence. An inside-the-park home run doesn't leave the playing field; it is a fair ball that eludes fielders for so long that the hitter is able to circle the bases before a play can be made on him. Other terms for the home run include *homer, dinger, jack, going yard, dial 8, long-ball, round-tripper, 'tater, four-bagger, going downtown,* and *clout.*

Homestretch: The final month of a season.

Home team: The host team in a baseball game. Mutual agreement determines who will be the home team when a game is played on neutral ground.

Hoover: An expert infielder who fields or "vacuums" ground balls. Hoover was also the nickname of third baseman Brooks Robinson, a perennial Gold Glove winner.

Hot corner: Third base.

Hot dog: A player who shows off. (For example, a hitter who stands at home plate admiring his own home run.) Players who field their positions with flamboyance are often said to be *hot-dogging* or *cutting the pie.*

Human rain delay: A hitter who takes a long time settling in the batter's box.

Ice cream cone: A ball caught in the top of a glove's webbing so that the top half is visible.

Incentive clause: A clause in a player's contract that awards him for achieving certain goals.

Incomplete game: Any game that ends before the visiting team finishes batting in the fifth inning.

Indifference: Allowing an opposing base runner to advance a base without attempting to stop him.

In his kitchen: A pitch that jams a hitter on the bat handle. Yankee outfielder Lou Piniella once hit such an offering from Red Sox lefthander Bill Lee for a game-winning double. Afterwards Piniella told Lee, "Bill, you can come into my kitchen, but don't sit down to eat."

In jeopardy: A term that indicates the ball is in play and the offensive player can be put out.

Infield fly rule: With less than two out, a fair fly ball (that is neither a line drive nor an attempted bunt) that can be caught with ordinary effort by one of the infielders when first base and second base are occupied by runners (or when runners are on all the bases). The umpires call this rule. The batter is automatically out even if the fielder misses the ball. (This rule is designed to keep infielders from missing fly balls on purpose in order to make an unfair double play — with less than two out, runners don't try to advance if they think a ball is going to be caught!)

Inning: A unit of a baseball game consisting of a turn at-bat and three outs for each team. Regulation games consist of nine innings. A game can have fewer innings if it is called (canceled) by the umpire (due to inclement weather or some other circumstance) and more innings if the game is tied after the regulation nine.

Inside baseball: Strategy such as the hit-and-run, stealing, bunting for base hits, squeeze plays, sacrifices, hitting the cutoff man, and defensive positioning. All involve a degree of savvy and teamwork. Also known as *little ball.*

Inside-the-park home run: A home run that does not leave the playing field. To achieve it, a batter must race around all four bases before the fielder's throw beats him to home plate. During the last game of the 1999 season, Tampa Bay's Randy Winn smacked a genuine rarity against the New York Yankees: an inside-the-park grand slam.

Insurance runs: Any runs scored in the late innings by the team that is already ahead.

Jamming: When a pitcher throws the ball inside and near the batter's hands, he is *jamming* the batter.

Journeyman: A serviceable player, rarely a star, who bounces around from club to club. The prototypical journeyman: right-handed pitcher Robert Miller, who was traded or sold 12 times to 10 different teams.

Juggle: To mishandle a throw or a fielding chance.

Junk: Off-speed pitches such as the change-up, the slow curve, the palmball, and the knuckleball. Relief pitcher Stu Miller was a renowned junkballer during the 1960s. He was said to throw at three speeds: slow, slower, and slowest.

K: Another term for a *strikeout.*

Keystone: Second base. A team's shortstop and second baseman are known as the *keystone combination* for their double-play collaboration.

Knock: A base hit. ("Tony Gwynn had five knocks today.")

Laugher: A lopsided victory, as in "The Braves won an 11–1 laugher." Also known as a *blowout.*

Launching pad: A ballpark where home runs are plentiful. Camden Yards in Baltimore is considered a launching pad.

Lead-off hitter: The hitter who bats first in the batting order.

Left-handed specialist: A relief pitcher who is usually brought in solely to get out one to three tough left-handed hitters.

Leg hit: What a hitter earns when he gets a single on a batted ball that doesn't travel beyond the infield. Also, an *infield hit.*

Let the ball play him: Said of a fielder who waits for a batted ball to reach him rather than aggressively charging it.

Line drive: A ball that is hit, usually hard, on a straight line. Also known as a *bullet* or *frozen rope.*

Lineup: The nine players (or ten if you are using a designated hitter) who start a game.

Live ball: A ball that is in play.

Long reliever: A relief pitcher who enters in the early innings after a starter has been bombed or injured. Also known as the *long man,* he usually pitches three innings or more.

Looper: A fly ball that carries just over the infield for a base hit.

Lord Charles: Uncle Charlie has long been a nickname for the curveball. Lord Charles is the *curveball maximus.* It doesn't merely break; it dives and is as fast as most pitchers' sliders.

Loud foul: A ball that is hit hard and far, but foul.

Lumber: A baseball bat.

Magic number: You hear this term mentioned frequently as the season winds down. The number represents any combination of wins and losses by the first- and second-place teams that clinches the top spot in the standings for the first-place club. For example, the Atlanta Braves lead the National League East with a record of 100–60; the Florida Marlins are in second at 99–61. With only two games left in the 162-game season, Florida cannot possibly win more than 101 games. Therefore, the magic number for the Braves is two; if Atlanta wins both of its remaining games, it will have 102 wins, a total Florida cannot reach. Atlanta can also clinch by winning one game while Florida loses once because the Braves would have 101 victories while the Marlins could not win more than 100.

Make-up game: A game that has been rescheduled due to inclement weather or some other postponement.

Men in blue: Umpires.

Mental error: A mistake made by a distracted player such as forgetting the number of outs.

Middle reliever: A relief pitcher who enters (usually) in the fifth or sixth inning of a close game.

Money player: A player who performs his best in critical games.

Mop-up man: You don't want to see him pitching too often for your favorite team. Mop-up men pitch when their team is losing by a lopsided score.

Mr. October: A player who excels during post-season play. The nickname was first hung on Yankee right fielder Reggie Jackson after he clouted three successive home runs in the final game of the 1977 World Series. It has since been applied to Yankee super sub Jim Leyritz and Atlanta pitching ace John Smoltz.

Must-win: A game a team must win to stay alive in the pennant race or post-season play.

Nab: To throw out a runner, usually on a close play.

National Pastime: Another name for the sport of baseball.

Nightcap: The second game of a doubleheader.

No-hitter: A nine-inning complete game in which a pitcher does not allow a hit to the opposing team. The opposition can have base runners through fielding errors or walks. (See *Perfect game.*)

No man's land: An area on the base paths so far from any base that the runner is usually tagged out once he hazards into it.

Non-roster invitee: A player who is invited to spring training by a team without any guarantee of a roster spot.

Obstruction: A call made by the umpire when a fielder, who neither possesses the ball nor is about to field the ball, impedes the progress of the runner.

Offensive interference: Any act by the offensive team that interferes with or confuses a fielder attempting to make a play, such as if a base runner deliberately runs into the second baseman while he is fielding a ground ball.

On-deck circle: The circle between the dugout and home plate where a player awaits his turn at-bat.

Oh-fer: What a batter takes when he fails to hit in a game or series. ("Jones took an oh-fer last night when he went 0-for-five.")

Open stance: A hitting stance in which the front foot is farther away from the plate than the back foot.

Opposite field: That side of the field that is opposite the batter's hitting side. For example, left field is the opposite field for a left-handed hitter like Barry Bonds who bats from the right side of home plate.

Out: One of the three required retirements of an offensive team during its half-inning turn at bat.

Out pitch: A pitcher's best pitch; the one he is most likely to throw to get an out or finish off a hitter.

Outright: To sever a player from a team's major league roster, either by sending him to the minors or releasing him.

Overslide: The act of a base runner sliding past and losing contact with a base.

Passed ball: Any ball that eludes a catcher which, in the official scorer's opinion, he should have controlled with ordinary effort.

Payoff pitch: A pitch thrown on a full count (three balls, two strikes).

Peg: A fielder's throw.

Pennant: The flag awarded to the champion of each league.

Pepper: A fast-moving (soft) hitting and fielding game designed to improve a player's reflexes. The fielder and hitter stand 20 feet apart. The hitter hits the ball to the fielder, who catches it and immediately pitches it back. The hitter hits that offering, and play continues.

Perfect game: A complete game in which the pitcher does not hit any batter with the ball and does not allow any hits, walks, or errors.

Phantom double play: A double play called by the umpire, even though the second baseman or shortstop did not step on second base for the force out.

Phenom: An ultra talented rookie. In 1999, Kansas City Royals outfielder Carlos Beltran was an American League phenom. Also spelled *pheenom*.

Pick it: To catch a ball. Players who can really pick it are good fielders.

Pick-off: A throw by a pitcher or catcher to nab a runner off base.

Pinch hitter: A hitter who substitutes for a teammate in the batting order. Managers often ask this hitter to come through in a pinch (a crucial situation).

Pinch runner: A runner who substitutes for a teammate on the bases.

Pine tar: A dark, viscous substance spread on the bat handle so that a hitter can get a better grip.

Pitch around: Refusing to throw a pitch into the strike zone of a dangerous hitter.

Pitcher of record: A game's winning or losing pitcher. You must throw at least five innings in a game to qualify for a win.

Pitcher's duel: A low-scoring game usually decided in the late innings.

Pitchout: When a pitcher intentionally throws the ball outside the strike zone so that his catcher has a better chance to catch a base runner trying to steal.

Plate appearance: Any trip to the plate by a hitter. Plate appearances include at-bats, walks, sacrifices, interference calls, and hit-by-pitches.

Platoon: A system in which players are alternated at a position. It is usually based on what side of the plate batters swing from. Left-handed platoon hitters generally start against right-handers; their right-handed counterparts usually take the field against lefties.

"Play!" or "Play Ball!": The umpire's order to start the game or to resume play following a dead ball.

Play-by-play: Any verbal or written account of every play that occurs in a given game. Also, a broadcaster's verbal description of a ball game broadcast on TV or radio.

Player-manager: A player who also acts as his team's manager. No one has held that title in the major leagues since the Cincinnati Reds' Pete Rose in 1986.

Pop fly: A high but weakly hit fly ball that rarely goes beyond the infield.

Portsider: A left-handed pitcher.

Productive out: Any out that advances a runner, or, even better, scores a run. Productive outs are at their most productive in close ball games. Whitey Herzog's St. Louis Cardinals were perennial leaders in this unofficial category during the mid-1980s.

Protest: Managers play games *under protest* when they believe an umpire has made a call that contradicts the rule book. No one can protest an umpire's judgment call. Managers must announce their protests to the umpire immediately following the disputed action, before the next play begins. The league office is the arbiter of all protests. Protests are rarely allowed.

Pull: To hit the ball early enough so that the bat meets the ball in front of the hitter. Right-handed hitters pull the ball to the left side; left-handers pull to the right. Pull hitters usually hit for power.

Pull the string: To throw an off-speed pitch.

Punch-and-Judy hitter: A batter who sprays softly batted hits to all fields; also known as a spray hitter.

Punchout: A strikeout. Also called a *whiff* or a *K*.

Purpose pitch: A pitch thrown close to the batter with the purpose of moving him off home plate.

Quality start: Any game in which the starting pitcher works six or more innings while allowing three or fewer runs.

Question mark: A player whose status with a team is uncertain because of injury, a recent poor season, or a general decline in skills.

Quick pitch (or quick return): A pitch made before the batter is set. An umpire must judge whether the batter was set. A quick pitch is illegal. If the umpire rules that the pitcher threw the ball before the hitter was set in the batter's box, he can declare the pitch a ball (if no runners are on base) or a balk (if a runner is on base).

Rabbit ears: Any player, manager, or umpire who is hypersensitive to criticism.

Radar gun: The device used by baseball scouts to measure the speed of pitches, also know as the *JUGS gun*. Scouts refer to these guns as either fast or slow, depending on their make and how they record ball speed.

Rain check: The detachable portion of a ticket that guarantees you admission to another game in case the contest you are attending is rained out or postponed.

Regular season: In the major leagues, the 162-game season that determines each division's final standings and playoff participants.

Regulation game: A baseball game that is played to its completion.

Release: A pink slip. What a player reluctantly obtains when he is permanently cut from a team's roster.

Relief pitcher (reliever): Any pitcher who enters a game after the *starter* (the starting pitcher) has been removed.

Retired number: A uniform number worn by some baseball immortal that is no longer available to current players.

Retouch: The act of a runner returning to a base.

Rifle: A powerful throwing arm.

Rookie: A first-year player.

Rosin bag: A cloth bag containing a powder called rosin. Kept at the side of the mound, it is used by pitchers to dry their fingers to improve their grip on the ball. Applying rosin directly to the ball is illegal.

Rubber: A 6-x-24-inch (15.5cm x 61cm) rubber slab on top of the pitcher's mound.

Rubber game: The third game of a three-game series in which the opposing teams have split the first two contests.

Run: A scoring unit posted by an offensive player who touches first, second, third, and home plate in that order.

Run Batted In (RBI): A batter is credited with a run batted in when he drives a runner home (helps him score a run) via a hit, a sacrifice bunt or fly, a walk, a hit batsman, a fielder's choice, or on an error if the official scorer rules the run would have scored had the error not been made. (For example, a runner scores from third with less than two out on a long, catchable fly ball that is dropped by the center fielder. The center fielder is charged with the error. However, the official scorer credits the batter with a run batted in after deciding that the runner would have scored on a sacrifice fly had the ball been caught. Had the ball been hit to shallow center, and the scorer ruled it was not hit far enough to score the runner without the error, the batter would not receive an RBI.) You also credit a batter with an RBI if he drives himself in with a home run. Batters do not get *ribbies* when they drive runners in while grounding into double plays.

Run-down: Members of the defense chase a runner back and forth on the base paths in an attempt to put out the runner.

Runner: An offensive player who is advancing toward, returning to, or occupying a base.

Sacrifice bunt: When the hitter willingly bunts into an out in order to advance a base runner. Also known as "giving yourself up."

Sacrifice fly: A ball hit deep enough to score a runner from third base with less than two out.

Save: The statistical credit awarded to a relief pitcher who finishes a game on the victorious side but does not get the win. (To discover how saves are calculated, see Chapter 16.)

Scatter arm: A pitcher or fielder who throws wildly.

Scorecard: The graph that allows you to track every play in a game, inning by inning.

Scoring position: A runner on second or third base, where he can score on almost any hit to the outfield. (Sluggers like Mark McGwire, Ken Griffey, Jr., and Frank Thomas seem to be in scoring position the minute they step in the batter's box.)

Scout: The person who evaluates talent for a professional baseball organization. Most scouts scour high schools, colleges, and minor leagues for players. Advance scouts monitor other major league clubs to pinpoint opposing players' strengths and weaknesses.

Season tickets: Tickets for an entire season of home games.

Seeing-eye grounder: A ground ball that barely eludes an infielder for a base hit.

Set position: The position the pitcher takes on the pitching rubber just before going into the wind-up.

Set-up man: A relief pitcher who usually arrives in the seventh or eighth inning, preferably when his team is winning. He sets up the ninth inning for the closer.

Seventh-inning stretch: A brief pause in the action between the top and bottom of the seventh inning. It allows time for fans to stand and stretch their legs. One story, perhaps apocryphal, claims that the practice began in 1910 when President William H. Taft stood up to stretch in the seventh inning of a Pittsburgh Pirates game. The rest of the crowd stood up with the president out of respect. However, research has uncovered numerous earlier references to the ritual.

Shoestring catch: A running catch made at the top of a fielder's shoes.

Show, The: The major leagues. A term popularized in the film *Bull Durham,* starring Kevin Costner.

Shutout: A pitcher's complete game victory in which the opposition doesn't score.

Signs: Managers, coaches, and players use these coded signals to pass information to each other during a game.

Single: A one-base hit. Also known as a *knock.*

Slugfest: A high-scoring game.

Slugger: A hitter who is usually among the home run leaders. Mark McGwire is the quintessential slugger.

Solo homer: A home run with the bases empty.

Southpaw: A left-handed pitcher.

Spectator interference: What an umpire should call when a fan reaches out of the stands or enters the playing field and touches a ball that's still in play.

Squeeze play: When a hitter attempts to score a runner from third with a bunt. If the runner leaves third before the hitter makes contact with the ball, it is called a *suicide squeeze;* if the hitter misses the pitch, the runner is dead. In the *safety squeeze,* the runner waits for the hitter to make contact before racing toward home.

Starting rotation: A team's group of regular starting pitchers who pitch in sequence.

Strawberry: A pinkish abrasion on the hip or leg, usually caused by sliding.

Stretch drive: The final lap of a horse race, or the final weeks of a season when teams are driving toward the pennant.

Strike: What occurs when a) a batter swings and misses the ball, b) the batter hits a foul ball (unless he already has two strikes on him), c) the ball crosses the plate in the strike zone and the batter doesn't swing, or d) the players' union and the major league baseball owners can't reach an agreement and the players refuse to come to work.

Strike zone: The area a ball must pass through to be called a strike by an umpire. According to the rules, this zone is the width of home plate and extends from the bottom of the kneecap to the uniform letters across a player's chest. In practice, it varies, sometimes widely, from umpire to umpire.

Strikeout: An out made by a batter who accumulates three strikes during an at-bat.

Striking out the side: Perhaps the most misused phrase in baseball. To strike out the side, a pitcher must strike out every batter he faces in an inning rather than merely strike out three batters in an inning. If the pitcher allows a base runner of any kind during the inning, the phrase does not apply.

Suspended game: A game that is called but is scheduled to be completed at some future date.

Sweet spot: The best part of the bat to hit the ball. The sweet spot is a few inches from the end of the barrel.

Switch-hitter: A batter who hits from both sides of the plate.

Tag: The act by which a fielder retires a base runner. The fielder either touches a base with his body or the ball before the fielder arrives, or the fielder touches the runner with the ball (which can be in the fielder's glove or hand) before the runner reaches the bag.

Take: To let a pitch go by without swinging.

Tape-measure home run: A long home run, usually one that travels 450 feet or more. Mark McGwire and Juan Gonzalez regularly hit tape-measure shots. The term was first applied to the long home runs hit by Mickey Mantle in the 1950s.

"Time": The umpire's declaration that interrupts play. The ball is dead.

Tools of ignorance: The catcher's equipment. The term implies that one has to be lacking intelligence to want to wear them. Actually, the converse is true. A good catcher is usually one of the smartest people on a team.

Trade: An exchange of players between two or more teams.

Triple: A three-base hit.

Triple play: Any defensive play that produces three outs on the same batted ball. In an *unassisted* triple play, one fielder records all three outs.

Twin killing: A double play.

Umpire: The on-field baseball official who declares whether a batter is safe or out, a pitch is a ball or a strike, or a batted ball is foul or fair. He also interprets the rule book on all plays.

Umpire's interference: An act by the umpire that obstructs a catcher as he's attempting to throw out a base stealer. This call is also made when a fair ball strikes an umpire in fair territory before passing a fielder. The ball is dead.

Uniforms: What players wear on the field.

Utility player: A player, usually a substitute, who has the versatility to play more than one position. Though it rarely happens, utility players can get enough plate appearances at their various positions to qualify as regulars. Billy Goodman started at six different positions for the 1950 Boston Red Sox and won an American League batting title.

Walk: When a hitter receives four balls during a plate appearance, he is entitled to take first base. All other base runners advance if they are forced in by the walk. See *Base on balls*.

Warning track: A dirt path in front of the outfield fences, which warns the outfielders of their proximity to the walls.

Waste pitch: A pitch deliberately thrown outside the strike zone in the hope that the batter will chase it. Pitchers usually throw them if they are ahead of the batter in the count (on 0–2 or 1–2 counts). This pitch really is a waste if you throw it to a *bad-ball hitter* who hammers it for extra bases.

Wheelhouse: A hitter's power zone — an area that is usually waist-high and over the heart of home plate.

Wheels: A player's legs.

Whitewash: A shutout.

Wild pitch: A pitched ball that is thrown so far from the target that it gets past the catcher. If the official scorer decides the catcher should have caught the pitch, he can rule it a *passed ball.* Wild pitches and passed balls are charged only when they advance a base runner or allow a batter to reach base safely on a third strike.

Winter league: A baseball league that plays during the winter months. Most winter leagues are based in Florida, Arizona, or Latin America. Many Latin American big leaguers play winter ball for their hometown teams as a matter of local pride. American major leaguers usually play in these leagues to sharpen their skills after an injury-plagued season or to learn a new position.

Worm-burner (worm-killer): A ground ball that rolls over the infield without taking a bounce.

Appendix B

Baseball Organizations

The Major Leagues

Office of Major League Baseball
245 Park Avenue
New York, New York 10167
Phone: 212-931-7800
Fax (PR Department): 212-949-5654
Web site:
www.majorleaguebaseball.com

American League
245 Park Avenue
28th Floor
New York, New York 10167
Phone: 212-931-7600

National League
245 Park Avenue
New York, New York 10167
Phone: 212-339-7700

Major League Players Association
12 East 49th Street
New York, New York 10017
Phone: 212-826-0808
Fax: 212-752-4378
Web site: www.bigleaguers.com

Major League Umpires Association
1735 Market Street
Suite 3420
Philadelphia, Pennsylvania 19103
Phone: 215-979-3200
Fax: 215-979-3201

Major League Alumni Association
3637 4th Street North
St. Petersburg, Florida 33704
Phone: 813-822-3399
Fax: 813-822-6300

National Baseball Hall of Fame and
Museum
25 Main Street
Cooperstown, New York 13326
Phone: 607-547-7200
Fax: 607-547-2044

Negro Leagues Baseball Museum
1616 East 18th Street
Kansas City, Missouri 64108
Phone: 816-221-1920
Fax: 816-221-8424
Web site: www.nlbm.com

Media

Baseball Writers Association of America
78 Olive Street
Lake Grove, New York 11755
Phone: 516-981-7938
Fax: 516-585-4669
E-mail: bbwaa@aol.com

National Association of Baseball Writers
and Broadcasters
P.O. Box A
St. Petersburg, Florida 33731
Phone: 727-822-6937
Fax: 727-821-5819

Publications

Baseball America
P.O. Box 2089
Durham, North Carolina 27702
Phone: 919-682-9635
Toll Free: 800-845-2726
Fax: 919-682-2880
E-mail: ba@interpath.com
Web site: www.baseballamerica.com

Baseball Digest
990 Grove Street
Evanston, Illinois 60201
Phone: 847-491-6440
Fax: 847-491-6203
E-mail: century@wwa.com

Beckett Baseball Card Monthly
15850 Dallas Parkway
Dallas, Texas 75248
Phone: 972-991-6657
Fax: 972-991-8930

ESPN The Magazine
19 East 34th Street
7th Floor
New York, New York 10016
Phone: 212-515-1000
Fax: 212-515-1290

Junior Baseball Magazine
P.O. Box 9099
Canoga Park, California 91309
Phone: 818-710-1234
Fax: 818-790-1877
Web site: www.juniorbaseball.com

Sport Magazine
110 Fifth Avenue
New York, New York 10011
Phone: 212-880-3600

The Sporting News
10176 Corporate Square Drive
St. Louis, Missouri 63132
Phone: 314-997-7111
Fax: 314-997-0765

Sports Illustrated
Time & Life Building
1271 Avenue of the Americas
New York, New York 10020
Phone: 212-522-1212
Fax: 212-522-4543

Sports Illustrated For Kids
Time & Life Building
Rockefeller Center
New York, New York 10020
Phone: 212-522-4876
Fax: 212-522-0120
Web site: www.sikids.com

Spring Training Baseball Yearbook
Vanguard Sports Publications
P.O. Box 667
Chapel Hill, North Carolina 27514
Phone: 919-967-2420
Fax: 919-967-6294
Web site: www.springtraining-magazine.com

Street and Smith's Baseball Yearbook
342 Madison Avenue
New York, New York 10017
Phone: 212-880-8698
Fax: 212-880-4347

Street and Smith's Sports Business Journal
120 West Morehead Street, Suite 310
Charlotte, North Carolina 28202
Phone: 704-973-1400

Total Baseball
445 Park Avenue,19th Floor
New York, New York 10022
Phone: 212-319-6611
Fax: 212-319-3820
E-mail: info@totalsports.com

USA Today Baseball Weekly
1000 Wilson Boulevard, 21st Floor
Arlington, Virginia 22229
Phone: 703-558-5630
Fax: 703-558-4678

Statistics and Research

Elias Sports Bureau
500 Fifth Avenue
New York, New York 10110
Phone: 212-869-1530
Fax: 212-354-0980

Howe Sports Data International
Boston Fish Pier, West Bldg. #2, Suite 306
Boston, Massachusetts 02210
Phone: 617-951-0070
Fax: 617-737-9960
Stats Service: 617-951-1379

Society for American Baseball Research
812 Huron Road
Suite 719
Cleveland, Ohio 44115
Phone: 216-575-0500
Fax: 216-575-0502
Web site: www.sabr.org

STATS, Inc.
8131 Monticello Avenue
Skokie, Illinois 60076-3300
Phone: 847-676-3383
Toll Free: 800-63-STATS
Fax: 847-676-0821
E-mail: info@stats.com

American League Teams

Anaheim Angels
2000 Gene Autry Way
Anaheim, California 92806
Phone: 714-940-2000
Fax: 714-940-2205
Web site: www.angelsbaseball.com

Baltimore Orioles
333 West Camden Street
Baltimore, Maryland 21201
Phone: 410-685-9800
Fax: 410-547-6272
Web site: www.theorioles.com

Boston Red Sox
4 Yawkey Way
Boston, Massachusetts 02215
Phone: 617-267-9440
Fax: 617-375-0944
Web site: www.redsox.com

Chicago White Sox
333 West 35th Street
Chicago, Illinois 60616
Phone: 312-674-1000
Fax: 312-674-5116
Web site: www.chisox.com

Cleveland Indians
2401 Ontario Street
Cleveland, Ohio 44115
Phone: 216-420-4200
Fax: 216-420-4396
Web site: www.indians.com

Detroit Tigers
2100 Woodward Avenue
Detroit, Michigan 48201
Phone: 313-962-4000
Fax: 313-965-2138
Web site: www.detroittigers.com

Kansas City Royals
1 Royal Way
Kansas City, Missouri 64129
Phone: 816-921-8000
Fax: 816-921-1366
Web site: www.kcroyals.com

Minnesota Twins
34 Kirby Puckett Place
Minneapolis, Minnesota 55415
Phone: 613-375-1366
Web site: www.twinsbaseball.com

New York Yankees
Yankee Stadium
161st Street and River Avenue
Bronx, New York 10451
Phone: 718-293-4300
Fax: 718-293-8431
Web site: www.yankees.com

Oakland Athletics
7677 Oakport Street, Second Floor
Oakland, California 94621
Phone: 510-638-4900
Fax: 510-562-1633
Web site: www.oaklandathletics.com

Seattle Mariners
First and Atlantic
Seattle, Washington 98104
Phone: 206-346-4000
Fax: 206-346-4050
E-mail: mariners@mariners.org
Web site: www.mariners.org

Tampa Bay Devil Rays
1 Tropicana Drive
St. Petersburg, Florida 33705
Phone: 813-825-3137
Fax: 813-825-3300
Web site: www.devilray.com

Texas Rangers
1000 Ballpark Way
Arlington, Texas 76011
Phone: 817-273-5222
Fax: 817-273-5206
Web site: www.texasrangers.com

Toronto Blue Jays
1 Blue Jays Way, Suite 3200
Toronto, Ontario M5V 1J1
Phone: 416-341-1000
Fax: 416-341-1250
E-mail: bluejays@bluejays.ca
Web site: www.bluejays.ca

National League Teams

Arizona Diamondbacks
401 East Jefferson Street
Phoenix, Arizona 85004
Phone: 602-462-8500
Fax: 602-462-6599
Web site: www.azdiamondbacks.com

Atlanta Braves
755 Hank Aaron Drive
Atlanta, Georgia 30312
Phone: 404-522-7630
Fax: 404-614-1391
Web site: www.atlantabraves.com

Chicago Cubs
1060 West Addison Street
Chicago, Illinois 60613
Phone: 773-404-2827
Fax: 773-404-4129
E-mail: cubs@cubs.com
Web site: www.cubs.com

Cincinnati Reds
100 Cinergy Field
Cincinnati, Ohio 45202
Phone: 513-421-4510
Fax: 513-421-7342
Web site: www.cincinnatireds.com

Colorado Rockies
2001 Blake Street
Denver, Colorado 80205
Phone: 303-292-0200
Fax: 303-312-2116
Web site: www.coloradorockies.com

Florida Marlins
2267 NW 199th Street
Miami, Florida 33056
Phone: 305-626-7400
Fax: 305-626-7428
Web site: www.flamarlins.com

Houston Astros
8400 Kirby Drive
Houston, Texas 77054
Phone: 713-799-9500
Fax: 713-799-9794
E-mail: twinspin@astros.com
Web site: www.astros.com

Los Angeles Dodgers
1000 Elysian Park Avenue
Los Angeles, California 90012
Phone: 213-224-1500
Fax: 213-224-1269
Web site: www.dodgers.com

Milwaukee Brewers
201 South 46th Street
Milwaukee, Wisconsin 53214
Phone: 414-933-4114
Fax: 414-933-3251
Web site: www.milwaukeebrewers.com

Montreal Expos
4549 Pierre-de-Coubertin Avenue
Montreal, Quebec H1V 3N7
Phone: 514-253-3434
Fax: 514-253-8282
Web site: www.montrealexpos.com

New York Mets
123-01 Roosevelt Avenue
Flushing, New York 11368
Phone: 718-507-6387
Fax: 718-565-6395
Web site: www.mets.com

Philadelphia Phillies
3501 South Broad Street
Philadelphia, Pennsylvania 19101
Phone: 215-463-6000
Fax: 215-389-3050
Web site: www.phillies.com

Pittsburgh Pirates
600 Stadium Club Circle
Pittsburgh, Pennsylvania 15212
Phone: 412-323-5000
Fax: 412-323-5024
Web site: www.piratesball.com

St. Louis Cardinals
250 Stadium Plaza
St. Louis, Missouri 63102
Phone: 314-421-3060
Fax: 314-425-0640
Web site: www.stlcardinals.com

San Diego Padres
8880 Rio San Diego Drive, Suite 400
San Diego, California 92108
Phone: 619-881-6500
Fax: 619-497-5454
Web site: www.padres.org

San Francisco Giants
3Com Park at Candlestick Point
San Francisco, California 94124
Phone: 415-468-3700
Fax: 415-467-0485
Web site: www.sfgiants.com

The Minor Leagues

Appalachian League
283 Deerchase Circle
Statesville, North Carolina 28677
Phone: 704-873-5300
Fax: 704-873-4333
E-mail: appylg@i-america.net

Arizona League
5900 North Granite Reef Road
Suite 105
Scottsdale, Arizona 85250
Phone: 602-483-8224
Fax: 602-443-3450

California League
2380 S. Bascom Avenue
Campbell, California 95008
Phone: 408-369-8038
Fax: 408-369-1409
E-mail: cabaseball@aol.com

Carolina League
1806 Pembroke Road
Greensboro, North Carolina 27408
Phone: 910-691-9030
Fax: 910-691-9070
E-mail: office@carolinaleague.com

Dominican Summer League
Calle Segundo No. 14 Reparto Antilla
Santo Domingo, Dominican Republic
Phone/Fax: 809-532-3619

Eastern League
511 Congress Street, 7th Floor
Portland, Maine 04101
Phone: 207-761-2700
Fax: 207-761-7064
E-mail: elpb@easternleague.com

Florida State League
103 East Orange Avenue
Daytona Beach, Florida 32114
Phone: 904-252-7479
Fax: 904-252-7495
E-mail: bballleague@mindspring.com

Gulf Coast League
1503 Clower Creek Drive
Suite H–262
Sarasota, Florida 34231
Phone: 941-966-6407
Fax: 941-966-6872

International League
55 S. High Street
Suite 202
Dublin, Ohio 43017
Phone: 614-791-9300
Fax: 614-791-9009
E-mail: office@ilbaseball.com

Mexican League
Angel Pola #16 Col.
Periodista, Mexico D.F. CP 11220
Phone: 011-525-557-1007
Fax: 011-525-395-2454
E-mail: lnb@lmb.com.mx

Midwest League
1118 Cranston Road
Beloit, Wisconsin 53511
Phone: 608-364-1188
Fax: 608-364-1913
E-mail: midwst@inwave.com

National Association
210 Bayshore Drive SE
St. Petersburg, Florida 33701
Phone: 813-822-6937
Fax: 813-821-5819

New York-Penn State
1629 Oneida Street
Utica, New York 13501
Phone: 315-733-8036
Fax: 315-797-7403
E-mail: nypenn@dreamscape.com

Northwest League
5900 North Granite Reef Road, Suite 105
Scottsdale, Arizona 85250
Phone: 602-483-8224
Fax: 602-443-3450

Pacific Coast League
1631 Mesa Avenue
Colorado Springs, Colorado 80906
Phone: 719-636-3399
Fax: 719-636-1199
E-mail: pcloffice@earthlink.net

Pioneer League
812 West 30th Street
Spokane, Washington 99203
Phone: 509-456-7615
Fax: 509-456-0136
E-mail: baseball@ior.com

South Atlantic League
504 Crescent Hill
Kings Mountain, North Carolina 28086
Phone: 704-739-3466
Fax: 704-739-1974
E-mail: sal@shelby.net

Southern League
One Depot Street
Marietta, Georgia 30060
Phone: 770-428-4749
Fax: 770-428-4849
E-mail: soleague@bellsouth.net

Texas League
2442 Facet Oak
San Antonio, Texas 78232
Phone: 210-545-5297
Fax: 210-545-5298

Independent Leagues

Arizona Fall League
10201 South 51st Street
Suite 230
Phoenix, Arizona 85044
Phone: 602-496-6700
Fax: 602-496-6384

Atlantic League
31 Turner Lane
West Chester, Pennsylvania 19380
Phone: 610-696-8662
Fax: 610-696-8667
E-mail: atlge@aol.com

Frontier League
727 Market Street
Zanesville, Ohio 43701
Phone: 614-452-7400
Fax: 614-452-2999
E-mail: klee@y-city.net

Hawaii Winter Baseball
905 Makahiki Way
Unit C
Honolulu, Hawaii 96826
Phone: 808-973-7247
Fax: 808-973-7117

Maryland Fall League
4101 NE Crain Highway
Bowie, Maryland 20716
Phone: 301-805-6012
Fax: 301-805-6011
Web site: www.mdfallbaseball.com

Northern League
524 South Duke Street
Durham, North Carolina 27701
Phone: 919-956-8150
Fax: 919-683-2693
E-mail: northernlg@earthlink.com

Texas-Louisiana League
2801 North Third Street
Abilene, Texas 79601
Phone: 915-673-7364
Fax: 915-673-5150
E-mail: txlaops@txproball.com

Western League
426 Broadway
Suite 208
Chico, California 95928
Phone: 530-897-6125
Fax: 530-897-6124
E-mail: office@westernbaseball.com

Foreign Leagues

Australian Baseball League
48 Atchison Street, Level 2 St.
Leonards, NSW 2065, Australia
Phone: 011-61-2-9437-4622
Fax: 011-61-2-9437-4155

Caribbean Baseball Confederation
Frank Feliz Miranda No. 1 Naco
P.O. Box 21070 y 21416
Santo Domingo, Dominican Republic
Phone: 809-562-4737 or 562-4715
Fax: 809-565-4654

Central League (Japan)
Asahi Building 3F
6-6-7, Ginza
Chuo-ku Tokyo 104-0061, Japan
Phone: 03-3572-1673
Fax: 03-3571-4545

Chinese Professional Baseball League
2 F, No.32, Section 3 Pateh Road
Taipei, Taiwan
Phone: 886-2-2577-6992
Fax: 886-2-2577-2606
Web site: www.cpbl.com.tw

Dominican League
Estadio Quisqueya
Santo Domingo, Dominican Republic
Phone: 809-567-6371
Fax: 809-567-5720

Japanese Leagues
Imperial Tower 10 F
1-1-1 Uchisaiwai-cho
Chiyoda-ku Tokyo 100-0011, Japan
Phone: 03-3502-0022
Fax: 03-3502-0140

Korean Baseball Organization
946-16 Dogok-Dong, Kangnam-Ku
Seoul, South Korea
Phone: 82-2-3461-7887
Fax: 82-2-3462-7800

Mexican Pacific League
Pesqueira No. 401-R
Altos, Navojora
Sonora, Mexico
Phone: 52-642-2-3100
Fax: 52-642-2-7250
Web site: www.ligadelpacifico.com.mx

Pacific League (Japan)
Asahi Building 9F
6-6-7, Ginza,
Chuo-ku Tokyo 104-0061, Japan
Phone: 03-3573-1551
Fax: 03-3572-5843

Puerto Rican League
P.O. Box 1852
Hato Rey, Puerto Rico 00919
Phone: 787-765-6285
Fax: 787-767-3028

Taiwan Major League
2F, No. 214
Tunhua, North Road
Taipei, Taiwan
Phone: 886-2-2545-9566
Fax: 886-2-2514-0802
Web site: www.naluwan.com.tw

Venezuelan League
Avenida Casanova Central Comercial El
Recreo
Torre Sur, Piso 3, Oficinas 36-37
Caracas, Venezuela
Phone: 011-58-2-761-2750 or 761-4817
Fax: 011-58-2-761-7661

College Baseball

American Baseball Coaches Association
108 South University Avenue
Suite 3
Mount Pleasant, Michigan 48858
Phone: 517-775-3300
Fax: 517-775-3600

Community College League of California
2017 O Street
Sacramento, California 95814
Phone: 916-444-1600
Fax: 916-444-2616

National Association of Intercollegiate
Athletics
6120 South Yale Avenue
Suite 1450
Tulsa, Oklahoma 74136
Phone: 918-494-8828
Fax: 918-494-8841

The National Collegiate Athletic
Association
700 W. Washington St.
P.O. Box 6222
Indianapolis, Indiana 46206-6222
Phone: 317-917-6222
Fax: 317-917-6888

National Jr. College Athletic Association
P.O. Box 7305
Colorado Springs, Colorado 80933
Phone: 719-590-9788
Fax: 719-590-7324

High School Baseball

Eastern U.S. Baseball Showcase
P.O. Box 2126
Chapel Hill, North Carolina 27514
Phone: 919-962-2351

National Classic High School Tournament
El Dorado High School
1651 North Valencia Avenue
Placentia, California 92870
Phone: 714-993-5350
Fax: 714-777-8127

National Federation of State High School
Associations
11724 NW Plaza Circle
Kansas City, Missouri 64153
Phone: 816-464-5400
Fax: 816-464-5571
Web site: www.nfhsa.org

National High School Baseball Coaches
Association
P.O. Box 5128
Bella Vista, Arizona 72714
Phone: 501-876-2591
Fax: 501-876-2596

NCAA Summer Baseball
700 W. Washington St.
P.O. Box 6222
Indianapolis, Indiana 46206-6222
Phone: 317-917-6222
Fax: 317-917-6888

Spalding West Coast Classic
Archbishop Mitty High School
5000 Mitty Avenue
San Jose, California 95129
Phone: 408-252-6610

Sunbelt Baseball Classic Series
505 North Boulevard
Edmond, Oklahoma 73034
Phone: 405-348-3839

Westminster National Classic
Westminster Academy
5601 Federal Highway
Fort Lauderdale, Florida 33308
Phone: 954-771-4615
Fax: 954-491-3021

Alaska League (Summer College League)
601 South Main Street
Kenai, Alaska 99611
Phone: 508-432-1774
Fax: 508-432-9766

Alleghany Mountain Collegiate League
151 Beimel Lane
Kersey, Pennsylvania 15846
Phone: 814-885-8480
E-mail: aaaba@key-net.net

Atlantic Collegiate League
401 Timber Drive
Berkeley Heights, New Jersey 07922
Phone/Fax: 908-464-8042
E-mail:acbl@vs-inc.com

Cape Cod League
7 Nottingham Drive
Yarmouth, Massachusetts 02675
Phone/Fax: 508-996-5004
E-mail: capecod@gbwebworks.com

Central Illinois Collegiate League
RR 13, Box 369
Bloomington, Illinois 61704
Phone: 309-828-4429
Fax: 309-827-4652
E-mail: clclbb@aol.com

Clark Griffith Collegiate League
4917 North 30th Street
Arlington, Virginia 22207
Phone/Fax: 703-536-1729

Coastal Plain League
4900 Waters Edge Drive
Suite 201
Raleigh, North Carolina 27606
Phone: 919-852-1960
Fax: 919-852-1973

Great Lakes League
590 Parkside Drive
Bay Village, Ohio 44140
Phone: 440-892-2692
Fax: 440-871-4221

Jayhawk League
Five Adams Place
Halstead, Kansas 67056
Phone: 316-835-2589
Fax: 316-755-1285

New England Collegiate League
P.O. Box 415
Jamestown, Rhode Island 02835
Phone: 401-423-9863
Fax: 401-423-2784

Northeastern Collegiate League
28 Dunbridge Heights
Fairport, New York 14450
Phone: 716-223-3528

Northwest Collegiate League
23737 SW Pincone Avenue
Sherwood, Oregon 97140
Phone: 503-625-4044
Fax: 503-625-0629

Northwoods League
P.O. Box 482
Rochester, Minnesota 55903
Phone: 507-289-1170
Fax: 507-289-1866

Pacific International League
504 Yale Avenue
North Seattle, Washington 98109
Phone: 206-623-8844
Fax: 206-623-8361

Shendandoah Valley League
Route 1, Box 189J
Staunton, Virginia 24401
Phone: 540-886-1748
Fax: 540-885-2068

Senior Leagues

Men's Adult Baseball League
One Huntington Quadrangle
Mellville, New York 11747
Phone: 516-753-6725
Fax: 516-753-4031
E-mail: info@msblnational.com

Men's Senior Baseball League
One Huntington Quadrangle
Mellville, New York 11747
Phone: 516-753-6725
Fax: 516-753-4031

National Adult Baseball League
3900 East Mexico Avenue
Suite 330
Denver, Colorado 80201
Phone: 303-639-9955
Fax: 303-753-6804

Youth Baseball

All American Amateur Baseball Association
331 Parkway Drive
Zanesville, Ohio 43701
Phone: 740-453-8531
Fax: 740-453-3978

Amateur Athletic Union
P.O. Box 10000
Lake Buena Vista, Florida 32830
Phone: 407-828-3459
Fax: 407-934-7242

American Amateur Baseball Congress
118-119 Redfield Plaza
P.O. Box 467
Marshall, Michigan 49068
Phone: 616-781-2002
Fax: 616-781-2060

American Amateur Youth Baseball Alliance
12919 Four Winds Farm
St. Louis, Missouri 63131
Phone: 573-518-0319

American Legion Baseball
National Americanism Commission
P.O. Box 1055
Indianapolis, Indiana 46206
Phone: 317-630-1213
Fax: 317-630-1369

Babe Ruth Baseball
1770 Brunswick Pike
P.O. Box 5000
Trenton, New Jersey 08638
Phone: 609-695-1434
Fax: 609-695-2505

Continental Amateur Baseball Association
82 University Street
Westerville, Ohio 43081
Phone/Fax: 614-899-2103

Dixie Baseball
P.O. Box 231536
Montgomery, Alabama 36123
Phone: 334-242-8395
Fax: 334-242-0198

Dizzy Dean Baseball
P.O. Box 202
Chickamauga, Georgia 30707
Phone: 706-866-1904

Hap Dumont Baseball
P.O. Box 17455
Wichita, Kansas 67217
Phone: 316-721-1779
Fax: 316-721-8054

Little League Baseball
P.O. Box 3485
Williamsport, Pennsylvania 17701
Phone: 570-326-1921
Fax: 570-326-1074

National Amateur Baseball Federation
P.O. Box 705
Bowie, Maryland 20718
Phone/Fax: 301-262-5005
E-mail: nabf1914@aol.com

National Association of Police Athletic
Leagues (PAL)
618 U.S. Highway 1 North
Suite 201
Palm Beach, Florida 33408
Phone: 561-844-1823
Fax: 561-863-6120

PONY Baseball
P.O. Box 225
Washington, Pennsylvania 15301
Phone: 724-225-1060
Fax: 724-225-9852
E-mail: pony@pulsenet.com

Reviving Baseball in Inner Cities (RBI)
245 Park Avenue
New York, New York 10167
Phone: 212-931-7897
Fax: 212-949-5695

T-Ball USA Association
915 Broadway
Suite 607
New York, New York 10010
Phone: 212-254-7911 or 800-741-0845
Fax: 212-254-8042
E-mail: teeballusa@aol.com

USA Baseball
Hi Corbett Field
3400 East Camino Campestre
Tucson, Arizona 85716
Phone: 520-327-9700
Fax: 520-327-9921
E-mail: usabaseball@aol.com

U.S. Amateur Baseball Association
7101 Lake Ballinger Way
Edmonds, Washington 98026
Phone/Fax: 425-776-7130

Youth Baseball Athletic League
301 Alma Street
Palo Alto, California 94306-0350
Phone: 650-856-4900

Index

• C •